GLORY IN THE FALL

THE GREATEST MOMENTS IN WORLD SERIES HISTORY

Edited by PETER GOLENBOCK

UNION SQUARE PRESS

An imprint of Sterling Publishing Co., Inc.

New York / London
www.sterlingpublishing.com

STERLING and the distinctive Sterling logo are registered trademarks of
Sterling Publishing Co., Inc.

Library of Congress Cataloging-in-Publication Data
Glory in the fall : the greatest moments in World Series history/edited by Peter Golenbock.
p. cm.
Includes index.
ISBN 978-1-4027-7756-1
1. World Series (Baseball)—History. I. Golenbock, Peter, 1946–
GV878.4.G58 2010
796.357'640973—dc22

10 9 8 7 6 5 4 3 2 1

Published by Sterling Publishing Co., Inc.
387 Park Avenue South, New York NY 10016
© 2010 by Sterling Publishing Co., Inc.
Distributed in Canada by Sterling Publishing
c/o Canadian Manda Group, 165 Dufferin Street
Toronto, Ontario, Canada M6K 3H6
Distributed in the United Kingdom by GMC Distribution Services
Castle Place, 166 High Street, Lewes, East Sussex, England BN7 1XU
Distributed in Australia by Capricorn Link (Australia) Pty. Ltd.
P.O. Box 704, Windsor, NSW 2756, Australia

Sterling ISBN 978-1-4027-7756-1

For information about custom editions, special sales, premium and corporate purchases, please contact
Sterling Special Sales Department at 800-805-5489 or specialsales@sterlingpublishing.com

CONTENTS

INTRODUCTION

I was just a boy when I discovered living baseball history in the stacks of the Stamford (Connecticut) Public Library. I had no idea who Frank Graham, Fred Lieb, or Roy Stockton were, but, because of them, I was able to get to know Babe Ruth, Ty Cobb, the Gas House Gang, and "Tinker to Evers to Chance." I read about the Black Sox scandal, and how Judge Landis saved baseball. I wasn't told that Landis had single-handedly kept Negroes, as they were called then, out of baseball, but this was the late 1950s, before the civil rights movement had even begun.

I recall watching baseball on television for the first time in 1954. We had a Dumont TV, a big hunk of a box. The picture was in black and white, and that year I watched Willie Mays make his incredible catch against the Cleveland Indians in the World Series. The next year I watched my Yankees lose the Series to Johnny Podres, Sandy Amoros, and the rest of the Brooklyn Dodgers.

An October later, in 1956, when I was ten, my Uncle Justin took me to the fourth game of the World Series. The game was played at Yankee Stadium, and I watched as the Yankees defeated the Dodgers 4–2. Mickey Mantle hit a home run. After the game, Uncle Justin said that he had to go see Jackie Robinson before we went home. Uncle Justin was Jackie's lawyer; Jackie was moving into a new home in Stamford, and there was something they had to talk about. I shook hands with Jackie. He was a large man with huge hands. I felt as though I were meeting royalty. I have spent the rest of my life thinking about him and what he went through.

Despite becoming a TV addict, I never stopped reading. In high school I discovered *SPORT,* a magazine that boasted some of the best writers ever to put pen to paper. Roger Kahn, Arnold Hano, and Ed Linn were my heroes. (Kahn and Linn later became friends.) They wrote biographies of the star baseball players. Around this time, a series of terrific books came out: *The Pennant Race,* by Jim Brosnan; *Eight Men Out,* by Eliot Asinof; and *The*

Glory of Their Times, by Larry Rittner, which I still feel is the greatest book on baseball ever written.

I admit it: All my life I have been a baseball junkie. No sport has a richer history than baseball, and no sport has such a treasure trove of books, magazine articles, and newspaper accounts. Over the years, I have tried to read everything I could.

And no sport has provided as many moments in its championship series as baseball. There is no sporting event quite like the World Series. During those two weeks in October—and now extending into November—time stands still. Nothing else matters.

Off the top of my head, if you asked me which were the greatest World Series moments, I'd have to start with Don Larsen's perfect game; Willie Mays's catch; Carlton Fisk's home run; Babe Ruth's called shot; Bill Mazerowski's home run; Ron Swoboda's catch; the ball that went through Bill Buckner's legs; Joe Carter's home run; and the Tampa Bay Rays playing in the 2008 World Series. I know. Kirk Gibson's home run off Mitch Williams is far more important, but if you had been a Rays fan as long as I had, you'd understand. For those of us who live in Tampa Bay, we will always have the 2008 World Series.

My guess is that you have another list, equally worthy. There hasn't been a book that combines the writing of the acclaimed sportswriters with the high drama and the rich history of the World Series until now. *Glory in the Fall* is that book.

On these pages we get to read the work of Roger Angell, Peter Gammons, Robert Creamer, Stephen Jay Gould, and David Halberstam, to name a few among many, many other talented writers, as they bring alive great moments in World Series history. We can read about Boston's Royal Rooters and their impact on the very first World Series in 1903, and relive what in 1904 was called "the most costly wild pitch in history," Jack Chesbro's throw, which cost the Yankees a chance to go to the Series that year. Of course, that Series never took place, because New York Giants manager John McGraw didn't want to risk losing to the Red Sox, the team that had won the year before. As a result, the Red Sox could claim that they were still world champs.

I had the good fortune to interview Joe Cashman, a reporter who remembered the 1912 World Series. He covered the Red Sox, and he claimed that the outfield of Duffy Lewis, Tris Speaker, and Harry Hooper was the greatest of all time. Eliot Asinof was able to interview a number of the players accused of throwing the 1919 World Series. It is because of Asinof that we know the details of that sordid story.

Robert Creamer recalls the heroics of Giants outfielder Casey Stengel in the 1923 World Series. Not only did Stengel hit two home runs to win games, but as he was scoring after hitting the second one, he thumbed his nose at the Yankees dugout. That winter Stengel was "the most famous man in America." A month later, manager McGraw traded him to the Boston Braves. Stengel would return to the World Series twenty-six years later. He would return time and time again.

The World Series has been full of surprises, the most astounding perhaps the time A's manager Connie Mack started journeyman Howard Ehmke in Game 1 of the 1929 World Series against the powerful Chicago Cubs. Mack had Lefty Grove, George Earnshaw, and Rube Walberg, but the Cubs were a fastball-hitting team, and Ehmke threw junk; Mack figured that the Cubs would be thrown off their game. Ehmke struck out 13 and won the game. Later in that Series, the Cubs would lead Game 4 by a score of 8–0, only to see the A's score 10 runs in the seventh inning. This was the greatest rally in World Series history.

Babe Ruth's so-called Called Shot came off Charlie Root in the third game of the 1932 Series. The story was that Ruth was furious with the Cubs for not giving former Yankee teammate Mark Koenig a full share of the World Series proceeds. But that may not be the real reason. The essay herein says Ruth didn't really care for Koenig; he just wanted to badger the Cubs. At the plate, he called them names. He pointed somewhere—to the dugout or to the center-field bleachers?—and then he hit a home run. This was the most famous home run in World Series history, and we get to read Paul Gallico and Westbrook Pegler's account of what happened.

The most dazzling performance by two brothers occurred in the 1934 World Series when Dizzy and Paul Dean won all the games for the Cardinals against the Detroit Tigers. Ten years later, the Cardinals again were in the Series, this time against the St. Louis Browns. Once again, the surprise choice of Denny Galehouse to start the first game for the Browns was the talk of the Series. In 1946, the Cards' Enos Slaughter made himself immortal with his mad dash from first on a single.

What was the biggest surprise in Series history? Stephen Jay Gould argues that it was the sweep by the New York Giants of the powerful Cleveland Indians in the 1954 Series. Arnold Hano brilliantly discusses Willie Mays's catch of Vic Wertz's long fly ball, and Gould tells of the heroics of one Lamar "Dusty" Rhodes, a boozer the manager Leo Durocher wanted to dump during the season. When no one wanted him even for a dollar, the Giants had to keep him, and in the '54 Series Rhodes had three pinch hits that helped win ballgames for the underdog Giants.

In 1955 the Series was won by the Brooklyn Dodgers when Sandy Amoros robbed Yogi Berra and saved Johnny Podres's 2–0 lead for a seventh-game win. The next year, Larsen made headlines with his Perfect Game. After the game, a reporter asked Larsen if it had been the best game he had ever pitched.

In 1960, Mazerowski hit his ninth-inning, seventh-game home run to beat the Yankees, and in 1964 Bob Gibson made himself immortal by beating the Yankees three times to win the Series. David Halberstam, a terrific reporter, chronicles how Gibson, a black man, felt about racism in America during a time before the civil rights movement.

Sandy Koufax wouldn't pitch on Yom Kippur during the 1965 World Series. Don Drysdale took his place and was shelled. As Walter Alston was taking him out, Dandy Don said to his manager, "Hey, skip, bet you wish I was Jewish today, too." Jane Leavy writes about Koufax's toughness and reclusiveness.

In 1969, the Mets beat the Baltimore Orioles in the Series. The Mets in 1969 were the Tampa Bay Rays of 2008. Their appearance surprised everyone. Ron Swoboda made a catch that saved a game in the biggest World Series upset since 1954. A year later, in 1970, Brooks Robinson played an uncanny third base against the Big Red Machine, and in 1975 Carlton Fisk hit a home run against the Pesky Pole in the twelfth inning to give the Red Sox what at the time was the most impressive victory in their history. Who threw the pitch? Pat Darcy.

Two years later Reggie Jackson, Mr. October, had three home runs on three pitches against three different pitchers. I took my parents to that game, and the next year I spent the 1978 season with Sparky Lyle, so I saw a lot of baseball. In April of 1978, Reggie came out with a candy bar. It was chewy and came in an orange wrapper with Reggie's picture on it. During the first home stand, the Yankees gave one to every fan entering the stadium. When Reggie hit a home run in his first at bat, 30,000 fans threw their Reggie! bars from the grandstands. This didn't occur during the World Series, but I had to tell you about it anyway.

The worst call by an umpire was made by Don Denkinger in the 1985 World Series. It cost the Cardinals the Series. The next year, the top attraction was Roger Clemens of the Red Sox against Dwight Gooden of the Mets. Of course, both were forgotten after Mookie Wilson hit a two-hopper that went through Bill Buckner's legs to cost the Bosox Game 6. Roger Angell was there and recounted the sad tale for all of New England as only he could.

Jim Murray describes Kirk Gibson's improbable home run against the Dodgers in the 1988 Series. In 1991, Kirby Puckett gained fame with his game-winning home run, and in 1993 Joe Carter lifted Toronto to a Series win with his game-winning three-run home run off Mitch Williams in the ninth inning. It was only the second time Carter had hit a ninth-inning home run in eleven seasons.

There was no World Series in 1994. The Montreal Expos, who were in first place, never recovered and were moved to Washington, where they became the dreadful Nats. Yankee fans have bitched about 1994 for years.

Tom Glavin pitched a one-hitter to beat Cleveland in the final game of the 1995 World Series. You could argue it was the second-best Series game ever pitched. The next Series were won by expansion teams. The Florida Marlins won in 1997 and again in 2003, and in 1998 Luis Gonzalez of Arizona blooped a ball over Derek Jeter's head to defeat the Yankees.

Boston won in 2004, its first Series win since 1918. Half the people living in New England fired their shrinks. Stephen King and Stewart O'Nan re-create the mojo, Curt Shilling's bloody sock, "Dirty Water," Pedro, Manny, and the final out as Keith Foulke threw to Doug Mientkiewicz to retire Edgar Renteria.

Jayson Stark, that long-suffering Phillie fanatic, completes the journey with his account of how the Phillies beat the Rays in the pouring rain in 2008. The Phils led all of Game 6 until right at the end when the Rays tied it up, allowing Commissioner Bud Selig to postpone the game until the next day. What if the Phils had been leading? Would he have called it after six? It would have been the first World Series decided by a rain-shortened game.

Open *Glory in the Fall* to any page and the history of the game of baseball comes alive. Who knows who will compete in the next fall classic? The Yankees and Red Sox, with their huge advantage in resources, certainly will be favored. But you can't count out the Phils and the Cardinals, and small-market teams like Minnesota, Seattle, and Tampa Bay have shown they know how to build a contender. We can't predict the future, but promise *Glory in the Fall* will certainly entertain you with the past.

In 1903, Pirates pitcher Deacon Phillippe was presented with a diamond stickpin in the middle of the final game as he batted against Cy Young. Phillippe pitched five complete games against the Red Sox in that first World Series, but couldn't win the final game. Had he won it, Phillippe would have been the most famous man in America. Instead, Phillippe lost 3–0. Bill Buckner would have understood.

Peter Golenbock

1903: Americans vs. Pirates

The First World Series

from *When Boston Won the World Series* by Bob Ryan

On October 9, 1903, Jimmy Collins received a telegram at his Pittsburg Hotel:

TO JAMES J. COLLINS,

MANAGER AND CAPTAIN OF THE

BOSTON BASEBALL TEAM, PITTSBURG, PENN:

The *Boston Globe*, believing that victory is within the grasp of you and your comrades, offers to present to each player of the Boston team of the American League, if it brings to Boston the world's championship, a valuable gold medal, which can be worn as a watch charm, and be treasured as a reminder of the most notable achievement upon the diamond.

CHAS. H. TAYLOR, Editor

1

Underneath the text of the telegram, the *Globe* offered additional explanation:

"Never before have the leaders of two great leagues battled for supremacy in the national sport. The public interest in the final result is therefore unusual.

"The *Boston Globe* shares in the general desire of New Englanders that Captain Collins and his men, who have made such a fine and somewhat uphill fight in the series with the Pittsburg* players, should bring the World's Championship in triumph to Boston. It belongs here, for this long has been the best ball town in the country. The prize should be ours, for ours is the highest talent this year that the diamond has seen.

"Beautiful gold medals, one for each of the Boston players if the series is won by Boston for Boston, are offered by the *Globe* as an added incentive to strenuous endeavor. Those medals will be worth the gaining because of their beauty, but they will be most prized by their possessors in the years to come as souvenirs of the most famous series of baseball games ever played."

The story would take on a predictable life of its own, especially inside the pages of the *Boston Globe*, which was now actively selling the idea that winning the medals was the incentive the Boston team needed to boost itself over the top in the grand struggle with the boys from Pittsburg.

First, of course, there was the requisite thank-you from Captain Collins, printed in you-can't-miss-it bold type:

I fully appreciate the sentiment expressed in your telegram. It is simply following out a policy that has made the *Globe* a great factor in the national game. It is pleasing to get such recognition, and such loyal and liberal support. The boys will do everything in their power to win the honor for

---

* In 1903, the city the Pirates called home was spelled Pittsburg. The current spelling—Pittsburgh—was the official spelling throughout the city's history except for the period from 1890 to 1911.

Boston, which has given us the best treatment, even when we were not having the best luck.

James J. Collins, Captain Boston Americans

And how could Fred Clarke not play the proper gentleman and add his own comments?

It looks well to see the press recognize the game and the players in this way. The *Boston Globe* has, for years, been recognized as the authority on the game, and the Boston boys are to be congratulated upon having such a supporter, but Pittsburg intends to take this series and prevent any handing over of the *Globe's* gold medals.

Fred Clarke, Captain Pittsburg Nationals

On the morning of Game 7, the *Globe* could not resist patting itself on the back. "Whenever in Boston men gathered last evening, whether in hotels, in theatres, clubs, bowling alleys, billiard rooms or street corners, the general topic of conversation was baseball—the championship series between the Boston Americans and the Pittsburg Nationals; the closeness of the series and the gold medals which have been offered to the Boston players by the *Globe*," wrote someone, quite possibly loyal *Globie* Tim Murnane.

"The excitement is more widely spread and more intense over this contest between the champions of both the great leagues than was ever known before in the history of baseball in this city. The offer of the *Globe* to present each member with a valuable gold medal if the team brings to Boston the world's championship has intensified the local interest, if such a thing were possible in the present context."

Truly desperate now, Fred Clarke did what any man in his position would have done. He played the weather card, declaring that Game 7 would have to wait another day due to inclement weather.

It wasn't rain, but wind and cold that made it impossible to play, he said. Collins was livid. "What's the matter with you people?" he demanded.

"Nothing," replied Clarke. "But it's too cold to play today."

Fred Clarke needed another day for Deacon Phillippe; that's all there was to it. Jimmy Collins would have followed the same path, were he in Clarke's shoes.

There was one other consideration. Pushing the game back from a Friday to a Saturday enabled Barney Dreyfuss to take advantage of a Westinghouse offer to purchase 1,000 tickets the giant firm would not have purchased on a weekday.

A gigantic crowd of 17,038 poured into Exposition Park, so once again there was a guarantee of ground-rule triples by somebody. Win or lose, this was going to be the last day of baseball in Pittsburg for the 1903 season, so the fans had come ready to make some noise.

The Boston players now had the extra incentive of the gold medals being offered by the *Globe*'s Charles Taylor. Pittsburg owner Barney Dreyfuss responded in the finest American way, by dangling dollar bills in front of his own players' eyes.

"If the Pittsburg team beats Boston in the championship series now on they will receive every cent of money coming to Pittsburg less expenses incurred," Dreyfuss announced on the eve of Game 7.

The translation was that he would take no money from the Series for himself or his franchise, per se. Every cent of the Pittsburg profits would go to the players. The estimate of the bounty was $25,000. It was later revealed that the generous Pittsburg owner had made the offer to Fred Clarke back on September 28 before it was definitely settled that the Series would be played.

Back in Boston, things were far from tranquil, as the morning paper revealed.

TROUBLE OVER TICKETS

COMPLAINTS ABOUT SPECULATORS CORNERING THE SUPPLY, AND PATRONS ARE INDIGNANT

The Americans, of course, said they had no idea how anything could have gone amiss. According to Mr. H. A. McBreen, the assistant manager, the box office was opened in the morning in order to sell tickets for Games 8 and 9*, but it was closed as soon as "substantial evidence was reported that speculators were practicing their cunning to get hold of large blocks."

Well, that's exactly what was going on, and vox populi was incensed. According to the *Globe*, "Several exceedingly vexed men who delight in a good game of ball were so hot under the collar when they called at the *Globe* office to complain that only the speculators had seats to sell that the rain of the forenoon hissed when it ran down their backs."

Angry baseball fans were complaining that tickets by the hundreds were in the hands of speculators who "hawked their 'cornered' goods in front of the shops where patrons of the game should get their cards of admission for the laying down of a single 'punk.'" The *Globe*, which a year hence would actually own the team, went into a 1903 version of damage control on behalf of the beleaguered club officials.

"The same at the ground was closed down early," the *Globe* reported, "for the reason that orders from all over New England had arrived by telegraph. First orders, of course, received first attention. A goodly number of tickets had to be reserved for the players, who buy for their friends. There are no free tickets."

There still aren't. A century later, all playoff tickets are paid for by someone. And a century later, there are still moans and groans at every big sporting and entertainment event that gobs of tickets fall into the nefarious hands of ticket speculators, or as we call them today, "scalpers." No one ever knows how they get them. It is one of American life's eternal mysteries, right there with how a man's socks are somehow gobbled up by his wife's washing machine.

However the good people of Pittsburg obtained their tickets, a record number of them packed Exposition Park hoping that the noble Deacon Phillippe had one more victory stored in his trusty right arm. But though he pitched fairly well, the strain of a fourth start in 10 days was evident as the

---

*In 1903, the World Series was the best 5 out of 9 games.

Americans reached him for 11 hits, bunching enough of them to come away with a 7–3 victory and a 4–3 lead in the Series.

Such an overflow crowd meant there would be bogus extra base hits, and this time the Fates turned on Pittsburg, as it was the Boston squad that benefited most handsomely from the necessary ground rules. The Americans smacked five triples, two of which, by Captain Collins and Chick Stahl, came during a two-run first inning.

The rain had stopped, it had warmed up some, and the wind had shifted, but the field was in predictably poor condition and the whole affair looked more as if there should have been an English soccer match taking place that a baseball game.

"The scene was a weird one," declared Murnane. "Clouds of black smoke from the large steel works came sailing down the two rivers that meet here from the Ohio, while a bright sun shot heedless through the whirling sheets of light and heavy smoke, and every face was focused on the home plate as Boston's curly-haired boy and his favorite club stood ready for business."

The beauty of a game that featured seven errors was clearly in the eye of the beholder. Whereas an envoy from the *Pittsburg Post* declared the game to be "sad, chilly and tedious," and the Pittsburg papers, when not (legitimately) bemoaning Phillippe's worn-out state, made reference to exhausted players slipping all over a slick surface, Murnane saw only elegance, beauty, and Boston dominance.

"The last play of the day by Ferris and Parent was worth a trip to Pittsburg to see," he gushed. "The young men to shine with the greatest brilliancy during the day were Collins, Ferris, Criger, Young, Stahl, and Freeman, with Uncle Cyrus the brightest star of all.

"For Pittsburg Bransfield, Phelps, Ritchey and Clarke did some extra fine work. The umpiring of Tom Connolly and Hank O'Day was simply great. Tonight the series stands 4 to 3 in Boston's favor, and Boston people will have a chance to see the finish of a wonderful series."

Ol' Uncle Cyrus was touched for 10 hits, but they were too scattered to do enough damage.

Typical of the afternoon's game flow was the seventh. With one out Young walked Phelps. "The crowd set up a din to rattle the Boston pitcher," Murnane reported, "but the old boy refused to quit, and fanned Phillippe and forced Beaumont to raise one out to Dougherty. Then came 'Tessie, my darling, how I love you,' and a rousing three times three from the Boston contingent."

By now the game had almost become secondary to the rousing Battle of the Bands.

The whole "Tessie" business had embarrassed Pittsburg into action. By now Pittsburg had produced its own band, and its first official action early in the day was to make an attempt to drown out a Boston rendition of "Tessie" by playing "Yankee Doodle" concurrently.

Among the musical selections played by the bands were "America," "Wearing of the Green," "Dixie," "Annie Laurie," and "My Maryland."

The Pittsburg fans surely had given their all. There had been a procession of some 500, armed with horns and megaphones, that had made its way to the park, and included among the marchers were some prominent Pittsburg businessmen. It was reported that trains had disgorged people from Wheeling, Steubenville, Uniontown, Connellsville, Blairsville, Indian, Charleroi, Beaver Falls, and Monangahela City, among other locales.

"The home players came out to the field at 1:45, and they were received with a roar of applause," Murnane said. "The crowd seemed fairly wild and cheered every move of the local players. At 2:10, when the Boston players pushed their way through the spectators, they were greeted with a combination of cheers and hoots."

There just wasn't anything Captain Clarke, Dreyfuss, or any of those rabid fans could do about the fact that the Pittsburg team only had one pitcher to count on, and he was wearing out. Said one neutral observer, "It is too bad that the Pittsburg club should be so sorely handicapped in the pitching department. With Leever and Doheny in shape, there is no doubt they could have made a better showing than has been the case. President Dreyfuss was advised not to play the series with the team in a crippled condition, but he insisted upon doing so."

Frank B. McQuiston of the *Pittsburg Dispatch* put it this way on the morning of Game 7: "The Pittsburg club did not win the championship of the National League with one pitcher, nor had they the right to defend it with but one. . . . It would not have been an act of cowardice for the owners of the Pittsburg club to announce plainly that, owing [to] the falling of Doheny and the bad cold in the shoulder of Sammy Leever, they did not feel able to fight against the American League club.

"Should the American League be the loser," he continued, "people will be sore indeed, and will have reason to be, because they will have been beaten by a one-man team. Phillippe will, if he wins, be the most famous player in the history of baseball. He will be famous even if he loses out now, for he alone has been the man."

The Sunday *Pittsburg Post* had run a photograph of Phillippe with a caption saying that "he went to the rubber too often." The fans appreciated the great effort Phillippe was putting forth, so much so that when he came to bat against Cy Young in the third inning, a man named Barney Arena, representing a group of Pittsburg followers, came to the plate to present Phillippe with a diamond stickpin. The crowd applauded tremendously, and Phillippe showed his gratitude by lashing a single to left.

Back on the gold-medal front, Captain Collins had responded to Charles Taylor by telegram on behalf of the team.

EXPOSITION PARK,
PITTSBURG, OCT. 10
GEN. CHAS. H. TAYLOR, THE *BOSTON GLOBE*
On behalf of the Boston players I thank you for your liberal offer. I assure you the boys appreciate your kindness, coming as it does from one who has always been a friend of the national game.

JAMES COLLINS, CAPTAIN OF THE BOSTON AMERICANS

And the players got into the act, as well:

PITTSBURG, PENN., OCT. 10

TO GEN. C. H. TAYLOR, EDITOR OF THE *BOSTON GLOBE*:

We, the undersigned members of the Boston American baseball club, thank you for your graceful compliment and tender of medals. Win or lose, we appreciate your courtesy and remembrance.

SIGNED: CAPT. COLLINS, YOUNG, CRIGER, DOUGHERTY, FREEMAN, GIBSON, HUGHES, LACHANCE, PARENT, FERRIS, C. STAYHL, J. STAHL, FARRELL, O'BRIEN, DINNEEN, WINTER

The *Globe* printed a design for the medals, which, the readers were assured, "represent the reversion from the type of huge, shapeless masses of metal which were popular a few years ago. These are almost tiny, being designed to hang as an ornament to a watch chain, but their meaning is weighty enough to make up for any lack of size. In fact, the smaller they are the more substantial."

At any rate, the Series momentum had swung toward the Americans, who now only needed to win one of two games at the Huntington Street Grounds in order to wrap things up and become the first official baseball World Champion of the twentieth century. The first seven games had aroused deep passions, not only in the competing cities but across the country. It was clear that the idea of an annual meeting between the champions of the two major leagues was a worthy idea.

"It has surprised me to see the amount of interest that is being taken in this Series," said Captain Collins. "I never thought that it would arouse so much enthusiasm. I am glad Pittsburg won the National League pennant, for this series with the Pirates has been the most exciting of any in which I have participated. It will certainly be an honor if we can succeed in winning the world's championship from such a bunch of sterling ballplayers as Fred Clarke has here."

Collins took the occasion to reaffirm his admiration for the great Cy Young. "I felt confident Cy would do the trick and that we would bat Phillippe enough to win. Cy pitched grandly."

We were, of course, still waiting for even one person on the Boston side to acknowledge the obvious pitching handicap under which the Pittsburg side was operating. Or did the Americans think it was normal to see one man start against them four times in seven games spread over 10 days?

Fred Clarke, Gentleman of the Plains, would let others make the appropriate excuses. "I am much disappointed," he said. "I felt all confidence we would win today, and that meant, in my opinion, the Series. I have not given up yet. Look out for Monday."

The Royal Rooters came away from the game feeling the Series would not last more than one game back on home turf. They cheered and so mobbed the ballclub after winning Game 7 that it took the team 15 minutes to break through them and return to the hotel.

Captain Collins was thoroughly impressed by the backing his team had received on the road, where 200 Royal Rooters had held their own against upwards of 17,000 Smoky City enthusiasts.

"The support given the team by the 'Royal Rooters' will never be forgotten," the skipper said. "They backed us up as only Bostonians could, and no little portion of our success is due to this selfsame band of enthusiasts. Noise—why they astonished all Pittsburg by their enthusiasm, and all Pittsburg rejoiced in the interest shown in the team by our fans."

The Rooters were becoming as famous as the players. The folks back home knew all about their Pittsburg exploits, and they were grateful. When Nuf Sed McGreevey, the acknowledged leader of the Royal Rooters, returned to his saloon, he discovered that several of his friends had decorated it in honor of his return.

The one big discovery on the trip had been "Tessie." No one had the song on his or her mind when the team and the Rooters had embarked for Pittsburg a scant five days before. Now it was the new Boston anthem.

"'Tessie' did the trick," the *Globe* quoted one of the Rooters as saying. "Ever since we began to sing that song the boys have played winning ball."

The *Globe* had reached new depths of shamelessness.

Rather than a cartoon with a strict baseball theme, the morning paper of October 12 offered its readers an over-the-top depiction of a well-upholstered gentlemen representing the *Globe* (his cummerbund proclaiming the paper to have "The largest circulation in New England") holding out to some dancing ballplayers a box containing some medals. In the background a pirate is sitting atop a mast, all that is left of his ship, and he is yelling "Help! Help! I'm sinkin'!" The caption below the cartoon reads, "Now, Boys, Down Him again and Line up For Your Medals."

The only problem was that everyone was going to have to wait one more day. It was raining in Boston. There was no debate about postponing the game, since it was to Pittsburg's advantage. For Captain Clarke had penciled in Sam Leever as his starting pitcher, and poor Sam could barely raise his right arm.

Captain Clarke was continuing to put up his brave front. "Talk about the Bostons' receiving medals from General Taylor," he said. "I know this offer was very sportsmanlike, and I admire him for his enthusiasm and interest in the team, but I do not really believe the Boston players will wear these souvenirs."

The truth is that the situation was now borderline hopeless. For in addition to his severe pitching woes, the great Pittsburg leader was also getting little production from his franchise player at shortstop. Wagner had not been very Wagnerian, either at the plate or in the field, and had actually been outplayed by Boston's diminutive shortstop, Freddy Parent.

Wagner wasn't feeling good. His arm was giving him trouble, and his arm was his personal pride and joy. He was so publicly despondent that he talked about quitting the game for good. One devilish Boston patron saw that quote and immediately dispatched a copy of the morticians' trade journal entitled *American Undertaker* to Wagner, who, by all accounts, was not amused.

Back home in the Smoky City, some people still could not get over the idea that Boston just might be better, especially considering the Pirates' well-publicized pitching woes. So it was that a rumor was being floated that the reason for Pittsburg's 3–4 situation was because the fix had to be in. The Pirates were extending the Series to the full nine games in order to make more money from the gate receipts.

The teams spent a leisurely day off. Many players on both teams attended the evening performance of "The Billionaire" at the Colonial Theatre. The house band did not forget to play "Tessie."

The day of rain led to one obvious lineup change. Clarke was able to scratch Leever as the starter and replace him with—who else?—Phillippe.

Captain Collins was ready with Big Bill Dinneen, who, when last seen, was in full command of the situation "in the box," and who would be working with a whopping and, by the standards of the day, a shamefully exorbitant four days' rest.

Tim Murnane had on his Boston hat as he sat down to the typewriter. "Billy Dinneen was in grand form against Pittsburg," he wrote, "and will throw his best curves today, and try hard to give the visitors a chance to catch a late train for home, thereby saving them one day's expense."

Murnane concluded his dispatch by saying, "The game should be a good one to watch. Take along your rubber cushion and cheer for old Boston and the gold medals."

But everything was not so jolly among the fans. The ticket situation was not good. Something was terribly amiss. People wished to buy tickets for the grand occasion, but the club claimed there were none to be had. But there certainly seemed to be some in the hands of unscrupulous speculators, as one A. E. Miller of Malden informed the *Globe* and its readers with a letter that was printed in the morning paper.

After recounting fruitless trips to both the team's downtown offices and the Huntington Avenue Grounds the day before, and claiming that Mr. McBreen, the ticket manager, had seen a crowd of 400 people gathered and had "turned on his heel and said that Mr. McBreen was gone for the day" (and when cornered, Mr. McBreen said all the tickets had been put on sale downtown and then vanished), Mr. Miller concluded by saying, "Speculators were around there with their pockets full of tickets. It looks like a game of bunco, as I could find no tickets for sale by anyone except speculators."

Plus, ca change, plus c'est la meme chose, eh?

The *Globe* certainly knew that something was up. "Speculators had tickets in plenty," wrote Murnane, "and were asking $2 and $3 for them. Where they got them is a mystery to Mr. McBreen, so he said, but those who had gone to a lot of trouble to call early are willing to swear that the public was not given a fair deal.

"That someone blundered badly, or stood in with the ticket speculators, is the honest opinion of the people who follow the game closely, and were deprived of the privilege of purchasing grandstand seats at a premium of 25 cents to a speculator.

"After the experience of the club in the ticket business during the opening series here this state of affairs should not exist. It was manager [Joseph] Smart's business to investigate and show the baseball public where the American club stands regarding ticket speculators."

What happened to cause this reprehensible situation has never been determined. But the fact is that on what turned out to be a glorious day for all Boston baseball followers, only 7,455 were present to see the game. It was, by far, the smallest gathering at any of the eight 1903 World Series games, and it was not because the fans had suddenly stopped loving either the Boston Americans or the game of baseball. True, the weather was threatening, but that was a secondary issue.

The repercussions were enormous. American League president Ban Johnson was so upset by the way the Americans had handled crowds throughout the Series that he practically forced Henry Killilea to sell the team when the season was over.

What the crowd meant for the players was that they could actually play baseball. "The players had all the room they wished," reported the *Globe*, "although the ground rules were in force just as if there had not been a clear field beyond the bases."

It was a nice, crisp 95 minutes of baseball (doesn't it seem as if some at bats take that long today?). The Americans broke a scoreless tie with two runs in the fourth on a two-run single by Hobe Ferris, and that would be all Big Bill Dinneen would need. He gave Pittsburg four hits, and only in the sixth did they have more than one. A double play helped him out, and from then on he was completely in charge, retiring the final seven men after walking Ritchey in the seventh, and striking out Honus Wagner to end the game. With his team providing him an insurance run in the sixth (LaChance triple, Ferris single), Big Bill Dinneen pitched the Boston Americans to the first twentieth-century World Championship, 3–0.

"There was no anticlimax in the game of yesterday," reported Murnane. "A theatrical manager could hardly have worked the incidents better as to gradually warm up the crowd. The game opened nicely, evenly and smoothly, with a chance to yell every once in a while. But not until the fourth inning, not until the crowd had become thoroughly imbued with the intensity which appeared in the features of every player, was the opportunity for a grand, tumultuous outburst."

The fourth inning was superb theater. The gritty Phillippe, making his fifth start of the Series, had managed to blank the Americans for three innings and the natives were getting fretful. But Freeman opened with a triple over the ropes in center to the accompaniment of "Tessie." Parent was safe when catcher Phelps bobbed his dribbler, Freeman holding at third. LaChance grounded out, first baseman to pitcher covering, moving Parent to second as Freeman, in the fashion of countless Red Sox sluggers to come, cautiously remained anchored at third.

That brought up Hobe Ferris, who singled sharply to right-center, bringing home Freeman and Parent, at which time, according to Tim Murnane (clearly as pumped up as he'd ever been while covering a baseball game), "the rooters tipped over their chairs in their eagerness to rise to the occasion."

Continuing on, Murnane reported that "It seemed as if every man on both bleachers was on his feet, waving his hat and roaring. A party of six at the end of the first base bleachers released large American flags to the breeze. More 'Tessie' with the band accompanying, and more shouting took place."

After the third run came across in the sixth, Murnane said the fans "anxiously watched Dinneen hurl the ball with a speed he had not attempted at any previous part in the game."

Reaching the ninth, he dispatched Clarke and Leach on fly balls. That brought up Wagner, who was experiencing a miserable (6 for 26, one extra-base hit) Series. Big Bill reacted as if he were protecting a one-run lead with the bases loaded in the ninth.

Again, from the fertile brain of Mr. Tim Murnane:

"How Dinneen did rip that black ball over the plate! Three times did Wagner try to connect, but not a sound from the rooters until the last swing, which nearly carried him off his feet, proclaimed the downfall of the mighty men and his nine."

Dinneen's own take was a bit tamer: "I threw him a fastball, and he took a cut and missed for the third strike, which ended the Series."

The Boston Americans were champions of the known baseball world.

Lou Criger hurled the baseball in the air, and the crowd stampede was on. As the band cranked out yet another "Tessie," thousands swarmed on the field as Captain Fred Clarke attempted to extend his congratulations to both his counterpart, Jimmy Collins, and the Boston players. But soon the fans had every player in the air but Ferris, who somehow eluded them. Collins was placed at particular risk. "Jimmy Collins was nearly dismembered," reported Murnane, "because the crowd that had his right leg insisted on going in a different direction than the party which held possession of his left one. Sympathetic grandstand shouters had to admonish his captors to let him down."

According to *Reach's Official American League Guide*, "The world's champions were borne to their dressing rooms on the shoulders of thousands and the cheering lasted many minutes."

Before leaving the field, the band struck up "The Star Spangled Banner," after which time the patrons left the field and continued to celebrate on their way home.

Everyone seemed to be in agreement that the teams had done honor to the game of baseball.

"This shows that baseball is the greatest outdoor sport that has ever been known," Murnane proclaimed, "and is thoroughly American, combining everything in the way of athletic skill, nerve, grit and honesty, and all that is best in our national character."

From the *Pittsburg Dispatch* came the following: "The series of ball games for the world's championship honors came to a close in Boston yesterday, when the team representing that city signalized its fourth consecutive victory over the National champions by a shutout in a contest marked by much brilliant playing. . . .

"While such a result was unlooked for by the loyal followers of the home team, and while their disappointment is consequently keen, the truth must be acknowledged that the National leaders were fairly and squarely outplayed. A test of ability involving eight games was sufficiently ample to give both organizations all necessary opportunity to show their best, and no unfair advantages were taken on either side from start to finish. In nearly all essential features of high-class play the [Bostons] showed themselves the superiors of their opponents during the series and their success was merited."

Collins went into the locker room, sat down, and attempted to collect his thoughts. It had been a long and stressful season, and the great player-manager was physically and mentally exhausted. Then the door swung open and in walked Senator M. J. Sullivan, followed by a few of Collins's friends. Mr. Sullivan walked over to Collins, produced a box, and motioned for the players to join him.

"I have been selected to present you with a slight token of esteem from the players whom you have so successfully led to victory this year," Sullivan intoned. He then presented Collins with an open-face gold watch, to which was attached an attractive fob, and suspended from that was a gold locket, in the center of which was a large diamond.

The inscription read "To James J. Collins. From the players of the Boston baseball club, American league, Oct. 15, 1903."

"I thank you," said Collins. "I cannot express what this means to me. Boys, I wish you all a splendid winter."

Collins took time to laud his opponents. "In Pittsburg we found a worthy opponent and a grand ball team," Collins said. "Every man on the team is a fine player and the spirit of true sportsmanship was never better exemplified than in the series just closed."

There was one other person to thank, and that would be a lass named

"Tessie," who jumped on the Boston bandwagon in the fifth game and became even more important than Nuf Sed and the Royal Rooters.

Tim Murnane summed it up. "'Tessie,' an obscure maiden whom somebody loved in a ragtime melody, wasn't much in the place which the librettist and the composer built for her," he wrote. "But she has a place in history. She will go tunefully tripping down the ages as the famous mascot that helped the Boston Americans win three out of four in Pittsburg, capture the final game in Boston and with it the title—champions of the world.

"Sang by the thundering ensemble at the Huntington baseball grounds yesterday afternoon, 'Tessie' was there when anything worth doing was done. 'Tessie' was never caroled for any four-flush proposition; her chaste salutes were only for that which wins the royal wreath.

"Just as the claim of the heroine is to a high place on the first page of the history of the most famous post-season series, the words of the song have about as much to do with baseball as they did to the operation of stoking in the roundhouse across the field. But the effect is the thing; so 'Tessie' is a four-time winner."

1904: Americans vs. Giants

The World Series That Wasn't

from *The Year They Called Off the World Series*

by Benton Stark

Of the remaining six games on the Giants' schedule in October, five were home against the Cardinals. It was difficult to make a sound judgment regarding which was the pennant winner and which the fifth-place team on the basis of the play in this series. Four times the Cardinals were victorious against the team John Brush said had captured the "championship of the United States." "GIANTS STILL IN DEPRESSING FORM," read the *New York Herald*'s headline. The *New York Times* complained about Mertes's playing center field for the absent Bresnahan, characterizing his fielding as bordering "on the ridiculous." And the *New York Daily Tribune* deplored the fact that "It looked as though the [Giants] put no interest in their work. Calls of 'It's too bad you won the championship!' were frequent, and on days that double-headers were played, many spectators left the grounds after the first game." The Giants' losing streak had reached six games, but this did not cut into the enjoyment of the splashy benefit given them on Sunday, October 2, at Klaw and Erlanger's New York Theater. Jockey Tod Sloan, a close friend and business partner of [John] McGraw's, served as the master of ceremonies. A large number of celebrities were on hand, some even traveling in from out of town. As a group, the politico–show business set gravitated toward baseball and especially the talented players collected by the infamous and therefore all-the-more-attractive management team of McGraw and Brush (whose second wife, Elsie Lombard, was herself a former actress). Here was a telling recognition of which performers, relying on the adulation of an audience, held the top spot in New York at the time—an acknowledgment that the baseball field, with its honestly engaging characters and largely unpredictable drama, as well as its sizable crowd of uninhibited cheering and jeering fanatics, had emerged as the greatest show in town. Brush encouraged this following by providing politicians and show business personalities with special free passes, such as the one designed by Lambert Brothers, the jeweler, in the form of a penknife with a picture of the Polo Grounds set back into the handle. Sports announcer Joe Humphries presented McGraw with a huge loving cup for the organization as well as personal mementos, which included a watch charm set with 68 diamonds from his stage friends, a set of diamond cuff buttons from Harry Stevens, and, as Blanche McGraw put it, "less brilliant items bestowed with equal pride and affection." The benefit itself brought in an astonishing $25,000, all of which was distributed to very grateful players, many of whom didn't earn very much money in salary.

Fewer than 1,000 turned out the next afternoon, October 4, for the doubleheader against the Cardinals that would formally end the season. McGinnity pitched and lost the opener, 7–3, winding up with a record of 35–8. His teammates made five errors in their halfhearted, go-through-the-motions performance. The second game was a total disaster. The trouble began in the bottom of the first when Dan McGann, who thought he had hit a home run over the right fielder's head, was called out on an appeal play for not touching first base. McGann and acting manager William "Doc" Marshall cornered umpire Jim Johnstone and argued loudly and abusively enough to be ordered off the field. Three innings later, Dahlen started on Johnstone over a safe call at second, and he also was ejected. This was too much for the Giants, who appeared unwilling to resume their positions, forcing Johnstone to forfeit the game to St. Louis. The 2,000 spectators were so worked up by this time, the *New York Times* declared, that they were making "as much noise as could be made by five times that number." As Johnstone attempted to leave the field, he was rushed by a number of these juiced-up Giant loyalists sitting in the grandstand, and violently shoved. Just after this, a fire broke out in the area of the home team players' bench.

Under the headline "DISGRACEFUL END," W. M. Rankin blasted the Giants in his *Sporting News* column:

> [In] the closing scenes on the Polo Grounds, this city . . . was a mix-up of enthusiasts, umpire, players, police and general dissatisfaction. It was the most disgraceful way for a champion team to end so grand and successful a campaign. . . .
>
> To forfeit the last game of the season was not the proper thing for them to do. Their actions during the past few weeks have not been all they should have been or was expected of them. They have acted entirely too indifferent to the duties they were expected to perform. . . . The public should have had a run for its money. It has supported them in grand style this year and was certainly entitled to better treatment from them.

Rankin was an influential journalist commenting in a periodical regarded as "the bible of baseball." If the religious imagery is appropriate, the 80-year-old man they called "Father," Henry Chadwick, had to be considered the game's guardian angel. Chadwick had been the first great promoter of the game, the developer of the box score, the author of numerous manuals and books, and the editor of the indispensable annual *Spalding's Official Base Ball Guide*. The most venerable sportswriter of them all couldn't stand what he had witnessed on October 4. He wrote a letter to the *Sporting News* stating that it was "with pained regret" that he had "to record the closing scene of the last game of the New York team at the Polo Grounds for 1904." That evening a specially arranged performance took place at the Majestic Theater, during which a silver-mounted bat, suitably inscribed, was presented to John McGraw and the Giants. Given the day's events, at least some of those present must have been a little uncomfortable.

As the month of October began, the Highlanders held a .003 first-place lead over the Pilgrims. The continued prospect of winning the American League pennant inspired President Joseph Gordon of the Highlanders to make one last attempt to get John Brush to change his mind about playing a World Series:

John T. Brush, Esq.
President New York National League Club

Dear Sir:

In behalf of the Greater New York Baseball Club of the American League, I hereby challenge the New York National League Club to play a series of seven games for the world's championship in the event of the winning of the American League pennant by the Greater New Yorks. In view of a general popular demand in the interest of true sportsmanship, I believe that such a series should be arranged forthwith.

As far as the Greater New York Club is concerned, gate receipts cut an insignificant figure. The New York public which has supported the game loyally through years of vicissitudes, is entitled to consideration, and the time has now arrived, in my estimation, when this support should be rewarded by the playing of a series that will be memorable in baseball history.

The American League won the title of world's champions when the Bostons defeated the Pittsburgs last year. If the Greater New Yorks defeat the Bostons in the American League race, we will have a right to defend the title. If you wish to prove to the baseball public that the New York Nationals are capable of winning these added laurels from the Greater New Yorks, we will pave the way. The responsibility will rest upon you,

Mr. Brush, to accept or decline this fair, square proposition, made in the interests of the national sport.

In stipulating the number of games to be played, we would suggest that three be played at the Polo Grounds, three at American League Park, and the place of the seventh, if it becomes necessary to play it, to be decided by the toss of a coin, the winner of four games to be the champions of the world.

Very truly yours,

Joseph Gordon,
President, Greater New York
Baseball Club of the American League

When Brush failed to reply to his letter, Gordon told the press that although he had sent his challenge by registered mail, if the Giant owner had not received it, he would be only too willing to mail another one—and, he added, "I think I shall do it." On October 6, Brush responded, giving as the reason for not acting sooner an illness that kept him from his office. He had decided to turn the question over to John McGraw. The Giant manager then issued a statement of his own:

I want to go clearly and emphatically on record in the matter of the refusal of the New York club to play a post-season series. The people of New York have been kind enough to give me some credit for bringing the pennant to New York, and if there is any just blame or criticism for the club's action in protecting that highly-prized honor the blame should rest on my shoulders, not Brush's, for I alone am responsible.

When I came to New York three years ago the team was in last place. Since that time, on and off the field, I have worked to bring the pennant to New York. The result is known. Now that the New York team has won this honor, I for one will not stand to see it tossed away like a rag. The pennant means something to me. It is the first I have ever won [as a manager]. It means something to our players, and they are with me in my stand. We never stopped until we clinched the pennant, even if it did rob the game of the interest of a pennant race. The club never complained. When the fight was hot we played to thousands. After the race was won we played to hundreds. But that was square sport and the stockholders never complained. If we didn't sacrifice our race in our own league to the box office we certainly are not going to put in jeopardy the highest honor in baseball simply for the box office inducements.

McGraw knew firsthand how the honor of a pennant can be lost in a postseason championship series. He had horrible memories of the pennant-winning Orioles of 1894 and 1895 losing the Temple Cup Series two straight years. McGraw and his teammates heard many hurtful remarks from the baseball public. "Fake champions!" "Quitters!" and "Can't take it when the chips are down!" are the ones he and his wife remembered. McGraw reacted very badly. "John went to bed," Blanche McGraw wrote, "and under a doctor's care for the rest of the year. At first his affliction was called nervousness, a sort of breakdown, and then it was diagnosed as malaria. He was weak, had recurring fever and regular headaches." The situation in 1904—the possibility of losing the glory he always needed to a Ban Johnson American League team, and perhaps the hated New York rival at that—was dangerously similar to the one he could not handle in the 1890s. Was he going to chance it? The answer was no!

The baseball press did not think much of McGraw's statement. The *Chicago Sunday Tribune,* typically, thought it "makes him ridiculous. He practically admits the Giants would be defeated in such a series. . . . Truly McGraw must be hard pressed by public opinion when he makes 'breaks' like that." The *New York World* chastised McGraw for "entirely ignoring the almost unanimous opinion of the baseball public that the Giants should play either Boston or the Highlanders for the honors won last year by the Boston team," and added that "a careful perusal of his letter fails to show a reason of any kind, good or bad, for the stand he has taken. . . ." The *New York*

Daily Tribune concurred: "What the baseball public, not only in this city but throughout the country, wishes now is a meeting of the winning teams of the National and American Leagues."

But nothing was going to change the minds of Brush and McGraw, not even a petition signed by 10,000 New York fans. What they did do, as an answer to criticism, was to bar the very outspoken Sam Crane, veteran newspaperman and former major league infielder, from the Polo Grounds. Back in the 1890s, in Cincinnati, Brush tried a similar punitive tactic when he took the press pass away from a troublesome sports editor named Ban Johnson. He didn't accomplish anything then either.

St. Louis was the site of the penultimate series for the Highlanders. When they left Sportsman's Park on October 5, they trailed the Pilgrims* by half a game. They were coming back East for the last five games on their schedule to play their season-long archrivals from Boston. Three out of five is what they needed for the American League flag: Win the series, win the pennant.

If "Dame Fortune" operates on an even-up basis, the Highlanders would have things their way back home because they sure weren't having much luck leaving the West. For hours, they sat on the train because of a wreck on the line at Terre Haute, Indiana. Finally, Griffith was able to switch his players to a second line, but because of the time lost, they arrived in New York only three hours before game time. Sharing the early portion of this frustrating journey with the Highlanders was New York's Governor Benjamin Odell, who, upon reaching Albany, sent a telegram to Griffith:

> Despite your running away from our sweeping challenge for a way station
> championship and laurels of our special train, the undersigned hope you and
> your splendid athletes of the diamond defeat the wily Boston beaneaters
> and achieve the world's championship as well as the American League

---

*Boston's American League franchise was known as the Pilgrims and the Americans in the early twentieth century.

pennant, for the great Empire State and for the City of New York. Foxily you hired a special train and ran away from us—worse than John T. Brush. However, the Gubernatorial staff admire your pluck and grand playing, and sincerely hope you win the big American League race.

When the Highlanders' brief rest ended in the early afternoon of Friday, October 7, and the opening contest with the Pilgrims at Hilltop Park was to begin, it was Jack Chesbro (40–10)—who else?—who got the call. According to *Sporting Life*, Chesbro told Griffith that, if necessary, he would work every day of the upcoming week. Facing him would be Norwood Gibson (17–13). Although Gibson had pitched exceptionally well lately, the New Yorkers might have been swinging against their old teammate Jesse Tannehill (21–11, 2.04 ERA) had he not suffered a strained groin in Cleveland in late September and been forced to leave the club for the season. The visitors drew first blood in the top of the third. With two out, "Kip" Selbach hit a roller just wide of shortstop "Kid" Elberfeld, so that although he made a fine stop on the ball, he could not throw it. When catcher "Red" Kleinow could not handle a Chesbro spitter, Selbach moved into scoring position. Freddy Parent then blooped one in front of center fielder John Anderson, and Selbach chased home with the game's initial score. The Highlanders, in their half of the inning, came right back. Elberfeld was hit by a Gibson pitch and scored on Anderson's double down the left-field line. Two innings later, Patsy Dougherty led off with a flare that fell between Parent, the shortstop, and Selbach, the left fielder. Keeler, still playing with a bandaged right forefinger as a result of being hit by a pitched ball a week before, then slapped a ground ball to manager–third baseman Jimmy Collins, who got the throw over to first in time, but "Candy" LaChance could not hold on, creating a second and third situation for the Highlanders. Elberfeld followed with a fly ball to right, driving in New York's second run. In the bottom of the seventh, the Highlanders added a third tally: Dougherty reached first on another LaChance error, advanced to second on a base on balls to Elberfeld and crossed the plate on a single to left by Jimmy Williams. Although the

Pilgrims got one more in the eighth, the tired hometown heroes hung on for a tremendously important triumph. "That the 'rooters' appreciated the work of Chesbro," reported the *New York Times*, "was shown after the last Boston man [catcher "Duke"] Farrell, was thrown out at first by Conroy. Rushing pell mell on the field, they picked the 'Happy One' up and carried him down the field to the clubhouse amid the wildest enthusiasm." Actually, both pitchers deserved special attention, each allowing but four hits. However, the 3–2 edge in runs gave Chesbro win number 41 and his New York team first place by half a game. "HIGHLANDERS HOME AND TAKE THE LEAD," announced the *New York World*.

> It now looks as if the title of "World's Champions," so coveted by baseball players, will be passed over to the Highlanders by Monday afternoon next. The teams have four more games to play. Boston must win three of them to retain the championship, while an even break will suit the Highlanders.

"Nothing is easy in war," wrote Dwight Eisenhower. "Mistakes are always paid for in casualties. . . ." Back in mid-July, the Highlander management agreed to allow the Columbia University football team to use Hilltop Park for its October 8 game against Williams. At the time, the Highlanders trailed the first-place Pilgrims by 3½ games, with half the season to go. It did not seem incredibly significant that the baseball game scheduled for Hilltop that afternoon would have to be shifted elsewhere. But, by October 8, the single game had become a doubleheader, and the significance had become tremendous. The Highlanders had moved ahead of the Pilgrims by a half-game, thanks to their home victory on Friday, October 7, with four games left in the war for the American League banner. Now, thanks to that casual decision made nearly three months before, the critical Saturday doubleheader was to be transferred—to Boston! What this meant to those who knew the atmosphere pervading the Huntington Avenue Grounds was the very real possibility of a total shift in fate for the New York club. Over on Boston's Columbia Avenue, near Ruggles Street, was a Roxbury saloon run by Michael T. McGreevy, known as "Nuf Sed" to all the locals. The nickname came about because, as Pittsburg third baseman Tommy Leach heard it, "any time there was an argument about anything to do with baseball, he was the ultimate authority. Once McGreevy gave his opinion that ended the argument: nuf sed!" McGreevy headed a large group of Pilgrim fans who called themselves the "Royal Rooters." But these were not just fans. In fact, these were not just enthusiastic fans. These were monstrous, dominating, indefatigable, deciding fans. Tommy Leach believed that these "Royal Rooters" actually won the 1903 World Series for the Boston Pilgrims:

> We beat them three out of the first four games, and then they started singing that damn "Tessie" song. . . . They must have figured it was a good luck charm, because from then on you could hardly play ball they were singing "Tessie" so damn loud.

> "Tessie" was a real big popular song in those days. . . .

> "Tessie, you make me feel so badly,
> Why don't you turn around.
> Tessie, you know I love you madly,
> Babe, my heart weighs about a pound. . . ."

> Only instead of singing "Tessie, you know I love you madly," they'd sing special lyrics to each of the Red Sox players: like "Jimmy [Collins], you know I love you madly." And for us Pirates they'd change it a little. Like when Honus Wagner came up to bat they'd sing:

> "Honus, why do you hit so badly,
> Take a back seat and sit down.
> Honus, at bat you look so sadly,
> Hey, why don't you get out of town."

> Sort of got on your nerves after a while. And before we knew what happened, we'd lost the World Series.

Thirty thousand Bostonians showed up on Saturday, October 8, for this relocated doubleheader, and several thousand gathered around the downtown newspaper offices to keep track of the score. Every reserved seat had been sold the previous week, and the bleachers were packed an hour and a half before the action was to begin. Temporary seats were erected in front of the grandstand so that several hundred more could be squeezed in, but fans directed to this section blocked the view of those in the permanent boxes, causing such an outcry that some of the newly positioned benches had to be quickly removed. Still the rooters poured in, necessitating the opening of the field for standing areas. So close to the outfielders were the standees that it was agreed that anything hit fair into their roped-off midst would be a ground-rule double. Incredibly, the native of North Adams, Massachusetts, Jack Chesbro, with less than 24 hours' rest, was to pitch again for New York. Facing him would be last year's World Series hero, Bill Dinneen. This was Chesbro's 50th start, one-third of his team's total games this season. However, the hard work did not appear to bother him through the first three innings. At this point, the Highlanders owned the only run, ex-Pilgrim Dougherty scoring that one. Then, in the Boston fourth, the fatigue Chesbro must have felt began to show. Six hits, a base on balls, and errors by Dougherty and Elberfeld cost the visitors six runs. Into the fray came Walter Clarkson, but the former ace of nearby Harvard College did no better, giving up two runs in the fifth, four in the sixth, and one in the seventh. At the end of this first game, the score read 13–2 and the American League standings showed Boston by a half-game over New York.

The second game's pitchers were Jack Powell and "Cy" Young. This would be a darkness-halted seven-inning contest, with only one run being registered. The lone tally occurred in the bottom of the fifth. Pilgrim second baseman Albert "Hobe" Ferris pushed a little grounder over second, which Williams reached but could not convert. Catcher Lou Criger sacrificed Ferris to second. "Cy" Young then helped his own cause by smacking one deep enough to right to permit Ferris to tag up. When third baseman Conroy failed to handle Keeler's throw, allowing the ball to roll into the crowd, Ferris was waved home amid deafening cheers. Regarding Young's shutout performance,

Jacob C. Morse wrote in *Sporting Life* that "nothing finer has been chronicled than the work of our 'grand old man' . . . who keeps on pitching famous ball, despite the attempts to write him out of it. . . ." Actually, something finer had been "chronicled" by Young earlier in the year—a perfect game against the Philadelphia Athletics. The all-time leader in games won, an astounding 511, had much written about him, including a little panegyric by Grantland Rice:

> *Fame may be fleeting and glory may fade—*
> *Life at its best is a breath on the glade.*
> *One hero passes, another is made.*
> *New stars arise as the old ones pale.*
> *So when a stalwart steps out from the throng*
> *On with the tribute, let garlands be flung—*
> *Here's to the king of them all, Denton True Young.*

The Highlanders now trailed by 1 1/2 games. "I am still confident we will land the flag," Clark Griffith told the press, "and the boys are too. Chesbro will go against the champions on Monday. He usually does that when he has been hit hard, and turns the tables. We are all cheerful."

The two clubs had Sunday to travel back to New York, repair and dry out their ripped and sweat-soaked uniforms, and rest up for the doubleheader on Monday, the last day of the season. Accompanying the Pilgrims were 200 "Royal Rooters," prepared to do to the Highlanders what they had done to the Pirates the previous year. On the rear of the railroad car that they stuffed themselves into was a banner that read: "WE WANT THESE TWO GAMES. 'NUF SED'" When they reached New York, they headed for the Hotel Marlborough, where they joyously milled about, sporting red badges with the words "WORLD'S CHAMPIONS" written across. The *New York Times* noted that "quite a number of the visitors carried suitcases and satchels which they took with them to Pittsburg last fall 'just for luck.'" The word at the hotel was that Dinneen and Chesbro, as Griffith had promised, would be the pitchers in the first game. "The Boston men," said the *Times*, "think Chesbro has been worked too hard, and that the drubbing he got on Saturday marked the beginning of his downfall." New York City was electric with excitement over the American League showdown. "Probably no such interest ever was taken in a baseball event in this city," thought the *Times*.

Monday, October 10, began with threatening weather but cleared up by the time the crowd of 28,584 lucky ticket holders pushed through the entrance gates of Hilltop Park. The "Royal Rooters" positioned themselves at the extreme left of the grandstand. They brought along the Lew Dockstader's Band, which, together with the megaphones and tin horns held to many agitated mouths, kept up a continuous din throughout the ballgame. "Tessie" was on hand, also. One of the "Rooters" stood above the Boston bench and led his comrades in the rallying tune until, the *Boston Herald* noted, the performers must have been as tired as the auditors, some of whom inquired innocently enough if that was the only air the band could play."

Chesbro hadn't lost much in 1904—in fact, only 11 times in 52 decisions—and after four of those times, he bounced right back to take the next contest from the team that did him in. Today, in the first game, he could make it five quick avengings with a triumph over Boston. "I am willing to bet my last dollar that I trim Collins' boys," he told the *New York World*. And so it appeared that trimming was what he was up to when the first three Pilgrims he faced were retired in order. Patsy Dougherty led off the Highlander half with a base on balls and took second on a Willie Keeler sacrifice. However, neither "Kid" Elberfeld nor Jimmy Williams was able to cash in this potential run, and the game was scoreless after one. In the second, "Buck" Freeman and "Hobe" Ferris singled, but were left stranded by Lou Criger. When John Anderson, John Ganzel, and "Wid" Conroy went down quietly in the second against Bill Dinneen, this crucial game showed all the signs of being exactly what it should be: a classic pitchers' duel. Ground balls got rid of Dinneen and "Kip" Selbach in the third, and Chesbro, for the second time, struck out Freddy Parent. After "Red" Kleinow continued the afternoon's dismal hitting exhibition by grounding out to begin the Highlander third, Chesbro stepped to the plate. Time, however, was called. At this point, it was decided to allow "Happy Jack's" fans to present him with a fur overcoat and cap. "He'll strike out for sure on account of that fur overcoat," predicted a superstitious fan within earshot of the *New York Herald*'s reporter. "But," the reporter wrote, "Chesbro this time made an exception in the case of players who go to bat and do nothing after having received a present. He slammed the ball along the right field line for three bases." With Chesbro ninety feet away from a New York lead, Dougherty and Keeler—the most consistent hitters in the Highlander lineup—did something not even the most loyal Pilgrim krank could have expected: They both struck out. Still, Griffith could take heart at the way Chesbro was pitching. He seemed to be getting stronger as the struggle progressed. Dinneen, on the other hand, faltered in the bottom of the fifth. Although he got Ganzel and Conroy out, Kleinow singled sharply to right and Chesbro smashed one right back through the middle past Dinneen. Dougherty, who had a knack for heroics, followed with a line single to right, driving in Kleinow with the first run of the game. Shaken by three straight hard hits, Dinneen proceeded to walk Keeler to fill the bases—perhaps he just didn't want to pitch to him anyhow. "Such cheering!" declared the *New York Herald*. "One had to stuff cotton in his ears in order to think. The cheering became a roar when Elberfeld walked, forcing Chesbro over the plate." But the fun ended there as Williams hit softly back to Dinneen for the long-delayed third out. Two runs constituted a good lead, with Chesbro doing his thing on the mound.

However, despite the attention pitchers naturally get, it is a fact that they cannot win all by themselves. This basic baseball truth was made evident in the top of the seventh. Chesbro got two strikes on "Candy" LaChance, but the big first baseman reached out and poked the next pitch just over Chesbro's head. Second baseman "Buttons" Williams got to the ball but couldn't make the throw in time. Ferris, the next hitter, chopped a routine ground ball directly at Williams, who just couldn't find the handle. Criger advanced both runners with a fine sacrifice bunt. Pitcher Bill Dinneen seemed to be helping Chesbro out of this mess when he followed with another routine grounder to Williams, who fielded this one all right, but then fired the ball into the dirt in front of catcher Kleinow, allowing both runners to score and even the contest, 2–2. Williams's poor play had allowed Boston to get untracked and put the game up for grabs.

In the top of the eighth, Charley "Chick" Stahl, Freeman, and LaChance got hits, and Boston was poised to jump into the lead. However, the Highlander defense came to the rescue, cutting down Stahl at the plate on a pretty relay play from center fielder Anderson to shortstop Elberfeld to Kleinow. So, toe to toe, Boston and New York went into the ninth inning looking for that little opening that would allow the deciding blow to land. In the top half of the inning, slow-footed, weak-hitting (.208) Lou Criger beat out a roller to short. Dinneen did his job, sacrificing Criger to second. Selbach, at the top of the lineup, was in a storybook position to bring home his relatively new club a winner, but Chesbro threw that spitter of his and "Kip" tapped the ball back to the mound. This made two outs, with Criger still on third. The second spot on the Boston card belonged to shortstop Freddy Parent. Twice this day Parent was a strikeout victim. And, for all the world, it appeared that Parent was about to go down a third time when Chesbro blew two strikes past the little 5-foot-5 $^1/_2$-inch guy on the first two pitches. The "Book" says that an 0–2 count calls for a pitch out of the strike zone to make the hitter, who is in an extremely defensive position, swing at something he cannot hit solidly. Was the next toss by Chesbro a "waste pitch"? What is known is that it was one of his spitballs and that it was high, wild, and beyond Kleinow's reach. Back it went to the foot of the grandstand and in trotted Criger with the go-ahead run. Although Parent hit the next pitch into center field for a single, that does not necessarily mean that the run would have scored anyway because game conditions, including pressure and pitching strategy, would have been different and such things clearly have great effects on performance.

So, although no more damage was done, the visitors were up that big one tally, 3–2, and it all came down to what the home team could do in its "last licks." Ganzel, the number six hitter, darkened the already gloomy picture for the New Yorkers by striking out for the second consecutive time.

But then Conroy drew a walk. Next came Kleinow, who had two hits this game. However, he popped out to second baseman Ferris. Chesbro's spot in the order had been reached. What were the Highlanders to do in this critical situation? Chesbro, too, had two hits off Dinneen, including that post–fur-overcoat-gift triple. The 1904 season had been Chesbro's best as a hitter (.236 average) as well as a pitcher. But, this was the most important at bat of the Highlanders' season, and it could not go to a pitcher. Griffith made a move. Hitting for Chesbro would be Jim McGuire. The "Deacon," however, was hitting only .210 and was unlikely to beat out an infield hit if it should come to that. Nevertheless, the substitution paid off in that the patient veteran catcher worked Dinneen for a walk, sending Conroy to second as the tying run. The lineup turned over to the top of the order. What a spot for Dougherty, the former Pilgrim left fielder. He could have the sweetest revenge baseball offers: snatching away the pennant from the organization that traded him. Patsy was hitting .279 and already had an RBI this afternoon. Meanwhile, Dave Fultz went out to run for McGuire at first. The dramatic tension couldn't be any higher—but it wasn't sustained long: three pitches, and nothing but air! Dougherty struck out. "No man in this land wanted to have the Highlanders humble the champions as much as Dougherty did. Then to be finally out-generalled by his ex-clubmates with two men on bases waiting to be brought home—it was simply awful," commented the *New York World* with appropriate sympathy.

Suddenly, it was all over. What had been a seemingly endless and gut-wrenching war, requiring triumph after triumph, had ended in the flash of one empty swing. Conroy, who would have been mobbed with supreme joy under other circumstances, walked dejectedly toward the clubhouse. The facts were brutal in their simplicity and would admit no change: The Highlanders had come in second and the Pilgrims had won their second American League pennant in a row. The "Royal Rooters" were delirious. They, the Lew Dockstader's Band, and other Bostonians in town celebrated with a torchlight parade down Broadway. What a humiliating scene that was for the proud Highlanders and their loyal supporters.

There was a second game that day, which the Highlanders won, 1–0, in extra innings, behind Ambrose Puttman. "Today, after the first game of the doubleheader had been won by Boston," wrote T. E. Sanborn in the *Sporting News,*

> there was absolutely no reason for playing the second game, as nothing depended on it. McGraw and his Giants would undoubtedly have made a farce of it and driven the patrons away. Not so the Bostons and Highlanders. They fought out a 10-inning game as sharply as if it mattered who won it and showed the kind of spirit that wins baseball fans of all degrees.

But, aside from showing "class" in playing despite a shattered spirit, it really did not matter to the Highlanders. The real issue had been decided in the ninth inning of the first game. That loss was to be a demon that destroyed all the pleasure Jack Chesbro should have derived from his dazzling 1904 season. He had started 51 games and completed 48 of them, pitched 454.2 innings, posted a 41–12 record, and finished with a 1.82 ERA—and all he could think about was that wild pitch, what has been called the most costly wild pitch in history. Several weeks after the close of the season, Chesbro and Griffith went on a hunting trip. Lee Allen tells the poignant story:

> "Why don't you look for something to shoot?" Griffith said to him in the woods.
> "I was thinking," Chesbro replied.
> "About that wild pitch?"
> "Yes."
> "Now, look here," Griff said. "If you ever mention that wild pitch again, I'll shoot you as I would a muskrat. Now shut up and hunt."

But Chesbro could not forget and neither, later, could his widow, who attempted to blame "Red" Kleinow for letting it get behind him. Fred Lieb asked "Kid" Elberfeld about the possibility of Kleinow catching that infamous pitch. Elberfeld exploded: "The only way Kleinow could have caught that ball would have been while standing on top of a stepladder." "Deacon" McGuire, who caught two-thirds of the Highlander games that year, was asked if he might have been able to grab "the wild pitch." "There wasn't a chance of stopping that spitter," he asserted. "It might as well have gone over the top of the grandstand."

But the criticisms and "what ifs" of baseball are part of its great fun and provide good kindling for the long "hot-stove league" season. The winter of 1904–1905 would be much longer and much less satisfying than the last because there was no World Series to analyze over and over again. One final try—probably to taunt the Giant management—had been made by Pilgrim owner John Taylor, when, on October 10, he announced an offer for a series of games between the two championship teams, with all the receipts to be divided among the players. According to the *Boston Herald*, a number of the top Giant players would have leaped at the chance. The journal reported that at the deciding Pilgrim-Highlander doubleheader, McGinnity complained that "It is just like taking money out of our pockets to prevent us from playing the winners. The players are willing enough, I tell you. I think McGraw has the best ball tossers ever got together and I think they can beat any aggregation when in trim." Then, he added, "Of course, they are out of training now, and cannot play the ball they did two months ago."

The "Royal Rooters," in their special fashion, made it known that they wanted a chance to see their Pilgrims play the Giants. As they left Hilltop Park for their hotel, they carried two brooms supporting a long banner that read: "Mr. Brush, we're on plush. Where are you? Don't be vain. Give us a game." Nevertheless, there was a benefit for the Boston club in the Giant management's stubbornness. As the *New York World*'s headline proclaimed: "THE BOSTONS STILL HOLD TITLE OF WORLD CHAMPIONS, GIANTS REFUSING TO PLAY. "As there is no challenge for the greater title," the journal explained, "Jimmy Collins's men will retain it for another year. Possibly in 1905 the National League winners may at least try to take the honors from the Boston boys."

1912: Red Sox vs. Giants
Red Sox Game 7 Extra-Inning Win
from *Red Sox Nation* by Peter Golenbock

The Birth of the Green Monster

In 1911, John I. Taylor announced he was building a new ballpark for the Red Sox. It would be located in an undeveloped area called the Fenway, close to Kenmore Square and only several miles from the center of downtown Boston. At the time, fans wondered why the team was moving from the Huntington Avenue Grounds. The answer: money.

The likelihood is that the man behind the move was John I.'s father, General Taylor. Ban Johnson was upset because of the rift between John I. and Jimmy Collins—and the negative publicity that resulted—and he was putting pressure on John I. to sell. The question became: How can we sell to our best advantage?

The Taylors' biggest liability in selling the Red Sox was that they did not own the Huntington Avenue Grounds. As long as they had to rent their field, buyers for the team would be limited and so would the asking price, because a new owner would also be at the mercy of the field's landlord.

At the same time the Taylors, under the name "Fenway Realty Company," owned a huge tract of undeveloped land in the Fens. By moving their team into a new ballpark built on their own property, the Taylors were not only making the land more attractive to buyers, but the club as well.

Before the construction of the park, the area was best known as being part of the Back Bay. The site of the ballpark had been a mud flat referred to as "the Fens," and the area surrounding the Fens was called Fenway. Once the Taylors let it be known that the new stadium would be called Fenway Park, the area immediately assumed a new identity in the minds of Bostonians.

The plan to move the team to Fenway Park paid off quickly. As soon as construction began and it was clear that the Taylors intended to complete the new park, they sold half their interest in the Red Sox, reportedly for $150,000—getting their original investment back while remaining owners of the ballpark.

The sale took place on September 16, 1911. The new part-owners were James McAleer, secretary of the American League and a close friend of Ban Johnson, and Robert McRoy. In a newspaper article the next day, Ban Johnson was quoted as saying, "Both are versed in baseball and have marked ability and they ought to greatly strengthen the organization."

Johnson was at the meeting announcing the sale. He "is in full sympathy with the new conditions," the article said. Johnson expressed "great satisfaction after the deal was closed to find a man of McAleer's experience connected with the local club."

In the interests of his league, Johnson had wanted John I. Taylor out and a baseball man to run the team. Taylor didn't want to go. This appears to have been the compromise.

When Fenway Park opened on April 9, 1912, the Red Sox defeated Harvard University in an exhibition game played during a snowstorm. In its major-league opener, Boston beat the Yankees 7–6 in eleven innings, as spitball pitcher Bucky O'Brien won in relief of Charles "Sea Lion" Hall (so called because of his deep voice).

The park was only partially finished at the time. There was a small section of center-field bleachers, but the bleachers in right had yet to be built and there were no stands at all down the left-field line. The area out beyond the right-field wall was a parking lot for cars during that season. (In fact, there was more parking for fans back in 1912 than there is today.) Not until the Red Sox got into the World Series of 1912 were the rest of the bleachers added.

When the park finally took shape, it featured a single-deck grandstand of steel and concrete. There were wooden bleachers in left, a right-field pavilion, and large wooden bleacher sections in extreme right and in center field.

The park was askew, built in seventeen facets, with walls and barriers breaking off at odd angles. The left-field fence was only 320½ feet from home plate down the line, and behind it was a high wall. The left-field turf sloped steeply from the wall toward the infield. The center-field fence was 390 feet away, and the right-field fence was only 313½ feet. (In the 1920s, the right-field fence was placed 358 feet from home plate, when a new bleacher section was built.)

Legend has it that the park was built with those dimensions because of the layout of the surrounding streets, and the fear that batted balls would strike nearby structures. But back in 1912, nobody ever hit the ball even as far as a fence. It was the dead-ball era, and the only home runs hit landed between the outfielders. If General Taylor had wanted to make his park symmetrical, he well could have. But first he designed the offices, and then he laid out the fences. Exactly where the fences were didn't matter, because, some experts say, they were constructed for one purpose: to keep out nonpaying fans.

The 10-foot embankment in left field was erected not to create excitement during a ballgame, but to make it easier for spectators sitting out there to see the action. On days when ticket demand was great, the ballclub sat the overflow crowd behind the left fielder. If the area had been flat, the fans in the back rows would not have been able to see over the heads of the fans in front of them. For the 1912 World Series, for instance, seats on the slope were made available. The cost was $1, the same as the left-field bleachers.

In later years, when more grandstand seats had been built and balls were regularly hit this far, the on-field seats were sold only in the rare event of huge crowds.

In 1934 owner Tom Yawkey removed the slope and erected a 28-foot-high fence behind the left fielder, affectionately known as the Green Monster, or the Wall. It is part of the legend of Fenway Park, one of the holy shrines in American sports.

Roy Mumpton, sportswriter, *Worcester Telegram*: "I still think at the old strange ballparks, Fenway Park, Ebbets Field, which is the reverse, and Tiger Stadium, you get a much better ballgame. It sounds crazy, but you do. The games are never over until the last man is out, because you have that chance to win because of the park."

John Updike: "I had small kids for a while, and we used to go in together as a family, and though I have kept up, I have always lived in a suburb, maybe an hour away from the park. It's a headache to park around the park and sort of a headache to go in general, although once you're there, you're rewarded by the timeless American pastoral of those men in whites spaced out in that meadow. It is a wonderful thing, like entering into an Easter egg. Suddenly after the hassles and traffic jam and getting in, you do enter this world where peace and order is reigning."

Anthony J. Lukas, author, *Common Ground*: "Everybody always writes about the Wall and the size of the field and the way it hunches in, but the thing that is almost as much a symbol of Fenway Park as anything else is the Citgo sign in Kenmore Square. Over the left-field wall is this famous sign, large, flashing, neon. It's almost become a part of Fenway Park. It's the most beloved sign. A song has been written about the sign. A three-minute movie has been made of it.

"Particularly when you go there at night, that sign . . . it's too far away for even Jim Rice to hit with a ball, but it is part of the experience of going to Fenway Park.

"Also, I love the street that runs right by Fenway Park. There's something nineteenth century about that little thoroughfare, the way you come in off this little, tiny street right into that lobby. Every other stadium in this country you approach from a large parking lot with a huge facade. Here it's almost medieval. You come in off the street right into this dark, smelly warren of a lobby. It's great."

1912

There aren't many Red Sox fans alive today who were there when the Boston Red Sox won the 1912 American League pennant. Frank Gendreau, Jr., who was born in 1903, was the son of a Boston jeweler who did a lot of business with the Red Sox players back then. The elder Gendreau had a summer home on the beach at Hough's Neck in Quincy, about 10 miles south along the shore from Boston. The Red Sox players used to drive their cars there after the games on Saturday or for the entire day Sunday, when playing baseball was prohibited in Boston. Frank Gendreau remembers an age that has long disappeared.

Frank Gendreau, Jr. (age 88): "My dad, I think, tried out with the Baltimore Orioles years ago, before the turn of the century. He was very friendly with the Red Sox players as a team. They were customers of his in those days, a lot of them, and they would come into the store at the corner of Summer and High streets and buy jewelry. One time, after the Sox won the pennant in 1912, at the Old Fenway Park he presented the captain, Heinie Wagner, with a large loving cup as a gift from the fans before a game.

"They were always coming down to the beach to visit with us. I can remember Forrest Cady arriving in his Hupmobile and Dutch Leonard arriving in his Stutz Bearcat, and one of the other players had a Thomas Flyer. These were high-speed cars. And the players would come down and spend the day and have steamed clams. I used to go out in front of the house and dig up the clams.

"They used to play a little ball on our front yard, hit grounders to each other, and then I'd get out in a 10-foot rowboat and row 100, 200 feet offshore, and they would pitch to each other, and they'd hit the balls into the bay, and I would row out and retrieve them.

"Then they would clean out all the liquor there was by late afternoon, and they'd head down to a well-known bar in Nantasket or go to Hough's Neck, which featured Taylor's ballroom, three dance halls, two bowling alleys, and also Crystal Lake, in front of the Pandora Hotel, with a bandstand in the middle, where the musicians used to play on the bandstand with the lake all around it. Hough's Neck was *the* place to go.

"Smoky Joe Wood seemed to be very close to me. I can remember one night in 1912—I was nine—it was announced that the Red Sox were going to be at Taylor's. When the locals knew that, it would bring a crowd down. Two or three streetcars at a time would be filled with people heading down there. And this one night Joe Wood was supposed to be watching me, and he lost me. The players were throwing baseballs at the African Dodger, and I was underneath the dance hall watching the bowling.

"The African Dodger got paid to duck baseballs. It was a very popular attraction with the players. They had a black fellow, and he would stick his head out of a piece of canvas, and the canvas was loose, so he had room to maneuver. I'd say this distance was about the same as from the pitcher to home plate. They'd get three balls for a quarter and they'd take the baseballs and try to hit the African Dodger in the head, and if they hit him, they got a prize.

"The trouble was the Red Sox players put a couple of them in the hospital. Because their heads weren't hard enough to stop those balls.

"Anyway, while the guys were throwing baseballs at the African Dodger, Joe Wood lost sight of me, and there was quite a commotion until they found me looking in the window of the bowling alley.

"We had a big Boston bulldog, and he used to drink beer with the players, and every once in a while one of them would spike the beer. One night they got the dog so drunk, when the dog wanted to go up the front stairs, he would start up and fall back down. We had to carry him upstairs to put him to bed. After that we kept an eye on the players.

"The players I can remember were Forrest Cady, a catcher, Smoky Joe Wood, Speaker, Duffy Lewis, Hooper I think, Dutch Leonard. My father and Forrest Cady were very close. Cady had never seen a clam before he came to Boston. I can remember the first time he ate them, he was pushing the clams around with a knife and fork, and he said, 'How the hell do you open these G.D. things?' My father had to show him. When those players left the team, which wasn't too many years after, that was the end of my relationship with the Red Sox. It was a long time ago. It sure was."

Joe Cashman, who was born in 1900 and grew up in South Boston, was a youngster who observed the 1912 Red Sox from a longer distance—a seat in the stands. What Cashman, who was a longtime Boston sportswriter, remembers best about that team was its incomparable outfield of Duffy Lewis, Tris Speaker, and Harry Hooper. It has been said that the three formed the greatest outfield of all time. They have become the standard for outfield play, much as Tinker to Evers to Chance defined infield play for the same period.

Joe Cashman: "The ball was different in those days. It wasn't lively like it is today. You never played near the walls. Few balls were hit out there.

"I don't think there was ever the equal of Tris Speaker going back for a ball. Speaker was a fifth infielder all the time. A base runner would be on second base, and that runner would look around and see the second baseman and then the shortstop, and the next thing he knew, Speaker would sneak in from center field and take the throw from the pitcher and pick him off. That's how shallow he played. There were balls hit over his head, but not many. He was uncanny the way he went after them. He would turn his back on the ball and run. He'd run to a spot, turn around, and catch the ball.

"The three of them could field, and they could throw. You couldn't run on them, couldn't take an extra base. Your life wasn't worth a nickel. Lewis was right-handed. Hooper batted lefty, but threw righty. Speaker was left-handed. Speaker started out as a right-handed pitcher. Down in Texas he broke his arm and had to learn to throw left-handed, and he became this great ballplayer.

Funny thing about him: If you were going from first to third, and if he was in center field and he had the ball, he would get you out at third base. The ball leaving his hand would come toward the infield, you'd think it was crazy, but the ball would be coming directly toward second base, and when it got to second it would curve right down the line into the third baseman's hands.

"And the other guys? If you ever got hit by one of Lewis's throws right in the air, you'd get killed. Lewis, in left, never bounced the ball. It was in the air all the way. And Hooper played in a tough field. There was no night ball then. That right field was the worst in the country, for one reason. In Boston we had single-decked stands, and the sun would come in over the top, and Hooper had to play that sun field.

"All three were good base runners, and all could hit home runs. And they were consistent. I don't know why it was, but back then the players were much more consistent. Every single year you could bet your house on the first day of April on how the batting race would end: Ty Cobb, Eddie Collins, Tris Speaker. I remember one year Speaker won it and the other two finished two and three. But it was uncanny. Usually, it was Cobb, Collins, Speaker."

(The records show that Cobb, Collins, and Speaker finished one, two, and three only in the year 1914. However, it was rare during that decade that the three Hall of Famers weren't all in the top five.)

In addition to their outstanding outfield trio, the Red Sox of 1912 had another hero of legendary proportions. His name was Joe Wood.

Wood was born in 1889. At age 16 he was paid $20 dollars a game to dress up like a woman and pitch for the Bloomer Girls, the most famous women's team of the day. He began his professional career pitching for the Hutchinson Salt Packers of the Western Association, and at age 19, in 1908, he played for the Kansas City Blues. That summer John I. Taylor bought him for the then-substantial sum of $7,000.

In his first three full years with the Red Sox, Wood won 11, 12, and 23 games. No one could have expected what he did in 1912: He compiled a 34–5 regular-season record with a 1.91 earned-run average. His pitching velocity was equal to that of the legendary Walter Johnson, whose American League record of 16 wins in a row was within Wood's grasp that year.

On September 5, 1912, Wood faced Johnson in one of the legendary pitching performances in baseball history. Johnson had the record. Wood had won thirteen in a row. Could Johnson stop Wood and protect his record? Thirty thousand curious fans invaded Fenway Park that day to see which pitcher was superior. Thousands more were turned away at the gate.

Manville E. Webb, Jr., sportswriter: "The crowds packed the stands and the bleachers and trooped all over the outfield inside the stand and bleacher boundaries. In the grandstand the broad promenade was packed solid 10 rows deep with fans on tiptoes to see what was going on. The playing field was surrounded completely by a triple, even quadruple, rank of humanity, at least 3,000 assembling on the banking in left field, and the mass of enthusiasts around in front of the huge concrete stand.

"So thickly were the spectators massed, and so impossible was it for the squadron of police to keep them back, that the players' pits were abandoned, the contestants bringing their war clubs out almost to the baselines."

The only run of the game came in the sixth inning. Speaker doubled past third, and Lewis hit an opposite-field high fly to short right field, which fell near the foul line. Washington outfielder Dan Moeller ran a long way for the ball, dove, got his fingers on the ball, but couldn't hold it. Speaker scored. Wood was credited with the victory that day, allowing him to continue to chase Johnson's record. He would later tie the record, but he did not break it.

The 1912 pennant was an easy one for the Red Sox. Under manager Jake Stahl, the Red Sox finished 14 games ahead of the Washington Nationals. Their World Series opponents were John McGraw's New York Giants, with their star pitchers Christy Mathewson and Rube Marquard, who himself had won 19 games in a row during the 1912 season.

The Giants knew that if they could beat Smoky Joe Wood, they could beat the Red Sox. Wood received a half-dozen death threats from Giant fans prior to the opening game. Each letter had a New York postmark. One letter was written in red ink, with a knife and gun drawn at the bottom of a sheet of paper. It read: "You will never live to pitch against the Giants in the World Series! We are waiting to get you as soon as you arrive in town."

Wood was unaffected. He beat the Giants in the first game. Wrote Damon Runyon: "When all is said and done, it was the chilled steel nerve of 'Smoky Joe' that lifted the Sox to a 4 to 3 victory."

The day after Wood won the opener, reporters cornered him in the lobby of the hotel and asked him for an interview.

"No," said Wood, "I have never given out an interview in my life and won't do it now or never!"

"Why?"

"It's a jinx. If I began talking and bragging about myself when I'm having a good year, then next season I would pitch rotten. I know, I tell you, and I am not going to say a word."

After a tie in Game 2 and a Marquard win to tie the series, Wood won Game 4 by the score of 3–1. In a column in one of the New York papers, Christy Mathewson wrote: "In spite of the fact that Wood beat us, I have nothing but admiration for Wood. His was the work of an artist."

In Game 5, Red Sox pitcher Hugh Bedient gave the Red Sox a 3-to-1 lead in games. After a one-day hiatus, Wood was scheduled to pitch Game 6 in New York. One more win, and the Red Sox would be world champs. A typical performance from Wood would almost surely have done the trick. But there is suspicion that Red Sox owner James McAleer, who had arranged the Wood–Walter Johnson duel, didn't want the Series to end so quickly. Owner McAleer may have had his eye on the balance sheet as much as on the scoreboard. If the Red Sox were to lose Game 6 in New York, with Wood resting on the bench, McAleer knew he would have one more huge gate in Boston, with Wood on the mound and 30,000 fans buying his tickets for the game.

McAleer's maneuvering may have almost cost the Sox the Series.

Sportswriter Fred Lieb was riding the train to New York with the Red Sox after Game 5. The Red Sox players, figuring Wood would be pitching Game 6, were confident of victory.

Fred Lieb: "There was jubilation in the two Pullman cars occupied by Red Sox personnel on the leisurely Sunday daytime trip to New York. They could smell the sweet scent of victory and those fat World Series checks. In the midst of the laughter in the first Boston car, Jim McAleer, president and part-owner of the club, stepped into the stateroom occupied by player-manager Stahl.

"'Who are you going to pitch tomorrow, Jake?' asked McAleer.

"Stahl looked at his boss in surprise and said, 'Who else but Joe Wood?'

"'Well, let's talk that over a bit,' said McAleer. 'Remember that Bucky O'Brien pitched real well in the third game. If he holds them to two runs again, I think we can win; and should he lose, it would give Joe another day's rest and he could finish it for us in Boston.'

"Stahl demurred. 'Why, all the boys are expecting Wood to pitch. Joe had told me he's ready and wants to pitch.' They discussed it some more. When McAleer left the stateroom he said, 'Think it over, but I think O'Brien deserves another chance. And remember, we always would have Wood available if we have to return to Boston.'

"There was a lot of bitterness and recrimination on the train when word spread around that Bucky O'Brien, not Wood, would pitch the Monday game in New York.

"Perhaps the feelings of his teammates upset O'Brien. He showed none of the stuff he had in Boston and was knocked out in the first inning [actually, he completed the first].

"There was more bickering and name-calling in the Boston cars of the Owl train sleeper to Boston. I heard that Paul Wood, Joe's brother, had a fistfight with O'Brien on the train and blackened one of O'Brien's eyes. Paul, expecting his brother Joe would pitch, had bet and lost $100 dollars on the day's game."

The Red Sox still led 3 games to 2 going into Game 6, but then came the incident in which McAleer and McRoy stripped the Royal Rooters of their customary seats. A riot ensued, Wood's arm tightened up, and the Giants won that one 11–4, to tie the Series.

By losing in Game 6, McAleer got a bonus. In addition to getting his gate for the game Wood pitched, he got yet another payday when he won a coin toss to determine the location of the final game. Unfortunately for him, only 17,000 fans showed up at Fenway because of their anger at the team's treatment of the Royal Rooters.

The final game has long been part of baseball's legendary past. There have been bizarre endings to World Series games, including Hugh Casey striking out Tommy Henrich to lose the second-to-last game in 1941 and the Red Sox losing to the Mets in the sixth game in 1986 on a ball that went through the first baseman's legs. This was a bizarre *final*-game ending.

Boston's Hugh Bedient and Giants legend Christy Mathewson were locked in a 1–1 duel after seven, and Wood came on in relief in the eighth. Harry Hooper had robbed Larry Doyle of a home run in the sixth inning when he threw himself back into an open-field box and, with some of the spectators holding him up, caught the ball in a prostrate position and grasped it tightly.

The Giants broke the tie in the first half of the 10th when Red Murray doubled and scored on a single by Fred Merkle.

New York needed three outs to be champions. Christy Mathewson was still on the mound. He induced the first Boston batter, Clyde Engle, to lift an easy fly to center fielder Fred Snodgrass.

Fred Lieb: "Any high schooler could have caught it with ease. The only possible excuse for Fred Snodgrass's finally dropping it for a two-base error was that he'd had too much time to think while the ball was in the air."

Duffy Lewis: "He [Mathewson] had us beaten when we came to bat for our last half of the 10th. A fly ball—the kind which most outfielders could take behind their back—landed in Fred Snodgrass's hands and bounced out. That started our rally. When the inning ended, we had sent two runs across the plate and Mathewson, McGraw's ace, was humbled.

"Mathewson left the park with drooping shoulders, but [was] too much of a sport to blame anybody."

On the very next play after his mishandled fly, Snodgrass atoned by making a spectacular running catch of Hooper's long line drive, almost doubling Engle off second base. Mathewson then walked Steve Yerkes, a weak hitter, the potential winning run.

With runners on first and second, Tris Speaker lifted a high foul ball about five feet from the first-base coach's box. It was clearly Merkle's ball, but it was a windy day, and the wind had been playing tricks with foul flies. Giants catcher Chief Meyers came down from the plate to take it.

Fred Lieb: "Mathewson moved over just into foul territory, and I thought it was he who called out, 'Take it, take it, Chief, you take it.' I later learned it was Speaker who offered this 'advice.' Anyway, confusion reigned and the ball fell in foul territory in the middle of the triangle formed by Merkle, Meyers, and Mathewson.

"In returning to the batter's box, Speaker passed Mathewson and whispered, 'Matty, that play will cost you the game and the Series.'

"Tris then hit a long single to right, easily scoring Engle with the tying run and sending Yerkes to third."

Tris Speaker: "Merkle should have caught the ball, but Matty kept yelling for Meyers to take it. The old Chief was chasing the ball, and I saw he couldn't get it, and I was going to yell for him to keep after it too, but Matty was yelling so loud I didn't have to. Merkle couldn't go for it for fear of running into Meyers, and the ball fell in the coach's box.

"I singled, driving in the tying run, and took second on the throw to the plate."

Giants manager John McGraw ordered Mathewson to walk Duffy Lewis to set up the double play, and with the bases loaded and one out, Red Sox third baseman Larry Gardner hit a long fly to right, and Yerkes scored after tagging up.

Snodgrass's muff was recorded into the history books, even though it was the missed pop-up hit by Speaker that really cost the Giants the victory. Nevertheless, the Red Sox were 1912 world champs.

It was miraculous that the Red Sox won that final game and the 1912 World Series. The Red Sox would win three more World Series— in 1915, 1916, and 1918. After that, any luck the Red Sox would have would be bad. More than 70 years later, loyal Red Sox fans, always hopeful, inevitably disappointed, would await another big break and another world championship.

1919: White Sox vs. Reds

Black Sox Scandal
from *Eight Men Out* by Eliot Asinof

On Monday, September 27, 1920, the Philadelphia *North American* ran a story that startled millions of readers: "THE MOST GIGANTIC SPORTING SWINDLE IN THE HISTORY OF AMERICA!" Jimmy Isaminger reported his interview with Billy Maharg.

"We were all double-crossed by Abe Attell," Maharg asserted, "and I want everybody to know the truth. I guess I'd better get to the start: I am a friend of Bill Burns, the veteran southpaw. After quitting baseball, Burns, who is a Texan, bought oil leases and cleared over $100,000. In the middle of September last year, I received a wire from Burns in New York. I hopped a train and met Bill at the Ansonia. . . ."

Maharg related the story of his involvement in the fix, exactly as he had experienced it. Isaminger's article concentrated on five major points of Maharg's experience:

1. The first, second, and final games of the Series were "thrown" by eight members of the White Sox.

2. The offer to "fix" the series was volunteered to Bill Burns and himself by Eddie Cicotte.
3. The ballplayers were promised $100,000 to lose the Series, but actually received only $10,000.
4. Abe Attell manipulated the fix, but betrayed them all.
5. He and Burns lost every cent they had betting on the third game, which they thought was fixed like the first two.

"Then I took my medicine and came back to Philadelphia and went to work," Maharg concluded. "This is the first time I ever opened my mouth on the subject."

On that afternoon, the White Sox played their last home game of the year. Dickie Kerr shut out Detroit, 2–0. Buck Weaver, Joe Jackson, and Eddie Collins combined base hits to win the game. Significantly, Cleveland also won, holding onto their $1/2$-game lead.

Before the game had finished, the Maharg story was repeated in Chicago afternoon papers. Several copies were waiting for the players as they filed into the locker room. They gathered around to read them. Nobody said a word. Joe Jackson, the illiterate, glanced at the faces of his cohorts, dressed hurriedly, and went out to get drunk. Happy Felsch rushed out after him. He, too, wanted to get drunk.

Another story, prominently displayed on an inside page, seemed inconsequential: A "mystery woman" had been uncovered by the State's Attorney's office. She was believed to have vital information to give the Grand Jury.

Eddie Cicotte returned to his hotel, only to face the tall detective with the smile and soft-spoken manner. Cicotte wanted to run away and hide. The detective told him there was no way to hide from what was going to happen to him. Everybody knew that evidence was piling up. The Grand Jury already had more than enough for indictments. The thing to do was to come clean. That would help Cicotte and everyone else. The State always takes care of its witnesses. Besides, Cicotte would feel better if he talked. . . .

Cicotte turned and went up to his room.

The following morning, Charles Comiskey came early to his office at the ballpark as he always did. But this day would be different. He had nursed this problem for a full year, and now the end was near. That much was apparent. He had not been able to separate himself from it. He had twisted and turned, attacked and retreated, shouted and bluffed. He had prepared himself as cleverly as he could to face any eventuality. On this morning, however, all these tactics provided no ease for his anguish.

Kid Gleason was waiting for him, ready for the funeral. "Commy, do you want the real truth? I think I can get it for you. Today."

"How?" Comiskey asked. The question choked him.

"Cicotte. I know he's ready to break down. He's weak. I've seen him stewing with this all summer." Then he paused before asking. "Shall I get him?"

Comiskey sighed. Well, there it was. Finally, there it was. The end of his pennant hopes, the end of his ballclub. The end of God knows what else!

What was he supposed to do? Now that he faced the real issue, he wasn't any more confident of [a] decision than he ever was. It crossed his mind that maybe there was a way of stalling this thing for a while. . . .

"Go get him," he mumbled finally. Then he turned to call Alfred Austrian.

Gleason found Cicotte in his hotel room. He told him that Comiskey wanted to see him. Cicotte nodded. He didn't bother to ask the manager what it was all about.

Together they went downtown to the law offices of Alfred Austrian. On their arrival, Cicotte was asked to wait in the reception room. The pitcher sat there alone for over 20 minutes while his hands grew clammy with sweat. Then a secretary asked him to follow her into one of the inner rooms. Cicotte entered, but found this room empty as well. He sat there for another 20 minutes. By that time, he was shaking, sick with guilt and hopelessness. When he was finally led into Austrian's office, he was a beaten man. He confronted Comiskey, Gleason, and Austrian. They did not need to ask him a question. He crumbled into a chair and broke down.

"I know what you want to know—I know . . ." he sobbed. "Yeah—we were crooked—we were crooked. . . ."

Comiskey could not face him. He didn't want to hear the words that would trigger his own destruction.

"Don't tell me!" he snapped. "Tell it to the Grand Jury!"

At 11:30 a.m., the Criminal Courts Building was crowded with reporters and the usual band of baseball buffs and curiosity-seekers. Cicotte, escorted by Alfred Austrian and two bailiffs, pushed their way in. Cicotte walked stiffly through the gauntlet, a smile frozen on his face. He ignored the flood of excited questions. At first, it was believed that the pitcher had come to clear himself of the charges. Someone shouted at him: "Hey, Eddie, you gonna get an immunity bath?" Cicotte seemed not to hear. He merely held his smile and moved on, Austrian's hand tight on his arm. He was led to an empty office on the sixth floor. Austrian introduced him to Hartley Replogle.

"This is the man handling the Grand Jury investigations, Eddie. He has the goods on you. Come clean with him and he'll take care of you."

A few more comforting words were spoken to him as a sheet of legal print was placed before him. It all looked complicated and legalistic.

"Sign it," Replogle said. Cicotte hesitated. "Don't worry," Replogle encouraged him. "We'll see that you'll be all right."

Cicotte signed. Since he wasn't up to reading the paper, he did not know it was a waiver of immunity.

They took him to another room, Judge MacDonald's chambers. The judge looked him squarely in the eye. "Are you going to tell us everything, Cicotte?" The pitcher nodded. "We want to know about the gamblers. . . ." Cicotte swallowed thickly, nodded again. The judge then instructed Replogle to indict him. The word had Cicotte worried. He turned to Replogle and asked, "What's that mean? Don't this go—what you promised me?" Replogle reassured him everything was going to be all right.

Then they took him down to the Grand Jury room. He had acted totally without benefit of counsel.

The members of the Grand Jury sat breathlessly still as the ballplayer began talking. "I don't know why I did it . . . I must have been crazy!" He had trouble finishing his first words; his voice was all choked up. "Risberg, Gandil, and McMullin were at me for a week before the Series began. They wanted me to go crooked. I don't know. I needed the money. I had the wife and the kids. The wife and the kids don't know about this. I don't know what they'll think." He stopped, suddenly buried his head in his hands. For a moment, it seemed as if he could not go on. When he raised his head, his eyes were wet with tears.

"Before Gandil was a ballplayer, he was mixed up with gamblers and low characters back in Arizona. That's where he got the hunch to fix the Series. Eight of us, we got together in my room three or four days before the Series started. Gandil was master of ceremonies. We talked about it, and decided we could get away with it. We agreed to do it.

"I was thinking of the wife and kids. I'd bought a farm. There was a $4,000-dollar mortgage on it. There isn't any mortgage on it now. I paid it off with the crooked money. I told Gandil I had to have the cash in advance. I didn't want any checks. I didn't want any promises. I wanted the money in bills. I wanted it before I pitched a ball. We talked quite a while about it. Yes, we decided to do our best to throw the games at Cincinnati.

"Then Gandil and McMullin took us all, one by one, away from the others and we talked turkey. Gandil asked me my price. I told him $10,000. And I told him $10,000 was to be paid in advance. It was Gandil I was talking to. He wanted to give me some money at the time, the rest after the games were played and lost. But it didn't go with me. Well, the argument went on for days, the argument for some now, some later. But I stood pat. I wanted that $10,000 and I got it.

"The day before I went to Cincinnati I put it up to them squarely for the last time that there would be nothing doing unless I had the money. That night I found the money under my pillow. There was $10,000. I counted it. I don't know who put it there. It was my price. I had sold out 'Commy.' I had sold out the other boys. Sold them for $10,000 to pay off a mortgage on a farm and for the wife and kids . . . $10,000 . . . what I had asked, cash in advance, there in my fingers. I had been paid and I went on. I threw the game."

The Grand Jury questioned Cicotte in detail as to the manner in which the games were thrown.

"It's easy. Just a slight hesitation on the player's part will let a man get to base or make a run. I did it by not putting a thing on the ball. You could have read the trademark on it the way I lobbed it over the plate. A baby could have hit 'em. Schalk was wise the moment I started pitching. Then, in one of the games, the first I think, there was a man on first and the Reds' batter hit a slow grounder to me, I could have made a double play out of it without any trouble at all. But I was slow—slow enough to prevent the double play. It did not necessarily look crooked on my part. It is hard to tell when a game is on the square and when it is not. A player can make a crooked error that will look on the square as easy as he can make a square one. Sometimes the square ones look crooked.

"Then, in the fourth game, which I also lost, on a tap to the box I deliberately threw badly to first, allowing a man to get on. At another time, I intercepted a throw from the outfield and deliberately bobbled it, allowing a run to score. All the runs scored against me were due to my own deliberate errors. In those two games, I did not try to win. . . .

"I've lived a thousand years in the last 12 months. I would not have done that thing for a million dollars. Now I've lost everything, job, reputation, everything. My friends all bet on the Sox. I knew it, but I couldn't tell them. I had to double-cross them.

"I'm through with baseball. I'm going to lose myself if I can and start life over again."

Cicotte testified for two hours and eleven minutes. He sobbed bitterly through much of his testimony. Part of the time, he was barely audible. The jury listened raptly, deeply moved by his anguish. There was not one moment during which the jury pressed him in order to elicit further evidence. By the time they recessed for lunch, Cicotte had exhausted himself.

Judge MacDonald, however, was not satisfied. He was looking to break down the door that would expose the whole frame-up. He wanted to catch all the big boys involved and run them through his mill. He wanted evidence, not a statement of mea culpa. He wanted Cicotte to tell him of meetings with Arnold Rothstein *et al.*, of a well-integrated, highly organized plot, naming names and dates and places. He wanted to lead the Grand Jury to a spread of indictments that would bunch them all into one big net, an ironclad case for the State to prosecute.

But Cicotte had failed him. For gamblers, Cicotte had mentioned Burns and Maharg. Did Cicotte expect the judge to believe this whole project was manipulated by those two punks? He accused Cicotte directly: "I thought you were going to tell us about the gamblers!"

Cicotte had nothing to say about gamblers. He insisted that this was all he knew. He had told them enough to reveal the plot, hoping, thereby, to satisfy their need for exposure and his own need for expiation. For his own protection—and that of his wife and children—he told them no more.

Ray Schalk, White Sox catcher, spent most of the morning outside the Grand Jury room, waiting to testify. He did not know what was keeping them. Then he heard that Cicotte was inside.

Schalk's first encounter with Cicotte had been back in 1912. Cicotte was already a veteran when Schalk first came to Chicago, a small, baby-faced 20-year-old who might have passed for 16. At training camp, down in Texas, Schalk was resting a sprained ankle, watching the proceedings from the grandstand. He saw Cicotte talking to a park policeman, pointing in his direction. The policeman then came over to the stands and told him to move out. "No kids allowed here, sonny!" Schalk had protested, trying to convince him he was a big leaguer. The policeman grabbed him by the arm, with some wisecrack about his being the president of the United States, and threw him out. Schalk looked back, hoping for the support of the others, but all he saw was their laughter, especially Cicotte's.

Schalk looked forward to the day when he could be a major-league manager. From his earliest awareness of his own talent, he decided that that was right for him.

Comiskey appreciated ballplayers like him, the smart, aggressive, willful men. He didn't like Comiskey, but he always tried to stay on his side. Comiskey was cheap. Comiskey underpaid him. Every year, Schalk hated to face signing that skimpy contract and the cold-turkey dictums of Harry Grabiner. But he never argued salary. He never wanted Comiskey to think he wasn't loyal.

When the Grand Jury convened, he faced the question as squarely as he could: What should he do? He didn't relish the prospect of talking, but what else could he do? If he didn't talk, could he be punished as an accomplice? Was it still worse to be a stooly? What, in the long run, was best for himself?

Then he heard the excitement as the door of the Grand Jury room opened. In a moment, the news was out: Cicotte had confessed!

Schalk turned and quickly left the building. He felt no great sense of relief, even though this took the onus off him. He merely wondered about what was going to happen now.

He was mobbed by reporters. "What were you going to tell them, Ray?"

"We're still in a pennant race. But at the close of the season, I'll have plenty to tell."

"How about reports that *this* season's games were fixed?"

"I won't say anything at all now!" Schalk snapped, and walked away.

After leaving Comiskey Park following Monday's ballgame, Joe Jackson had gotten himself good and drunk. If he was going to be confused, he figured he might as well be confused and drunk. When he awoke on Tuesday morning, he was confused and hung-over. The Sox had the day off. He thought maybe he'd call Lefty Williams and go to a movie. Nothing much else was happening. But he knew that this was crazy; trouble was brewing all over the place, bubbling over the rim of the pot. Sooner or later, he'd have to do something.

He missed his wife, Katie, who was home in Savannah. He needed someone to talk to. Katie would tell him what to do. He knew he was in trouble, serious trouble.

He reached for the phone and called the Criminal Courts Building, asked for Judge MacDonald. The judge was in session with the jury and could not be reached. He spoke briefly to the bailiff and told him who it was. In a few minutes, the judge was on the phone.

"This is Joe Jackson, Judge . . ."

"What is it, Jackson? Are you ready to talk?"

"Look, Judge, you've got to control this thing . . . whatever they're digging up, I can tell you, I'm an honest man!"

"I can tell *you*, Jackson, I know you are not!"

Jackson heard the phone go dead. That worried him. He went downstairs for coffee and ran into Risberg and Felsch. The word was out that Cicotte had gone over and was spitting up his guts. So that was how the judge knew so much. Jackson started to sweat. Risberg studied him. "Just keep your own mouth shut, that's all, Joe," the Swede barked. "I swear to you, I'll kill you if you squawk!"

Jackson spent the rest of the morning kicking himself around his room. Finally, too desperate to do otherwise, he called Judge MacDonald again. This time, the judge did not hang up on him. He asked Jackson to come over and tell his story.

Before he got there, Jackson fortified himself with another coating of alcoholic armor. The rube from Brandon Mill, South Carolina, knew he was walking into a den of lions. He wanted to make the feast as painless as possible. Like Cicotte, it never occurred to him to get his own lawyer.

And, as with Cicotte, Alfred Austrian was waiting for him. He took Jackson into a vacant office and talked to him like a Dutch uncle. He asked him if he was going to confess. Jackson mumbled his innocence. He had nothing to confess. He merely wanted to tell what he knew. He repeated that he'd wanted to talk right from the start. He had tried to get to Comiskey after the Series. He even had his wife write letters.

Austrian shook his head. He told Jackson it would go bad for him for him to lie about anything. Cicotte had already told them the whole story. To deny his involvement would prejudice the Grand Jury. Did Joe understand that?

Sure, he understood. But he had to stay out of trouble. That's what mattered to him. He just didn't want to get into trouble. Austrian assured him he would be safe if he told everything he knew. That was the only way to protect himself. It was the honest way, to make a clean breast of it. The State was only interested in clearing out the gamblers, not the ballplayers. This was the way to clean up baseball. Joe's confession would help the State. They would all appreciate his cooperation. This way, he would never be prosecuted. The only way he'd be used would be as a witness.

Jackson finally agreed. He would talk. Just as long as nothing would happen to him.

Austrian put a large sheet of paper in front of him, handed him a pen. He pointed to a line on the bottom, told him to sign his name. Jackson hesitated; he didn't want to sign anything. Austrian told him not to worry. His signature was not going to change anything. The Grand Jury wanted it from all witnesses. Again, Jackson was too confused to argue. He was batting in another man's ballpark. He signed.

Then Austrian, with the waiver of immunity in his briefcase, took him downstairs to Judge MacDonald's chambers.

Hartley Replogle sat through the meeting in Judge MacDonald's chambers and said nothing. The events of the past few weeks were coming to a climax; the headlines would be big and shocking; the confessions would lead to new exposures. He had reason to feel excited over the leading part he had played. But this was saddening. These confessions rocked him. He looked at Jackson, pathetic and helpless. Replogle had seen him play ball a number of times, responded to the incredible power of the man at the plate. Now, with a shirt and a tie on, the ballplayer was nothing. Red-eyed, unshaven, smelling of alcohol, the great man on spikes was just another frightened pigeon in the judge's chambers. Jackson sat there dumb and helpless, and they did what they wanted with him.

To Replogle, the players were victims. The owners poured out a stream of pious, pompous verbiage about how pure they were. The gamblers said nothing, kept themselves hidden, protected themselves—and when they said anything, it was strictly for cash, with immunity, no less. But the ballplayers didn't even know enough to call a lawyer. They only knew how to play baseball.

The judge was stern with Jackson. He warned him not to deceive the jury about anything, for if he did, they could get him for perjury. Jackson promised. He would tell what he knew. They took him downstairs to the Jury Room, Replogle leading the way. The great ballplayer approached the crowded corridor and seemed to shudder. Replogle patted him on the shoulder, trying to reassure him. He saw the battery of newspaper photographers with their harassing flashbulbs. He called to them to back away, to leave Jackson alone. But they set up a wall in front of the doors and began the agonizing process of picture-taking. Jackson hung his head, covering his face from the brilliant flashes of light. Then he suddenly exploded. He began cursing them, cursing gamblers, cursing baseball, cursing the whole damn world. He charged through the crowd like a plunging fullback, ironically seeking sanctuary in the Grand Jury room.

After they swore him in, he began talking. They asked him questions, leading into the story of the fix. He told them of the gradual feeling-out by Gandil and Risberg. They'd been at him for days. They could make some big dough. They would give him $20,000 for helping out. It was easy; all he had to do was go along with it; let a ball drop a few feet in front of him; don't hit the big one with men on. He could look good and still play badly. Twenty thousand dollars.

Finally he'd agreed, but he got only $5,000—$5,000 in a dirty envelope, delivered to his room by Lefty Williams. He'd get the other $15,000 after the Series—after he had delivered the goods. He took Lefty's word for it.

Then, after the Series, he'd protested to Gandil and Risberg about that. He wanted the rest of his dough. If not, he was going to squawk. They told him: "You poor simp, go ahead and squawk. Where do you get off if you do? We'll all say you're a liar. Every honest ballplayer in the world will say you're a liar. You're out of luck. Some of the boys were promised more than you and got less!"

Jackson rambled on for almost two hours. He told the jury how he hadn't played good baseball, despite his incredible .375 World Series average, and record 12 base hits. The judge thanked him for his testimony. He came out smiling. The jury had made him feel honest again. "I got a big load off my chest!" he told the two bailiffs beside him.

Again Replogle was protective. "Leave him alone," he demanded of the reporters. "He's come through beautifully and we don't want him bothered."

But Jackson still felt like talking. It was as if he had to pour it all out; his confusion, his anger, his bitterness, his fear. "They've hung it on me. But I don't care what happens now. I guess I'm through with baseball. I wasn't wise enough, like Chick, to beat them to it. But some of them will sweat before the show is over." Jackson was like a little boy, hitting wildly back at the big adult world. "They" were all the people who were causing his troubles: the legal machinery of Cook County, Illinois; the reporters; the club magnates—all lumped together into one word. His admiration went to Gandil, the man who got away with it.

Then he added, "Now Risberg threatens to bump me off if I squawk. That's why I've got the bailiffs with me. I'm not under arrest yet, and I've got the idea that after what I told them, old Joe Jackson isn't going to jail. But I'm not going to get far from my protectors until this thing blows over. Swede is a hard guy."

[Cicotte and Jackson recanted their confessions, and were acquitted. However, the day after their acquittal, Kenesaw Mountain Landis, the first Commissioner of Baseball, banned all eight implicated White Sox players from Major League Baseball for life, as well as two other players believed to be involved.]

1923: Yankees vs. Giants

Casey Stengel's Inside-the-Park Home Run

from *Stengel: His Life and Times* by Robert W. Creamer

The opening game of the 1923 World Series was played in Yankee Stadium, the first World Series game ever played in the stadium, then in the first year of its existence. The glamour of the new ballpark and the continuing internecine rivalry between the Giants and the Yankees drew a record crowd of 55,307 to the stadium, at that time the largest ever to see a major-league game. Ordinarily, on such an auspicious occasion, the game itself turns out to be a dud, a mild affair that generates little fire or drama. But not this time. The first World Series game ever played in Yankee Stadium was a thriller from the first inning to the last, and the hero of the piece was Charles Dillon Stengel.

The Yankees got a run in the bottom of the first inning when Ruth scored from first base on a double by Bob Meusel. In the top of the second, Stengel almost tied the game when he hit a long fly toward the right-field bleachers that Ruth ran back to the fence to catch. In the bottom of the second, the Yankees scored two more to go ahead 3–0, but the Giants came back in the top of the third with four runs to take the lead. The Yankees put men on second and third with one out in the fourth, but a sensational double play by the Giants, from pitcher to third base to second base, ended the inning. The Yanks came close to scoring again in the fifth after Ruth tripled, but Frank Frisch, running with his back to home plate, made a great catch of a little looping fly ball, then turned and threw Ruth out at home. In the seventh the Yankees finally did tie the game when Joe Dugan drove in a run with a triple. Ruth followed with a vicious grounder down the right-field line that should have put the Yankees ahead, but George Kelly, the Giant first baseman, made a stunning stop and a great throw to the catcher to nip Dugan at the plate. In the eighth a Yankee base runner was picked off second just before another player hit a single to center that would have scored him.

The game was still tied 4–4 in the top of the ninth when Stengel came to bat with two men out and the bases empty. Casey had walked in the fourth inning and singled in the seventh but each time had been wiped off the bases by a Yankee double play. Joe Bush, the Yankee pitcher, had given up only three singles in the $6\frac{1}{3}$ he had pitched since coming on in relief in the four-run Giant third.

The count on Stengel went to three balls and two strikes. The next pitch was a fastball, in the strike zone but high and on the outside corner. Bush said later, "The count was 3 and 2 and I threw just as hard as I could. He crashed it good and plenty."

Stengel hit the ball on a hard line to left center field, the vast "Death Valley" of Yankee Stadium. It went between left fielder Bob Meusel and center fielder Whitey Witt and all the way to the outfield fence. As Heywood Broun wrote, "The outfielders turned and ran toward the bleacher wall, the ball sailed and hopped and skipped, and Casey sprinted."

Witt got to the ball first and tossed it to Meusel, who had one of the best arms in the majors. Meusel fired the ball in to shortstop Ernie Johnson, a replacement that inning for the regular Yankee shortstop, Everett Scott, who had been lifted for a pinch hitter. Johnson relayed it toward catcher Wally Schang at home plate, for by this time Stengel, churning his way around the bases, was well past third on his way home. The ball and Casey arrived at the plate at the same time, but the throw was a little bit up the line toward first base. As Stengel deftly slid across home plate the ball skipped past Schang and rolled toward the Giant dugout.

"Casey slid into the plate," reported James Harrison of the *New York Times*, "and up onto one knee in a single motion. Then he waved a hand in a comical gesture that seemed to say, 'Well, there you are,' and the game was as good as over." (It was. The Yankees went down in order in the last of the ninth and the Giants won 5–4.)

The Giants poured across the field toward Stengel, mobbed him and escorted him triumphantly to the dugout. The huge crowd had begun roaring the moment Stengel hit the ball, had roared for the quarter of a minute or so it took him to run the 120 yards around the bases with his inside-the-park homer, and it was still roaring. The excitement of the moment was almost indescribable, but the press tried.

Grantland Rice milked the theme of "Casey at the Bat," who had struck out for the Mudville Nine, saying Casey had gotten his revenge at last. Heywood Broun's story had more facts in it than Rice's, although Broun got caught up in the windstorm of hyperbole swirling through the Yankee Stadium press box, starting his copy with the declaration, "It was the best baseball game ever played," and going on to describe Casey's circuit of the bases this way: "Stengel proceeds furiously in all directions at the same time when he runs. He doesn't point very well and seems to need a center board. The dust flew as Casey tossed one loose foot after another, identified each one and picked it up again. Perhaps he didn't go so fast but he ran determinedly. It would have been a thrilling sight to see him meet an apple cart or a drugstore window."

Joe Vila wrote, "Stengel, eyes bulging and mouth wide open, kept on sprinting as if to save his precious life." Frank Graham wrote, "There was very little breath left in his body and that was hammered out of him by his mates as he staggered to the dugout." Hype Igoe called Stengel "a little old man of baseball, gimpy, crooked-fingered, spavined, halt, squint-eyed and mebbe a grandfather." Walter St. Denis said, "The old boys had their day when 'Old Case' Stengel came through."

And then there was Damon Runyon, whose story in the *New York American* pulled out all the stops. Part of baseball lore now, Runyon's story has been quoted and requoted and misquoted for 60 years and has come to be accepted as the authoritative account of Casey's famous homer. Appearing on the front page under a huge banner headline that read, "STENGEL'S HOMER WINS FOR GIANTS, 5-4," it was the lead story in that day's *American.* Below the big black headline were subheads that said, "60,000 Frantic Fans Screech as Casey Beats Ball to Plate. Warped Legs, Twisted, Bent in Years of Campaigning, Last Until He Reaches Goal."

Beneath the bold byline, "By Damon Runyon," the copy read:

This is the way old "Casey" Stengel ran yesterday afternoon, running his home run home.

This is the way old "Casey" Stengel ran running his home run home in a Giant victory by a score of 5 to 4 in the first game of the world's series of 1923.

This is the way old "Casey" Stengel ran, running his home run home, when two were out in the ninth inning and the score was tied and the ball was still bounding inside the Yankee yard.

This is the way—
His mouth wide open.
His warped old legs bending beneath him at every stride.
His arms flying back and forth like those of a man swimming with a crawl stroke.

His flanks heaving, his breath whistling, his head far back.

URGES HIMSELF ON

Yankee infielders, passed by old "Casey" Stengel as he was running his home run home, say "Casey" was muttering to himself, adjuring himself to greater speed as a jockey mutters to his horse in a race, that he was saying: "Go on, Casey! Go on!"

People generally laugh when they see old "Casey" Stengel run, but they were not laughing when he was running his home run home yesterday afternoon. People—60,000 of them, men and women—were standing in the Yankee stands and bleachers up there in the Bronx roaring sympathetically, whether they were for or against the Giants.

"Come on, Casey!"

The warped old legs, twisted and bent by many a year of baseball campaigns, just barely held out under "Casey" Stengel until he reached the plate, running his home run home.

Then they collapsed.

"Casey" Slides

They gave out just as old "Casey" Stengel slid over the plate in his awkward fashion with Wally Schang futily [sic] reaching for him with the ball. "Billy" Evans, the American League umpire, poised over him in a set pose, arms spread wide to indicate that old "Casey" was safe.

Half a dozen Giants rushed forward to help "Casey" to his feet, to hammer him on the back, to bawl congratulations in his ears as he limped unsteadily, still panting furiously, to the bench where John J. McGraw, the chief of the Giants, relaxed his stern features to smile for the man who had won the game.

"Casey" Stengel's warped old legs, one of them broken not so long ago, wouldn't carry him out for the last half of the inning, when the Yankees made a dying effort to undo the damage done by "Casey." His place in center field was taken by "Bill" Cunningham, whose legs are still unwarped, and "Casey" sat on the bench with John McGraw.

And so on. It is florid, exaggerated, mildly inaccurate (where Runyon got the broken leg from, I don't know) and shamelessly overwritten, and at the same time it is stirring and unforgettable. Runyon was a gifted writer—his tales about Broadway guys and dolls became part of the American scene—and journalists are impressed by the fact that his memorable account of Stengel's homer was written under the gun in time for the morning editions.

The stories about his home run made Stengel the most famous man in New York for the moment, and possibly in the country. From the tone of the various reports you could have assumed that Stengel had barely survived the game and might never be able to play again, maybe not even be able to walk without a cane. But he was fine—no muscle pulls, no strained tendons, the bruise on his heel no worse for the experience. The rubber pad had shifted as Stengel rounded second and, he said, "I thought my shoe was coming off." The scrabbly style of running so remarked upon by the press was partly a result of Casey's efforts not to let that happen. McGraw sent Cunningham to the outfield in Casey's place in the last of the ninth because Stengel was all in after the homer. Cunningham started in center field the next afternoon, when the Series shifted across the Harlem River to the Polo Grounds, but only because the outstanding left-hander Herb Pennock was on the mound for the Yankees, and McGraw was playing the righty/lefty percentages. Cunningham went hitless against Pennock; McGraw used a pinch hitter (not Casey) for him late in the game and sent Stengel to center as Cunningham's fielding replacement in the ninth. The Yankees won 4–2.

The teams returned to the stadium, and Stengel played center and had another unforgettable day. It was Columbus Day, and the holiday crowd was even larger than the one at the first game. This one too was a jewel of a contest, not as wildly thrilling but almost impeccably played. Art Nehf of the Giants threw a six-hit shutout, and Sam Jones of the Yankees did even better than Nehf, except for one pitch—to Stengel. Casey had hit the ball hard off Jones the first time he batted in the game, lining a fly ball to Witt in center field. His next time up, in the fifth inning, he worked Jones for a walk but for the third time in the Series was eliminated by a double play.

When Casey faced Jones again in the seventh inning the score was still 0–0; only four Giants had reached base—one on a bunt, one on an error, and two on walks. With the count on Stengel two balls and one strike, Jones threw a screwball, trying to get it to break away from Casey on the outside edge of the plate. "It didn't break the way I expected it would," Jones said. "It broke in too close." Stengel jumped on it and lofted a high fly down the right-field line that carried into the bleachers for another game-winning home run.

This time Casey had time to savor his feat. As the ball landed in the seats, Casey glanced over at the Giants' dugout and held up two fingers, as though to say, "That's *two*." Between first and second he looked at the disconsolate Jones and, beyond Jones, at the Yankee dugout beyond the third-base line and merrily thumbed his nose at them. Rounding third he blew a kiss at the Yankees, but he was all business as he crossed home plate in full stride and veered toward the Giant dugout. Nehf held the Yankees scoreless, the Giants won 1–0, and the papers shouted exultantly that Casey had done it again. "Stengel 2, Yankees 1" was the most common gag. Fans on a lower Manhattan street watching the action of the game as it was re-created on a large mechanical scorecard on the side of an office building cheered mightily when Stengel's homer became apparent as a little light made a circuit of the bases. "Casey, you lulu! You darb!" shouted a delighted fan. "Hey, maybe that McGraw don't know how to run a team!" In Kansas City, Lou Stengel went around saying to people, "Did you hear about my boy Charley? My boy Charley hit another home run!"

It was the first time a player had broken up a 0–0 game in the World Series with a home run. It was also the first time a player had won two Series games with homers. And Casey's two home runs were the first World Series homers ever hit in Yankee Stadium. All in all, it was indeed an auspicious occasion.

Through the triumph and adulation and publicity Stengel managed to stay remarkably unaffected. He loved the attention—when he came to bat again in the ninth inning of the 1–0 game and was greeted with wave after wave of cheering he stood at home plate grinning from ear to ear—but he wasn't seduced by it. A young woman named Zoe Buckley interviewed him during the Series in a parlor of the ornate Hotel Ansonia at 72nd Street and Broadway in Manhattan, where many ballplayers (Babe Ruth among them) lived during the season. Casey didn't want to be interviewed. Buckley persisted, and he finally gave in and agreed to talk to her. Her reaction to the Runyonesque accounts of his inside-the-park home run are revealing: "From descriptions we'd read of Casey Stengel's performance in winning the first game we expected to see a large loose person of hayfoot, strawfoot awkwardness. But no. Your modern ballplayer is no roughneck. He is trim and immaculate, wears a $90 suit and a camel's hair overcoat. His skin is clear and rosy, his features well cut, his body lithe, with modest bearing but high-proof masculinity."

She asked him why ballplayers disliked being interviewed. "I guess we're scared of getting swelled heads," he said. "We know the hazards—we're the hero today and the goat tomorrow." She asked him about his home run in the first game, and he said, "It only goes to show you that good luck is as sure to stumble your way as bad luck. You've got to learn how to take both. You have to remember that nothing lasts—neither the good nor the bad." He echoed that existential philosophy nearly four decades later when, after winning 10 pennants in 12 years, he summed up his life by saying, "I'm a man that's been up and down."

"Baseball's a business," he told Zoe Buckley. "Some of us are plugging sorts, like bookkeepers, and some are plungers—flying high, doing wonderful things by spurts and then slumping."

"Which are you?" she asked. She described his reaction: "Stengel stroked a neatly shaved chin with a well-groomed hand and considered, closing one blue eye and raking the horizon of the big red-and-gold parlor with the other, as though to catch a reflection of himself in the light of 13 years of professional ballplaying."

"I wonder," he said finally. "I'm not so doggone sure. I've had a pretty checkered career. They call me superannuated now. I'm 33. I'm no wonderful runner and I wouldn't expect to set the Mississippi River afire with my brains. I guess I'm a bookkeeper that had a lucky day."

Stengel's second homer against the Yankees was the high-water mark for the Giants in the Series (they lost the next three games) and in a sense the high-water mark for McGraw in his managerial career. Since losing the first two games in the 1921 Series, his Giants had defeated the Yankees 11 times in 13 games (not including the tie in 1922) and he was within two victories of achieving his ambition of winning three straight world championships, something no other manager had done. But that was as close as he was to come; he did win a fourth straight pennant the next year but failed again in the Series and never won another pennant after that.

As for Casey, even though the Giants lost the next three games he continued to do well, adding two walks and two singles the next day before McGraw methodically sent Cunningham in to bat for him in the ninth inning when the left-handed Pennock came in to relieve. At that point Stengel had been to the plate a dozen times in the 1923 Series, had reached first base safely nine times, and two of his three outs had come on hard-hit fly balls. Nonetheless, McGraw stuck with the percentages, and Cunningham struck out.

Casey went hitless in the next game and didn't play in the last game of the Series—Pennock again—until the eighth inning, when Jones relieved Pennock. The Giants were losing by two runs and there were two out when McGraw sent Stengel up to bat for Cunningham, but there was a runner on first base. The Giant fans in the crowd cheered Casey wildly as he approached the plate, hoping that he'd hit another homer and tie the game. But Casey lifted a high foul fly to the third baseman, and that was that. The Giants went down quietly in the ninth inning, and the Series was over.

Defeat is always disappointing, but Stengel had had the satisfaction of performing heroically for McGraw and the Giants in New York before huge crowds and under intense observation by the press. He batted .417, led the Giants in runs batted in and tied for the lead in runs scored. His home runs were the dramatic high spots of the Series. True, his nose-thumbing after the second homer had upset Jacob Ruppert, the Yankee owner, but nothing came of it. Ruppert complained about Stengel to Judge Landis in the lobby of the Hotel Commodore the night after the game, saying rather stuffily, "I don't think Stengel's actions were a credit to baseball." A Ruppert cohort named Billy Fleischman added, "It was an insult to all our fans."

Landis listened but did nothing. Asked later by a reporter if he was going to take action against Stengel, the commissioner grinned and said, "No, I don't think I will. A fellow who wins two games with home runs has a right to feel a little playful, especially if he's a Stengel." Casey used to say later on that Landis bawled him out for the nose-thumbing and others say he was fined $50, but it wasn't so. Babe Ruth, asked what he thought of Casey's behavior, summed up the general feeling by saying, "I didn't mind it. Casey's a lot of fun."

McGraw had said after the first game of the Series, "There isn't anyone I'd rather have seen make that homer than Casey," but a month later he traded Stengel, sending him to the seventh-place Boston Braves, who had lost 100 games that season, along with Cunningham and Dave Bancroft. It was a perplexing trade, because McGraw received relatively little in return: Billy Southworth, an ordinary outfielder, and Joe Oeschger, a fading pitcher. But Christy Mathewson, who had left Saranac Lake, had been made president of the Braves by the Boston owner, Judge Emil Fuchs, and McGraw said publicly that he was trying to help out his old friend. Bancroft was to be Boston's playing manager, and Stengel and Cunningham would be regular outfielders.

As usual, there were subtleties about the deal that McGraw didn't mention. He knew that Bancroft was no longer the superb player he had been and that the Giants had an outstanding young infielder named Travis Jackson ready to take over for Bancroft at shortstop. He knew that Cunningham was never going to cut the mustard as a big-league outfielder, and he knew that Stengel, for all his brilliance in the Series, *was* old and fragile and close to the end of his career. In Southworth he was getting a full-time player who could give the Giants everyday stability in center field, and behind Southworth he had a power-hitting rookie named Hack Wilson, who had played a few games in center for the Giants late in 1923. McGraw was cleaning house, sweeping out players who were no longer needed in the continuing scheme of things. And there was another ramification. Fuchs had put money into the deal, quite a bit of money. This time McGraw and the Giants were on the receiving end of a bunch of cash.

Casey, who had gone home to Kansas City, moaned a little about the trade ("What do you have to do? I suppose if I'd have hit three homers they'd have sent me to the Three-Eye League"), but he kept his equilibrium. He wrote to [his wife] Edna about the change in his life and suggested she come to Boston on her vacation the following spring. He is also supposed to have commented philosophically on his departure from New York so soon after his World Series exploits by saying, "The paths of glory lead but to the Braves."

1929: Athletics vs. Cubs

Athletics' 10-Run Inning

from *Connie Mack's '29 Triumph* by William C. Kashatus

The Chicago Cubs were the A's opponents in the 1929 World Series. After threatening for several years in the National League, the Cubs finally overcame a series of close races to win their first pennant since 1918. Their manager, Philadelphia-born Joe McCarthy, had grown up rooting for the Mackmen. But the loyalties to his boyhood team ceased once he crossed the foul lines for the opening game of the Fall Classic.

The Cubs' awesome lineup came into the Series batting .303 as a team, seven points higher than the A's. McCarthy had an explosive outfield of Kiki Cuyler who hit .360 in right, Riggs Stephenson who hit .362 in left, and Hack Wilson who hit .345 and played in center. Though small in stature, being only 5'6" and 190 pounds, Wilson was a deceptively strong power hitter with 39 homers to his credit. He was especially dangerous in the clutch. The trio was considered the most fearsome right-handed-hitting attack in baseball history, combining for 71 homers, 337 runs, and 271 RBIs. Nor was the infield lacking for production, with National League MVP Rogers

Hornsby, at second. Hornsby hit .380, slugged 39 homers, and drove in 149 runs. Additionally, the infield was bolstered by shortstop Woody English, who scored 131 runs.

Chicago's pitching staff, like its batting order, was dominated by right-handers. The only southpaw was 36-year-old Art Nehf who was already past his prime. Pat Malone was the ace of the staff, leading the National League with 22 wins. Charlie Root contributed another 19, and Guy Bush 19 more.

Many baseball writers were either unable or unwilling to declare a Series favorite. But none doubted that both teams would demonstrate a high quality of play. "If this year's World Series draws weather fit for baseball, it should produce the best competition seen in the Fall Classic for many a year," predicted Tom Swope of the *Cincinnati Post*. "Both are good teams which won their pennants far enough in advance of closing day to get thoroughly rested and prepared for a mighty effort in the big games. So it seems folly to attempt to pick one to defeat the other." Sam Carrick of the *Boston Evening American* believed the team that won the first game would win the Series. "Past results have shown that the initial contest winner has come out on top in somewhat more than two-thirds of the Series," he insisted. "One game is 25 percent of the victories to be accomplished and that is a considerable margin."

Others favored the Cubs. Archie Ward of the *Chicago Tribune* gave four good reasons for his choice: "(1) The Cubs have been favored by the schedule, which will enable them to play a possible four out of seven games on their home field; (2) They have been exceptionally successful against left-handed pitching; (3) They have more men experienced in World Series competition and consequently will stand up better under the strain; and (4) The Cubs have a more devastating attack." Not all Cub partisans were from Chicago either. Arthur Mann of the *New York Evening World* gave the Cubs a slight edge in "six or possibly seven games." He based his prediction on the "A's mad quest for victories in the last weeks of the season" which has "shorn the team of its best pitchers and has leveled the sluggers to a point approximating mediocrity." Mann went on to write, "This disintegration is bound to tell in the Series. The Cubs, on the other hand, have swung along with no pretense at invincibility, winning three or four and losing one or two, since midseason they have accelerated and they are finishing in a blaze of hitting." Paul Gallico of the *New York Daily News*, evidently still smarting from the Yankees' recent fall from first place, seamed to give his vote to the Cubs based on little more than a personal animosity for the Athletics. "The whole thing apparently is a put-up job to advertise Wrigley's chewing gum and Connie Mack's elephants—I believe it is elephants Mr. Mack sells— and I will have nothing to do with such out-and-out publicity schemes," he wrote in mock derision. "Our Yankees at least were playing for good Ruppert beer. The Cubs will win the Series in four straight games, so that a lot of sportswriters can perpetuate tear jerkers about poor old Connie Mack."

The A's had their devotees as well. Stuart Bell of the *Cleveland Press* made his prediction on the strength of the A's superior pitching: "If the best team wins, the Athletics will be the champions. Their pitchers, with the lowest earned run average in their own league, and lower than those of the Cub pitchers, are much better than the Chicago curving corps." Predictably, the Philadelphia press echoed his reasoning. "The Cubs may have hammered National League southpaws with enthusiasm, but there are no portsiders in the older circuit with the skill and cunning of Grove and Walberg," wrote Myron Huff of the *Public Ledger*. "And as for right-handers—well, there isn't a better pitcher in either league than Earnshaw and it happens he is with the A's." James Isaminger of the *Inquirer* went even further: "In my opinion, the Athletics have the batting power, pitching and defensive strength to beat any team in America. They have swept everything before them and in September were as irresistible as they were at any time during the race. I'm not saying there will be any four-game mop-up, but I do believe the A's will triumph in six."

Of course, there were still others in Philadelphia and Chicago who picked the hometown team out of self-defense. "Never having qualified as a baseball expert," wrote Joe Cunningham of the *Philadelphia Record*, "it doesn't matter who I pick so long as I say the A's will win. About the only reason I give is that I know most of the Athletics personally and do not know the Cubs, but do chew Mr. Wrigley's gum." Harry Neily of the *Chicago*

American was even more forthright. "Who do I pick in the Series?" he asked rhetorically. "Naturally—one guess. I live within a mile of the Cubs' park and don't want to sneak home nights up back alleys if I should dare to suggest the A's would take the Series." If nothing else, both Cunningham and Naily deserved to be admired for their candor.

Charlie Root received the starting assignment for the opening game at Chicago on October 8. Mack purposely refused to announce his starting pitcher until moments before the game, but the sellout crowd of 50,740 fans who jammed into Wrigley Field on that cold, rainy day assumed it would be one of his three star hurlers, Grove, Earnshaw, or Walberg. To everyone's great surprise, the Tall Tactician gave the nod to his 35-year-old right-hander, Howard Ehmke. It was the most daring ploy in World Series history.

Ehmke had only pitched 62 innings and two complete games during the 1929 campaign. He had compiled a record of seven wins and two losses, hardly the kind of numbers one would expect to see from the starting hurler in a Series opener. What's more, Ehmke hadn't pitched for nearly a month before the Series. But a heart-to-heart conversation between Mack and his veteran pitcher resulted in the decision.

Shortly before the A's left on their last western trip, Mack called Ehmke to his office in the tower at Shibe. "Howard, there comes a time in everyone's life when there has to be a change," he began, "and I think we've reached the point where we must soon part company."

Ehmke regretfully admitted that his manager was correct. "All right, Mr. Mack," he said. "I haven't helped you much this year, and it's lucky you didn't need me. But I've always wanted to pitch in a World Series, and I'd like to get the opportunity, if only for a few innings."

Flexing his arm, Ehmke added: "I honestly believe that I've got one more good game left in this arm. I know I'm not as fast as I used to be, but I'm a lot smarter."

Impressed by the veteran pitcher's confidence, Mack, to Ehmke's amazement, agreed. "All right, Howard," he said. "You govern yourself accordingly. Stay at home during this last road trip. Train yourself as you see fit. Keep the arm nice and loose. Go to the Phillies' ballpark and watch them play the Cubs when they come to town. Spend time studying those big hitters. Find out what they like to hit, their weaknesses, and see how we can stop them." Enthusiastic about the prospect of baffling the baseball world at the height of its glory, Mack offered his hand to seal the agreement. "And Howard," he added, "let's not talk to anyone about this. It's between us."

Mack knew exactly what he was doing. The Cubs were intimidated by Grove, Earnshaw, and Walberg because of their masterful pitching during the last month of the season. He realized that if the Cubs, playing on their home field, defeated one of these star hurlers, they might break the A's powerful spell, giving them a decided advantage when the Series moved to Philadelphia. A major surprise, on the other hand, might break their spirit, rendering them incapable of any comeback. At the same time, however, Mack, was taking a calculated risk. If his strategy didn't work, his detractors would be quick to claim that he was slipping in his old age and that it was time to retire.

The night before the Series was to open in Chicago, Jimmie Foxx, who was rooming with Ehmke at the Edgewater Beach Hotel, confided, "I have an idea that the old gentleman is going to pitch you tomorrow!"

The remark took Ehmke by complete surprise. He hadn't said a word about the ploy to anyone, not even his wife. He also knew that Mack was as good as his word. Choosing to ignore Foxx, he replied, "Go to bed and forget about it." But Foxx persisted, "Well, if he does pitch you, I'll hit one out, for you."

The next day, shortly before game time, Ehmke approached Mack and asked, "Is it still me?"

"Yes, Howard, it's still you," he replied.

When Ehmke pulled off his jacket to warm up, the sportswriters, the spectators, and the Cubs' players couldn't believe it. The shock carried as far as Philadelphia, where hundreds of A's fans gathered on the streets outside the *Bulletin* newspaper building to watch an electronic scoreboard and listen to an announcer with a direct wire to Wrigley. Even the A's players themselves were dumbfounded. Al Simmons, who was sitting next to Mack on the bench, managed to ask, "Are you going to pitch him?"

Keeping a straight face, Mack turned, stared at his star outfielder, and replied, "Yes I am, Al. Is that all right with you?"

Simmons retreated. "Yes, Mr. Mack. If you think he can win," he said rather sheepishly, "it's all right with me."

Ehmke performed magnificently. Pitching off his right hip, close to his shirt, his submarine delivery baffled Cubs' hitters like Wilson, Cuyler, and Hornsby who liked to take hefty cuts. They never could get a good look at the ball and by the time they did see the pitch, it was obscured by the white shirts in the center-field bleachers.

The Cubs failed to capitalize on a third-inning scoring opportunity, when, with one out, McMillan singled and English doubled. But Ehmke struck out both Hornsby and Wilson on a total of seven pitches to retire the side. Ehmke seemed to get stronger as the game unfolded. In the sixth inning, he single-handedly retired the side, striking out English on three pitches and getting Hornsby and Wilson for the second time each.

With the score deadlocked at 0–0 in the top of the seventh, Jimmie Foxx delivered on his promise. The Beast caught hold of a Charlie Root fastball, sending it into the center-field bleachers for the first run of the game and a 1–0 A's lead. In the bottom of the inning, the Cubs threatened again. Cuyler singled up the middle, and Stephenson collected another base hit. Charlie Grimm laid down a sacrifice bunt, advancing both runners while accounting for the first out. Pinch hitter Cliff Heathcotte followed with a towering fly to left center field, but Simmons caught it, wielded, and threw to the plate to hold Cuyler at third. When Gabby Hartnett struck out on three straight curveballs, Ehmke had pitched himself out of the inning.

The A's added two more runs in the ninth. They loaded the bases for Dykes, who singled in Cochrane. Ehmke then helped himself by knocking home Foxx for the third run. With the score 3–0 in favor of the Athletics, Chicago was down to its last three outs.

Again, the Cubs threatened. Wilson led off and smacked a vicious line drive back to the pitcher. The blow knocked Ehmke off the mound, but he recovered and threw the center fielder out at first. Cuyler followed with a hard-hit grounder to third base. Dykes fielded it cleanly but threw wildly to first, allowing Cuyler to race to second. Stephenson's base hit to center scored the speedy Cuyler. Grimm followed with another single, advancing Stephenson to second. Footsie Blair came in to pinch hit. He grounded to Dykes who threw to second to get Grimm. With two outs and runners on first and third, McCarthy sent Chuck Tolson to the plate to pinch hit for Guy Bush, who had replaced Root in relief. Ehmke worked a full count on him. Having already lost his shutout, the veteran hurler faced the possibility of losing the game. He called time and motioned for his catcher, Mickey Cochrane, to come to the mound.

"When you get back there, delay as much as you can," he ordered his backstop. "The longer he stands in the box the more nervous he's going to get. With $60,000 on the line I can't afford to fool around."

Umpire Bill Klem got tired of waiting and ordered an end to the conference. Cochrane returned behind the plate and gave his pitcher a sign. Ehmke shook him off. Cochrane gave another sign, and again Ehmke shook it off. They continued the ritual for five minutes in an attempt to frazzle Tolson. It worked. Ehmke took the sign for one last time, shook it off, and quick-pitched a strike right down the middle of the plate. As he released the ball, Cochrane yelled at the top of his lungs, "Hit it!" Tolson took the cue and whiffed. The game was over. The A's had won their first World Series game in 16 years. And Ehmke had established a new Series record by striking out 13 hitters in a single game. Mack, largely because of his risk in pitching the veteran right-hander, called the game his "greatest thrill in baseball."

The A's duplicated their success in Game 2. This time, however, there was no secret as to who would start. Earnshaw pitched for the Mackmen and Malone for the Cubs. Another huge crowd of 49,987 packed Wrigley to watch the contest. Foxx began the A's attack in the third when he blasted a three-run homer, scoring Cochrane and Simmons ahead of him. The A's doubled their score in the fourth when Dykes singled, Haas walked, and Boley advanced the runners on a sacrifice bunt. Earnshaw walked to load the bases and Bishop singled in Dykes with the A's fourth run of the game. Cochrane followed with another walk to load the bases again, and Al Simmons singled to center, scoring Earnshaw and Haas. Malone was finished for the afternoon.

With a 6–0 lead, Earnshaw became careless. With one out in the fifth, Hornsby and Wilson broke out of their hitless streaks with singles. After Earnshaw fanned Cuyler for the second out of the inning, Stephenson singled to right, scoring Hornsby. Wilson advanced to second and later scored on Grimm's single to left. Stephenson, who had advanced to third on the hit, scored on Taylor's single through the box. When the dust had settled, the A's lead was cut by half, 6–3. Grove replaced Earnshaw, limiting the Cubs to three scattered hits for the remainder of the game. The A's padded their lead in the seventh when Foxx singled to right, Miller sacrificed him to second, and Dykes singled him home. Simmons added two more in the eighth when he hit his first home run of the Series, scoring Cochrane ahead of him.

The Series moved to Philadelphia on Friday, October 11. The Athletics faithful were ready and waiting. "Fans lined up two and three deep outside of Shibe, waiting for the ticket windows to open," recalled Bill Brendley. "To be eligible for a World Series ticket, you had to show 50 rainchecks from regular season games. During the season when each game was over, I used to go around and pick up all the rainchecks I could find. Most people just threw them away. I'd collect 10 to 15 rainchecks a game and pray that the A's would clinch the pennant." Those fans who weren't lucky enough to get a ticket found other, more enterprising ways to enjoy the Series. Residents along North 20th Street hired barkers to advertise their wildcat bleachers, overlooking the diamond from right field. Because the right-field fence was only 12 feet high, residents could see the entire park from their front bedroom. During the 1929 World Series, many not only constructed portable bleachers on their rooftops, but also removed all four windows from their front bedroom and packed another dozen spectators there as well. Mothers made lemonade and sent their children to buy hot dogs from the local street vendors. The kids would purchase a dozen at a nickel each and return home to sell them for a dime. John Rooney, another resident of the Shibe Park neighborhood, found another way to turn a profit. "I would simply sit out on my front porch step well before game time and wait for a car to park in my territory," he said. "Then I'd wave the motorist into the space and ask, 'Want me to watch your car, Mister?' Usually, I'd get a nickel or a dime when the game was over."

When the A's clinched the pennant, the neighborhood residents planned to make a killing. Soon, however, word spread that the tax collectors planned to close down their makeshift bleachers unless they paid $50 per house. After negotiating the price down to $30, they were permitted to continue their operations. Rooney's father somehow coaxed the officials down to $20. "That money was quickly recouped threefold from our paying customers," mused the son. "We got even more income when one of the cameramen from the Pathé Newsreel Service asked what we would charge to let him film the home games of the World Series from our roof. 'Twenty dollars,' was Dad's quick reply. We soon made similar arrangements with Fox Movietone News and Universal News."

Meanwhile, Connie Mack was making plans of his own. On the train ride east, the Spindly Strategist, acting on a hunch, summoned Earnshaw to his car. "George, I'm going to pitch you again in Philadelphia," he told his big right-hander. "You were working too fast yesterday when they knocked you out of the box. I want you to take more time between pitches tomorrow. Step off the mound, look around at your outfielders, rub the ball, pick up some dirt. Just slow down your rhythm and you'll beat those Cubs."

Earnshaw followed Mack's instructions and pitched brilliantly, allowing the Cubs just six hits and striking out ten. Cochrane scored the A's only run of the game in the fifth, but Chicago struck back in the sixth. Earnshaw's free pass to Cub pitcher Guy Bush and Dykes' error on a hard ground ball by English began the rally. Hornsby followed with a single, driving in Bush with the tying run. A single by Cuyler added two more. When all was said and done, the Cubs had won, 3–1, to snap a 10-game National League losing streak in the Fall Classic.

Game 4 was played on a perfect autumn day. A warm sun and gentle southerly breeze greeted the nearly 30,000 fans who packed Shibe Park to witness a game that has no parallel in World Series competition, producing the most spectacular rally in the annals of baseball history. Mack sent Jack Quinn to the mound against Charlie Root, the hard-luck loser of the first game. Again, Root delivered a masterpiece through the first six innings, holding the A's to just three scattered hits. The Cub hitters, on the other hand, gave the fans their greatest power display of the Series. Chicago scored twice in the fourth on Grimm's homer. Quinn was knocked out of the game in the sixth after serving up successive singles by Hornsby, Wilson, Cuyler, and Stephenson. Rommel, who replaced him, fared no better. By the time he fanned Root and McMillan for the final outs, the Cubbies had added another five runs to their lead. Rommel surrendered yet another run in the top of the seventh. To add insult to injury, every time Chicago scored, pitcher Guy Bush placed a blanket over his head and did a mock Indian war dance.

With Philadelphia down by a score of 8–0 going into the bottom half of the seventh, Mack planned to give his regulars one last chance to put the A's on the board. They did more than that. Simmons opened the inning with a towering home run onto the roof in left field. Foxx and Miller followed with singles. Then Dykes drove in Foxx with a base hit to left, adding a second run. Boley continued the rally by bringing home Miller on a fly ball to center field that Hack Wilson lost in the sun. Rommel was lifted for pinch hitter George Burns, who popped up for the first out. But the A's would not be denied. Max Bishop singled to left, scoring Dykes and cutting the Cubs' lead in half, 8–4. Though the A's had made the game respectable, no one really expected the rally to continue, least of all Cub manager Joe McCarthy.

Determined to squelch the A's momentum, McCarthy pulled his starter and brought in his southpaw Art Nehf. Mule Haas, the powerful, free-swinging center-fielder, was the first to face him. Jumping on Nehf's first pitch, Haas hit a screeching liner into dead center field. Wilson started in for the ball, but then, seemingly blinded by the sun, he hesitated and the ball shot past him into deep center field. The A's bench came to life. Players jumped to their feet and began cheering on the base runners as Boley crossed the plate, then Bishop. Wilson finally retrieved the ball as Haas was rounding third and heading home. But the throw was late and the Mule had himself an inside-the-park home run. The fans went berserk. Dykes, who was standing at the top of the dugout steps, was so overcome with excitement that he slapped the man next to him across the back, knocking him clear out onto the field. "We're back in the game, boys!" he screamed. Horrified to learn that the person he'd decked wasn't a player at all, but his manager, Connie Mack, Dykes jumped out of the dugout and helped the Tall Tactician to his feet. As he apologized profusely for his indiscretion, Mack simply smiled, dusted himself off, and in his own quiet way replied, "That's all right, Jimmy. Anything you do right now is all right. Wasn't that wonderful?"

The score now stood at 8–7, but the A's rally wasn't over yet. Noticeably shaken, Nehf walked Cochrane before he was replaced by right-hander Fred "Sheriff" Blake. Simmons and Foxx were not to be denied though, knocking out singles to tie the score. McCarthy was infuriated. He called in big Pat Malone who promptly hit Bing Miller with his first pitch, again loading the bases. Up stepped Jimmy Dykes, who nailed a high line drive to left. Stephenson overran the ball and it flew past him for a double. Simmons and Foxx scored to give the A's a 10–8 lead. Malone somehow managed to regroup, striking out Boley and Burns to retire the side, but the damage had already been done. Mack brought in Grove, who proceeded to snuff out the Cubs in order in the eighth and ninth, fanning four of the six batters he faced.

Not only had the Mackmen taken a commanding lead in the Series, but they had staged the greatest rally in World Series history. In earning the victory, the A's established a new World Series record for runs scored in a single inning, scoring 10 in the seventh. They also broke the previous record for hits in one inning, with 10, as well as the record for at bats, with 15.

Though the Cubs' Hack Wilson proved to be the goat of the game, he still managed to retain his sense of humor. That evening, as news spread of his misplayed fly balls, Wilson entered a Philadelphia restaurant, pulled down the window shades near his table, and sardonically asked the maitre d' to dim the lights so he wouldn't misjudge the soup.

Game 5 had to wait until Monday, October 14, since the Blue Laws prohibited Sunday baseball in Philadelphia. When the Series resumed, the A's snatched yet another victory out of the jaws of defeat. President Herbert Hoover traveled from Washington, D.C., to see the fifth and deciding game. It was one of the greatest occasions Philadelphia had ever witnessed. "People didn't see the president of the United States at all back in those days," recalls Joe Barrett, a lifelong A's fan. "When Hoover attended the final game of the '29 World Series, it was a big occasion. Schools were off. People lined Lehigh Avenue. This was the only opportunity the great majority of Philadelphians would ever have to see the president." Thirteen-year-old Wayne Ambler, who would later go on to play for the Athletics, witnessed the event from the left-field bleachers. "That World Series was exciting and colorful," he said. "The bad baseball in it—the way the Cubs lost the eight-run lead in the fourth game—made it exciting. The good baseball—the way the A's came from behind to win the fourth and fifth games—proved how great baseball can be. I don't believe that Philadelphia has produced as great a ball club as those A's since."

Hoover's presence unquestionably added to the pomp and ceremony surrounding the Series. If nothing else, it provided a forum for the public expression against the government's restrictive policy on alcohol distribution and consumption. As the president made his way to his box seat, the fans began chanting: "Beer! Beer! We Want Beer!" It wasn't that Prohibition stopped the sale and consumption of alcohol in the Irish-dominated North Penn District where Shibe was located, but rather that the fans couldn't legally consume beer at the ballpark. In fact, illegal distilleries, warehouses, and speakeasies flourished in the neighborhood. Even the local kids participated, roaming the streets for empty paint bottles for the illegal brew. Worse, some residents were directly engaged in the gangsterism associated with the bootleg industry. But the seriousness of the problem didn't hit home until 1928 when bootleggers gunned down Hughie McLoon near his speakeasy at 10th and Chestnut streets. McLoon, a gnome-like figure with a hunched back, lived at 25th and Lehigh and had been the A's mascot for years before becoming involved in the bootleg industry. His was the first of 20 murders associated with Prohibition, generating a grand jury investigation which exposed the links between Philadelphia politics, corrupt police, and the manufacturing and distribution of alcohol.

Philadelphia's problems were mild compared to Chicago, however, where Prohibition made murder synonymous with the Windy City. Chicago was home to a crime syndicate that grossed $100 million a year and deployed an army of nearly 700 thugs and gunmen. Among them were such gangsters as the infamous Johnny Torrio, Jack "Legs" Banion, "Machine Gun" Kelly, and, of course, public enemy number one, Al Capone. Thus, between Philadelphia and Chicago, the 1929 Fall Classic might have just as well been called the "Bootleggers' Series." Though no game fixing was ever uncovered, America's greatest annual sporting event seemed to invite the bribery, gambling, and gangsterism associated with the illegal industry.

Aside from the crime and violence that Prohibition threatened to cast on the Series, Mack was greatly disturbed by the fans' treatment of the president. "It was a most regrettable occurrence," he stated after the game, "and I am sorry any of our Philadelphia fans were guilty of it. I never have been a party man. I vote for the man, not the party; and in my day I have voted for good men of both parties. But every good citizen should show proper respect for the president and his office." Though he stopped short of saying it, Mack also felt the fans' behavior reflected poorly on the Athletics' organization at a time when it claimed the national spotlight—something that was of great embarrassment to him. True to form, however, the players from both clubs did their fair share to embarrass each other.

The bench jockeying was so severe that Commissioner Judge Kenesaw Mountain Landis, who was seated between the two dugouts and was caught in the crossfire, issued a warning to "cease and shut up." Fearing that the ladies in attendance might be offended by the earthy language, Landis summoned both managers to his box. "If the vulgarities continue," he told them, "the culprits will be fined their full World Series share." When Mack passed the warning on to his players, Cochrane, who had been the ringleader, sarcastically cried out, "After the game, we'll serve tea in the clubhouse!" Landis, clearly within earshot, was not amused by the remark. But rather than acknowledge it, he stared straight ahead as if he had heard nothing.

Mack apparently chose to turn a deaf ear to the sultry banter of his players. It wasn't his style to allow such profanity. Instead, he insisted that "There is room for gentlemen in baseball." To that end he would "not permit" his players "to indulge in rough jockeying." "There always is an exchange of joshing before and during a game," he admitted. "The average player is a good-natured chap and a practical joker. But I have told our boys that there never can be anything personal or malicious shouted at our opponents." But the Tall Tactician suspended his policy that day. Game 5 would be a hard-fought grudge match between the two teams. McCarthy and his Cubs were smarting from their ten-run collapse of the fourth game and the Mackmen certainly did not appreciate the way Guy Bush and his fellow bench jockeys had ridden them or the eight-run barrage Chicago's "Murderer's Row" unleashed against them in their own ballpark.

Howard Ehmke started the game, but lost his earlier magic and was knocked out in the fourth. With two out, he surrendered a double to Cuyler, a walk to Stephenson, and singles to Grimm and Taylor. The A's were down 2–0 and Mack replaced the veteran right-hander with southpaw Walberg. The Rube retired the side by fanning Malone and held the Cubs to only two more hits for the remainder of the game.

Pat Malone, who started for the Cubs, was impressive through the eight innings, giving up only two hits to the 26 batters he faced. Going into the A's ninth, it seemed as though the Series would return to Chicago for a sixth game. With the A's down 2–0, French came in to pinch hit for Walberg and struck out. Bishop followed with a single and Haas, the hero of Game 4, smashed a line-drive home run over the right-field fence, tying the score at 2–2. Everyone in the park was on their feet as Cochrane came to the plate. But the rally would have to wait, as Black Mike was retired on a ground ball to second base for the second out of the inning. Al Simmons brought the fans back to life with a towering shot that just missed clearing the center-field scoreboard, falling instead for a double. McCarthy, feeling the lead slip away once again, ordered Malone to walk the always dangerous Jimmie Foxx. But Bing Miller didn't disappoint the fans, knocking a 2–2 curveball off the scoreboard for another double. Simmons bounced home with the winning run, giving the A's their first world championship since 1913.

The crowd went berserk. Philadelphia Mayor Mackey leaped from the field box where he had been hosting President Hoover and hugged every A's player he could lay his hands on. When he finally returned to the presidential box, Mackey was reprimanded by a secret service agent for leaving the chief executive. "Don't be silly, man," replied the mayor. "A Philadelphian does as he pleases on a day like this." Meanwhile, in the Athletics' clubhouse, Landis offered his congratulations to all but Cochrane. Just before he was ready to leave though, he elbowed his way to the A's backstop and, with a straight face, said "Hello, Sweetheart, I came in after my tea. Will you pour?"

As all of Philadelphia celebrated, Connie Mack quietly retreated to his private office in the Shibe Park Tower. When they saw him entering, three secretaries rushed towards the 66-year-old manager, fighting to plant a kiss on him. But graciously refusing them the privilege, he closed the door, lay down on his battered couch, and fell sound asleep. The Tall Tactician could now rest peacefully. He had just captured his fourth world championship, a record at the time, and one that placed him head and shoulders above all other managers in the history of the game. It also vindicated his judgment, proving that his advanced age did not blunt his reasoning or his ability to win. It also proved that the so-called advanced ideas ushered in by the lively ball era did not belong solely to younger men.

1932: Yankees vs. Cubs

Babe Ruth's Called Shot

from *The Big Bam: The Life and Times of Babe Ruth* by Leigh Montville

On July 6, 1932, a 21-year-old woman named Violet Valle went to the room at the Hotel Carlos at 3834 Sheffield Avenue in Chicago where 24-year-old Cubs shortstop Billy Jurges lived. Ms. Valle, a jilted lover, was upset with Jurges and had a .25-caliber revolver to prove it. Her plan was to kill Jurges and then kill herself.

"To me, life without Billy isn't worth living," she wrote in a good-bye note she left for her brother. "But why should I leave this earth alone? I'm going to take Billy with me."

Her execution of the plan, once she was admitted by the shortstop into his room, was a bit slow. Jurges was able to wrestle her for the gun. He was shot twice, once in the ribs and once in the hand, and she was shot once, but neither of the combatants was seriously injured. They both were taken to the hospital.

Jurges, the gentleman, refused to press charges. Violet, passions subsided, signed a 22-week vaudeville contract for shows that billed her as "Violet

(What I Did for Love) Valle—The Most Talked-About Woman in Chicago."
The story had a reasonably happy ending for everyone concerned except for
the Cubs, who needed a shortstop to replace Jurges while his injuries healed.

They settled on Mark Koenig, the shortstop on the 1927 Murderers' Row
Yankees, who had been released by the Tigers in the spring and now was playing
for the minor league San Francisco Seals. Koenig, who had thought his big league
days were done, hurried to Chicago, hit like a madman, never left the lineup,
even when Jurges returned, and finished with a .356 batting average as the Cubs
outlasted the Pittsburgh Pirates and won the National League pennant.

In voting for World Series shares, dividing up the money that would be won
in the next week, a perilous moment in many teams' intrapersonal relationships,
the Cubs, alas, disregarded his fine effort and voted him only a half-share as they
prepared to face the Yankees. (It was, after all, the Depression.) The Yankees,
most of whom knew Koenig, of course, took this as great catcalling ammunition
for the Series, a chance to tell the Cubs many times how cheap they were.

The chief catcaller was Ruth. He was no great friend of Koenig's—indeed,
they'd had a locker-room fight in 1929 when Koenig made a deprecating
remark about Claire shortly after Ruth's marriage—but Ruth always had
an active mouth on the bench. He riddled the Cubs with comments about
Koenig and cheapness during the first two games of the Series in New
York. The Cubs riddled him back with questions about his parentage, his
increasing weight, his racial features, his sexual preferences, and whatever
else they could invent. The "nigger" word from long ago surfaced. It was all
familiar baseball stuff for the time, but with an exaggerated edge.

The Yankees won the first two games at the Stadium and traveled to a
packed Wrigley Field to try to take care of the rest of business. Newspaper
accounts of the back-and-forth bench jockeying had stirred the local public.
The Yankees had been subjected to insults as they made their way to the
Edgewater Hotel, especially Ruth, who was walking to the hotel with Claire.
The back-and-forth resumed as soon as the third game started, with a crowd
of over 51,000 in the stands.

Ruth had one hole card in all arguments on this afternoon. A terrific wind was blowing out toward right field. In batting practice, both he and Gehrig had hammered a bunch of shots over the wooden temporary stands.

"The Babe is on fire," Gehrig said after batting practice. "He ought to hit one today. Maybe a couple."

The first one came in the first inning off Cubs starter Charlie Root, with two men on base, to give the Yankees a 3–0 lead. In the third inning, Root won the battle, getting Ruth to fly deep to right-center. All of this time, the back-and-forth with the Cubs dugout continued. Ruth also had established communications with the fans in right. They hooted at him when he was too slow to reach a soft line drive by Jurges in the fourth and Jurges wound up on second base. (Koenig had injured a wrist in the first game of the Series.) Ruth hooted back, tipping his cap. His entire day was a happy, malevolent dialogue with somebody. Two lemons had been thrown at him when he went to the plate in the first inning.

All of which was prelude to his at bat in the fifth. Root was still on the mound. The score was tied, 4–4. Nobody was on base. Ruth came to the plate, and another lemon rolled his way. While the umpire disposed of the lemon, Ruth did more gesturing with the fans. He then settled in to face Root.

The first pitch was a called strike. The players in the Cubs dugout were yelling, particularly pitcher Guy Bush, a native of Aberdeen, Mississippi, who was standing on the top step. Ruth looked toward Bush and the dugout and put up one finger, as if to say, "That's just one strike." Root then delivered two balls, followed by a second called strike. More yelling. Bush was out of the dugout, onto the grass, and yelling. Ruth held up two fingers this time as if to say, "That's just two strikes." He then pointed. Where he pointed is a question, but legend has it that he pointed to dead center field.

Cubs catcher Gabby Hartnett later said that Ruth said, "It only takes one to hit." Gehrig, in the on-deck circle, said Ruth said to Root, "I'm going to knock the next one down your goddamned throat." A pair of 16mm home movies discovered more than half a century later seemed to indicate that Ruth might have pointed at the Cubs bench and at Bush rather than dead center field (maybe Ruth wanted to knock the ball down Bush's goddamned throat?), but both films were taken from angles that left room for doubt.

Whatever happened, the next part was not debatable. Root threw a slow curve. Ruth slammed the baseball up and into the big, carrying wind, and the ball left the park somewhere between the scoreboard and the edge of the right-field bleachers, one of the longest and prettiest home runs in Wrigley history. He circled the bases as happy as he ever had been, saying, "Lucky, lucky, lucky," and imparted wisdom to each of the Chicago infielders as he passed and raised four fingers at the Cubs bench as he rounded third and laughed and laughed all the way home. Four fingers. Four bases. Four games.

When all the celebrating calmed down, Root took a fresh baseball and served it to Gehrig, who swung on the first pitch and hit a homer deep, deep to right, and the Yankees were off to a 7–5 win. The next day they won again, 13–6, to close out the Series in four games. Gehrig was the undeniable star of the show with three home runs and a .529 batting average, but it was the Ruth home run—the "Called Shot"—that was remembered.

"It was a privilege to be present because it is not likely that the scene will ever be repeated in all its elements," Westbrook Pegler wrote for the next morning's *Tribune Syndicate*. "Many a hitter may make two home runs or possibly three in World Series play yet to come, but not the way Babe Ruth hit these two. Nor will you ever see an artist call his shot before hitting one of the longest drives ever made on the grounds, in a World Series game, laughing and mocking the enemy with two strikes gone."

Did he call his shot? Didn't he? Though not mentioned in most immediate deadline accounts of the game, the moment would be gilded two and three and four days later, embellished, built into Johnny Sylvester deathwatch proportions. Then, years later, it would be debunked, seen as pure fable. Proof would be requested and questions asked of participants and bystanders, everything taken as seriously as if this were the examination of a final miracle needed from the Vatican for sainthood.

The moment became quite overblown.

"He shouted to his enemies," Paul Gallico wrote two days later in the *Daily News*. "He pointed like a duelist to the spot where he expected to send his rapier home and then he sent it there. His second home run in the face of the razzing he was taking from the Cubs camp was a stroke of genius. He went so far out on his limb with his gestures and his repartee and his comportment at the plate that if he had missed he never would have been able to live it down. But the point is he didn't miss."

Did it happen exactly that way? Probably not. Did it happen? The Babe always was predicting home runs. He had that itchy feeling that he was going to hit a home run for Lindbergh. He told Mark Roth, the traveling secretary, that he'd end the game so the team could make the train. He once told Ford Frick's father, at an exhibition in Fort Wayne, Indiana, "You look like you want to get home for supper," and hit a home run. In 1930 he hit three home runs against the Philadelphia A's, then came to the plate the fourth time, batted right-handed for two strikes, then stepped across the plate and swung with a fury to strike out on the next pitch. What if he had connected? Where would that have gone down in the lore?

He called shots all the time. He loved to create situations. It was for other people to determine what they meant. Did he call a shot here? That probably never will be answered to every nitpicker's satisfaction. He definitely created a situation. He challenged his entire environment, whipped up all parties, then made them shut up. The specifics might be hazy, but the general story was not wrong.

Ruth himself gave different versions through the years of what happened that day, which did nothing to help historians. He said more than once that he absolutely pointed at the flagpole to indicate where he was going to hit the ball. He also said more than once that "only a damn fool" would do something like that. Rather than make the moment into the mythical event that it became, he seemed inclined to have fun with it.

His best description probably came at a cocktail party held by sportswriter Grantland Rice in the spring of 1933. This was a dignified affair. The wife of Walter Lippmann, the famous political columnist, asked Ruth what happened with that famous home run in the 1932 Series. Rice printed the Home Run King's answer in his 1955 autobiography, *The Tumult and the Shouting*, leaving blanks for words that can be quite easily filled in now.

"It's like this," the Babe said, dressed in white and waving his cigar. "The Cubs had fucked my old teammate Mark Koenig by cutting him for only a measly fucken half share of the Series money.

"Well, I'm riding the fuck out of the Cubs, telling 'em they're the cheapest pack of fucken crumbums in the world. We've won the first two and now we're in Chicago for the third game. Root is the Cubs' pitcher. I pack one into the stands in the first inning, but in the fifth it's tied, 4 to 4, when I'm up with nobody on. The Chicago fans are giving me hell.

"Root's still in there. He breezes the first two pitches by—both strikes! The mob's tearing down Wrigley Field. I shake my fist after that first strike. After the second I point my bat at these bellerin' bleachers—right where I aim to park the ball. Root throws it and I hit that fucken ball on the nose, right over the fence for two fucken runs.

"'How do you like those apples, you fucken bastard?' I yell at Root as I run towards first. By the time I reach home I'm almost fallin' down I'm laughin' so fucken hard—and that's how it happened."

The details, of course, were a bit messed up. The count was 2–2, not 0–2. The home run scored one run, not two. Perhaps some of the dialogue had been embellished. The spirit of the moment, though, was probably better preserved here than in all other descriptions by all historians and literary lions. Mrs. Lippmann soon grabbed her famous husband and they left the party in a hurry.

"Why'd you use that language?" Rice asked Ruth.

"What the hell, Grant," Ruth replied. "You heard her ask me what happened. So I told her."

The best piece of empirical evidence that *something* out of the ordinary happened was delivered by Guy Bush the next day. He was the Cubs starter for what turned out to be the fourth and final game. With runners on first and second, nobody out, first inning, he drilled the Bambino with a fastball on his very first pitch.

1934: Cardinals vs. Tigers

The Gashouse Gang

from *The Dizziest Season* by G. H. Fleming

Monday, October 8

On October 7, in St. Louis, the Cardinals lost Game 5 of the World Series, 3–1. Winning pitcher, Tom Bridges; losing pitcher, Dizzy Dean.

Bill DeLancey last night was reportedly fined $200 by Umpire Brick Owens for uncomplimentary remarks in yesterday's game, but Commissioner [Kenesaw Mountain] Landis said he alone could assess a fine and knew nothing of the matter.

Announcement of the fine was made by Mickey Cochrane, who said it was inflicted while DeLancey was fanning on three called strikes in the ninth.

When Owens called the first strike on DeLancey, according to Cochrane, the Redbird catcher snapped out a few short cuss words, and Owens told him it would cost him a $50 fine.

"Why don't you make it $100, you thievin' bum," DeLancey yelled back.

"A hundred it is," Owens retorted.

"Make it two," DeLancey screamed.

"Two it is," came back Owens.

Cochrane ended the argument by reminding DeLancey he'd better keep his mouth shut or he wouldn't have any World Series check coming. [*Since Landis did not levy a fine against him, and since the umpire had no right to do this, Bill DeLancey did not lose any money because of this incident.*]

St. Louis *Globe-Democrat*

Tuesday, October 9

On October 8, in Detroit, the Cardinals won Game 6, 4–3. Winning pitcher, Paul Dean; losing pitcher, Schoolboy Rowe.

The Schoolboy flunked his homework, and the big baseball debate will go into the final clinch. Oklahoma won out over Arkansas when Daffy of the Deans outpitched the El Dorado scholar and tied up the Series in a bitter battle.

What hurt Lynwood T. Rowe was that he could not suppress Lippy Leo Durocher, whose batting record long ago earned him the sobriquet of "The All-American Out." Through the early games of this Series there were some queries as to why Lippy Leo carried all that lumber when he went up to the plate. It was a weight on his shoulders. He is none too strong. He could have done just as well bare-handed. [*In the first four games of the World Series, Durocher had one hit, a single, in 16 times at bat. The jeering remarks concerning Durocher, the weakest-hitting regular on the St. Louis team, might be contrasted with the relatively mild tone of the press and television response to Mike Schmidt, the Philadelphia Phillies' most powerful hitter—who earns an annual salary of $900,000—after he had completed the 1983 World Series with one bloop single and no RBIs in 20 times at bat.*]

Then Lippy Leo came up with a good hit on Sunday, and yesterday he really got into the spirit of things. He went up there as though he meant to hit. He didn't hem and haw or pull down his cap or scratch the dirt from his cleats. He took a toehold like a determined hitter and pounded the ball solidly for three hits. He scored two runs and paved the way for another. Now he has something to talk about, not that it makes any difference to Lippy Leo. At all times he talks fluently with or without cause or reason. Lippy Leo will never be crippled until his voice gives out.

Gordon Stanley (Mickey himself) Cochrane was sitting in the driver's seat. Now he is in a depression, if not a deep hole. Coming back to the jubilant home city of the Tigers, he figured to shoot the Schoolboy at the Cardinals and clinch the Series. Well, the Schoolboy didn't pass his test, and the seesaw Series goes into the final game with the Cardinals holding an edge in the eyes of most observers.

When Rowe wavered, Manager Mike did his best to win the game single-handedly. He was all alone in his early attack on Daffy of the Deans. He singled in the first, singled in the third, and singled again in the sixth. Up to that time he was the only Detroit batter to hit safely. They were hot smashes that burned the fingers of the Cardinals' infielders.

The Cardinals teed up on Rowe in the very first inning and scored a quick run on Rothrock's double and Medwick's single. The Tigers evened the score in the third when Daffy walked Jo-Jo White with two out. It's always a mistake to walk White because as soon as somebody walks him he starts running.

Jo-Jo tore down toward second in an attempt to steal. Finding Frank Frisch there waiting for him with the ball, Jo-Jo took out the old Fordham Flash with a rolling block. Those Tigers have been hitting the bases and the basemen hard since Manager Mike spoke to them about their ladylike sauntering in the first three games.

So Jo-Jo White knocked Frisch for a row of revoking samovars and continued to third base when the ball dribbled away from the scene of the crime. It was easy for him to score on Cochrane's smash to Rip Collins that went for a hit.

That run tied the score, but it may have cost the Tigers ultimate victory because Manager Mike crashed heavily into first base running out his hit and was spiked on the knee by Daffy Dean, who had run over to cover.

There was some fear that they would have to gather up Mickey and trundle him off in a barrow, but the injured leg was the same one that Muscles Medwick had battered earlier in the Series. Mike still had one leg left. He was determined to hobble along on that one.

Where it really hurt was in the sixth inning. The Cards jumped on Rowe again in the fifth, led by Lippy Leo Durocher. On hits by Durocher and Pepper Martin and a bad throw by Goslin, they had scored two runs and were leading, 3–1.

In the Tiger sixth, White was first man up, and Daffy of the Deans presented him with another free ticket to first, despite the foolishness of such a procedure as proved in the third inning. Cochrane nearly tore the glove off the hand of Ripper Collins with a wicked smash for a single, and White waltzed around to third. Gehringer dribbled a grounder through the box that Daffy muffed, and the Tiger rooters were in a frenzy of delight. White had scored, Cochrane was on second, Gehringer on first, and none out.

A sacrifice bunt was the play, and Goslin tried it. But limping Mike with the game leg couldn't get down to third before Catcher DeLancey had picked up the bunt and ferried it to Pepper Martin for a force play. Hank Greenberg's smashing single sent Gehringer home to tie the score, but Cochrane's lameness spoiled a great chance for the Tigers to clinch the Series then and there.

The Cardinals came right back and added a run in their half of the seventh. With one out, Durocher banged a rousing double to deep right-center and rode home in style when Daffy either accidentally or on purpose singled to right. In any event, he did single, and the boys might as well have gone to the showers right there. The game was over.

It was an exciting festival for Dean the Younger, and he had himself to blame for the hot spots. He gave two bases on balls that were turned into runs. But he came through right side up with a wide grin. He had beaten Schoolboy Rowe, he had tied up the Series, and he had won his own game with a hit to right that drove in the deciding marker.

Seeing that the Deans have accounted for the three Cardinals' victories, Dizzy and Daffy are trying to talk Manager Frisch into letting them pitch the seventh game, separately or together. As Dizzy remarked, "This is a family matter."

John Kieran, New York Times

Kids out of school, a torrent rushing over a dam, madmen on the loose, that's how the Cardinals stormed into the dressing room. Uniforms were all but torn off, sweaty bodies engaged in bumping matches that threatened the permanency of the very walls.

"You can have anything I got," screamed Dizzy Dean. He hurled himself on his brother, and wrestled him to the floor. "Oh, baby, what a guy you are! What a guy, what a pitcher!"

Arms wrenched "Diz" free from Paul's body, not to let the youngster rise but to serve as a fresh outlet for a frenzy of emotions. Orsatti, Martin, Collins flung themselves on the younger Dean to pound home their congratulations. Ol' Mike Gonzalez, his gold teeth outglaring the blinding flashlights, stood in the center of the room, repeating, "Who says we're dead?"

Frankie Frisch sat in sodden fatigue, his shirt half off, his locks matted into porcupine quills. He was too tired even to breathe, but a wan little smile testified to his joy over Paul's victory that may save the world's title for the Cardinals.

"Dean tomorrow, the other Dean?" we asked.

"If I last till tomorrow, maybe," he said. "Dean or Hallahan. I don't know yet."

Dean or Hallahan, but it will be "Dizzy" you can bet all the tea in China. Wild horses won't keep him on the bench. In the end Frisch will say yes because he can't say no. It's his best bet, and after tomorrow there is no tomorrow at all. Under a sputtering shower the "Dizzy" one washed soap from his eyes and hollered, "The greatest pitcher the Dean family ever had, that kid brother of mine. Didn't he prove it? Didn't he?"

Over in a corner, "Rip" Collins sat, opening a letter. It was an anniversary card. "Married 12 years ago today," he smiled. "I couldn't give my wife a better present."

John P. Carmichael, Chicago Daily News

In the Tiger clubhouse the ludicrous expressions on the faces of Graham McNamee and the moving picture men was a stiff admission price. [*Graham McNamee was the first nationally known sports broadcaster. He was behind the microphone in Yankee Stadium in the first month of its first season, April 1923, for the initial broadcast of a major league baseball game, and later in the same year he was the announcer for the first World Series broadcast.*] They had a setup worthy of a Belasco. [*David Belasco was a theatrical producer who had died in 1931.*] Kleig lights, wires, huge cameras, and other paraphernalia were scattered all over the place, waiting to have Mickey Cochrane say for posterity just how he won the World Series.

Instead, there was poor Mickey lying on a table with a doctor and trainer working over the long cut on his kneecap inflicted by Daffy Dean's spikes.

St. Louis Post-Dispatch

Wednesday, October 10

On October 9, in Detroit, the Cardinals won the baseball world's championship by beating the Tigers, 11–0. Winning pitcher, Dizzy Dean; losing pitcher, Eldon Auker.

The dizziest, maddest, wildest, and most exciting World Series game played in recent years began with a seven-run batting rally in the third inning that gave the Cardinals the championship of the world for 1934, was interrupted by one of the wildest riots ever seen in a ballpark in the sixth inning, and wound up, of all things, with the spectators engaging in an old-fashioned pillow fight in which for a half an hour the populace stood around and hurled seat cushions at one another. For the first time that I know of, the crowd forced a manager to remove a player from the field. Twenty thousand people massed a-slant in the left-field bleachers turned into a deadly and vicious mob. Only the barrier of a steel screen and locked gates prevented them from pouring into the field and mobbing Outfielder Joe Medwick, who bears the incongruous nickname of Ducky Wucky.

In the sixth inning, with Pepper Martin on second and two out, Medwick hit a triple against the center-field fence and slid into third base.

Marvin Owen stepped on him, but whether by intent or accident, no one could tell. But there was no mistaking Medwick's ideas as he lay on the ground on his back and suddenly began lashing out at Owen's legs with his spiked feet. One-two-three, his feet flashed, and then he kicked with both together like Joe Savoldi. [*A former Notre Dame fullback. "Jumping Joe" Savoldi was then a professional wrestler, noted for his "flying drop-kick," in which he hurled himself feetfirst at his opponent.*]

Then they were at one another, with Umpire Bill Klem in the middle. The coaches stepped in. The other players ran over, and what is known as "cooler heads" prevailed. The Cardinals swarmed from the dugout, a red mob, but returned immediately. Klem must have seen provocation for Medwick, for neither man was punished. Medwick held out his hand to Owen. The Tiger third baseman refused it petulantly and returned to his station. Medwick remained on third and scored on Collins' single. DeLancey struck out, ending the inning. The teams changed places, and without the slightest warning the dangerous storm broke.

Medwick began to jog out to his position in left field. In an instant the entire bleacher section, a tall, sloping stand holding 20,000, was on its feet blasting him to a standstill with a wave of booing that broke over his head like a comber curling over a lone swimmer. He came closer, and 40,000 arms were lifted against him, waving him back. Then a single red apple flew from the crowd and rolled at his feet, and Medwick fielded it lazily and gracefully, the way an infielder scoops up an easy grounder, and threw it back to the fence. The next moment the air was full of flying fruit—apples, oranges, bananas— and beer and pop bottles, the fruit squashing and breaking into little bits, the ugly brown and white bottles striking the turf and rolling over and over.

I watched the crowd and Medwick and the pelting missiles through my field glasses, and it was a terrifying sight. Every face in the crowd, women and men, was distorted with rage. Mouths were torn wide, open eyes glistened and shone in the sun. All fists were clenched. Medwick stood grinning with his hands on his hips, just out of range of the bottles. A green apple rolled to his feet, and he fielded that, too. Umpires and attendants rushed out to left field and began picking up the mess. Medwick came back to the diamond. One cameraman ran out and leveled his box at the patch of inflamed and angry people all afire with mob hatred. In a moment cameramen were all over the field. Medwick and Pepper Martin began to play a little game of pop-ball between themselves, Martin making the ball bounce off his biceps into Medwick's hand and Medwick whipping it up behind his back to Martin. The crowd began to chant in a swelling, choleric chorus, "Take him out, take him out!"

For the second time Medwick started for his position, and the storm broke with renewed fury, with more bottles and less fruit. The outfield was covered with attendants with bags picking up the glassware as fast as it landed. One of them narrowly escaped being hit on the head. Someone in the dugout had sense enough to send out a sweater to Dizzy Dean, whose arm was getting cold.

Again Medwick returned to the diamond while the field was cleared and then for the third time he tried to take his position. And he did a pretty brave thing. He trotted out and turned his back on the stands. Mobs are rank cowards, and the sight of courage inflames them beyond all reason. By far the most dangerous peal of rage broke from them this third time. Heavy milk bottles flew onto the field. The police stood quietly by against the fence along the bottom row and did nothing. "Take him out! Take him out!" The chant echoed and re-echoed like a football yell. Mickey Cochrane ran halfway into left field, and with one gesture tried to pacify the mob. It had no more effect than throwing a pebble into the ocean. Cochrane returned to the diamond. The umpires walked around helplessly.

Judge Landis from his box beckoned to Medwick, Frisch, and Owen. They trotted into his box between home and first base. Umpire Klem joined them. There was a short discussion. Landis did the sane and reasonable thing. Flames were creeping near a powder mine. He extinguished that flame by asking Frisch to remove Medwick. Then only did this mad game continue.

During the next inning, Medwick, with a police escort, walked across the field and into the dugout. Once more the boos thundered. One more bottle was hurled at him, and then he vanished and the crowd was satisfied.

Unheard-of in the annals of baseball, IT had worked its will, IT had taken an active and potentially terrible part in the game. When the thing was done, the poor Tigers had been soundly whipped by the humiliating score of 11 to 0.

Paul Gallico, New York Daily News

In the wake of Western dust blown up by the two cyclonic Deans, the St. Louis Cardinals take their place today on the top plateau of baseball.

Riding along on the rubbery, loose-jointed arm of the dazzling Dizzy, they cut their way to the front through six Tiger pitchers and a wild and savage barrage of beer bottles, oranges, and other hurtling implements composed of fruit, wood, iron, and glass thrown from the left-field bleachers, which turned the game into a woolly riot that looked like the two battles of the Marne, with Verdun and Tannenberg thrown in. [*The reference is to battles waged in World War I.*]

Slingshot Dizzy slaughtered the Tigers as he held them to six scattered hits, but it remained for Ducky Wucky Medwick to steal a big part of the show and start one of the neatest young riots that any World Series has ever known.

After the riot or whatnot it was the two country kids from Oklahoma who took charge of this show with all the mastery of a Booth or a Barrett, a George M. Cohan or a Walter Huston, a Mansfield or an Arliss. [*Edwin Booth and Laurence Barrett were nineteenth-century actors; Walter Huston and George Arliss were popular actors during the first part of the 20th century; George M. Cohan was America's most famous song-and-dance man; and Richard Mansfield was a noted nineteenth-century English actor.*]

In spite of fines and suspensions and brotherly strikes, they carved their way to 49 victories. On top of this the two kids from the brush and the bush, from the dust and sage of the Southwest, won all four Cardinal victories—four winning charges in five starts—for one of the most amazing dramatic drives beneath the great white spotlight that sport has ever known—and you can go back 4,000 years if you have the energy and time.

"I've got to keep up with Paul," Dizzy said before the game. "I'd like to win anyhow—I always like to win—but I can't let Paul down. He carried us to the seventh game. It's my time now, and if I have to I'll just throw my arm off to show the two Deans still move together. I wouldn't let Paul down for the world. A great pitcher? Sure, I know that. But he's a great kid on the side. They don't come along like Paul. He's the finest kid you ever met."

As the bulky figure of Babe Ruth fades out of the picture, an old-fashioned schooner fading into the fog, two kids from the dust of the Western trail take his place as the greatest sensations baseball has known—matching the glamour of Mathewson, Hans Wagner, Ty Cobb, and Babe Ruth.

But these two country kids have come along with a sudden blaze and flame that surpasses in its dramatic flourish the leaders of the old parade. In one brief six months, they have called upon two strong right arms to write one of the greatest of all sporting classics.

And in the midst of the Dean triumph, don't overlook Pepper Martin, who came back with a rushing, rowdy, ripping attack to regain the place he held a few years ago as one of the best ballplayers who ever carved and slashed and ripped his way from goatdom to the purple toga. Except that the Pepper's interest in a purple toga would be less than nothing with his baggy trousers, open shirt, and a front piece that has only casual interest in a razor.

What a ballplayer!

And in spite of his banishment I'll say the same for Ducky Wucky Medwick, the Cardinal Cossack, who plays the game up to the hill of flying spikes. Did Detroit ever see Ty Cobb along the base paths?

The Tigers today know how Bill Terry's Giants and the rest of the National League must have suffered. The twin poisons of sport carried their venom to the final out.

Grantland Rice, New York *Sun*

1941: Yankees vs. Dodgers

Mickey Owen's Dropped Third Strike

from *The New York Times,* "Owen, Henrich, Say Casey
Threw a Curve," by Dave Anderson

*Nearly half a century later, they were together again, two old actors reliving their
roles in one of baseball's most theatrical scenes.*

Mickey Owen let a third strike get away, letting Tommy Henrich
hurry to first base with two out in the ninth inning at Ebbets Field just
when the Brooklyn Dodgers appeared to have squared the 1941 World
Series with the Yankees at two games each. Afforded that life, the Yankees
erupted with a four-run rally for a 7–4 victory. And listening to the radio in
Brooklyn, a Dodger fan erupted by throwing his small dog off his lap and
out his apartment-house window. If the dog survived, the Dodgers didn't.
The Yankees closed out that World Series the next day.

In later years, Hugh Casey, the Dodger pitcher, insisted that he had
thrown an illegal spitball for the strikeout that wasn't.

"But if Casey threw a spitball, he threw it on his own," Mickey Owen
was saying now. "It never looked like a spitball to me. It was a curveball.
That's what I called for."

"That's right," Tommy Henrich said. "Spitballs drop down. I swung at
a big breaking curveball."

"Casey had two kinds of curveballs," Owen said. "One was an overhand curve that broke big. The other one was like a slider, it broke sharp and quick. But we had the same sign for either one. He just threw whichever one was working best. From the fifth inning when he came in, he had stopped the Yankees using his quick curve. He never tried the big overhand curve. When we got to 3 and 2 on Tommy, I called for the curveball. I was looking for the quick curve he had been throwing all along. But he threw the overhand curve and it really broke big, in and down. Tommy missed it by six inches."

"As soon as I missed it, I looked around to see where the ball was," Henrich said. "It fooled me so much, I figured maybe it fooled Mickey, too. And it did."

The spry 72-year-old Owen and the laughing 75-year-old Henrich each will be inducted into the Brooklyn Dodger Hall of Fame today along with Cookie Lavagetto, Gene Hermanski, George Shuba, Cal Abrams, Eddie Miksis, and two other "distinguished opponents" named Bobby Thomson and Tommy Holmes. So will Irving Rudd, once a Dodger executive, Marty Glickman the announcer, and four sportswriters: Gus Steiger, Sid Friedlander, Stan Isaacs, and another, now a columnist, who was the last to cover the Brooklyn Dodgers for the *Brooklyn Eagle*.

Since there's no hall for this fame yet, the 12:30 p.m. ceremony will be held outside the Brooklyn Museum near Grand Army Plaza, a long foul ball from where Owen had to chase the pitch that got away with the Dodgers leading, 4–3.

"The big mistake I made," Owen said, "was not going out to the mound to tell Casey that I blew it. I just stood there behind the plate. I should've gone out to tell Casey that I blew it and to settle him down. But all of us were in shock from what happened."

"When I got to first base, Dolph Camilli never said a word to me," Henrich said, referring do the Dodger slugger. "Not a word."

"I couldn't believe what happened, none of us could," Owen said. "Then Joe DiMaggio hit a fastball, a screaming line drive over Pee Wee Reese's head into left field, then Charlie Keller hit a quick curve high off the right-field screen."

"That was a soft screen above that angled wall," Henrich said. "The ball came straight down off that soft screen, hit the wall, bounced up in the air to give DiMaggio another two seconds and he slid across with the go-ahead run."

"That was as good a play," Owen said, "as Enos Slaughter scoring from first base for the Cardinals in the 1946 Series."

"Bill Dickey walked," Henrich said, "then Joe Gordon doubled over Jimmy Wasdell's head in left field for two more runs."

"I don't remember Leo Durocher saying much in the clubhouse," Owen said, referring to the Dodger manager. "We were still in shock when Larry MacPhail came in. Larry was the general manager and he always had something to say. I thought, 'I'm going to hear something now.' But he was feeling no pain. He came over and hugged and kissed me. I thought, 'I can't believe this.'"

In the Yankee clubhouse, Henrich's locker was near DiMaggio's.

"Even with all the noise," Henrich recalled, "I can still hear Joe saying, 'They'll never come back from this one.'"

"Joe was right," Owen said. "We didn't come back."

Months later, Owen asked Casey about that pitch.

"He told me, 'It just happened,'" Owen said.

Now a great-grandfather, Owen is a livestock auctioneer in Springfield, Mo., where he was once the county sheriff. Henrich lives in Dewey, Ariz., where he swings at golf balls.

"When people ask me if I was the batter when Mickey missed the pitch," he said, laughing, "I tell 'em, 'You mean the swinger.'"

In the 1949 World Series opener, the Yankee known as Old Reliable hit a ninth-inning home run for a 1–0 victory over Don Newcombe of the Dodgers.

"But people remember me being in the Mickey Owen play," he said, "more than they do that homer."

As they reminisced the other night at the Downtown Athletic Club, where they were honored by Guinness Stout for a memorable achievement that doesn't qualify for the Guinness Book of Records, each remembered watching Bill Buckner's error at first base that enabled the Mets to go on and win the 1986 World Series after the Boston Red Sox had been within a strike of winning it in the sixth game.

"Right away," Tommy Henrich said, "I thought, 'He'll never get over this.' But you never know. Look at the way Mickey has handled it. He turned it into a plus."

"I would've been completely forgotten if I hadn't missed that pitch," Mickey Owen said. "But I really felt sorry for Buckner. The way he was hobbling on his bad ankle, he was a cripple, he shouldn't have been out there. But if I'd seen someone miss one like I did, I'd have kicked him in the backside."

1944: Browns vs. Cardinals
The Hapless Browns Meet the Legendary Cardinals

from *The Boys Who Were Left Behind* by John Heidenry and Brett Topel

Bob Broeg was a 25-year-old Marine who had a problem—in fact, two or three problems, and one was worse than the other. In June 1943, only fifteen months earlier, he had gotten married. His first year of marriage with Dorth had been idyllic, until Broeg received notification, without any advance warning, that he had been transferred from St. Louis to Marine headquarters in suburban Washington. Leaving Dorth had been tough. Now he was lovesick and homesick, missing not only his young bride but also his mom's lemon meringue pie. To make matters worse, the Cardinals had once again wrapped up the National League pennant, meaning that some games of the World Series would once again be played in his hometown. Wonder of wonders, there was even the possibility of a first-ever Streetcar Series if the Browns, that other St. Louis team, did the impossible and won the American League pennant.

Broeg's love for the Cardinals had begun when he was 12 years old and took a streetcar to see Frankie Frisch and his Gashouse Gang for $1 a ticket.

Broeg's parents subscribed to all four local papers so he could devour every detail of each Redbirds game. After attending a local South Side high school, he graduated from the University of Missouri in Columbia with a journalism degree and went to work for the Associated Press bureau in Boston in 1941. Later, before he was drafted, he got a job covering sports for the *St. Louis Star-Times*.

Dorth, like her husband an apprentice sportswriter in civilian life, loved baseball. The previous year, when they were still courting, he had taken her to the Browns' home opener against the Chicago White Sox. He quickly noticed, as he later wrote, something about the ball: "The Spalding Company had manufactured an ersatz ball, called the 'balata,' a poor green-tree substitute for precious war-time rubber." The balata ball was "mushy," and as a result home runs became scarce. Even Dorth noticed that there was something wrong with the ball. "We were always kidding about it," Cardinals star shortstop Marty Marion later recalled. "But nobody really questioned it. If that's what we were going to play with, that's what we were going to play with."

On another day, watching the Cardinals sweep a doubleheader over the Dodgers, Broeg and his fiancée saw Brooklyn right-hander Les Webber irritate slugger Stan Musial, who was then en route to his first batting championship. Webber decked Musial with his first pitch, then forced him to back away from three high-and-tight deliveries. For the first and only time in his career, an enraged Musial headed out to the mound, only to be restrained by catcher Mickey Owen and plate umpire Al Barlick.

In Washington, Broeg had followed the Cardinals from afar and also caught a few Senators home games. During the Browns' momentous struggle against the Yankees in the last four games of the regular season, he was sitting at his desk, listening to the Senators-Tigers game. "They were feeding in results," he later recalled. "My brother-in-law had come in with a rare bottle of scotch from Canada and we were nibbling on that and, of course, I was pulling for the Browns."

Just then, his boss, a major, came into the office. Marine "researchers," the major told the disbelieving young soldier, had discovered that four members of the Baseball Writers' Association of America were in the corps. Three of them were in the Pacific, presumably all combat correspondents. So the Marines' entertainment monthly, *Leatherneck*, wanted Broeg to cover all the Series games for their special Pacific editions, wherever the games might be held, at their expense!

That was the first miracle. Broeg could only hope against hope for a second—a pennant win by the Browns. After Sewell's swashbucklers won three straight from the third-place Yankees, he could hardly contain himself, but when he heard that Sig Jakucki was going to pitch for the Browns on the final-day showdown, his heart sank. Jakucki, he remembered, was "the grizzled guy who had angrily draped a semi-pro ump off the bridge at Wichita's Arkansas River." But after "Bill DeWitt's carefully contrived roster of castoffs and cutthroats, 4-Fs, and players able to escape from war plants" won the pennant, as Broeg later wrote, his impossible dream came true. St. Louis was going to play host to an all-Midwest World Series.

As a Marine, Broeg also knew that this World Series was not just a game. For a few precious moments, as he later recalled, it would help people forget there was a war on. "It was as if time stood still for a week." The daily deprivations everyone had to put up with could temporarily be forgotten, though no doubt the hearts of some would ache that a "father didn't live to see the Browns win or that a brother, son, nephew, and dear friend was tied down in a European hedgerow or Pacific foxhole."

Broeg told his hometown folks that if they did not mind, he would have to spend most of his time downtown at a hotel. For press parties, Browns owner Don Barnes was somehow able to put on a lavish display of whiskey, beer, gin, and champagne. Broeg did not want to miss out on any of the celebrations—the lemon meringue pie would have to wait.

Another sportswriter, Jack Hand of the Associated Press, who at the start of the season had picked the Browns to finish at the bottom of the standings, was still dismissive of the American League team. His reasons were unassailable. "With a standout outfield built around Stan Musial, an infield hinged on 'Mr. Shortstop,' a catching department that includes

Walker Cooper, and a strong arm mound staff of Mort Cooper, Ted Wilks, and Harry Brecheen, the Redbirds stick out in all departments with the possible exception of pitching."

The Browns' stellar pitching staff was only one reason to give some sportswriters second thoughts, the Cardinals management ulcers, and Browns fans hope. Another possible reason was a fear that perhaps the Cardinals had gotten so complacent that they could not possibly fight their way out of their end-of-season slump. If the Browns had scratched and clawed their way to the top berth on the very last day of the season, the Redbirds had spent the entire month of September coasting—mostly downhill. That month, they had won only five games, while losing 15.

On the other hand, a cynic might have pointed out, perhaps the Cardinals were simply bored with winning. Even with that September record, they had still run away with the National League pennant, finishing 14½ games ahead of Pittsburgh, their nearest competitor. During one week in the regular season, they stood 73–27, and eventually finished with a 105–49 record, for a .682 winning percentage. They had won their 90th game (or more than the Browns won in the entire season) on August 28, earlier than any other team since the Chicago Cubs accomplished that same feat in 1906. Not even the Cardinals, though, or any other team, has ever been able to equal or better the Cubs' winning percentage of 76.3 percent of its games—a record that still stands.

Among the fans who had no doubt that the Browns could do the impossible was a contingent from Cape Girardeau, where the Browns had been training for the past two years. "It took Cape Girardeau just two years to do what Florida and California couldn't do in 40 years," Mayor Raymond E. Beckman proudly boasted. The *Southeast Missourian* quoted local fans as saying, "They'll take those Cardinals like Patton took France!" Unfortunately, wartime restrictions on travel made it impossible for most out-of-town rooters for either the Browns or the Cardinals to get to St. Louis to see the Series, even if they could get tickets. Both teams had to adhere to Office of Defense Transportation restrictions and sell virtually all their tickets in the immediate metropolitan area of St. Louis.

One observer who wondered whether the Cardinals just might be in trouble was John Drebinger of the *New York Times*. As "the game's outstanding academic minds" pondered the relative merits of the two teams, he noted that if the Series had been played even a month earlier, the outcome would never have been in doubt. The Cardinals, "rocketing to their third straight flag," would have been the unanimous, unqualified choice to win, no matter who their opponent was. Until August, he went on to say, "the Redbirds were so thoroughly the class of anything either league had to offer that a comparison would have been ridiculous." Nor had the military draft depleted their roster as it had that of virtually every other team. One exception was second baseman Lou Klein, but the Cardinals had come up with Billy Verban as his replacement, and as it turned out he was just as good as Klein.

The Redbirds were flying high, Drebinger ominously reported, until "suddenly, almost overnight, something passed out of [manager] Billy Southworth's array of 'invincibles.' They began to lose." Even though their overwhelming lead kept them out of danger of losing the pennant, they were nevertheless beginning to play an awful lot like "vulnerables." Perhaps that was true, but as *The Sports Encyclopedia* later noted, the 1944 Cardinals team won its third pennant in a row "in the most one-sided race in the [National League] in 40 years."

If the Browns' winning the American League pennant had been improbable enough, for them now to go ahead and take the Series against the Cardinals seemed simply inconceivable. After all, the Cardinals did not appear to have any weaknesses, whether in hitting, pitching, or defense. The team boasted a composite .275 batting average, 100 home runs, and a .402 slugging percentage—all three the best in the major leagues. Its pitchers had tossed 26 shutouts, or nine more than the next National League team, while the pitching staff's 2.67 ERA was well below the 3.09 that the Detroit Tigers recorded to lead the American League.

Only once before had a team racked up three straight hundred-win seasons, and that was back when the venerable Connie Mack accomplished that feat with the Philadelphia Athletics in 1929–31.

More statistics only added to the mystique of the Cardinals as a team that was all but invincible. For example, not only was their .982 fielding percentage the best in either league, but their 112 errors committed broke the all-time record for fewest errors by one team in a season.

The Browns did have a few statistics on their side, especially—or rather, almost exclusively—regarding their pitching. In the last nine games of the regular season, the team had allowed only 10 runs and finished with a 3.17 ERA and 16 shutouts (second only to Detroit), and led the league in strikeouts. The Browns' fielding was a respectable .972, and both Christman and McQuinn led the league in fielding at their respective positions.

Other statistics were not so favorable. The team's collective batting average of .252 was the second worst in the league. No other team had ever made it to the World Series with such a low percentage except for the Red Sox, who in 1918 squeaked by with a .249 average. The Browns also would have become the first team in history to win the pennant without a single .300 hitter or a 20-game winner on the squad if Kreevich had not collected two hits on the final day of the season to bring his average up to .301.

The Cardinals' 1944 lineup was virtually the same as the 1943 team that had fallen to the Yankees in the World Series. The two most notable changes were Johnny Hopp, a backup outfielder and first baseman in 1943, who now took over in center field for Harry "The Hat" Walker, and Emil Verban at second base. Verban, the Redbirds' third second baseman in three years, was generally regarded as the team's weakest link, with a batting average of only .257.

Ray Sanders, at first base for the Cardinals, had batted .295 with 12 homers and 102 RBIs, for a tie for fourth place in the league. His .994 fielding percentage also led the National League at first base, and equaled that of McQuinn for the Browns. At shortstop was the stellar Marion, the league's MVP for 1944. Affectionately known as "Slats" or "The Octopus," the 6-foot-2 Marion had hit a modest .267 with only six homers and 63 RBIs during the season. But his .972 fielding percentage led the league at shortstop.

Rounding out the infield were steady-as-she-goes Whitey Kurowski at third base and catcher Walker Cooper. In the regular season Cooper had hit

.317 with 13 homers and 72 RBIs, while Kurowski turned in a respectable .270 percentage with 20 homers. Hopp had posted some fantastic numbers for his first year as a starter—a league-leading fielding percentage of .997 at third base, and a .336 batting average that placed him fourth in the standings. He also hit 11 home runs, scored 106 runs, drove in 72, and stole a team-high 15 bases. Marty Marion later explained the relatively low base-stealing number this way: "Back in our day we didn't do much running. We had a pretty fast team but our manager believed in first and third and all that kind of stuff. We didn't do much stealing."

Danny Litwhiler, a power hitter picked up in 1943 to replace the irreplaceable Enos "Country" Slaughter, who had entered military service before the opening of the season, now owned left field. Though he hit only .264 with 15 homers, his RBI average was a respectable 82.

Right field, of course, belonged to one of the greatest players in the game, Stan Musial. Only 23 years old, Musial was eligible to be drafted, but because his hometown of Donora, Pennsylvania, had more than enough eligible draftees already, he had yet to be called—much to the relief and delight of the fans. In 1943 Musial had won the MVP award, and this season had hit .347, the second highest in the league. He also led the league with 197 hits, 51 doubles, and a .549 slugging percentage. His 14 triples tied for fourth in the National League, and he had also chalked up 12 homers, 112 runs (second in the league), and 94 RBIs while drawing 90 walks (third best in the league) and striking out only 28 times.

The Cardinals' pitching staff was virtually intact from its pennant-winning 1943 season; only one new pitcher had a chance of starting a game in the Series—rookie Ted Wilks. Mort Cooper, Walker's older brother, who led the rotation, had won the 1942 MVP award when he went 27–7 with 10 shutouts and a 1.78 ERA. The 1944 season marked the third straight time he had compiled a 20-win season, finishing with a 22–7 record, a 2.46 ERA, and a league-high seven shutouts. In short, three Cardinals players had been named MVP for three years in a row.

The other pitchers on the starting staff were Max Lanier (17–12, 2.65),

Harry Brecheen (16–5, 2.85), reliever Blix Donnelly (2–1, 2.12), Freddy Schmidt (7–3, 3.15), and Al Jurisch (7–9, 3.39), who split his time between starting and relief.

"Goddamn," the Browns' Ellis Clary was later to recall, reflecting on a Cardinals roster that boasted Musial, Kurowski, both Coopers, and Marion, "they had a hell of a team."

Unlike the previous two World Series, the first six games of the Browns-Cardinals matchup were to be played on six consecutive days, because the two teams played in the same park. The only off day, if one became necessary, was scheduled to take place before the seventh game. From a strategic point of view, that meant the pitcher who started in game 1 would most likely not pitch three games, unless he pitched on only two days' rest for the deciding seventh game. That left Sewell with a serious decision to make about who would start on Wednesday, October 4, the first day of the Series.

Most sportswriters and baseball connoisseurs thought Nelson Potter was the obvious choice to get the nod. Despite his 10-game suspension earlier in the year for throwing an illegal spitball, he led the Browns with 19 wins and also had a 2.83 ERA. In the stretch he had performed admirably, going 6–1 in September. Both of his final two starts were shutouts. One sportswriter who begged to differ was New York–based Dan Daniel, who in a story filed October 3 opined that Jack Kramer was the probable choice to face Mort Cooper in Game 1. Like Potter, Kramer had piled up an enviable record during the Browns' stunning September drive, finishing all six games that he started and winning five of them. In that month, he had also pitched a total of $58^2/_3$ innings, allowing only 8 runs on 39 hits, and 5 walks, while striking out 26. Though his season record stood at 17–13, his 2.49 ERA was the lowest among the Browns starters.

The choice, then, was a toss-up. Both Kramer and Potter had pitched one game each in the Browns' doubleheader sweep over the Yankees on September 28, and now both were rested. Thus the announcement Sewell made on October 3, the day before the opening of the Series, came as a complete shock to just about everyone—except to Denny Galehouse, who had been sworn to secrecy when the manager told him he was going to start. Sewell's surprise choice had finished the season with a 9–10 record, and for September was just 3–4, but he had allowed only two runs in his last three regular starts, and Sewell had a hunch.

Galehouse had not even been with the team at spring training. A man who had started his major-league career in Cleveland back in 1934, he had failed to distinguish himself in one mediocre season after another before being traded to the Boston Red Sox in December 1938. He proved to be no better in Bean Town, and two years later, when the Browns came shopping, Boston sent him to St. Louis. According to one account, the desperate Browns paid $30,000 for Galehouse and pitcher Fritz Ostermueller, but the purchase was hardly much of a bargain. Galehouse's pitching did get a little better, and in 1941 his record was 9–10, with a career-best 3.64 ERA. In 1942 he finished with a 12–12 record and a 3.62 ERA, and then topped that with an 11–11 record and a 2.77 ERA in 1943. That same year, he threw two shutouts and held opponents to two or fewer runs 11 times. But when spring-training time came around in 1944, Galehouse sent word that he was going to continue working at his Goodyear aircraft job in Akron and retire from baseball. In his spare time he coached a high school baseball team in nearby Cuyahoga Falls, and that was enough to keep his hand in the game.

That seemed to be that until pitcher Steve Sundra was drafted and the Browns, finding themselves in an even more desperate pickle than usual, persuaded Galehouse to reconsider. Galehouse did his own spring training, playing catch with friends in the neighborhood and running around on local streets to get into condition. Despite his best efforts, as he later admitted, he was not nearly in as good physical shape as his teammates when, on May 14 in Philadelphia, he made his first appearance. On that day, he did well enough, pitching 1¹/₃ innings of scoreless relief. But thereafter his troubles began. He lost two games in May, including one start, and the following month started three times but lost twice. During that latter period he had given up 11 runs on 17 hits while striking out just 3.

But Galehouse had spirit and determination and was not a quitter. Let go by the team, he went back home and signed up with the Akron Orphans of the Akron–Barberton–Cuyahoga Falls League, pitching for them in a kind of catch-up spring/summer training program. On June 21, when he led his team to an 8 to 2 victory over the Barberton Genets, the Genets groused about having to face a major-league pitcher and lodged an official complaint to the league office shortly after the contest. Two weeks later, league officials ruled that Galehouse was an ineligible player.

In mid-July Galehouse finally rejoined the Browns as a full-time player after receiving an assurance from his draft board that he would not be inducted into the army until after the season ended. Though he still never recaptured his peak pitching form, he did win three games that month, and ended the season with a 3.12 ERA. Clearly, his record was spotty at best, and no doubt everyone had to wonder just what Sewell was thinking when he nominated this part-time, home-conditioned, lackluster pitcher as the man who would face the formidable Cardinals in Game 1. Maybe it was because Sewell knew that Galehouse had something to prove, once and for all, to himself—and to the fans, the sportswriters, and his teammates.

On the second-to-last day of the season, after Galehouse had shut out the Yankees while allowing just five singles, Sewell approached him in private in the locker room. Galehouse was just the opposite of Jakucki, who made a point of being out of the ballpark as quickly as possible. The big Ohio pitcher was a heavy sweater, and he preferred to take his time showering. When he finally emerged, his teammates were usually gone or getting dressed. Sewell came over to Galehouse while he was alone, and told the pitcher that if the Browns won the pennant, he was going to start.

"If we're in it, you're it," Sewell said.

"Okay, fine," Galehouse merely replied.

He knew that everyone on the team was speculating who would be the starter, but Sewell told him to keep mum about it. "We were told to keep quiet, yeah," Galehouse later recalled. "She [his wife] knew enough to keep quiet."

Sewell even kept up the suspense after the Browns won the pennant, and waited for two days, until after the Browns had completed a 2 ½ hour workout on October 3, before making the announcement that Potter, who had won 19 games, would not be the starter. Instead, as any baseball statistician knew, a man who had the worst season winning percentage of any pitcher ever to start a World Series opener was going to be given that honor. The baseball world was stunned.

GALEHOUSE SURPRISE CHOICE TO PITCH FOR BROWNS, an understated *Post-Dispatch* headline reported the next day. Another local paper, the *Star-Times*, was not so timid, calling the selection of Galehouse "the first bombshell of the 1944 World Series." Pressed on who might pitch in Games 2, 3, or 4, Sewell wisecracked, "It might rain all winter, and we may not get to use anyone."

Young Broeg reported the surprise to his fellow Marines in the Pacific this way: "In the language of the baseball dugout, where the polysyllable is of unknown quantity, Luke Sewell had 'more guts than a burglar' by taking a gamble unequaled in 15 years in the choice of an opening-day selection for a World Series. But a tall, thin man with a high collar and watery blue eyes, sitting less than 100 feet away from the Browns' bench, could have told him that the risk isn't always as great as it seems."

Broeg was referring to the legendary Connie Mack. Before the opening game of the 1929 World Series between his Philadelphia Athletics and the Chicago Cubs, Mack had confounded the experts by passing up his pitching aces, Lefty Grove and George Earnshaw, to start a graying veteran who for months, as Broeg quipped, "had sat around just listening to his arteries harden." But mentally and physically the Chicago sluggers had trained for the blistering fastball of Earnshaw and Grove. Mack had a hunch that Howard Ehmke's slow curve and half-speed ball would throw the Cubs off stride. He gambled—and won, with Ehmke giving up only three hits and striking out 13 batters for a Series record that still stood, and beating the puzzled Chicagoans, 3 games to 1.

Sewell also announced that catcher Red Hayworth and outfielders Chet Laabs and Mike Kreevich would play in every game, no matter what.

For Game 1, on October 4, a few dark clouds appeared in the sky just after sunrise, and by 8:15 a light rain had begun to fall.

Concessionaires were prepared for a capacity crowd, having loaded up with 40,000 frankfurters, a truckload of peanuts, 10,000 cases of soda, and 5,000 cases of beer. Blake Harper, the man in charge of concessions, maintained strict neutrality by making sure that an equal number of Browns and Cardinals pennants were on sale to the public.

Assigned to seat the crowd were 250 ushers, who arrived at 7:30 a.m. and began lining up chairs in their proper places and drilling for the big job ahead. At 9:50, workmen swarmed onto the field and began removing the tarpaulins to give the damp earth underneath an opportunity to dry out. One groundskeeper spent more than an hour currying the pitcher's mound. At 10:00 a 20-piece band took the field and began tuning up for the great day ahead.

The long line of fans waiting to purchase tickets were all in a partying, festive mood. Some played cards or craps, while others danced to jitterbug music provided by students from nearby Soldan High School. A few enterprising neighborhood children took advantage of the situation by selling cartons or boxes as makeshift seats. The *Post-Dispatch* reported that "a Negro boy rented 19 of 25 collapsible chairs for 50 cents."

One baseball eminence who would not be attending the Series was none other than Judge Kenesaw Mountain Landis, the first baseball commissioner, who was suffering from a bad cold. A former U.S. district court judge from Illinois, Landis had come into power in 1920 in the wake of the Chicago Black Sox gambling scandal of 1919, taking the place of a three-man commission that had overseen baseball since 1903. Back in 1907, Landis had earned a national reputation as an incorruptible magistrate who imposed a $29 million fine on Standard Oil for accepting illegal rail-freight rebates. The decision was later reversed, but Landis's integrity and character were never questioned.

Despite missing the Series for the first time since he was hired, Landis still made sure that the Series was not called by radio broadcaster and ex-

Cardinals pitcher Dizzy Dean. Much as the colorful Dean contributed to enthusiasm for the game, Landis arranged for a more professional announcer to sit in the upstairs booth.

The Series was being covered by reporters from 21 states, as well as by three Canadian papers and one in Panama, along with three G.I. papers, seven movie studios, and several national weekly magazines, including *Newsweek, Life,* and *Look.* The Mutual Radio Network was broadcasting the games on a nationwide hookup, numerous local and out-of-town broadcasters were set to give live play-by-play descriptions or summaries of the contests, and American troops abroad were able to hear the games live via broadcasts over short-wave radio. The novice sportswriter assigned to cover the Series for Panama was a 17-year-old-boy named Rafael Aleman, while the oldest veteran in the broadcast booth was Joe Page, 84 years old, a reporter for the *Montreal Star,* who had covered every Series since 1884, back when the Browns played Providence.

Among the big-name sportswriters in attendance was Grantland Rice, the man who had memorably described the Notre Dame backfield as the "Four Horsemen of the Apocalypse." He was there on assignment from the North American Newspaper Alliance. Others included Orlo Robertson and Charles Dunkley of the Associated Press, Bob Considine of International News Service, Sgt. Charles Kiles of *Stars and Stripes,* and Bob Broeg, the St. Louis native now with the Marines, who had lucked into the assignment for *Leatherneck,* the official publication of the Marine Corps.

In all, about 250 reporters were keeping 70 Western Union telegraph operators busy on direct wires to their newspapers during and after each game. In addition, another 25 telegraph operators were stationed at the park to take stories directly after the game. In the mornings and evenings, 20 to 30 operators were stationed at the Hotel Jefferson in downtown St. Louis, where many of the journalists were staying, to transmit stories from a pressroom early each morning and late each night. On the day before Game 1, reporters filed 130,000 words, while on the first day of the Series the word count reached 175,000. Millions more words were being transmitted by radio. At war plants, factories, and other workplaces, many employees were allowed to listen to the games, or at least updates, while they worked. At one plant, a buzzer would sound, riveting would immediately halt, and over the loudspeaker would come a quick update about a recent score.

The American League was also making movies with sound of all the games. Immediately after the Series ended, 320 prints were to be developed and sent for distribution overseas to the armed services, with an expected delivery date of about November 1. Another 200 prints were to be made for showings to civilians in the United States, though those prints were not expected to be available until January 1, 1945.

Several newsreel outfits had also taken up positions on the roof of the grandstand to photograph highlights of the games. Among those represented were Paramount, Movietone, Pathé, News of the Day, and Universal Newsreel. Not to be outdone, the Missouri State Highway Department was also taking color film of the Series for use in advertising the state.

The Browns' World Series ticket, something never before seen in baseball, was identical to that of the Cardinals, except that it was printed with a brown background instead of cardinal red. The Browns' game tickets were for Games 3, 4, and 5. Proceeds of Games 3, 4, and 6 were to go the National War Relief fund.

The earliest "early bird" waiting to buy a ticket was Cardinals fan Arthur "Happy" Felsh, who had taken up residence in an oblong, canvas-covered cardboard shack outside the pavilion gate a week before. Felsh had been the first to wait outside the gate for the past 16 years, but in 1943 he had moved out of St. Louis and so been obliged to store his movable residence at a local YMCA after the Cardinals lost the previous year's Series. This year he furnished it with a cot, mattress, blankets, and even an electric light and promised that next year he would try to install a shower.

Another fan who lined up outside the park in the predawn hours was a die-hard Browns booster named Sisler Brown Futrell, a 22-year-old sailor who had been named not only for the team but for the great Browns first baseman. Sisler told reporters he had spent 3½ years in the South Pacific and that the submarine he was aboard had sunk 27 Japanese vessels. Other fans braved a chilling wind and temperatures in the low 60s, sleeping on boxes, chairs, and the sidewalk to be among the first in line to buy tickets to the bleachers and pavilions. By 3 a.m. their number reached only 300, but two hours later another 1,000 showed up.

"This rain don't bother me," 16-year-old Bill Schneider told a reporter. "A loyal baseball fan would sit through a snowstorm."

In the stands was the Browns' oldest fan, retired druggist Charles H. Zahn, 93 years old, who had been rooting for the team since 1869, four years after the Civil War ended. PFC. Bill Veeck, general manager of the champion Milwaukee Brewers, was another spectator. Now a Marine stationed in the Pacific, he had obtained leave to attend the Series. After the war, in 1951, he was to become the next—and last—owner of the Browns and to go on to make baseball history in a way no one ever had before, or ever has since. Sitting just a few rows away was nattily dressed Leo Durocher, manager of the Brooklyn Dodgers, the Browns' mirror image in the National League.

Enos Slaughter, the Cardinals' slugging outfielder, had also managed to get a furlough for the Series. Earlier he had stopped by the ballpark to work out with his old teammates. Currently, he was stationed at the army base in San Antonio, and during the season had led the San Antonio military league with a batting average of .419.

A few quarrels and shoving matches occasionally broke out in the bleachers among fans, most having to do with the relative merits of the two teams about to take the field, but on the whole, according to the *St. Louis Star-Times,* "the decorum of the crowd was excellent."

One man not pleased at all by the crowd was Walter Ridley, who earned his living selling peanuts to the fans at Sportsman's Park. Ridley had come to the notice of both baseball connoisseurs and a reporter for the *Sporting News* for his skill "at tossing the bags to the customers seated out of range." He was equally skillful at snatching the coin flung to him in payment. "Some of Walter's catches of flying coins in mid-air have been quite spectacular and have drawn favorable comment from the fans. And sometimes, particularly when Brooklyn is in town, odious comparisons are made between Ridley's defenses at retaining thrown objects and that of the athletes on the field. Walter rarely loses a nickel."

What bothered Ridley during the Series, surprisingly, was all the people. "With a big crowd you can't get through to make your sales," he explained. "When you can't get through a crowd you can only sell in a limited area. And any salesman can tell you that when you work a limited area you reach the saturation point that much sooner and are thus faced with a consumer shortage and a goods surplus." An artist, a businessman, and a philosopher, Ridley packaged each of the bags of peanuts he sold by hand.

Among the many sideshows at the World Series that Broeg described for his readers in the Pacific was "an aged Ohio screwball" named Harry Thobe, who showed up at the stadium dressed like a lunatic carnival barker with one red shoe and one white, a white suit, a red tonguelike tie, a flat-brimmed straw hat the color of the rainbow, a cane, and a parasol. A well-known gate-crasher (by invitation), he was a perennial presence at every World Series and Rose Bowl game, taking vacations from his regular job as a bricklayer. Once upon a time, he claimed, his teeth were filled with 14 diamond fillings, but when the Depression came along he had to hock the 11 that were now missing.

Also sitting in the stands were Sewell's brother Joe, and Southworth's son, Major Billy Southworth Jr., who in December 1940 had become the first professional baseball player to sign up for the military.

A tongue-in-cheek item in the *Star-Times*, datelined "Astride a Fence" in Sportsman's Park, reported on the predicament of Bobby Scanlon, who during the regular season served as batboy for both the Cardinals and the Browns. Who was he rooting for? a reporter named Stan Mockler wondered. "Step right up and pick a winner, Bobby." The "slim, nervous, black-haired 18-year-old" took a deep breath and shouted, "And lose my job—two jobs?"

As Scanlon headed into the Cardinals' clubhouse, pursued by Mockler, Blix Donnelly joined in the fun, saying, with a wink to the reporter, "I think you're for the Browns, Bobby. I saw you shining up to Denny Galehouse."

"Oh, no, I'm not," the boy sputtered. "You see, I—"

"That's fine, then," Donnelly replied, cutting him off. "Glad to know you are backing the Cardinals. We think it's good luck to have a batboy in our dugout."

"No, you don't, Blix," Scanlon plaintively replied. "That ain't playing fair. You mugs are putting me behind the eight ball. I gotta stay neutral."

Just then, somebody in the Browns' dressing room upstairs called for Scanlon, and with a weary sigh he took off. When he got there, second baseman Don Gutteridge greeted him with a question: "Got any bets on the Series?"

"I don't bet," said Scanlon.

"You mean to say," said Gutteridge, "that you're not willing to risk a bob on us after we went and voted you in on the Series melon? That's gratitude for—"

"Well," said Scanlon, "you see, I got inside dope the Cardinals are going to do that, too, and—"

"Oh, he's a money player," Vern Stephens chipped in. "And what were you doing in there shining Mort Cooper's shoes? Trying to play both ends against the middle, eh?"

Facing the most miserable and yet happiest days of his life, Scanlon threw up his arms in disgust and muttered, "If only there was some way this damn thing could end in a tie!"

Another devoted fan of baseball watching the Series was Dr. Alexander Paul, a longtime teacher and missionary for the Disciples of Christ Church in Japan and China, who had spent more than 20 years in Asia after sailing from Vancouver for the Far East in 1922, accompanied by a group of major leaguers who were touring and playing in Asia. The missionary had only recently returned to the United States after being interned for most of the war by Japanese forces. On the morning of December 8, 1941, Dr. Paul, then in Nanking, had been visited by a detachment of Japanese soldiers, who searched his home. Several of the soldiers who could speak English were especially interested in the American's pile of the *Sporting News*, representing more than a year's worth of issues.

"Baseball!" one of the soldiers shouted, and an argument quickly ensued over how the papers would be distributed. Dr. Paul was later held in solitary confinement in his schoolroom. To pass the time, he once decided to pick his all-time All-Star team. He managed to send his choices by Chinese servants to another missionary being held in another part of the building, who then sent back his own selections.

Back in September, when the White Sox played the Browns at Sportsman's Park during the home stretch, one reporter noted that the infield, badly torn up after being used nearly every day of the season, "resembled a wheat field that had been badly shorn by a mowing machine." In fact, in the fifth inning of that game, Chicago player Hal Trosky raised his hand to call time, and then stepped over a few paces to pick up a practice ball that had been lying there for half a game. But for Game 1 of the Series the field had been covered with new sod. Each blade of grass looked as though it had been individually trimmed. "A peanut could not have been hidden there today."

A sweltering crowd of 33,242 waited impatiently for the game to begin. Many of the fans, who had seen rain clouds in the morning, had arrived wearing coats, which were now quickly peeled off under the sizzling sun. Despite the record crowd, the attendance was a trifle under expectations, with the receipts totaling $149,268—slightly less than the figures for the two home games that the Cardinals had played against the Yankees in the previous World Series.

At 11:50 a.m. a roar went up as the Cardinals, dressed in home club white uniforms, walked slowly out onto the field for batting practice. A few boos were also heard, but the cheers predominated. In the bleachers, someone with a horn kept the early crowd awake with long, unmusical blasts at infrequent intervals. Also part of the pregame entertainment were the efforts of workmen testing the public-address system. Invariably, whenever a voice over the loudspeaker would inquire, "Can you hear me out there?" the crowd roared back, "No!"

Sportsman's Park had been among the last to install a loudspeaker system. Instead, before the start of each game, a deep-voiced official would stand at home plate and call out the lineups to the press box through a megaphone. Then he would walk first to left field, then to right field, and call out the lineups. Most of the day games began at 3 p.m., giving sportswriters for the afternoon papers virtually no time after the game to file their stories. To make matters worse for the press, the water cooler never really seemed to work.

Like many baseball stadiums of that era, Sportsman's Park had an odd shape dictated in large part by the layout of the surrounding neighborhood. Back in the 1920s, legendary sportswriter Red Smith, just finding his legs as a cub reporter, covered many Browns and Cardinals games for the *St. Louis Star*. He found the ballpark to have "a garish, county-fair sort of layout." Billboards in the outfield advertised such products as Ivory Soap and Philip Morris cigarettes. Nor was the ballpark kept in good repair. The wooden seats were wobbly, and so was the rickety ladder that sportswriters had to climb to get to the press box, which hung from the roof over the second deck of the stadium. And then there was the infield.

"We used to call it the rockpile," recalled Cardinals shortstop Marty Marion, one of the game's elite fielders. "They used to call me the pebble picker, because I was always picking up pebbles off the ground and throwing them off the field so I wouldn't get a bad bounce. It was a very hard infield and the ball went through there very fast. We got used to it though. It was part of growing up."

Pavilions extended from both sides of the infield down to the foul poles—351 feet down the left-field line, and 310 down the right-field line, with dead center 422 feet away from the plate. The fences stood 11$^{1}/_{2}$ feet high, though the right-field fence featured a 33-foot-high screen that was installed in 1929 after the Detroit Tigers hit eight home runs in four games.

On this day the ballpark was decked out in bunting. The only genuine wartime note came just before the start of the game when a massive bomber cruised overhead several times, then banked sharply, apparently to allow its occupants to catch a fleeting glimpse of the game about to be played below. Some fans remembered the moment during the previous year when a bomber swept so low over Yankee Stadium that it nearly hit a light tower—and almost gave New York mayor Fiorello La Guardia a heart attack.

Gone for the Series were the huge portraits of broadcasters Dizzy Dean and John O'Hara that usually hung over the scoreboard. They had been replaced by an advertisement for the St. Louis war chest.

The pregame ceremony was a simple one that ended quickly. "The folks of St. Louis are of the sort who like their baseball in the raw, so there was little pomp or ceremony to the launching of this third wartime World Series," Drebinger reported in the *Times*. White-haired Governor John W. Bricker of Ohio, who was the Republican vice presidential nominee that year, appeared on the field just before game time to shake hands with both managers, who happened to be Ohio natives as well. But there was to be no tossing out of the first ball. Partisan feelings about the two teams, reporters noted, seemed to be about evenly divided.

The only Browns who had ever appeared in a World Series game before 1944 were the club's three coaches: Sewell, Fred Hofmann, and Zack Taylor. If the Browns had decided to throw the dice and put long-shot Denny Galehouse on the mound, the Cardinals, in contrast, were taking no chances. The Browns would be facing Mort Cooper, probably the best pitcher in the National League, who had already won four World Series starts, including the first game of the 1942 series. When a reporter asked Cooper if he felt fit, the taciturn Missourian simply replied, "Uh huh."

Before the Series opener, the Cardinals exuded confidence, with most players telling reporters that they expected to defeat their hometown rivals in the fall just as they had in the exhibition series that spring. Pepper Martin, setting the tone for the Redbirds, opined, "I think we'll beat the hell out of the Browns. All my friendship for such pals as Don Gutteridge, Al Hollingsworth, a few others comes to an end, as of today."

With the Cardinals as the home team for the first two games, Gutteridge was first at bat for the Browns. He watched as a ball and then two strikes whizzed past him, then popped out to Marion at shortstop. Kreevich and Laabs then struck out.

Not only had Browns pitcher Denny Galehouse never appeared in a World Series game, he had never seen one either. "It's just another ballgame to me," he told reporters. "I never even saw a World Series game before, because I resolved long ago that I wouldn't see one until I was in it. I never thought I'd make it, but here I am."

Whether he was as calm and collected as he pretended to be, Galehouse had no trouble getting the first Cardinals batter, Johnny Hopp, to swing at his first pitch and fly out to Laabs in left field. He next struck out Roy Sanders on three pitches. The brass band in the stands then struck up "Take It Easy" as Stan Musial strode to the plate. He quickly got the first hit of the Series with a single up the middle, but then Walker Cooper flied out to center, with Kreevich making the final putout.

Mort Cooper continued to dominate the Browns in the second inning. Vern Stephens bounced to the pitcher for the first out. After Gene Moore walked, Cooper jammed McQuinn with an inside fastball that caused him to fly out to shallow left field. Mark Christman struck out on a called third strike.

Galehouse seemed on his way to returning the favor by retiring Kurowski and Litwhiler in quick succession. But then Marion doubled just inside the left-field foul line. Verban followed with a single over second, but Gutteridge, a Cardinals castoff, was able to collar the ball behind the bag and hold Marion on third. Galehouse closed the inning by fanning Cooper.

At the top of the third, Hayworth was up first and grounded out to third. Then Galehouse fell behind on the count 0–2, but luckily drew a walk. After Cooper got Gutteridge to fly out, Kreevich bobbled one to the mound, and once again the Browns were quickly left scoreless.

The Cardinals, though, used their bottom half of the third to unleash just a fraction of their awesome power. First up was Hopp, who drilled a grounder through the hole between first and second. Sanders then powered a liner to right field that Gene Moore leaped for, momentarily seemed to catch, but could not hold onto. But the play was close enough that Hopp, holding up until he saw how the ball would be played, could only make it to second. Southworth then signaled for ace hitter Musial to execute a sacrifice bunt, which the slugger almost beat out, to put runners at second and third base with only one out. That brought up Walker Cooper, who had hit an impressive .317 in 1944, not to mention a combined .289 in his two previous Series appearances.

Musial's deft bunt under Southworth's direction was strictly according to the playbook, but now it was time for Sewell to do a little masterminding of his own. Taking no chances, he had Galehouse intentionally walk Cooper to load the bases—and also set up a potential double play. Then it was all up to Galehouse. He never faltered, fanning the long-clouting Whitey Kurowski, whose homer had sunk the Yankees in 1942, with two fouls and a fastball. Next up was Litwhiler, a fearsome power hitter—and, in fact, the only player ever to hit a ball over the double-deck left-field bleachers at the Polo Grounds, where the Giants played, a distance of some 505 feet. But this time he only grounded to third baseman Mark Christman for an inning-closing force-out.

The top of the fourth seemed destined to be as anticlimactic for the Browns as the first three. Laabs flied out and Stephens hit a pop-up to Marion. But then Moore, the shopworn outfielder whom the Senators had jettisoned the previous winter, whacked a single to right field for the first-ever Browns hit in a World Series. That brought up George McQuinn. The ex-seminarian's back had been bothering him late in the season, causing him to get just 10 hits in his last 60 at bats, for a .167 average. McQuinn was shrewd enough to know, though, that he had a reputation as an opposite-field hitter. That was precisely why Cooper had thrown him the inside fastball on his first time up. This time Cooper let loose with a pitch that was low and away, outside the strike zone. McQuinn assumed that his opponent was setting him up for another inside fastball, but this time he was waiting for it and sent the ball streaking over the densely packed right-field pavilion. Suddenly, the Browns had a 2 to 0 lead, and bedlam broke out in the stands.

An inspired Galehouse kept the Cardinals in check, retiring the next three batters in order. In the fifth, the Browns also went down quickly, unable to extend their lead. In the Cardinals half of the fifth, with one man on base on a walk, Musial hit into a double play to end the inning.

In the top of the sixth inning the Browns managed to get only one man on base—Vern Stephens, who got a walk with two men out.

Things got more interesting when the Cardinals came up to bat in their half of the sixth, however. Pinch-hitting for Emil Verban, Augie Bergamo led off and drew a walk. Southworth then sent in another pinch hitter, this time Debs Garms, for Mort Cooper. When Garms grounded out, Bergamo advanced to second, and for the first time since the third inning the Redbirds had a man in scoring position. But Bergamo was left stranded on base when Galehouse got Johnny Hopp to fly out to center and Ray Sanders to line out to first.

Blix Donnelly, the new pitcher for the Cardinals, wasted no time putting down the Browns in order in the eighth and ninth innings. In the bottom of the eighth, Kurowski managed to get a single for the Cardinals with two out, but was left stranded on first. Then, in the bottom of the ninth—do-or-die time—Marion, the long, lean, accomplished shortstop known affectionately as "Slats," livened up the crowd with a line drive into center field. Kreevich, diving for the ball, could not come up with it. Suddenly Marion was standing on second base—his second two-bagger of the afternoon. Bergamo then grounded out to Gutteridge, who had to range to his left to make the play, while Marion advanced to third. Southworth then sent in another pinch hitter, Ken O'Dea, who sent a towering sacrifice fly into deep center field, easily scoring Marion from third and ruining Galehouse's shutout.

Momentarily, it looked as if the big Ohio country boy might be on the ropes. But Galehouse refused to relinquish his grip, and there was to be no come-from-behind victory for the Cardinals as the Browns pitcher retired Hopp with a fly ball to Kreevich to end the game. Only fittingly, it seemed, the Browns had won their inaugural World Series game, like the real champions they were. After pausing on his way to the dugout to get a kiss from his wife, Galehouse retreated into the Browns clubhouse with the rest of his team under police escort.

Never before had a World Series game been won with such a scarcity of hits—only two. Nor had any Series pitcher ever lost on a two-hitter. The two heroes of the game, of course, were McQuinn, with his two-run homer, and

Galehouse, who had pitched superbly, allowing seven hits while walking four and striking out five. As the game wore on, he had visibly gotten stronger. Five of the Cardinals' seven hits had come in the first three innings. In the ninth inning, he had thrown 20 pitches, and seventeen of those were strikes.

One of the reasons for Galehouse's success in the Series opener was summed up by catcher Red Hayworth, who said that the pitcher was throwing a fantastic "half-apple curve." The half-apple was a sweeping curveball, which broke—from twelve o'clock, near the batter's eyes, to six o'clock, below his knees—simulating half of an apple. It was Galehouse's calling card, and on this day it was the right number.

Back in the clubhouse, the gloriously happy, exultant Browns were yelling and screaming that the Series was theirs. The rooms were steaming hot with the showers going full blast, all the players were yipping and yelling, and Milt Byrnes, the alternate left fielder, was heard to cry out, "Just three more to go, boys. Just three more to go. We'll take 'em for sure."

Sewell was generous in victory, laughing off the failure of his team to get more than two hits and telling reporters, "We were lucky, we had the breaks, and I freely admit it. You have to be lucky when a pitcher holds you to two hits. But I'm proud of the game Galehouse pitched. George McQuinn's home run was really something and I'm proud of the way the entire Browns team performed." He also announced that he was starting Potter, the Browns' best pitcher, in next day's game.

The following day the *St. Louis Post-Dispatch* ran a cartoon showing a large baseball-shaped boulder labeled "Browns' momentum" rolling down a hill. At the bottom stood a worried Cardinals player, looking like he was afraid he was about to be run over. John Drebinger, in the *New York Times*, reported on an almost gleeful note that "Luke Sewell's amazing Browns, the 'Cinderella team' of nondescript castoffs which only last Sunday had bagged an American League pennant, downed Billy Southworth's supposedly all-powerful Cardinals in the opening clash of the classic."

[The Cardinals won the 1944 Series 4 games to 2.]

1946: Cardinals vs. Red Sox

Enos Slaughter's Mad Dash

from *The Spirit of St. Louis* by Peter Golenbock

Despite the departure of Lou Klein, Fred Martin, and Max Lanier to Mexico in the spring of 1946, the Cardinals didn't fold. One of the reasons was the outstanding play of second baseman Red Schoendienst, who made the All-Star team, shortstop Marty Marion, who led the league in putouts and assists; the hitting of Enos Slaughter (.300, 18 homers, 130 RBIs), Whitey Kurowski (.301, 14 homers, 89 RBIs), and Stan Musial (.365, 16 homers, 103 RBIs); and the pitching of Howie Pollet, a 21-game winner, and two 15-game winners, Harry Brecheen and Murry Dickson.

Marion remembered the upset felt on the team when the trio left for Mexico. But he also recalled that most of them accepted Sam Breadon's cheapness as a fact of life.

Marty Marion: "There was a lot of dissension on the club about Lou, Fred, and Max going to Mexico. Players were upset about this guy going, that guy going. The dissension wasn't over the low salaries, because we were used to that. That was nothing new. Everybody knew the Cardinals were a cheap club. You have to remember, back in those days it was an honor to be in the big leagues, and you didn't want to do anything to rock the boat. Most guys would have played for small amounts. We always called Mr. Rickey 'cheap' and Mr. Breadon 'cheap.' And they were cheap. We didn't see much of their money. But if you argued too much, you'd be back in Rochester again.

"Max had won six games when he left for Mexico. Max didn't say a word in the clubhouse to anyone about nothing. I never did talk to Max or Martin or Lou about it. But after they left, the dissension didn't last too long. In '46 we had a rookie manager, Eddie Dyer, and we went on to win the pennant.

"Dyer had been in the minor leagues managing for a while. He was a baseball man. He was a company man. He worked for the Cardinals, and you knew that. There was nothing fishy about him. He was very serious. He knew baseball. No question about that. He was more or less like Southworth: He tried to keep you happy. I always liked Dyer, and he always liked me.

"Dyer was Howie Pollet's mentor. When they were together in Houston, Dyer took Howie and raised him like a son. The year before when we played Houston in an exhibition, Dyer said, 'Boy, you guys got to see this Pollet. He can pitch.' We pooh-poohed him. But Pollet's ball really moved. It had something on it. He was a good pitcher.

"Howie was another of my roommates. He was a good Catholic boy who went to church like he was committed. He would go to bed every night with his arms folded across his chest, and he would wake up the same way. I never saw him turn over. He was the calmest person I ever saw. Howard Pollet, a good ol boy. And Dyer loved him."

According to Marion, the Cardinals were successful even though the team was split into the group that drank and played cards and the rest who didn't, including Marion. The cardplaying clique had once been the domain of the Cooper brothers. Even after they were traded away, the division continued.

Marty Marion: "We had cliques on the club. One group was the boys who drank a lot of beer and loved to play cards. Oh, my gosh. The guys who didn't play—me and Harry Walker and Pollet and Brecheen and those kind of guys—they called us 'the college kids,' although none of us probably went to college. But we were the 'nice' kids. We weren't the rough boys. Stan was kind of on our side. They had enough rounders. But practically the whole pitching staff—Mort, Beazley, and Lanier—they all loved to play cards, and they'd always have a card game going. When you went back to the hotel, they all went to the card games, and we all went to the movies.

"I would sit and watch them play a lot of times. Finally they had to stop. Mr. Dyer had to put a ban on cardplaying. Well, when you play cards, the loser is always the guy who can't afford to lose. And they were getting complaints from the wives at home, that they were losing money, so they must have been playing for pretty good stakes. I never gambled in my life, so I never played cards. But they used to play cards in the clubhouse all the time. They played pinochle before the games. Finally Dyer had to stop them from playing cards in the clubhouse.

"We called them 'the mean bunch.' They were a little bit more aggressive than we were. Kurowski loved to play cards and drink beer. Ol' George could drink beer. We definitely had two different types of people on that team, but when we got on the baseball field, it was a different thing. We had the will to win and the desire to do so, and we did. We had the ability, too. The writers talk about this team not getting together, the players not liking each other. Well, that's all a lot of baloney. We never had that problem."

In June of 1946, the Cards left St. Louis for a 15-game road trip. After winning 5 of 7, the team headed for Brooklyn. In three games Stan Musial went 8 for 12. Whenever Musial would come to bat, the Brooklyn fans would start a chant. Up in the press box, reporter Bob Broeg wondered what the fans were saying. That evening he asked traveling secretary Leo Ward about it.

Bob Broeg: "Leo and I were having dinner. I said, 'What in the hell were those people chanting?' He said, 'They were saying, "Here comes the man."' I said, 'Do you mean, "Here comes *that* man?"' 'No. No. Here comes *the* man.'"

"So I recounted what I had heard in my overnight. 'Stan the Man Musial.' I was a little surprised at how quickly it stuck. You didn't have to be a brain surgeon to figure that 'Stan the Man' was pretty good. And over the years he's been very proud of it."

In mid-July the Dodgers came to St. Louis for a four-game series. In the first game, Musial stole home and singled to start the winning rally; in the second game, he tripled and scored the tying run and then homered in the ninth to win it, 2–1; in Game 3 he had four hits—two singles, a triple, and a home run. On July 16, Erv Dusak's grand slam completed the sweep. A few days later, the Cards beat the Phils and took over first place.

At the end of the season the Cards won 23 of their last 31 games, but it was enough to only tie the Dodgers.

Mort Cooper, the former Cardinal ace, helped the Cards greatly when he pitched the Boston Braves to a last-day win over Brooklyn to force a three-game playoff. Danny Litwhiler, who played with Cooper on Billy Southworth's Braves ballclub in '46, recalled his role in the events leading to Cooper's crucial victory.

Danny Litwhiler: "Mort was a great pitcher. He pitched with sore arms. When he was with the Cards, after the game his arm would swell up, and Doc Weaver, the trainer, would hang it up by a strap, and he'd milk his arm, stick it in ice.

"Mort had pitched for us in Boston, and we were going into Brooklyn, and Brooklyn had to beat us to win the pennant. And Southworth didn't know who he was going to pitch. I asked Mort, 'Couldn't you pitch?' He had just pitched two days before. Mort said, 'Hell, yes. I have no place to go. I can pitch.' He really wanted to beat Leo and the Dodgers.

"I caught Billy going out on the subway, and I rode with him, and I said, 'Why don't you pitch Mort?' 'Oh no, he can't pitch. He just pitched two days ago.' I said, 'He won't have to pitch anymore after that. And he'd like to pitch. I know he'd like to pitch. He told me he wants to pitch the game. Why don't you just pitch him as long as you can?'

"So Mort pitched and won the ball game, and the Cardinals tied for the pennant."

Though the Cards had finished in a tie with the Dodgers for the 1946 pennant, observers blamed Sam Breadon for turning a sure winner into a horse race.

Bob Broeg: "On the closing day of the season, Biggie Garagnani and Henry Ruggieri, friends of Stan and catcher Joe Garagiola, threw a party for the team. Sam Breadon and a lot of the Cards players attended.

"J. Roy Stockton, the chief chronicler of the Gashouse Gang, a brilliant writer who wrote more *Saturday Evening Post* pieces than anybody trying to crack that market, had a few martinis."

Stockton, acting as toastmaster, told the crowd that it would be appropriate to stand for 10 seconds of silence in tribute to "the man who made the close race possible." All eyes turned on Breadon.

He mentioned Breadon's trades of Walker Cooper, Johnny Hopp, Emil Verban, and the three players who jumped to the Mexican League and suggested that if some of these men hadn't been lost to the team the Cards would have won in a runaway.

"All the glorious excitement would have been missed," Stockton said sarcastically. Then he added, "I hope Sam hasn't cut the baloney too fine."

Bob Broeg: "Which Sam had, for Christ's sake. We were a heavily favored team, and the season came down to a tie. Sam had miscalculated. Rickey was gone, and he just kept unloading. He made what I called 'The Cape Cod

Cardinals.' Two years later, the Boston Braves won the pennant, largely with acquisitions from the Cardinals.

"Everybody was furious at Roy. Harry Caray was one of them. But that didn't bother Stockton. He could have knocked Caray on his ass."

After Stockton sat down, Caray was invited to go up to the dais. He talked about how lucky the Cardinal players were, how being a Cardinal almost guaranteed each player a World Series check. Caray recalled how Sam Breadon had sent checks to Grover Cleveland Alexander long after the alcoholic pitcher had outlived any usefulness. Caray said that if any ballplayer ever had personal problems, Breadon was always there to help out.

After Caray was finished, Stockton glared at him. Breadon came over, shook Caray's hand, and told him, "Young man, that was awfully nice of you. I will never forget it."

Bob Broeg: "Harry Caray was a company man. He always knew when a Breadon or a Busch was in charge. But Caray could be very tough on anybody who didn't sign the checks."

The next spring Sam Breadon expanded his radio broadcasts to include road games. He had to choose between the team of Dizzy Dean, sponsored by Falstaff Beer, and the team of Harry Caray and Gabby Street, sponsored by Greisedieck Bros. Beer. Dizzy Dean had the bigger name and Falstaff had the bigger budget, but Breadon chose to go with Caray.

When Breadon told Caray of his decision, Caray was flabbergasted. Before he left the meeting, Breadon told him, "Young man, a few months ago at that testimonial dinner, I told you that I would never forget what you did. Well, consider this proof of that."

As a result, Harry Caray became "The Voice of the Cardinals" and would go on to broadcast Cardinal games for the next forty years.

The Cards had to get past the Brooklyn Dodgers in a best 2-out-of-3 series to reach the World Series.

Leo Durocher, the manager of the Dodgers, won the coin flip. Durocher, making a disastrous call, chose to play the first game in St. Louis and the next two at home in Ebbets Field. Leo didn't anticipate how tired the long train trip from Brooklyn to St. Louis would leave his players.

Marty Marion: "Leo was a gambler and he took the best odds. You get to play two games at home against one. That's why he made the decision. Everybody knows that. But he had to travel. A long way to play the first game, and all the way back to play the second. We beat 'em both games. Howie Pollet won the first one. We beat Ralph Branca, 4 to 2.

"What I remember about that game was Leo Durocher. He was standing along third base, and he said, 'Kurowski, Marion, Schoendienst, and Musial. You couldn't get a pint of blood out of your whole infield.' We were all skinny, you know. [Could Durocher have been commenting on the icewater in their collective veins?]

"I used to love ol' Leo. I used to argue with him all the time. 'Come on, Leo. Do something.' He was fun. He was a showman. He had Laraine Day for a wife. Ol' Leo did all right.

"We won the first game, and the star was Joe Garagiola. Joe was a lot better ballplayer than he gives himself credit for. He makes fun of himself, but it really wasn't true. Joe wasn't a bad hitter, not at all. And he wasn't a bad catcher. He didn't have a great arm, but other than that, he was a good ballplayer.

"We returned to Brooklyn after winning the first game, and Murry Dickson beat them by 8 to 4.

"Naturally, we never even got to play them in a third one."

The first game of the 1946 World Series was at Sportsman's Park. The Cards lost a heartbreaker in extra innings on a long home run by Rudy York. In this game, manager Eddie Dyer employed the "Boudreau Shift" on Ted

Williams. Third baseman Whitey Kurowski left his position and moved to the right side of the diamond.

Marty Marion: "I stayed at shortstop. Kurowski moved over to the right side. He and Schoendienst were over there. Ted didn't try to hit the ball my way. Bunting was against his code. He wanted to challenge everybody, try to hit the ball through there.

"Ted and I played in the All-Star Game that was held at Fenway Park that year. He hit two home runs, and the American League beat us pretty bad [12–0]. I'm playing shortstop, and he's coming around second base, and he gives me a wink and in that froggy voice says, 'Kid, don't you wish you could hit like that!' I just looked at him as he ran by. I was speechless."

The Cardinals won the second game, 3–0, behind a six-hitter by Harry Brecheen.

Marty Marion: "Ted didn't do a thing in the World Series. Brecheen crowded him with the ball the whole time. He didn't do a thing."

With the games tied at one apiece, the Series moved on to Boston for three more games. The final two, if it went that long, were scheduled for St. Louis.

Marty Marion: "We figured if we could win one game in Boston, we could beat them in St. Louis."

In the third game, Boston's "Boo" Ferriss himself pitched a shutout, and Rudy York hit a three-run home run off Murry Dickson in a 4–0 victory. In this game, Ted Williams finally gave in and bunted the ball.

Marty Marion: "He bunted one time. That was against his code. And the next day there were big headlines: 'Williams Bunts Safely!'"

The Cards won Game 4 by the score of 12–3. Joe Garagiola, Enos Slaughter, and Whitey Kurowski each had four hits as the Cards tied a one-game Series record with 20 base hits.

The Red Sox took a 3–2 lead in games with a 6–3 win in Game 5. Howie Pollet didn't get out of the first inning. It would remain to be seen whether the Cards could win the two remaining games as Marion had anticipated.

Harry Brecheen won Game 6 to tie the Series at three apiece when he defeated the Red Sox, 4–1. Game 7 would prove to be one of the most memorable in World Series history.

With the score tied at 3–3 and nobody out in the eighth inning, Enos Slaughter came to bat. Slaughter had been hit on the right elbow by a pitch in Game 5, and was thought to be out for the rest of the Series. Doc Weaver, however, worked on the elbow all day and night, allowing Slaughter to start the seventh game. Leading off in the eighth inning, the peppery Cardinal outfielder lined a single to center field off reliever Bob Klinger.

The next two batters were retired easily. With Slaughter still on first base, the Cardinals' Harry Walker then blooped a hit to shallow left-center. The fleet Slaughter, running even before the crack of the bat, flew around second, headed for third, ran through coach Mike Gonzalez's stop sign, and hustled his way home as he somehow scored to give the Cardinals a lead they never relinquished. It's not every day that a runner scores from first on what should have been ruled a single to left-center. (After the throw home, Walker went to second and was inexplicably credited with a double by the official scorer.) It was the singular play of Slaughter's distinguished 19-year career.

Marty Marion: "It wasn't an exciting play when it happened. Enos was on first, and Harry Walker hit the ball into short left-center. Leon Culberson was out there [Dom DiMaggio was the regular center fielder, but he pulled a muscle on a hit that tied the game in the top of the eighth], and he got the ball back to Johnny Pesky, the shortstop, who was on the edge of the grass. Enos was coming around third base. Mike Gonzalez was our coach, and he had an accent, and he was hollering, 'No no no.' Enos says, 'I thought he said, "Go go go." ' Anyway, Pesky hesitated—he dropped his arm and turned around to throw and had to double pump—and there was no contest. I could see right quick he didn't have a chance to throw Enos out at home. I didn't even have to tell him to slide. Roy Partee, the catcher, was way up the line as he slid across home plate.

"In the defense of Pesky, nobody told him where to throw the ball. His back was to the infield, and nobody was telling him what to do, which is a cardinal sin. The second baseman should be hollering 'Home, home, home.' I can't blame Pesky at all.

"And every time I see Harry, I say, 'Harry, nobody even says you hit the ball!' He got no credit for it at all.

"Later Enos said, 'I was going all the way.' I don't know whether he was or not. You never know what's in Enos's mind. He's a character. What did he say?"

Enos Slaughter: "A lot of people have asked me on that play, Was it the biggest thrill of my baseball career? To me it was just a routine play as far as baseball is concerned. I scored from first. They gave Harry Walker a double, but ordinarily it should have been a single.

"I was stealing. A 3–2 pitch, two men out. I was running on the play when Harry hit this little looping ball into left-center, and as I rounded second, I said to myself, 'I can score.'

"The reason I kept running was, in an earlier ballgame, the fifth game, a game we got beat, Mike Gonzalez, the third base coach, had stopped me too quick on a relay throw, and that's when they juggled the ball. I could have walked home. But I had stopped. To me, when you stop running on a play, the best thing to do is stay at that bag. And we didn't score in that game, and we got beat.

"I went to Eddie Dyer. He said, 'From now on, if you think you have a legitimate chance to score, I'll take the blame.' Well, this play came up. I was the winning run. And I knew Dominick DiMaggio had been taken out of the ballgame. And he had a great arm. When he was taken out, and Leon

Culberson replaced him, I knew Culberson didn't have a great arm, and I said to myself when I rounded second, 'I can score and score easy.'

"Culberson threw the ball in to Johnny Pesky. In baseball, word of mouth is important. Bobby Doerr was the second baseman, Pinky Higgins the third baseman, and they made Johnny Pesky the goat. Well, his back was to the infield when he took the relay throw.

"If either Doerr or Higgins had hollered 'Home with the ball,' Pesky could have been wheeling, and I think he could have maybe thrown me out by eight or 10 feet. But no one said a word, and he turned toward second. When he turned back to me coming home, it was too late. He threw the ball, and Roy Partee took a couple steps in front of the plate, and I slid across easy. Like I said, it was a routine play as far as I'm concerned."

1952: Yankees vs. Dodgers

Billy Martin's Game 7 Catch

from *The Era: 1947–1957* by Roger Kahn

For the first time ever, the Reliable Jersey House installed the Dodgers as favorites to win a Series from the Yankees. To bet Brooklyn, you had to put up $8 to win $5. For what seemed to have been eons, Brooklyn fans bleated in October, "Wait till next year." Now in 1952 it seemed that Next Year had arrived.

But on Monday at Ebbets Field, Stengel managed with triumphant desperation, and the Yankees won because Billy Loes, Brooklyn's starting pitcher, lost a ground ball in the sun. Stengel started Raschi and relieved with Reynolds. That meant he had no suitable pitcher for a seventh game. Tomorrow's problem. Today Stengel focused on making sure the Series actually went to seven games.

Duke Snider's home run in the sixth inning gave Loes a 1 to 0 lead. Berra tied the game with a home run in the seventh. Woodling singled. As Loes wound up to pitch to Irv Noren, the ball dropped out of his glove. Balk. Woodling took second.

Loes struck out Noren. Billy Martin popped to Cox. Two out, Woodling on second, Raschi up. The Yankee pitcher hit a bounding ball toward Loes. Late-afternoon sunlight flooded into Ebbets Field through arches behind seats on the third-base side. The grounder bounced up in front of the low October sun and Loes was blinded. The ball struck Loes's knee and skittered past Gil Hodges into right field. Running with two out, Woodling scored.

Eighth-inning homers by Mantle and Snider canceled one another. The Yankees won, 3 to 2.

"There were only 30,037 persons at Ebbets Field for this game," Rud Rennie wrote, "which would have had the effect of an A-bomb with noodles if the Dodgers had won. It was the smallest crowd of the Series, probably because many did not think they would be able to get tickets; or maybe because many people did not want to stand in line and preferred to stay at home and look at it on television."

Stengel next started Ed Lopat, whose left-handed slow stuff would not long stop a Brooklyn lineup consisting of seven right-handed batters in Ebbets Field. Stengel knew that. Lopat pitched three scoreless innings and, as soon as the Dodgers started to cuff him, Stengel summoned Allie Reynolds. Another three innings. Then Raschi again.

The Dodgers started Joe Black and relieved with Roe and Erskine. In the seventh, with the Yankees leading, 4 to 2, the Dodgers loaded the bases with one out. The batter was Snider, who had hit four home runs so far in the Series.

Stengel brought in a journeyman left-hander, Bob Kuzava, whose name reminded Red Smith of "some kind of melon."

"I knew Snider a little bit from the International League," Kuzava says, "and good as he was, I never had trouble with him." The count went full. Kuzava threw a rising inside fastball. Snider popped to second base.

"I thought," Kuzava says, "that Casey would lift me then for Johnny Sain, bring in a right-hander to face Jackie Robinson. Sain had pitched in the National League; he knew how to work Jackie. I turned and looked for Sain, but Casey kept me in."

Kuzava threw Robinson a snapping outside curve and Robinson hit a pop fly to the right side. "I saw the ball," Kuzava says. "I coulda caught it. But this is the major leagues. The World Series. Pitchers don't chase down pop flies.

"I hollered, 'Joe! Joe!'"

That was the call for first baseman Joe Collins. But Collins lost the pop fly, as Loes had lost the grounder, or he froze. Billy Martin, running at top speed, made a wonderful catch when the ball was barely shoelace high. That was the ballgame and the Series.

"Them Brooklyns is tough in this little park," Stengel said, "but I knew we would win today. My men play good ball on the road. Now, you are gonna ask me why I left in the left-hand fella [Kuzava] to face the right-hand fella [Robinson], who makes speeches, with bases full. Don't I know percentages and etcetera? The reason I left him in is the other man [Robinson] has not seen hard-throwing left-hand pitchers much and could have trouble with the break of a left-hander's hard curve, which is what happened."

Stengel now had managed four consecutive World Series winners. The benchmark managers, John McGraw and Connie Mack, won successive World Series on three occasions. No other manager matched Stengel and his lineal predecessor Joe McCarthy with four straight.

"Nice Series, young man," Rud Rennie said to Mantle, who batted .345. "What are you up to now?"

"Headin' back to Oklahoma. I got me a job working down in the mines."

"Work in the mines?" Rennie said. "You don't have to do that now."

"Yes I do," Mantle said. "You know my dad died and I got seven dependents who're counting on me." Mantle named three brothers, a sister, his mother, and his wife.

"That's six," Rennie said.

"A baby is due in March," Mantle said.

High above Ebbets Field, I looked at my Royal portable and quested for a lead. I was 23, about Mantle's age, and seated between two elegant veterans, Red Smith and Rud Rennie. My assignment was the lead story that would run on the front page of the *Herald Tribune*.

I thought of Brooklyn's bent dreams, but I thought, too, of how the Yankees had responded with power and endurance and great courage. I began with a short sentence: "Every year is next year for the Yankees."

Casey Stengel recalls the moment: "When Robinson hits that pop fly in the seventh, who makes the catch? My feller at first [Collins] is asleep and my feller behind the bat—I don't know what he's doin'. But that little 140-pound fresh kid on second comes tearin' in after the ball. It isn't his ball but that 135-pound kid races in and I can't swallow because my heart is in my throat. If that 130-pound kid don't make the catch we blow the World Series. He makes it."

Casey didn't attempt to explain how Martin could lose 10 pounds in one paragraph. Maybe he just shrank under the strain. But Frank Frisch said in slightly more lucid fashion later on that hustling Billy's remarkable catch of a dying pop fly was one of the greatest plays he ever had seen in a World Series. Two runs already had pattered over the plate and Pee Wee Reese was rounding third when Martin dived near the mound to grasp the ball for the third out.

1954: Giants vs. Indians

Willie Mays's Catch

from *A Day in the Bleachers* by Arnold Hano

And like wolves drawn to our fresh prey, we had already forgotten him, eyes riveted on Liddle, while off to the side of the plate Vic Wertz studied the new Giant pitcher and made whatever estimations he had to make.

Wertz had hit three times already; nobody expected more of him. He had hit one of Maglie's fastballs in the first inning, a pitch that was headed for the outside corner but Wertz's bat was too swift and he had pulled the ball for a triple. Then he hit a little curve, a dinky affair that was either Maglie's slider or a curve that didn't break too well, and drove it into left field for a single. Finally, he had pulled another outside pitch that—by all rights—he shouldn't have been able to pull, so far from the right-field side of the plate was it. But he had pulled it, as great sluggers will pull any ball because that is how home runs are made. Wertz hadn't hit a home run on that waist-high pitch on the outside; he had rifled it to right field for another single.

But that was all off Maglie, forgotten behind a door over 500 feet from the plate. Now it was Liddle, jerking into motion as Wertz poised at the plate, and then the motion smoothed out and the ball came sweeping in to Wertz, a shoulder-high pitch, a fastball that probably would have been a fast curve, except that Wertz was coming around and hitting it, hitting it about as hard as I have ever seen a ball hit, on a high line to dead center field.

For whatever it is worth, I have seen such hitters as Babe Ruth, Lou Gehrig, Ted Williams, Jimmy Foxx, Ralph Kiner, Hack Wilson, Johnny Mize, and lesser-known but equally long hitters as Wally Berger and Bob Seeds send the batted ball tremendous distances. None, that I recall, ever hit a ball any harder than this one by Wertz in my presence.

And yet I was not immediately perturbed. I have been a Giant fan for years, 28 years to be exact, and I have seen balls hit with violence to extreme center field which were caught easily by Mays, or Thomson before him, or Lockman or Ripple or Hank Leiber or George Kiddo Davis, that most marvelous fly catcher.

I did not—then—feel alarm, though the crack was loud and clear, and the crowd's roar rumbled behind it like growing thunder. It may be that I did not believe the ball would carry as far as it did, hard hit as it was. I have seen hard-hit balls go a hundred feet into an infielder's waiting glove, and all that one remembers is crack, blur, spank. This ball did not alarm me because it was hit to dead center field—Mays's territory—and not between the fielders, into those dread alleys in left-center and right-center which lead to the bullpens.

And this was not a terribly high drive. It was a long low fly or a high liner, whichever you wish. This ball was hit not nearly so high as the triple Wertz struck earlier in the day, so I may have assumed that it would soon start to break and dip and come down to Mays, not too far from his normal position.

Then I looked at Willie, and alarm raced through me, peril flaring against my heart. To my utter astonishment, the young Giant center fielder—the inimitable Mays, most skilled of outfielders, unique for his ability to scent the length and direction of any drive and then turn and move to the final destination of the ball—Mays was turned full around, head down, running as hard as he could, straight toward the runway between the two bleacher sections.

I knew then that I had underestimated—badly underestimated—the length of Wertz's blow.

I wrenched my eyes from Mays and took another look at the ball, winging its way along, undipping, unbreaking, 40 feet higher than Mays's head, rushing along like a locomotive, nearing Mays, and I thought then: It will beat him to the wall.

Through the years I have tried to do what Red Barber has cautioned me and millions of admiring fans to do: Take your eye from the ball after it's been hit and look at the outfielder and the runners. This is a terribly difficult thing to learn; for 25 years I was unable to do it. Then I started to take stabs at the fielder and the ball, alternately. Now I do it pretty well. Barber's advice pays off a thousand times in appreciation of what is unfolding, of what takes some six or seven seconds—that's all, six or seven seconds—and of what I can see in several takes, like a jerking motion picture, until I have enough pieces to make nearly a whole.

There is no perfect whole, of course, to a play in baseball. If there was, it would require a God to take it all in. For instance, on such a play, I would like to know what Manager Durocher is doing—leaping to the outer lip of the sunken dugout, bent forward, frozen in anxious fear? And Lopez—is he also frozen, hope high but too anxious to let it swarm through him? The coaches—have they started to wave their arms in joy, getting the runners moving, or are they half-waiting, in fear of the impossible catch and the mad scramble that might ensue on the base paths?

The players—what have they done? The fans—are they standing, or half-crouched, yelling (I hear them, but since I do not see them, I do not know who makes that noise, which of them yells and which is silent)? Has activity stopped in the Giant bullpen where Grissom still had been toiling? Was he now turned to watch the flight of the ball, the churning dash of Mays?

No man can get the entire picture; I did what I could, and it was painful to rip my sight from one scene frozen forever in my mind, to the next, and then to the next.

I had seen the ball hit, its rise; I had seen Mays's first backward sprint; I had again seen the ball and Mays at the same time, Mays still leading. Now I turned to the diamond—how long does it take the eyes to sweep and focus and telegraph to the brain?—and there was the vacant spot on the hill (how often we see what is not there before we see what is there) where Liddle had been and I saw him at the third-base line, between home and third (the wrong place for a pitcher on such a play; he should be behind third to cover a play there, or behind home to back up a play there, but not in between).

I saw Doby, too, hesitating, the only man, I think, on the diamond who now conceded that Mays might catch the ball. Doby is a center fielder and a fine one and very fast himself, so he knows what a center fielder can do. He must have gone nearly halfway to third, now he was coming back to second base a bit. Of course, he may have known that he could jog home if the ball landed over Mays's head, so there was no need to get too far down the line.

Rosen was as near to second as Doby, it seemed. He had come down from first, and for a second—no, not that long, nowhere near that long, for a hundred-thousandth of a second, more likely—I thought Doby and Rosen were Dark and Williams hovering around second, making some foolish double play on this ball that had been hit 330 feet past them. Then my mind cleared; they were in Cleveland uniforms, not Giant, they were Doby and Rosen.

And that is all I allowed my eyes on the inner diamond. Back now to Mays—had three seconds elapsed from the first ominous connection of bat and ball?—and I saw Mays do something that he seldom does and that is so often fatal to outfielders. For the briefest piece of time—I cannot shatter and compute fractions of seconds like some atom gun—Mays started to raise his head and turn it to his left, as though he were about to look behind him.

Then he thought better of it, and continued the swift race with the ball that hovered quite close to him now, 30 feet high and coming down (yes, finally coming down) and again—for the second time—I knew Mays would make the catch.

In the Polo Grounds, there are two square-ish green screens, flanking the runway between the two bleacher sections, one to the left-field side of the runway, the other to the right. The screens are intended to provide a solid dark background for the pitched ball as it comes in to the batter. Otherwise he would be trying to pick out the ball from a far-off sea of shirts of many colors, jackets, balloons, and banners.

Wertz's drive, I could see now, was not going to end up in the runway on the fly; it was headed for the screen on the right-field side.

The fly, therefore, was not the longest ball ever hit in the Polo Grounds, not by a comfortable margin. Wally Berger had hit a ball over the left-field roof around the 400-foot marker. Joe Adcock had hit a ball into the center-field bleachers. A Giant pitcher, Hal Schumacher, had once hit a ball over the left-field roof, about as far out as Berger's. Nor—if Mays caught it—would it be the longest ball ever caught in the Polo Grounds. In either the 1936 or 1937 World Series—I do not recall which—Joe DiMaggio and Hank Leiber traded gigantic smashes to the foot of the stairs within that runway; each man had caught the other's. When DiMaggio caught Leiber's, in fact, it meant the final out of the game. DiMaggio caught the ball and barely broke step to go up the stairs and out of sight before the crowd was fully aware of what had happened.

So Mays's catch—if he made it—would not necessarily be in the realm of the improbable. Others had done feats that bore some resemblance to this.

Yet Mays's catch—if, indeed, he was to make it—would dwarf all the others for the simple reason that he, too, could have caught Leiber's or DiMaggio's fly, whereas neither could have caught Wertz's. Those balls had been towering drives, hit so high the outfielder could run forever before the ball came down. Wertz had hit his ball harder and on a lower trajectory. Leiber—not a fast man—was nearing second base when DiMaggio caught his ball; Wertz—also not fast—was at first when . . .

When Mays simply slowed down to avoid running into the wall, put his hands up in cup-like fashion over his left shoulder, and caught the ball much like a football player catching leading passes in the end zone.

He had turned so quickly, and run so fast and truly that he made this impossible catch look—to us in the bleachers—quite ordinary. To those reporters in the press box, nearly 600 feet from the bleacher wall, it must have appeared far more astonishing, watching Mays run and run until he had become the size of a pygmy and then he had run some more, while the ball diminished to a mote of white dust and finally disappeared in the dark blob that was Mays's mitt.

The play was not finished, with the catch.

Now another pet theory of mine could be put to the test. For years I have criticized base runners who advance from second base while a long fly ball is in the air, then return to the base once the catch has been made and proceed to third after tagging up. I have wondered why these men have not held their base; if the ball is not caught, they can score from second. If it is, surely they will reach third. And—if they are swift—should they not be able to score from second on enormously long flies to dead center field?

Here was such a fly; here was Doby so close to second before the catch that he must have practically been touching the bag when Mays was first touching the drive, his back to the diamond. Now Doby could—if he dared—test the theory.

And immediately I saw how foolish my theory was when the thrower was Mays.

It is here that Mays outshines all others. I do not think the catch made was as sensational as some others I have seen, although no one else could have made it. I recall a catch made by Fred Lindstrom, a converted third baseman who had bad legs, against Pittsburgh. Lindstrom ran to the right-center field wall beyond the Giants' bullpen and leaped high to snare the ball with his gloved hand. Then his body smashed into the wall and he fell on his back, his gloved hand held over his body, the speck of white still showing. After a few seconds, he got to his feet, quite groggy, but still holding the ball. That was the finest catch I can recall, and the account of the game in next day's New York *Herald Tribune* indicated it might have been the greatest catch ever made in the Polo Grounds.

Yet Lindstrom could not have reached the ball Wertz hit and Mays would have been standing at the wall, ready to leap and catch the ball Lindstrom grabbed.

Mays never left his feet for the ball Wertz hit; all he did was outrun the ball. I do not diminish the feat; no other center fielder I have ever seen (Joe and Dom DiMaggio, Terry Moore, Sammy West, Eddie Roush, Earle Combs, and Duke Snider are but a few who stand out) could have done it for no one else was as fast in getting to the ball. But I am of the opinion that had not Mays made that slight movement with his head as though he were going to look back in the middle of flight, he would have caught the ball standing still.

The throw to second base was something else again.

Mays caught the ball, and then whirled and threw, like some olden statue of a Greek javelin hurler, his head twisted away to the left as his right arm swept out and around. But Mays is no classic study for the simple reason that at the peak of his activity, his baseball cap flies off. And as he turned, or as he threw—I could not tell which, the two motions were welded into one—off came the cap, and then Mays himself continued to spin around after the gigantic effort of returning the ball whence it came, and he went down flat on his belly, and out of sight.

But the throw! What an astonishing throw, to make all other throws ever before it, even those four Mays himself had made during fielding practice, appear the flings of teen-age girls. This was the throw of a giant, the throw of a howitzer made human, arriving at second base—to Williams or Dark, I don't know which, but probably Williams, my memory says Dark was at the edge of the outfield grass, in deep shortstop position—just as Doby was pulling into third, and as Rosen was scampering back to first.

I wonder what will happen to Mays in the next few years. He may gain in finesse and batting wisdom, but he cannot really improve much because his finest talent lies in his reflex action. He is so swift in his reflexes, the way young Joe Louis was with his hands when, cobra-like, they would flash through the thinnest slit in a foe's defense, Louis, lashing Paulino Uzcudun with the first hard punch he threw, drilled into the tiniest opening and crushing the man who had never before been knocked out. That is Mays, too. Making a great catch and whirling and throwing, before another man would have been 20 feet from the ball.

And until those reflexes slow down, Mays must be regarded as off by himself, not merely *a* great ballplayer, but *the* great ballplayer of our time.

(I am not discussing his hitting here; for some strange reason—National League-itis, I guess—when I discuss the native ability of a ballplayer, I invariably narrow my gaze to his defensive ability. DiMaggio was a better hitter in his prime than Mays is now, maybe than Mays ever will be, although no hitter was ever as good as Mays at the same stage of their respective careers—check Ruth, Wagner, Cobb, Hornsby in their second full year of play and you will see what I mean.)

Still, Willie's 1954 season at the plate may have been some freak occurrence. It happens sometimes that a ballplayer hits all season far above his norm. I am thinking of Ferris Fain who led the league a few years ago, though he had never been an impressive hitter before. My wife inquired about this man Fain, of whom she was suddenly hearing so much. I told her that he was a pretty good ballplayer, an excellent defensive first baseman, and a fair hitter. She said, "Fair? He's leading the league, isn't he?"

I said, "Yes, but that's a fluke. He's hitting way over his head. Watch what happens next year." [The following year Fain led the league again.]

Or take Carl Furillo hitting over .340 in 1953. Furillo is a fine hitter, a solid .300 hitter who can drive in nearly a hundred runs a season, but .340 is not his normal average. Possibly .345 is nowhere near Mays's norm; nothing in the past had indicated he could hit that high.

I do not list Mays among the great hitters, though I concede that one day we all may. As a fielder, he is already supreme.

So much for Mays and the catch.

1954: Giants vs. Indians

Dusty Rhodes Comes Through

from *Triumph and Tragedy in Mudville* by Stephen Jay Gould

Circumstance is the greatest leveler. In a world of too much predictability, where records by season and career belong only to the greatest players, any competent person in uniform may produce one unforgettable feat. A journeyman pitcher, Don Larsen, hurled a perfect game in the World Series of 1956. Does Bill Wambsganss, with his unusual name and strictly average play as an infielder, ever evoke any memory beyond the unassisted triple play that fortuitously fell his way in the fifth inning of the fifth game of the 1920 World Series?

All ship's carpenters are named "Chips," all radio engineers "Sparks." By a similar custom, anyone named Rhodes will end up with the nickname "Dusty." James Lamar "Dusty" Rhodes, an alcoholic utility outfielder from Mathews, Alabama, made me the happiest boy in New York when he won the 1954 World Series for the New York Giants, all by himself. (I will admit that a few other events of note occurred during these four short days—Mays's legendary catch off Vic Wertz among others—but no man, and certainly not a perpetually inebriated pinch hitter, has ever so dominated our favorite days of October.)

The 1954 Cleveland Indians were probably the greatest team of modern baseball (although we might also argue for the 1998 Yankees and a few others). They compiled the best record of the modern era, 111–43 for an incredible winning percentage of .721. People forget the ironic fact that the Yankees, who won the American League pennant in every other year from 1949 to 1958, actually compiled their best record of the decade by coming in second to the Indians at 103–51 in 1954. With a pitching staff of Bob Lemon, Early Wynn, and Mike Garcia (not to mention an aging, but still able, Bob Feller), Cleveland was an overwhelming favorite to slaughter my beloved Giants with dispatch.

The Giants won that World Series in the greatest surprise of modern history, matched only, perhaps, by the 1969 Mets, whose victory, or so George Burns tells us, was the only undeniable miracle since the parting of the Red Sea. Those two Series, 1954 and 1969, share two other interesting elements, but in each case the 1954 Giants provide the cleaner and more memorable case. First, both the Giants and the Mets were overwhelming underdogs, yet both won commandingly with four straight victories. But the 1969 Series lasted five games, because Baltimore beat Tom Seaver in the first contest; the Giants put the Indians away in four—clean, simple, and minimal. Second, both victories were sparked by the most unlikely utility ballplayer. Al Weis (remember Big Al?) won the Mets' first game with a two-out single in the ninth, then tied the last game with an improbable homer. Dusty Rhodes fared even better. He won, tied, or assured victory in each of the first three games. By then, the Indians were so discouraged that they pretty much lay down and died for the finale.

If Leo Durocher, the Giants' manager, had been able to call the shots, Rhodes wouldn't have been on the team at all. In fact, Durocher told Giants' boss Horace Stoneham that he would quit as manager unless Rhodes were traded. Durocher had two objections to Rhodes: He couldn't field, and he couldn't stay sober. Stoneham agreed and put Rhodes on the block, but no other team even nibbled. As Durocher said, "Everybody else had heard about Mr. Rhodes, too. Any club could have claimed him for a dollar bill. Thank the Lord none did." Durocher was appeased by Stoneham's honest effort, and even more by Rhodes's stellar performance as a pinch hitter in 1954, when he batted .333 in that role at 15 for 45.

Rhodes won the first game of the 1954 Series with a three-run homer in the 10th after Willie Mays had saved the game with his legendary catch off Vic Wertz. Rhodes's dinger wasn't the most commanding home run in the history of baseball, but they all have the same effect, whether Carlton Fisk grazes the left-field foul pole in Fenway Park or Mantle hits one nearly into orbit. I loved the old Polo Grounds, but the ballpark had a bizarre shape, with a cavernous center field and short fences down the lines to compensate. The right-field corner sat at a major league minimal distance of 258 feet from home plate. Dusty just managed to nudge one over the right fielder's outstretched glove—an out anywhere else.

In Game 2, Durocher called upon Rhodes earlier. Wynn held a 1–0 lead in the fifth, but the Giants had two on and nobody out. Rhodes, pinch-hitting for Monte Irvin, dumped a single to center, tying the score. In the seventh, he added an insurance run and silenced the grousing about his "cheapie" of the day before by blasting a massive homer that was still rising when it hit the Polo Grounds' upper facade, 350 feet from home.

Durocher, on a roll, inserted Rhodes as an even-earlier pinch hitter in Game 3. He came in with the bases loaded in the third inning and knocked in two more runs, including the ultimate game-winner, with a single.

All this happened long ago, but my memories of joy and vindication could not be more clear or immediate. I had taken all manner of abuse, mostly from Dodger fans, for my optimism about the Giants. I had also bet every cent I owned (about four bucks) at very favorable odds. I ended up with about $15 and felt like the richest kid in New York. I'd have bought Dusty a double bourbon, but we never met, and I was underage.

Dusty Rhodes, a great and colorful character, was a strictly average ballplayer who had a moment of glory. You will find him in record books for a few other items—he once hit three homers in a single game, two pinch-hit homers in a single inning, and has the most extra-base hits in a doubleheader. But he was no star during his seven-year career, all with the Giants. People tend to focus on great moments and forget averages. They then falsely extrapolate the moment to the totality. Thus, many fans think that Dusty was a great pinch hitter throughout his career. Not so. As Bill James points out, Dusty's career pinch-hitting average is .186. He could do no wrong in 1954, but his pinch-hitting averages in his other six years were .111, .172, .250, .179, .152, and .188.

Who cares? Our joys and our heroes come in many modes and on many time scales. We treasure the consistency of a Ted Williams, the resiliency of a Cal Ripken, but we hold special affection for the journeymen fortunate enough to taste greatness in an indelible moment of legitimate glory. We love DiMaggio because he was a paragon. We love Dusty Rhodes because he was a man like us. And his few days of majesty nurture a special hope that no ordinary person can deny. Any of us might get one chance for an act of transcendence—an opportunity to bake the greatest cake ever, to offer just the right advice or support, even to save a life. And when that opportunity comes, we do not want to succeed because we bought the lucky ticket in a lottery. Whatever the humdrum quality of our daily life, we yearn to know that, at some crucial moment, our special skills may render our presence exactly right and specially suited for the task required. Dusty Rhodes stands as a symbol of that hope, that ever-present possibility.

1955: Dodgers vs. Yankees

Jackie Robinson Steals Home

from *What I Learned from Jackie Robinson* by Carl
Erskine with Burton Rocks

The good times did roll along that summer, as we ended up winning
the pennant with a resounding resolve to "win it all" this time around against
the Yankees, and Newk was back in full form with another 20-win season.

Along the way, the Robinson knack for psyching out the opponent shone
bright in Chicago one day. Jackie had Sam "Toothpick" Jones of the Chicago
Cubs, a hard thrower with a nasty curve, in a fluster at Wrigley Field.

He knew just what to yell at Sam when he was standing inside the
batter's box.

"You can't get me out, you big slob! Throw the ball over!"

Sam was so flustered that he got wider with every pitch.

Jackie ended up on first base, and then the Robinson show was in full
swing.

"You can't pick me off! I'll steal second on you!" Robinson shouted to
the pitcher's mound from first base, knowing this would really put Jones over
the edge.

And after a few throws home, Robinson ran on Jones and stole second base.

Jackie was in his zone now.

He was always in the game, physically and verbally. He paralyzed Sam Jones that day, stealing third and then home. Sam threw down his toothpick in disgust. It was a harbinger of the Dodgers' ability to take it all that fall.

The Yankees had their own mystique, and we wanted to show we were tough enough to finally conquer it.

We couldn't wait to get the season over and face the Yankees in the World Series. Only this time, things would be different. We had bolstered our pitching staff mid-season by bringing up Roger Craig and Don Bessent. Alston conducted a series of strong clubhouse meetings to prepare us for the Big Dance. It was no understatement that we felt we needed this World Series championship to prove to the world that these Dodgers were true champions.

Jackie was in rare form, and he knew that this would be one of the last chances he'd have at a World Series championship.

Jackie always did his "I might steal home today" dance down the third-base line. The 1955 World Series was no exception.

Whitey Ford was on the mound for the New York Yankees, and once again Jackie kept moving off third base, taking big strides and moving back and forth from side to side. Ford gave Jackie a couple of looks and began his delivery. Jackie took off—not bluffing this time. In what seemed like a split second, he raced toward home. The throw arrived simultaneously. Yogi didn't have to reach for the ball—it was right there. Jackie was tagged just as he made contact with home plate, gliding into a very low slide with only his right toe crossing the front edge of home plate and his body toward the infield. Yogi's glove went down, and so did umpire Bill Stewart's arms—with hands held flat, indicating safe. Jackie had stolen home. He had done the unbelievable in a World Series, and Yogi went into orbit. He stomped around home plate out of his mind, but nothing was changing the mind of Stewart. Jackie was safe.

From our bench on the third-base side of Yankee Stadium we could not tell just how close it was. Yogi clearly thought he had tagged Jackie out.

Looking down at the play as the hitter, Frank Kellert, did, Jackie must have looked out, because when the writers asked Kellert about the play, he surprised the world by saying he thought Jackie was out. Jackie was none too pleased with Kellert's remarks.

In replays of the black-and-white footage, taken from the ground vantage point, it appears that Jackie deftly slid under the tag and was safe.

Yogi was far away from our bench, and so we couldn't hear what he was yelling at Stewart, but the Incredible Hulk in Yogi was ever present as he jumped up and down around the umpire, yelling everything in the book at him.

The funnier part of the story is that to this day, Yogi still believes, and says openly, that Jackie was out. We think umpire Bill Stewart was right.

Jackie was the quickest man on the bases I ever saw. He just had the intangible instincts that cannot be taught. He knew when to take the lead, how far off first or third to position himself, and exactly when to head out for the steal.

A harbinger of the sweet taste of the bubbly to come, the call stood.

Jackie and the rest of us were on our way to meet Destiny face-to-face. The fans prayed for our victory in every game, in every inning, and in every swing of our bats. . . .

The Yankees took Game 2 as well at Yankee Stadium, and when the scene shifted to Ebbets Field, it was crisis time—do or die. [The Dodgers won the 1955 Series 4 games to 3.]

1955: Dodgers vs. Yankees

Sandy Amaros's Game 7 Catch

from *Praying for Gil Hodges* by Thomas Oliphant

I remember watching Walter Alston slowly walk to the mound. Campanella was already there, Pee Wee Reese was on his way in from shortstop, and Podres was in the familiar pitcher's position for such meetings—head down, right foot kicking at the pitching rubber. Labine was throwing in the bullpen.

Podres says he does not remember what was literally said during those moments, only that the result was that he was still in the game, still throwing fast pitches, still trying to throw them away from spots from which they could be hit with power.

Later that day and until they died, Alston and Campanella had the same memory. The Dodger manager asked his catcher how Podres was doing before he reached the mound. The phrase he used, give or take a word, was, "Has he still got it?" Clearly, Campanella was trusted explicitly to make the judgment call. Campanella replied that Podres had lost none of his effectiveness. End of subject.

That left the matter of how to pitch to the most dangerous hitter imaginable to be coming up at a critical moment like this one—Yogi Berra. The Yankee catcher was not merely an excellent hitter. He was one of the best-hitting catchers of all time, because he not only hit for average and power but also could hit for average and power to all parts of a ballpark. His normal tendency was to pull balls sharply that he could reach easily; however, he was also famous for his eagerness to chase pitches that were outside the strike zone. He swung an unusually long bat.

At the mound, Alston and Campanella assumed Berra would be swinging away, not bunting. They each stressed the vital importance of keeping the pitches away from him and preferably low. They were intent on avoiding what the Yankees most likely would be seeking—a big inning. Alston slowly walked back to the dugout while Reese and Campanella returned to their positions.

At the plate, Berra was not content when he saw no bunt sign from the third-base coach, Frankie Crosetti. Berra walked toward the Yankee veteran. Crosetti was a regular on the championship teams of the 1930s and a fixture in the coaching box ever since. He had been on the field for more World Series games than anyone, ever. They met halfway down the third-base line, where Crosetti told him the instruction was to hit away. Casey Stengel confirmed after the game that he never for a moment considered a sacrifice, that he wanted the big inning the Dodgers assumed he wanted.

Behind the plate, Campanella called for a fastball that even Berra would not swing at—above the shoulders and inside, to set up the outside pitches that would follow. Berra took the pitch for ball one.

For Podres's second pitch, Campanella called for a curveball low and outside and set himself and his target accordingly. As usual, Berra held his long bat high. In the field, the Dodgers played him to pull the ball; everyone was farther toward right field than normal. In the outfield, Sandy Amoros was not playing Berra all that deep—about midway between the infield and the outfield wall. He was positioned way off the foul line in left-center field, roughly behind where Reese was at shortstop, which was shaded toward second base. From right after the game until he died in 1992, Amoros always insisted that before returning to the dugout Alston had motioned him a few more steps toward straightaway center field, which Amoros interpreted as meaning that Alston still worried that Podres might be tiring and was mostly concerned about Berra pulling the ball.

It made what was about to happen all the more improbable.

According to my stopwatch, it took 11.97 seconds from the instant the ball left Johnny Podres's left hand until it arrived in Gil Hodges's glove to complete the play.

The pitch from Podres came in fast and slightly higher than Campanella's low target. Berra swung at it—sort of. His swing was late, bordering on the tentative, the way a good hitter swings when he intends to foul off a pitch.

At the instant of contact, the frozen film frame shows the Yankee catcher with his weight back, almost facing third base, with his bat fully extended. Berra followed completely through with his swing, but the act supplied no additional power behind the ball. At that moment of contact, it was more as if he had punched at it. In a game often ruled by millimeters, he had also swung slightly under the pitch from Podres.

In the outfield, Sandy Amoros did what only ability and instinct formed by experience can produce in a baseball player. He shifted at the crack of Berra's bat to face the left-field foul line and exploded like a sprinter coming out of starting blocks.

From the mound, Podres sensed an out and turned to pick up the white rosin bag from the dirt behind him.

From the plate, Berra had no idea beyond a sense that he hadn't hit the ball hard. This was long before the free-agent era, when zillionaires could afford to stand at home plate to admire the flight of balls they had hit. He turned, discarding his bat, and started running to first base.

From behind the plate, Campanella discarded his mask as he stood up and began to mumble a prayer.

From a box next to the Dodgers' dugout on the third-base side of the field, Buzzie Bavasi was the instantaneous pessimist. The Dodger executive, aware that the left-field seats were a mere 301 feet away, next to the foul pole, thought Berra had hit a home run.

From the Yankee dugout on the first-base side, which afforded a clear view at field level, Tommy Byrne and the other players in the dugout thought: *Foul ball.* Berra had not truly sliced the ball, but it appeared to them on a gradual arc that would carry it well into the stands.

Down the foul line, the young Dodger assistant in the front office, Billy DeLury, was sitting by himself at the game and looking directly at Sandy Amoros, who seemed to be headed right at him. From the trajectory, he was certain the ball was not hit far enough to be a home run. What he could not be certain about was whether the ball would land foul, land fair, or be caught. If it landed fair, he was almost certain it would bounce into the stands for a ground-rule double—scoring Martin and leaving Berra and McDougald on second and third, still with nobody out. The only way for a complete disaster to unfold would be if Amoros tried for a catch and dropped the ball.

From second base, Billy Martin was uncertain. He trotted halfway to third base and stopped. From first base, Gil McDougald immediately decided, as he would say later, that there was no way Amoros could get to the ball before it hit the ground and began sprinting toward second base at full speed.

No one had a better view than the people in the press box, well behind and well above home plate. From this ideal perch, Vin Scully not only had the right view; he also was concentrating with special intensity because he had to describe to the television audience what was unfolding. Scully has a standard phrase that he uses for possible or actual home runs: "cut on and belted." He told me he is certain he said nothing of the kind; instead he said he described a fly ball that was hit very high (in fact, very, very high) down the left-field line.

Back on the pitcher's mound, Podres said his second thoughts began as he picked up the rosin bag and noticed no one in left field was nestling under the fly ball he had assumed would be an out; he called it a banana ball that seemed to be gradually moving beyond Amoros's reach. With deep misgivings, Podres turned and began jogging into foul territory behind third base to be in position to back up any throw from the outfield. Next to the Dodger dugout, Buzzie Bavasi now realized the ball did not appear to have been hit far enough to reach the seats for a home run; beyond that, he had no idea what would happen.

Down the line, DeLury stood up as he saw Sandy Amoros, looking larger with each sprinting step. DeLury saw the ball, too, and realized it was an open question which would get to it first—the dirt just in fair territory or Amoros's glove.

I remember the first camera shot that widened beyond the home plate–centered view when Berra completed his swing. It showed the outfield, with Amoros coming into view at a point directly behind the normal shortstop's position. It was a moment of intense suspense in the race to the corner between the baseball and the outfielder. It was a hold-your-breath moment; the crowd was not yelling.

Amoros did not stop sprinting. In a quotation after the game in some of the few English words he knew, Amoros said, "I don't know I get it. I just run like hell and stick out my glove."

Pete Reiser's tragic heroics aside, it is not natural to run full speed directly at a wall. With about 30 yards to go, Amoros's stride changed—from all-out sprint to choppy. Whether he was decelerating to survive a collision or already certain he could reach the ball is uncertain; what is certain is that he was decelerating.

About three strides from the foul line and perhaps 10 feet in front of the stands in fair territory, Amoros can be seen using his right heel as a brake, digging it into the ground. After another stride, he stuck the glove on his right hand straight out at about eye level, the inside of it facing him.

On television the ball was visible for the first time when it fell into the glove. Amoros's heel was planted in the dirt, but his left foot was at an anticipatory angle—pointed at third base. The play was at most half-completed. At that instant, Podres, head down, was just jogging across the third-base line to his backup position.

In the Dodger infield, Pee Wee Reese was the player with the responsibility to be on the move. On a ball hit into left field with runners on base, he had gone onto the grass in short-left field after the ball was hit. As it seemed to carry toward the foul line, he kept moving over as well until he was almost directly behind third base. His job would be to take a throw from the outfield and send it on its way with fresh gas toward home plate or to some other base, which demanded an accurate sense of where the base runners were.

With Martin stopped halfway from second, he was close enough to have an excellent chance to make it back to the bag if the ball was caught; though Martin was the lead runner, Reese decided on the spot to ignore him. McDougald, however, had run so far so fast that he had already rounded second base; he could not have been more exposed.

As the ball was falling into Amoros's outstretched glove, Reese began screaming to get his attention. At the same time, Reese held his own glove high above his head and waved it frantically.

Amoros heard him and saw the glove, he would say later. As he caught the ball, he pivoted, turning counterclockwise as his momentum from the long run took him into the left-field corner. In one motion he threw the ball straight at Reese's outstretched glove about 60 yards away.

From the press box, Vin Scully said he could see out of the corner of his eye that McDougald had stumbled as he realized the fix he was in and had begun moving to retag the bag and start the long sprint back to first base.

Reese was backing up as Amoros's beautiful perfect throw came toward his glove. When he caught it, he was one full step onto the infield dirt behind third base. With a graceful counterclockwise move of his own, Reese turned as the ball reached his glove and threw an equally beautiful line drive directly across the infield at Gil Hodges.

Hodges stretched to the limits of his long frame—left arm out stiff, right leg out stiff, left leg bent at the knee. He needn't have. The throw from Reese was in Hodges's glove while McDougald was still in the air before sliding.

Double play.

People who were in the stadium said that at first there was no great noise, as if the crowd was pausing to be sure it had actually seen what appeared to have just happened. This was followed by what was typically described as an excited buzz, a kind of "Did you see that?" reaction. The buzz got louder, there were many Yankee fans applauding in tribute, but there was never any roar of the sort there is after a game-winning hit or home run, and the buzz continued even after Hank Bauer stepped into the batter's box with Billy Martin still on second base.

Spent, I turned from the couch, half-wondering if the sphinx at the dining table would at last speak. I found him staring at me, eyes ablaze, lips pursed so tightly they seemed to disappear. I think I half-smiled at him, but he continued to look at me, even as we both heard Scully's voice in the background saying that Bauer had hit a routine ground ball at Reese, who cleanly fielded an in-between hop at shortstop and threw him out to finally end the inning—11 batters, two modest base hits, an error, a wild pitch, and a play that has survived for 50 years.

It is referred to as the Amoros Catch, but it really was a spectacular run, catch, and two picture-perfect relays—all directly connected to the bizarre events in the Dodger half of the inning.

Every Dodger that day and in the decades since has always made the same analytical point about the play. Junior Gilliam could not have made it had he still been in left field. Running directly at the short wall and needing to reach for the ball while moving forward, he would have had to reach across his body as a right-handed fielder to catch the ball backhanded. Even in the highly improbable event he could have done that, he would have had to stop, set himself, and then throw. Even in the highly improbable event he could have done that smoothly, precious instants would have been lost. The point is unanimous and apparently inarguable.

By contrast, very little attention has been paid to a final factor that may have had a significant influence on the play—the wind. It was a clear fall day, the wind was not strong and constant, but it blew hard in gusts. On a ball hit extremely high, there are informed eyewitness opinions that it played a role—both in keeping the ball in the air and in keeping it over fair territory.

That was Sandy Amoros's strong opinion after the game as he described the ball he never took his eyes off as he raced toward the left-field corner. To him it seemed to be trying to slowly curve into the stands but never managed to do so. That was also the considered view of Johnny Podres, once his second thoughts about the ball he first assumed was an easy out began. What he called a banana ball should have kept curving into foul territory, especially given the likely spin on a ball hit to the opposite field by a left-handed hitter.

Reflecting the view from the Yankee dugout, that was also Tommy Byrne's judgment. He told me that on windy days a breeze was often much stronger on the field and swirled intensely—especially in the left-field corner.

If the wind was in fact involved, it was a gift to the Dodgers that fate had rarely provided, helping keep a high fly ball aloft a little longer while Amoros ran toward it and helping keep it fair, which made possible the crucial double play. In the next day's *Daily News,* homage was paid to the wind as "a breeze that grew in the Bronx"—a nice play on Betty Smith's *A Tree Grows in Brooklyn.*

Nonetheless, for all the unforgettable drama, the score was still only 2–0 with three full innings to go. After the excitement began to wear off, the emotional residue is best described as relief, as people resumed the long vigil.

I have heard some people—Buzzie Bavasi, for example—say that from that moment on they had no doubt that the Dodgers were going to win the

World Series. I have yet to meet a player who confessed to such supreme confidence. I know I didn't feel it; the burden of history was too heavy. [The Dodgers won the 1955 Series 4 games to 3.]

Still, those who followed the Dodgers all over the country could sigh with a relief that was rare enough in their experience.

1956: Yankees vs. Dodgers

Don Larsen's Perfect Game

from *The Perfect Yankee* by Don Larsen with Mark Shaw

The Miracle Ninth

	1	2	3	4	5	6	7	8	9	10	R	H	E
Brooklyn	0	0	0	0	0	0	0	0			0	0	0
Yankees	0	0	0	1	0	1	0	0			2	5	0

At approximately 2:57 on October 8, 1956, Hall of Fame broadcaster Vin Scully told his international viewing audience: "Let's all take a deep breath as we go to the most dramatic ninth inning in the history of baseball." The Armed Forces Radio commentator between innings said, "I'm going to sit back, light up, and hope I don't chew the cigarette to pieces."

I tried to do what Vin Scully had suggested to his viewers once I reached the pitching mound. I fiddled around with the rosin bag. It suddenly felt like it weighed 50 pounds. Then I walked around the back of the mound trying to calm myself. My stomach was jumpin' and my head felt like it was going to burst wide open.

I watched Joe Collins throw ground balls to Billy, Gil, and Andy. They seemed pretty nonchalant, but I knew they were nervous as hell. Martin bobbled an easy chance. I'll bet he hoped that wouldn't happen if a grounder was hit to him.

I glanced up near the press boxes. I was sure the sportscasters were trying to figure out what type of ending they would write for this day. Writing about a near-no-hitter was one thing. If I could get through the ninth, their story would be one to tell about for years to come.

As I mentioned, I later had to tell reporters that while I knew I had a no-hitter going, I never thought about what was called a "perfect game." I didn't really even know what that was. And I had just a two-run lead. I just hoped to finish the game, get the victory, and get the hell out of Dodge.

It was great to learn later on that in addition to the pressure on me, my defensive fielders, the managers, and the Dodgers' hitters, Vin Scully was nervous as hell. In a later interview, he said:

In the early days of television . . . this was the fourth year for the Series . . . the press always said the television announcers talked too much. During the Series, I therefore tried to talk sparingly.

Scully, who first debuted as a Dodger announcer in 1950, as a protégé of Red Barber, also remembered that he was restricted with what he could say about the potential for a no-hitter that memorable day.

"We talk about no-hitters all the time now, but not back then," says Scully, who is head and shoulders above all of his colleagues in that he has broadcast the astounding number of 15 no-hitters and three perfect games. He added:

In 1956, we were afraid of garnering the wrath of the players and audience alike by talking about a no-hitter or perfect game. Therefore, I kept saying "that's the 22nd consecutive batter Larsen's retired" or something like that, but I never mentioned the no-hitter possibility.

Scully also recalled that the first few innings of the fifth game were rather dull. "Mel [Allen] didn't have much to say early on . . . since there were only the good defensive plays and Mantle's home run."

The veteran broadcaster added:

New York *Daily Mirror* writer Harold Rosenthal used to say he wanted to write a lead headline for a story. "It was a dull game . . . everybody struck out," Scully recalls, "until the last couple of innings that's what we had, because not much happened offensively."

Scully also said he was afraid he'd make the mistake of mentioning the possibility of a no-hitter or perfect game and then be blamed if someone broke it up.

In the 1947 Series, Red Barber was given a lot of flak when he mentioned that New York Yankee pitcher Bill Bevens had a no-hitter and then it was broken up. I remembered that game and kept saying to myself, "Please God, don't let me make a mistake," especially when we reached the ninth inning.

After Game 5, Jesse Katz, a Philadelphia mathematician at the Remington Rand Univac Division of Sperry Rand compounded the probability of establishing the odds on my throwing a perfect game on October 8, 1956.

According to Katz, he used the *Who's Who in Baseball* record book to figure out how frequently men got on base against me. Apparently he found that 3 percent reached first base.

Using this statistic and others, Katz figured that before I threw the first pitch of the game, the odds were against me, 76,000 to one. After six perfect innings those odds dropped to 41–1, and after seven, 11–1.

Katz told reporters that at the end of eight perfect innings the odds had dropped to 2-to-1 against me pitching the perfect game. After one out, those odds switched to 13–10 against, and after two, the odds were finally 19–10 is favor of me retiring the final batter and pitching the no-hit/perfect game.

I was later told that before the Yankee infielders took the field in the ninth Billy Martin took them aside and gave them a pep talk, saying, "nothing gets through." I was too nervous to realize it at the time, but apparently Casey and Frank Crosetti were also shouting out instructions and flapping their arms wildly to signal Slaughter, Mantle, and Bauer to their respective positions in the outfield. Stengel later told reporters, "I had more managers helping me than I knew what to do with."

After the game, some sportswriters questioned why Casey didn't put in a replacement for Enos Slaughter, who wasn't as fleet of foot as in his younger days. I never did find out, but Casey was superstitious. Maybe he just didn't want to do anything to shake up things.

There have been many stories written about the tension in that ninth inning as I readied myself to pitch to the first Dodger hitter, Carl Furillo. One of the best came from sportswriter Arthur Daley, who described what the atmosphere was like in Yankee Stadium as the two teams began the ninth.

For almost four innings, wily Sal Maglie had matched Larsen putout for putout. Folks were beginning to wonder if this would be the first double no-hitter since Fred Toney of the Cincinnati Reds and Hippo Jim Vaughn of the Chicago Cubs tangled almost 40 years ago [Vaughn lost in the tenth].

But then that precocious youngster, Master Mickey Mantle, tagged the ancient Barber for a homer in the fourth. Another run trickled in later. But the Barber, pitching far better ball than he had in his victory in the opener, was left holding an empty bag.

Somewhere in the middle of the game the crowd seemed to get a mass realization of the wonders that were being unfolded. Tension kept mounting until it was as brittle as an electric light bulb. The slightest jounce and the dang thing might explode.

Or perhaps it was more like a guy blowing air into a toy balloon. He keeps blowing and blowing with red-faced enthusiasm. But every puff might be the last. Larger and larger grew Larsen's balloon. It was of giant size at the start of the ninth.

Broadcaster Bob Wolff added, "You can hear the hum of the crowd in the background." Longtime Dodger publicist Irving Rudd was so upset, he jumped up on a table and yelled, "Get a hit . . . Get a f____ hit!" Reserve Dodger outfielder Ransom Jackson told me, "I kept thinking there had to be a hit. Nobody pitches a no-hitter in the World Series."

Most of what happened in that incredible ninth is difficult to recall. I do remember that after I completed my warm-ups, I turned around and faced center field, and said to myself, "Good Lord, I've got one more to go. Please get me through this."

Mickey Mantle described his feelings in the ninth in *My Favorite Summer 1956:*

> The crowd was on its feet and I was so nervous I could feel my knees shaking. I played in more than 2,400 games in the major leagues, but I never was as nervous as I was in the ninth inning of that game, afraid I would do something to mess up Larsen's perfect game. If I dropped a fly ball, it wouldn't stop his no-hitter, but it would end his perfect game, and that added to my nervousness.

In the ninth, every Dodger hitter looked like Joe DiMaggio. In fact, I might have felt better if Joe had been the batter, because when Carl Furillo took his place in the batter's box, his stare was enough to frighten me into surrendering a base hit to him on the spot.

Of all the Dodger hitters, Furillo was the most ferocious. Not the best, or the one with the most power, but a man whose very appearance made me uncomfortable. His half-shaven beard and steely demeanor gave me the creeps, and on this occasion his look seemed to say, "Larsen, I'm gonna stuff this ball right up your butt."

Why I looked at his face, I'll never know. But I did, and now my palms were sweaty and I hadn't even thrown the first pitch. Yogi looked out at me through his mask and I tried to concentrate once again.

"Throw strikes," I reminded myself, "throw strikes." But my brain was buzzing so much, and my arms felt heavy, and I wasn't certain whether I'd throw the first pitch five feet short of home plate or five feet over Furillo's head.

My warm-up tosses had gone by so quickly, I didn't even remember throwing them. Now Furillo was ready, and umpire Babe Pinelli was ready, and Yogi was ready, and I was set to throw the first pitch toward home plate.

Despite the roar in my ears, I tried to concentrate on recalling how to pitch to the Dodger right fielder. Thinking back, I remembered that I had retired him on a fly ball to Bauer in the third and a pop-up to Billy Martin in the sixth.

Of all of the Dodgers, Junior Gilliam and Furillo were touted as the "smartest" hitters on the club. Known as a contact hitter who sprayed the ball to all fields, I remembered that Furillo liked the ball down and preferably on the inside part of the plate.

All day long, Yogi Berra had led me through the maze of Dodger hitters. This time he placed his mitt toward the high outside corner. I knew that he wanted me to keep the ball up to avoid Furillo's sweet spot.

While I was paying attention, I'm sure if Yogi would have positioned the mitt 10 feet outside the plate or over the batter's head, I would have tried to throw the ball there. I intended to follow Yogi's instructions all the way.

Carl Furillo was 5 for 17 in the Series. Once again I wanted to establish myself with a good first pitch that would let him and the Dodger hitters know I was still on track. While most reporters wrote that I threw a curve or two in the ninth, the truth is that they were all hard sliders. I think Yogi believed that my fastballs were my best pitches, and that we'd go with them until the Dodgers showed us otherwise.

I threw that first slider a bit lower than I wanted to, and I have no doubt that it would have been a ball. But Furillo was an aggressive hitter, and had decided he wasn't about to let the first pitch go by if it was close. My ability to throw several first-pitch strikes in the seventh and eighth innings no doubt contributed to his decision.

I think Carl could have handled the pitch, but he was a bit late on it, and fouled it away for strike one. My second pitch was another slider and it headed straight for Berra's mitt on the outside part of the plate. Furillo decided to try his luck on this one and fouled it off to bring the count to no balls and two strikes.

Once again, I was in the driver's seat. Should I waste a pitch or go right after Furillo? I think my brain may have told me to throw one away, but my arm was almost on remote and I was just throwing as hard as I could to somewhere near the center of the plate. If I got too cute, I'd make a mistake. Yogi had confidence in the hard slider and so did I. Give 'em your best and make them hit it, was my creed.

I threw the pitch, but it was high from 10 feet out. Pinelli called it a ball and Furillo backed away for a few seconds. The fact that it was high might have been a blessing. Calling that slider a curve was a misnomer, because it certainly didn't move much.

Yogi's signal for the fourth pitch to Furillo was a fastball. It had a chance to be a called strike three, but just at the last moment, Furillo fouled it off.

A good hard slider followed, but Furillo fouled it as well. With the count now one ball and two strikes and the tension mounting with every pitch, I threw yet another slider. It was a tumbling pitch that moved across the lower part of the outside corner. Furillo liked what he saw and swung away. It was almost as if his bat was in slow motion, and I turned to see the ball sailing toward Hank Bauer.

All of the fielders after the game told me how they felt as the game progressed toward the ninth. On the one hand they wanted the ball to be hit to them because they had confidence that they could handle it. On the other, they were scared shitless they'd screw up.

None of that crossed my mind as I watched the ball float in the blue afternoon sky. Would it fall for a base hit? Would Bauer catch it? Misplay it?

Judging the distance the ball would travel was difficult for me to do. The sound of bat to ball wasn't distinguishable because of the crowd noise. To my relief, it ended up being a routine play that anyone could have made. Hank Bauer was rock-solid steady as he coolly and calmly collected the fly ball into his glove for out number one.

The pitch of the crowd noise went up an octave. I saw arms waving and people grabbing each other. The fans were going crazy. Twenty-five consecutive outs on pitch number 89 had left me with two more batters to face to gain the no-hitter.

While I was a nervous wreck, the fans were delirious. In the ballpark that day was my boyhood chum Joe Medina.

We sat behind home plate. Our mutual friends Charlie Graham and Clark Higgins were with me. The last two innings were really something . . . crowd on their feet . . . everyone knew Don had a perfect game. I kept score until the last two innings . . . then I got too excited.

You keep thinking it's not going to happen . . . then each pitch . . . each out . . . it gets closer, more exciting. I could tell Don was a nervous wreck. . . . You could see the pressure was really something.

My buddy Charlie Graham almost cost himself a bundle of money. He kept telling the beer vendor to stand by because if Larsen pitched a no-hitter, he wanted to buy everyone in the house . . . all sixty thousand of them . . . a drink!

With Furillo retired, I started to think about Roy Campanella. I don't know if he was as nervous as I was when he came to the plate, but I'm sure he felt a lot of pressure as well.

The Dodgers were losing the pivotal Game 5 of the World Championship, 2–0. If that wasn't bad enough, I hadn't given up a hit. Fifty-two World Series had been played before this one, and nobody had ever pitched a no-hitter.

And don't kid yourself, baseball teams hate to have a no-hitter pitched against them. It's bad enough to lose, but no team wants to think that a pitcher is that much better than they are on a given day.

Most times, when the no-hitter is still possible and the game gets into the late innings, the other team will try anything to scratch out a hit. Interestingly enough, nobody in the Dodger lineup tried to bunt on me. The Dodgers weren't known for their speed, but I was surprised they didn't try at least one bunt.

Of course, I knew that Roy Campanella wasn't going to do anything but try to get a solid base hit. I remember that Yogi and he exchanged words, and both had a good chuckle about something. There they were poking fun, and I was dying out there.

Our strategy with the great Dodger hitter was to pitch him inside, even though I had retired Campanella on two outside pitches in both the third and sixth innings.

This time around, I was determined to throw the pitches inside and keep the ball away from Campanella's power zone. My first pitch was a good fastball in close. The crack of the bat scared me, but Campanella came around too soon and fouled it into the left-field stands for strike one.

Yogi called for a slider on the next pitch. Since this was the ninth inning and I was approaching 100 pitches, I wasn't sure how much "stuff" I had left. But Yogi was the boss, and so I set up to throw the slider. It was more of a fastball and just a wee bit outside. I knew it would be ball one.

But while Roy Campanella was a very disciplined hitter, he decided that the pitch was hittable and swung the bat. Campanella said later he was trying to foul the pitch off, but instead the future Hall of Famer grounded the ball harmlessly toward an anxious Billy Martin who was positioned perfectly at second base.

There was never a doubt that Martin would handle the medium-speed grounder. Almost effortlessly, he scooped the ball into his glove, and threw easily to Joe Collins at first for consecutive out number 26 on pitch number 91.

Twenty-six up and 26 down. No runs, no hits, no errors, no walks, no passed balls, no wild pitches, no hit batters—nothing to spoil my day in the sun.

With just one more out standing between me and a no-hit, perfect game, it was difficult to know who was more nervous, Babe Pinelli, the official scorers, my defensive teammates, Casey Stengel, the players on the Yankee bench, the Dodgers, or yours truly.

Standing on the mound, I felt like I was in a dream world. I've heard players talk about the magic moment when something very special happens in a sporting event. It may be a great hit like Bobby Thomson's shot heard 'round the world, or The Catch in the NFC Championship Game by the 49ers' Dwight Clark, or the last-second shot by John Havlicek in the fifth game of the Celtics–Phoenix Suns playoffs in the mid-seventies. When players are asked to describe their feelings, most times they can't remember much, because they are so focused on the task at hand.

While the pressure had been building with every inning and every batter, I can honestly say that after I retired Roy Campanella, a bit of a peaceful feeling came to me. I had somehow reached a point where the challenge would be met, where I would find out if a miracle was truly going to occur. The stakes were clear now. If I retired the next batter, I would have a no-hitter and be the winning pitcher for the Yankees in the pivotal World Series game. Every athlete wants to be in a special situation like that, and I would get the chance.

The atmosphere on the field suddenly seemed in focus. Everything was moving in slow motion, but I focused and began to prepare for what I hoped would be the final batter.

The Yankee Stadium crowd had gone crazy after Campanella's out, but I would not allow myself to be distracted by them. I made up my mind I was going to focus on one thing—throwing strikes to whoever the Dodgers sent up to face me.

With this in mind, I kept my eyes peeled in the direction of the Dodger dugout. I knew Walter Alston would send up a pinch-hitter to bat for Sal Maglie. The Barber had pitched a great game, but Alston would want his best pinch-hitter at the plate so that he had every chance to not only break up my no-hitter, but come back and either tie up the score or hit me for a few runs and take the lead.

The choices to pinch-hit for Sal Maglie consisted of Dodger reserve third baseman Randy Jackson; outfielder/first baseman Dale Mitchell; outfield reserve Gino Cimoli; infielders Charlie Neal, Chico Fernandez, Don Zimmer, and Rocky Nelson; and catchers Rube Walker and Dixie Howell. The most logical choice was Mitchell, who ended up with a lifetime .300-plus average in ten seasons with Cleveland and one with the Dodgers.

From Colony, Oklahoma, the 6-foot, 195-pound, 35-year-old Mitchell, who had lazy gray eyes and close-cropped brown hair, first joined the Indians in 1946. A left-handed thrower and hitter, Mitchell had a number of good years with the club and led the American League with 203 hits in 1949.

In 1947, his first full year with the club, Dale hit .316, and in 1948 improved the average to .336. He played on the Indians' world championship team that year along with Joe Gordon, Lou Boudreau, and Larry Doby.

In a career where he ended up with 1,244 lifetime hits, Mitchell batted .317 and hit 23 triples in 1949, the most in the American League since 1939. A .308 and .290 average followed in 1950 and 1951, but in 1952, Mitchell hit .323, second in the league to Philadelphia's great hitter Ferris Fain.

Dale Mitchell's prowess at the plate fell off in 1954 and 1955, and he was traded to the Dodgers during the 1956 season. With the Dodgers, he hit .292, the most as a pinch-hitter in 19 games.

As I walked around the mound trying to ready myself, I saw that Dale was approaching the plate. I tried not to look at him too closely, but instead watched for Yogi to get in position. The break in the action had suddenly made my hands shake. I slapped the ball in my glove and tried to steady myself.

Later on, I'd read an interview with umpire Babe Pinelli. He recalled the moments just before the first pitch to Mitchell in the ninth:

When the last man in the ninth, pinch-hitter Dale Mitchell, stepped up, my blue suit was soaked with sweat. I noticed Commissioner Ford Frick in his box. He was pale as a sheet.

With two out, Larsen was just one man away from immortality. As he prepared to throw, I took a firm grip on my emotions. Everyone else could sympathize with him—but not me. Refusing Larsen anything he didn't earn 100 percent was the hardest thing I'd ever done in baseball.

In Mickey Mantle's *My Favorite Summer 1956*, he described Mitchell and his feelings when the Dodgers pinch-hitter came to the plate:

The Dodgers were down to their final out. It was Maglie's turn to bat, but Walter Alston sent up a pinch-hitter, Dale Mitchell, a veteran left-handed hitter. I knew him well. He had spent a little over ten seasons with the Cleveland Indians and had a lifetime batting average of .312. He had very little power, only 41 home runs in 11 seasons, but he was a good contact hitter. He sprayed the ball all over the field and that made it impossible to defend against him. . . . As Mitchell stepped in and went into his crouch, I shifted nervously in center field. "Please don't hit to me," I kept thinking. Then: "Please hit it to me." I worried about him hitting a sinking line drive or a bloop that would fall in front of me. I worried where I should play him. "Should I come in a few steps? Go into the bench for help," as an outfielder usually does in this kind of situation, but nobody was looking at me. They were leaving it up to me. They didn't want to be responsible if I should mess up. So I just stayed right where I was.

Writer Frank Graham Jr. wrote about Mitchell and my words to him (Graham) after the game:

Now Dale Mitchell was announced, pinch-hitting for Maglie. The Yankees knew the left-handed swinging Mitchell well; he had played against them often while he was with the Indians. They knew him as a threat to slash, slap or bloop a hit in any direction. Talking about it later, Larsen said, "He really scared me up there. Looking back on it, though, I know how much pressure he was under. He must have been paralyzed. That made two of us."

Yogi and I hadn't specifically discussed Mitchell that much, since he wasn't in the starting lineup. I'd faced him before in the American League and knew he was a good hitter.

Casting any strategy aside, I once again decided to throw the ball as hard as I could and hope for the best. While I was planning my attack, Mitchell told reporters after the game that he knew exactly what was at stake, but tried to focus on the importance of the outcome of the game. "My job was to get on base any way I could," he said. "It was still a 2–0 game, and if I could get on, I could bring the tying run to the plate. I was trying to look for a pitch I could handle."

As Mitchell readied himself by swinging two bats over his head like some sort of Neanderthal caveman, I looked at Yogi. I also took a deep breath, trying to somehow calm the nerves that threatened to blow my stomach apart. I read later that broadcaster Vin Scully told his viewing audience, "I think it would be safe to say no man in the history of baseball has ever come up to home plate in a more dramatic moment." He added, "Yankee Stadium is shivering in its concrete foundation right now." So was I.

Umpire Pinelli positioned himself behind Yogi as Mitchell stepped to the plate for what would be 103 of the most exciting seconds in baseball history. Yogi signaled No. 1 for a fastball, and at 3:05, I sent it spiraling toward the plate.

Mitchell, who stood slightly bent over when he batted, passed on the pitch, which was just a bit low and a little outside. The crowd loudly booed the call, but Pinelli was right.

Yogi next called for a slider, but for all practical purposes it was a fastball. It had good velocity to it and caught the outside corner. The roar of the crowd drowned out Pinelli's call of "Stee-rr-rrike One" to even the count.

If Mitchell disagreed with the call, he didn't let Pinelli know. He simply resumed his batting position, and I stared down at Yogi. He fired the Spalding baseball back securely to my glove.

Seconds later, the rotund, barrel-chested catcher I'd come to love resumed his squatting position. He carefully flashed me the sign for another slider. I took my catcher's directive and buggy whipped the deceiving pitch. But its trajectory was low, and it certainly would have been ball two. No call was made on the pitch though, because Mitchell aggressively swung and missed on pitch No. 95.

Looking back, I wonder whether the moment of truth really registered in my brain. One strike and I could go home with something every ballplayer dreams about—a no-hitter in the World Series.

Trying not to think about the possibilities, I prepared myself to throw what I hoped would be the most important pitch of my life. Up in the broadcast booth, Vin Scully's carefully chosen words added to the excitement: "Crowd's roaring now similar to the day Johnny Podres stood out last year. But there is so much more at stake."

If Yogi was feeling the strain, I couldn't tell. His eyes peered at me through the catcher's mask and his fingers indicated a fastball.

Using my newly discovered no-wind-up delivery, I somehow calmed myself and threw a dastardly fastball that wove in toward the inside back outer edge of the plate. Sensing strike three, Pinelli prematurely started to raise his hand to call the 27th and final Dodger batter out, but he wouldn't make the call. At the last possible second, Mitchell's powerful hands and arms lunged at the too-close-to-take fastball and fouled it straight back of the plate. The crowd's thunderous "Ooooohhh" captured the moment.

A sudden gut-wrenching hush fell over the stadium as Pinelli dug a new baseball out of his umpire's bag and placed it in Yogi Berra's right hand. Mitchell stood just outside the batter's box nervously waving his bat at the sky. No doubt his mind was racing in tandem with the others' as they all prepared to witness what I hoped would be a historic pitch.

They all expected me, the ol' Gooney Bird, to resume my position at the rubber and begin the sleight-of-hand motion that would deliver pitch No. 97. Every fan in the house that Ruth built craned their necks to get the best possible view, but I was just not ready. I stepped away from the rubber and off to the right side of the mound.

When I lifted up my left hand and took off my dusty blue hat with the white NY emblazoned on the front, every eye in the stadium was on me. As the seconds ticked by, I wiped my brow with my forearm and then put my cap back on.

I was still not ready to pitch. I stooped down and picked up the half-full, smudged rosin bag that lay a foot to the right of the pitching rubber. Caressing it in my right hand, I jiggled a mist of white powder out of the thin bag and peered down toward the ground.

For a few charged seconds, I just stood there, immobile. But then, I knew I was ready. I tossed the rosin bag, and after a quick glance toward center field turned and ascended the pitching rubber.

Behind me, the Yankee defense, forced to fidget in their respective positions as they awaited my next effort, now assumed their ready positions. Every Yankee player was determined not to ruin my chance at glory.

Catcher Berra, batter Mitchell, and umpire Pinelli returned to their respective crouched, close-knit positions surrounding home plate. Berra's eyes met mine, and the burly off-beat quipper and future Hall of Fame catcher went through the regimen of pitch signs for what he hoped would be the final time.

Not unexpectedly, Berra signaled for a fastball. Berra rose slightly from a deep crouch and positioned his catcher's mitt knee high and just to the outside lower position of the diamond-shaped plate.

The left-handed hitter Mitchell, sporting No. 8 on the back of his Dodgers uniform, now assumed his crouched position deep in the batter's box. Babe Pinelli, umpiring for what would be his final time behind the plate after nearly a thousand games and 22 years as a man in blue, kneeled touch-close behind Berra. Pinelli later admitted that he was so short of breath that he felt faint.

Gasping for air in the frenzy, the overflow crowd now focused on the mound. I raised my hands and arms to shoulder length, all the while hiding my ball inside the worn Wilson-model glove that covered my left hand.

I propelled the tiny sphere on its intended trajectory toward Yogi Berra's glove. While it took less than two seconds for that baseball to cut through the air and end up crossing the plate, those who witnessed my final pitch swore that time stood still.

I remember watching the ball turn over and over and head on a direct line with Mitchell's uniform letters. I saw Dale commit himself and make a futile half-swing. He didn't connect and then I saw the ball pop squarely into Yogi's mitt.

Instantly, Dale looked back at Pinelli. I watched the umpire's mouth open, and he said something I couldn't hear. A second later, Pinelli's right arm pointed upward toward the sky.

Next thing I knew Yogi rose up out of his crouch. I saw Mitchell flail his arms and protest to Pinelli, but he was long gone. Without Pinelli or Yogi there, poor Dale looked rather lost. He was probably cussing at himself, wishing he'd either held up and taken a chance on a Pinelli ball/strike call or swung full-out at my pitch.

All the while Yogi was racing toward me with a huge grin on his face. When it registered that Pinelli had called strike three, I do not know. I didn't fully realize what had happened until Yogi leaped into my arms.

Two hours and six seconds from the first pitch of the game had elapsed. Later I'd learn that Vin Scully had memorialized the moment when he was kind enough to say: "Ladies and gentlemen, it's the greatest game ever pitched in baseball history."

[The Yankees won the 1956 Series 4 games to 3.]

1960: Pirates vs. Yankees

Bill Mazeroski's Series-Winning Home Run

from *The Pirates Reader,* by Lester J. Biederman

MAZ, SMITH HOMERS KILL YANKEE HOPES

NELSON ALSO BOMBS AS HADDIX GAINS WIN IN 10–9 FINALE

Team of Destiny? Well, can you think of a better word to describe the brand new World Champion Pirates?

This surely was a team of destiny with tremendous spirit and unmatched desire. They bolted through the National League like true champions, then carried the power-packed Yankees to seven games before beating them yesterday at Forbes Field, 10–9, with their very own weapon, the home run.

And with it, they won the greatest prize baseball has to offer—the world championship in their first opportunity since 1927 when the same Yankee organization humiliated them in four straight games.

Mark it: Debt repaid in full.

Until yesterday, the Pirates had hit only one home run (Bill Mazeroski in the opener) to eight for the Yankees in their first six games. Then after the American Leaguers blasted a pair in this vital seventh game, the Pirates saved their best two shots until they needed 'em.

Hal Smith came through with a dramatic three-run blast over the left-field wall with two outs and the Pirates trailing 6–7 in the eighth inning that rocked old Forbes Field and brought the 36,683 fans up screaming.

The Yankees tied it in the top of the ninth but this was only temporary.

Then when Bill Mazeroski drilled Ralph Terry's second pitch over the left-field wall leading off the ninth inning to crack the 9–9 tie and bring Pittsburgh its first world championship since 1925 with a 10–9 victory, there was a thunderous ovation awaiting Maz and his teammates when he finally touched home plate.

There have been similar scenes at Forbes Field all season long but none that meant as much as this one.

The whirlwind finish was as dramatic as any World Series game in many years. Yet it seemed the Mazeroski game-winning homer was a little anticlimactic after Smith's two-out, three-run homer that came with such swiftness it almost numbed the fans before they really cut loose.

The Pirates and their fans figured the game was over then and there but the Yankees tied it in the ninth only to allow Maz to become the hero with his home run that sailed majestically over the left-field wall and sent the crowd into a frenzy never matched in this city.

This blow touched off a celebration in Pittsburgh that lasted far into the night and was heard round the world.

The Pirates simply had one more last-inning rally left in their systems and they gave the Yankees a dose of it. They won 23 games during the year in their final turn at bat and this time they proved that lightning can and does strike more than once.

By the time Maz circled the bases and was escorted to the dugout, the fans had started swarming on the field, making it difficult for the Yankees to drudge silently and solemnly to their clubhouse.

The game started out as a duel between Vern Law, trying for his third victory despite a lame right ankle, and Bob Turley, who won the second game here.

Rocky Nelson gave Law a fast 2–0 lead when he homered in the first inning after Bob Skinner walked and in the second inning, the Pirates chased Turley when Smoky Burgess led off with a single.

They filled the bases on Bill Stafford with a walk and Maz's safe bunt, but when Stafford took Law's bouncer and started a double play, it appeared he was home safe. However, Bill Virdon cracked a two-run single and now Law enjoyed a 4–0 lead.

Bill Skowron spoiled the shutout with a right-field homer in the fifth but when Bobby Richardson singled and Tony Kubek walked to open the sixth, Danny Murtaugh felt Law's ankle was acting up and he called in Roy Face.

Face retired Roger Maris but Mickey Mantle singled for one run and Yogi Berra drilled a three-run homer into right field and the Yankees had a 5–4 lead.

Bobby Shantz protected this margin expertly and then Face yielded two more runs in the eighth on a walk, Skowron's scratch single, John Blanchard's looping single to center and Cletis Boyer's double to left.

But in their half of the eighth, the Pirates got a break, a big break. Gino Cimoli dropped a pinch-single into right and Kubek waited for Virdon's grounder, but it took a bad hop and hit him in the throat.

Instead of one on or a double play, the Pirates now had runners on first and second and the fans were screaming. Dick Groat singled for a run and Jim Coates relieved Shantz. Skinner sacrificed but Nelson flied out and fans moaned.

Then came another real break. Roberto Clemente grounded to Skowron but Coates didn't cover first base and Clemente beat it for a hit, Virdon scoring.

This seemed to breathe new life into the Pirates and they took advantage of it as they've done so often during the season.

Coates had two strikes on Smith and even had him swing and miss strike two, but the husky catcher took dead aim on a 2–2 low fastball and the moment he connected everybody knew the destination—Schenley Park.

When Smith touched home plate with the run that gave the Pirates a 9–7 edge, the customers were limp from excitement.

But the Yankees still had some fight left. Bob Friend came in to pitch the ninth and Richardson singled and so did pinch-hitter Dale Long. Exit Friend, enter Haddix. Maris fouled out but Mantle singled for a run.

Berra hit a sharp grounder down the first base line but Nelson grabbed it, stepped on first and tried to tag Mantle, but Mickey slid back safely as the tying run crossed the plate.

Maz didn't keep the fans waiting long in the Pirate ninth. He took the first pitch for a ball, them met a high fastball and sent it sailing over the left-field wall and the Pirates became the champions of baseball.

No game today!

1964: Cardinals vs. Yankees

Bob Gibson's Gutty Game 7 Performance

from *October 1964* by David Halberstam

The sixth game [of the 1964 World Series] was in some ways a repeat of the third, with Jim Bouton again pitching against Curt Simmons. For the first seven innings it was a tight, well-pitched game. For the Yankees it provided a last World Series hurrah for the home-run tandem of Maris and Mantle, when they and Joe Pepitone flashed a demonstration of that vaunted Yankee power. Simmons did not feel he pitched that well; he preferred the cold, in which he had worked earlier at the Stadium, and he had sensed that his breaking ball was not sharp on this day. As for Bouton, he was delighted to be getting his second shot in this Series. Far more than most baseball players, he was an adrenaline player, and he liked pitching under this kind of pressure. He had pitched exceptionally well in the third game of the 1963 World Series, which he had lost to Don Drysdale, 1–0, a game in which both teams got a total of only seven hits; he had given up one run and six hits in the third game of this Series, and his combined World Series earned run average for his three starts after this day was 1.48.

Bouton was puzzled by the behavior of the Yankee ownership on the morning of the sixth game. The players had been told to pack their suitcases and check out of the St. Louis hotel before they left for the ballpark. If they lost, they would leave for New York right after the game; if they won, they would return to the hotel and check back in. Management clearly did not want to be charged for an extra day in St. Louis if they were going to lose the game and the Series. That stunned Bouton: In the past the Yankees had always been both arrogant and parsimonious, but this was the first time he could ever remember their parsimoniousness outweighing their arrogance. It was, he thought, the work of people with a loser's mentality. But Bouton felt good on this day; he loved being the center of attention and being given the ball in a game this big.

The Cardinals scored in the first inning. Curt Flood opened the game with a single to left, then went to third on Lou Brock's single to center. Brock scored when Bill White hit into a double play. The Yankees tied it in the fifth; Tom Tresh, who had hit the Cardinal pitching hard all week, lined a ground-rule double down the left-field line, moved to third when Clete Boyer grounded out, and scored when Bouton himself singled to left-center. In the sixth the Yankees nailed Simmons. Richardson, the team's leading hitter in the Series, popped up. Up came Maris, who had been a notoriously poor hitter in this and previous World Series games. Simmons hung a curve to Maris and Maris jumped on it, hitting it up on the roof in right, the ball landing just fair. Then Mantle came up and Simmons threw him a fastball; Mantle, batting righty, hit it on a line to the roof in right field. This gave the Yankees a 3–1 lead. Then, in the eighth, with Simmons out of the game and first Barney Schultz, then Gordon Richardson, on the mound for the Cardinals, the Yankees scored five more times, including four runs on a Joe Pepitone grand-slam home run. The final score was 8–3, and the Yankees had to check back into their St. Louis hotel.

In the seventh game Bob Gibson took the ball. There was a time, only recently past, when that would have surprised people, a black pitcher getting the call in a decisive seventh game of the World Series, for it had long been part of the myth of white America that blacks were not mentally as tough as whites and therefore could not be counted on in the clutch: It was the performances of such athletes as Gibson that destroyed that particularly scabrous fiction. In a way Gibson's very presence on the mound in so big a game showed how much baseball had changed in its ethnic makeup in so short a time. Only fifteen years earlier, in the final regular-season American League game that would decide the pennant, neither team had a black player on its roster, and when the Yankees took the field, four of the nine players, DiMaggio, Rizzuto, Berra, and Raschi, were Italian-American. Now four of the nine Cardinal starters were black, and if Julian Javier had not been injured, the total would have been five black or Hispanic players. The only black starter for the Yankees was Ellie Howard. Now Gibson, starting the seventh game of the World Series for the Cardinals, was a long, long way from the moment seven years earlier, when he had been pitching for Columbus in the Sally League, a brief unhappy stint lasting only eight games, and someone had yelled out at him, "Alligator bait! Gibson, you're nothing but alligator bait!" *Alligator bait*, he thought, *what the hell is that?* for he had no idea at all what it meant. Later he was told it was an old Deep South expression, and it recalled the good old days when the good old boys went into the swamps in search of alligators and tied a rope around a black man, or so they claimed, and threw him in the water as bait.

In the seventh game Bob Gibson was battling his own fatigue as well as the New York Yankees. [He had pitched Games 2 and 5.] He was determined not to give in to it. Most pitchers as tired as Gibson was on this day, with only two days' rest, slowed down their rhythm so that they could rest between pitches. Not Gibson. If anything he sped up his pace so the Yankees would not know that he was tired. He did not want to show even the slightest hint of weakness, and so he set a blistering pace. Gibby was struggling, Tim McCarver, who was catching him, thought. He was sure that Gibson was more tired than he had been when he pitched against the Mets in the final game of the season. Then, McCarver had been able to see the fatigue in his face, but on this day he could see it even more clearly in

Gibson's pitches. Against the Mets his breaking ball had been a little flat, but now, in his third World Series start in a week, it was not only his breaking ball that was flat, it was his fastball as well. It did not explode in the strike zone the way a Gibson fastball normally did.

And yet even with all that, he had the Yankees off balance. Gibson was still a very fast, very smart pitcher, and even more, a great competitor. The Yankees might be a great fastball-hitting team, but that did not mean that hitting Bob Gibson was going to be easy. When the Cardinals played against Koufax or Maloney or Bob Veale, Gibson used to tease his teammates: "Okay, all you fastball hitters, there he is, now just go out there and have a field day." It was like telling a kid who liked ice cream to eat a gallon of it at one sitting, McCarver thought. Gibson was going to do that on this day; he was going to make the Yankees earn every hit.

In baseball, thought McCarver, players admired the ability of a pitcher who could reach back and find something extra. More than anyone he had ever played with, Bob Gibson could do that. He might be exhausted, but he seemed to understand even on the worst days that he would be finished in $2^{1}/_{2}$ hours. That allowed him to force his body to do things it did not want to do. It was a triumph of the spirit over body; since he refused to be defeated, he was not defeated. He would walk off the mound after one of those games, his arm aching, and he would sit in the locker room icing his arm, saying that he was going to quit, that it was not worth it, that the pain was too great. The constant use of his slider had literally bent his arm out of shape. When Gibson and McCarver went to the tailor together, the tailor would tell Gibson to drop both his arms straight down so that he could measure their length; the left arm dropped normally, but the right arm remained bent just slightly. "Let your arm hang straight, Bob," the tailor would say, and Gibson would say, "It *is* hanging straight." That was as good as he could do. The slider had done it to him. He always knew the price he was paying for the success he sought.

Normally, the day after he pitched his arm was all right, and then on the second day, it ached terribly, and on the third day the ache began to go away. It was not the rest of his body that was tired, only his arm. In those days he, like other pitchers, took Darvon to kill the pain. Gibson thought he had rather good stuff early in the game, and he struck out three batters in the first two innings, including Mickey Mantle.

The Yankees went with Mel Stottlemyre, who had gone, in a few brief weeks, from ingenue to rookie sensation to ace of the staff. Yogi Berra and the coaches came to him and asked if he could pitch on two days' rest. The other possibilities were Ralph Terry, whom they had not used much late in the season and who had not had a good year, and Al Downing, about whom they clearly were uncertain. So Stottlemyre said yes, and he felt reasonably good when he went to the mound. He thought he was pitching fairly well, although his slider had less bite on it and his ball had less movement than usual. But the Cardinals were hitting the ball on the ground.

But in the fourth inning the Yankees self-destructed. They had fielded poorly throughout the Series, and though when it was over they were charged with nine errors to the Cardinals' four, in reality their fielding had been far worse than that. There had been numerous bad throws and bonehead plays, which were not counted as errors but which cost them dearly, just as their poor baserunning had cost them on offense. Ken Boyer started the home fourth with a single to center. Dick Groat walked on four pitches. Then Tim McCarver hit a bouncer to Pepitone that looked like a double-play ball. Pepitone made a good pickup and threw to Linz at second for the force on Groat. Stottlemyre covered first for the return throw, but the throw from Linz, which should have beaten McCarver easily, was wide of first and rolled to the stands. Backing up the play, Bobby Richardson picked up the ball and threw home, but Boyer scored for the first run of the game. Mike Shannon's single sent McCarver to third. So far in the Series, the Cardinals had been relatively cautious in their baserunning, but they decided in this game that they would challenge Howard and the Yankees, and they tried the double steal. Shannon broke for second, and behind the plate Ellie Howard double-pumped; then Howard bit and threw to second, but his throw was high and to the right, and Shannon slid in safely. When Howard threw, McCarver raced for home, and he scored when Richardson's throw was in the dirt and went through Howard. Dal Maxvill singled to right, and Mantle got to the ball quickly. A good throw from Mantle might have caught Shannon, but Mantle threw wide and Howard dove for Shannon and missed. The Cardinals had three runs on only one Yankee error, but four bad Yank throws. The once-great Yankees, wrote Dick Young, "had looked more like the Mets than the Mets. Linz made a bad play. Howard made a bad play. Richardson made a bad play. Mantle made a bad throw and up went three ragged runs for St. Louis and the Yankees were never in the ballgame again."

Worse, Stottlemyre jammed his shoulder diving for the ball from Linz, and it quickly stiffened on him. The Yankees sent up a pinch hitter for him in the fifth, and then sent Al Downing to the mound in the bottom of the fifth. Brock greeted Downing with a 400-hundred-foot drive to the pavilion roof in right-center. Then Bill White singled to center and Boyer doubled to right, sending White to third. That was it for Downing, and Roland Sheldon came in to pitch. Groat grounded to Richardson, who had to throw to first and had no chance to get White, who scored. Boyer went to third. That made it 5–0. Then McCarver hit a soft fly to right and Boyer beat Mantle's throw, which skidded through Howard again. That made it 6–0.

In the top of the sixth the Yankees began to struggle back. Richardson beat out a slow roller to Ken Boyer at third. Maris hit a ground single to right, with Richardson stopping at second. All during the Series Gibson had pitched Mantle outside, going against the book. McCarver had thought the scouting reports were right, but Gibson was Gibson—he did not like coming inside on power hitters; he believed the outside of the plate belonged to him, and he was not a man easily argued out of anything. So far his strategy had worked. Mantle had been 1–10 against him in the Series. But now Gibson was really beginning to tire and he came outside, and Mantle hit the ball into the left-center-field bleachers to make the score 6–3. It was Mantle's third home run of the Series and his record 18th in World Series competition.

But even then the Yankees could not hold the Cardinals. Ken Boyer hit a solo home run off Steve Hamilton in the home seventh. By the seventh inning

Gibson knew he was tiring, but Johnny Keane left him in, in part because he had a four-run lead, in part out of respect for Gibson as a competitor, and in part because of his anxiety about his own bullpen. Gibson hated to come out for a relief pitcher in any circumstance, and he most certainly did not want to come out of this game. But by the seventh inning he was finding it harder and harder to put the ball where he wanted. He had to put more effort into getting extra break on the ball, and as he did that, he lost location. There was a danger at a moment like this, he well knew, of slipping, of pushing rather than firing the ball, of losing both location and speed, and then of beginning to fall behind the hitters. The other danger, he thought, was that it was easy to become lazy without knowing it, to give in to your body and stop reaching back. So he spent those last three innings talking to himself on the mound, trying to keep himself alert: *Let's go asshole, don't quit now. . . . This is where you've always wanted to be, the seventh game of the World Series with you pitching for everything against the New York Yankees . . . this is not the time to get lazy and get soft.* Out on the mound his throat was dry because every time he threw, he grunted from the effort.

In the seventh the Yankees hit the ball relatively hard on him. With two out Richardson singled to center, and Maris hit a line shot to right field, but directly at Mike Shannon for the third out. The eighth was easier. Mantle flied to center. Ellie Howard struck out, which was a relief for it showed Gibson still had some pop on the ball. Then Pepitone popped up to Maxvill. The Cardinals did not score in the bottom of the eighth. Now it was time for the top half of the ninth. Rarely had Bob Gibson wanted anything so badly as to finish this game. When it was time to go out on the mound for the ninth, Johnny Keane, *who knew he was tired and knew he was wearing down*, came over to Gibson and told him he was going to stay with him, and reminded him that he had a four-run lead. "Bob, I'm going with you in the ninth. Just throw it over the plate," he said. "Don't be cute. Don't go for the corners. Just get it over. They're not going to hit four home runs off you." What Gibson had always wanted was the confidence of his manager, and on this day he had it more than any pitcher could ever ask for. He did not want to betray that trust in the ninth.

He struck out Tom Tresh, the first batter. Then Clete Boyer came up and hit a home run into the left-field bleachers. *That's one home run,* Gibson thought to himself. Johnny Blanchard batted for Pete Mikkelsen and struck out. Two outs now, both strikeouts. Then Phil Linz came up, and he hit the ball into the left-field bleachers, making it 7–5. *That's two home runs,* Gibson thought. *Maybe Keane is wrong.* Up came Bobby Richardson, who already had 13 hits in the Series. Out in the bullpen, Ray Sadecki was warming up. Aware that he had not pitched well in the Series, and that Johnny Keane was down on him, he wondered whether Keane would go to him if Richardson got on. Until then Keane said he never thought of lifting Gibson. But if Richardson had gotten on, he would have gone to Sadecki. Keane went out to the mound to talk with his pitcher for a moment. McCarver did not go all the way out because he knew Gibson hated it when the catcher came out, and besides, there was nothing to say. The count was 1–1. Richardson liked the ball high and out over the plate, and Gibson made a very good pitch to him, a fastball that moved in on him at the last instant. Richardson popped it up, and Dal Maxvill gathered it in a second.

Afterward Gibson realized for the first time how hard he had fought against his fatigue and how much his arm hurt. It would hurt on and off for an entire month, but it was a month in which he did not have to pitch. He had struck out nine men, which gave him a total of 31 for the Series, a Series record, which he would soon break. He was voted the Most Valuable Player in the World Series, just ahead of McCarver. After the game, when reporters crowded around Johnny Keane, they asked the manager why he had left Gibson in during the ninth when he was so obviously tiring. Keane answered with one of the nicest things a manager ever said about a baseball player: "I had a commitment to his heart."

1965: Dodgers vs. Twins

Sandy Koufax, Yom Kippur, and Game 7

from *Sandy Koufax: A Lefty's Legacy* by Jane Leavy

When, **on September 9, 1965**, Major League Baseball announced that the World Series would open on October 6 in the American League city, it wasn't at all clear that the Dodgers would be in it. But as they won 18 of their last 22 games, headlines began to appear: "Koufax Problem: Jewish Holiday." Koufax told reporters, lightly, "I'm praying for rain." He also said he would consult the rabbis (as Greenberg had done) to discuss a dispensation. He was joking. He never intended to pitch on Yom Kippur. He never had.

In the early Brooklyn days, management encouraged him to take off on Jewish holidays. It was a demonstration of good faith to their heavily Jewish fan base. And, given how much he was contributing, Koufax later said, "They were probably glad I was gone."

Alan Dershowitz, who knew him as a neighborhood legend, recalls the scene outside one Brooklyn synagogue when Koufax showed up for services with his father. He remembers people cheering and rumors spreading that

Koufax had been called to the Torah. When they met in later life, Koufax told him it never happened.

Twice, in the fall of 1960 and 1961, manager Walter Alston scheduled him to pitch on Jewish holidays. An hour after sundown marks the end of holiday observances in the Jewish faith. On September 20, 1961, after sundown, Koufax went to the mound and beat the Cubs 3–2 in 13 innings, striking out 15. Soon after, a fan sent Alston a 1962 calendar marked with all the Jewish holidays. From then on, the manager made sure to consult Danny Goodman, director of advertising and novelties, before making out his starting rotation.

Far from being distraught over Koufax's willingness to pitch that evening—even if it meant missing afternoon services—Jewish authors of present-day online encomiums salute his toughness. Imagine pitching 13 innings without eating or drinking! His observance of the fast is assumed without a shred of documentary evidence.

Koufax was presumptively devout. Teammates still testify to the strength of his faith. "Like Muhammad Ali's," Lou Johnson said. "His Jewish belief was bigger than the game." How else could they understand his decision not to pitch on Yom Kippur except as a reflection of compelling belief? Why else would anyone voluntarily skip the World Series? Others needled him about getting religion only after he got famous. "I used to jokingly say that Sandy didn't become Jewish until he had his first great years," Stan Williams said.

Their assumptions were rooted in ignorance. In fact, like Greenberg, Koufax was neither a devout nor a practicing Jew. "His Jewishness has nothing to do with whether he wears a yarmulke every day," Fred Wilpon said. "And I will tell you this—he is very Jewish. He is a Jewish being. And unlike most of us who aren't very religious, he is very Jewish in his thinking because he's very New York in his thinking and his background."

It's a sensibility. To wit: One night in Philadelphia, Koufax and the Sherry brothers went out for Chinese food. They got in a cab and told the driver to take them to a good place. Norm Sherry remembers: "The cab pulls up at a restaurant and Koufax says, 'This is not where I want to eat.'" So, the cabbie takes them to another and another and another. "Finally, Koufax says,

'This is okay!' Larry says, 'What the hell is the difference?' Koufax says, 'You don't go to a Chinese restaurant unless it has an awning like they have in New York. It's gotta have an awning.'"

The Jewish boys from southern California didn't get the humor.

He never spoke publicly about religion except to acknowledge his Jewishness, no small fact. After years of traveling with Koufax, Phil Collier could not recall a single conversation on the subject until one day at Los Angeles International Airport when a fan interrupted Koufax at a urinal to ask, "Would you mind settling an argument for me?"

"Sandy said, 'No, I don't mind.'

"The guy waited until we washed up. I swear to God, we walked halfway across the terminal. He introduces us to five or six people. He says to Sandy, 'Are you Jewish? I bet money you're Jewish.'

"I wanted to knock the guy on his ass, dragging him across the airport for that. Sandy couldn't have been nicer about it. He said, 'Yes, I am. It was nice to meet all of you. I hope you'll forgive us. We have a plane to catch.'"

Yom Kippur is a day of denial. It is why Jews fast. In fact, Koufax's sacrifice was greater than his teammates knew. Rabbi Hillel Silverman, who annually invoked Koufax's name in his Yom Kippur sermon, spoke with him about it once. "He said to me, 'I'm Jewish. I'm a role model. I want them to understand they have to have pride.' Not being observant and feeling a connection with his people, it's an even greater sacrifice."

The morning of the opening game of the 1965 World Series, the *St. Paul Pioneer Press* carried the following dispatch:

SANDY NOTES HOLY DAY

Dodger pitcher Sandy Koufax left the team's Hotel St. Paul quarters Tuesday evening to begin the 24 hour observance of Yom Kippur, the Jewish Day of Atonement. He planned to spend the night with friends in suburban Minneapolis, will attend services today and rejoin the team tonight for his starting assignment in Thursday's second game of the world series. He was asked whether he would view today's game on television or listen to radio accounts. "No," he said. "I don't think that's possible."

He was apocryphally seen at synagogues throughout the Twin Cities—and even in Los Angeles. Bonnie Goldstein, now a private investigator in Washington, D.C., was a young congregant at the Temple of Aaron in St. Paul, the synagogue closest to the ballpark. The crowd was strictly standing room only and unusually devout that day in deference to Koufax. "Everyone was in their chairs," she said. "None of the usual restlessness. There was so much speculation. Is that him? People who weren't Sandy Koufax were getting a lot of attention.

"Everyone agrees he was at the early service. Nobody got up and left. I was much more interested in boys than Sandy Koufax. But the boys were more interested in Sandy Koufax so I was a little interested."

The rabbi, Bernard Raskas, waited until afternoon services to address the issue, affirming to the congregation that Koufax had been there, seated in back, near an exit. In Raskas's recollection, they nodded to each other, the rabbi noting the pitcher's nice head of hair. He did not want to infringe on the pitcher's privacy. Nor did he want to make an example of him. After all, Koufax wasn't so observant.

In fact, Koufax did not attend services there that day or anywhere else. A friend may well have made arrangements for Koufax to attend, as Raskas was led to believe. But friends say he chose to stay alone in his hotel room. Raskas could not have seen him unless he was the room service waiter at midnight. Koufax never publicly contradicted the stories. He never commented at all—except for a mild written rebuke, in his autobiography, to Minnesota sports columnist Dan Riley, who wrote that the Twins were looking forward to eating matzo balls when Koufax pitched the next day.

Choosing not to work on Yom Kippur was not a difficult decision. It's what Jews do. His roommate, Tracewski, doesn't remember him agonizing over it. "It was a given with him." So, you pitch a day late. Big schmeer. And, as Osteen said, "It wasn't a real bad choice having Drysdale."

Drysdale started in his place and got hammered. The score was 7–1 when Alston came to the mound to relieve him. "Hey, skip, bet you wish I was Jewish today, too," Drysdale said. For Jews, the loss was a win. If Big D could joke about being one of the Chosen People, that was already something, a tacit acknowledgment of their acceptance into the mainstream. *Shtetl*, farewell.

Koufax started and lost Game 2. The flight back to Los Angeles was difficult, especially for Osteen, who was scheduled to start Game 3. He sat on the aisle and every coach and player walking by made sure to touch his left shoulder. With each reassuring pat and each pat rejoinder—"You'll get 'em!"—his shoulder got tighter. Koufax and Drysdale loosened everyone up with humor. "Don looks at Sandy and goes, 'Well, we sure got ourselves in a hell of a mess, didn't we?'" Jim Lefebvre said. "And they started laughing."

The Dodgers won three straight in Los Angeles—Osteen, Drysdale, and Koufax outdid themselves and each other. In the final home game of the Series, Koufax shut out the Twins, 7–0. After the game, Koufax cheerfully told Scully, "I feel like I'm a hundred years old."

The Dodgers needed only one more win but they needed to go back to Minnesota to get it. They were confident. Lou Johnson packed enough clothes for a one-day business trip. The Dodgers checked out of the team hotel the morning before Game 6 was played. Osteen lost, forcing management to scramble for rooms and Alston to make a difficult decision. Parker, the first baseman, went into the bathroom and cried. Alston summoned his coaches—Preston Gomez, Danny Ozark, Lefty Phillips—to a gloomy tribunal. Drysdale was the logical choice to pitch Game 7. It was his turn in the rotation. He would be pitching on a full three days' rest; Koufax on two.

The players were showering; no one had popped a beer. All three coaches put their heads between their knees when Alston broached the question. Ozark recalled the scene. "'Jeez,' Lefty Phillips says, 'Koufax does real well against them, maybe he can go.' Alston says, 'Who's gonna ask him?' Everyone got laryngitis. Me, the big dumb Polack says, I'll do it.' I find out later on that there were differences between him and Alston. They may have been going back to '57. I don't think he could overlook what happened. It was his career. They held him back."

His teammates knew how he felt. "He felt he always had something to prove with Walter Alston," Ron Perranoski said. "He wasn't used when he was young and when he was used he wasn't trusted. He always had this thing in the back of his mind about the way he was treated, that he didn't get a chance. He knew what he was made of, what he was capable of."

Those feelings endured. In 1985, 30 years after his rookie season, 20 years after his World Series triumph, there was a celebration in Vero Beach. "Buzzie was there and they were telling stories and Buzzie's laughing," Tom Villante recalled. "And then Sandy starts with Buzzie about why the hell didn't Alston pitch me. Buzzie was giving him some double talk but Sandy was getting mad all over again. I'll never forget it. Sandy was transformed into this 19-year-old kid again, puzzled why the hell Alston didn't pitch him."

When Ozark approached him at his locker at Metropolitan Stadium on the eve of the seventh game of the 1965 World Series, Koufax told him, "I'm okay for tomorrow." It would be his third start in eight days. "He didn't want to be known as a person who couldn't have the strength and the ability to take the ball on two days' rest," Wilpon said. He did so eight times in his career, winning six; three were complete-game wins with a combined total of 35 strikeouts. He never lasted less than seven innings. How much, if at all, this represented for him a refutation of stereotype is unknowable. How much it represented a retort to early doubters is easier to guess. But it spoke volumes to the Jewish community.

Alston told Mel Durslag, the Los Angeles writer, it was the hardest decision he ever made as a manager. Drysdale subsequently made it easier by volunteering to go to the bullpen. "He was worried about Drysdale's feelings and afraid of saying something anti-Semitic," Durslag recalled. "He was an uptight guy, not a loose guy. People intimated—he was a farmer from the middle of Ohio—that he might have been anti-Semitic. Maybe he felt if he didn't give it to Koufax, he'd look anti-Semitic."

The heart of bias is as intangible as it is corrosive. When he was interviewed by Charley Steiner for ESPN's *Sports Century* series, Koufax was asked, off camera, whether he believed anti-Semitism played a part in the way he was used early in his career. "I don't even want to think about that," Koufax replied. It violates his code of honor to argue with the dead or the past. He has never addressed the issue publicly and he won't. But as Steiner, now the voice of the Yankees, says, "When he says he hasn't thought about something, you know he's thought about it a lot."

Others have, too. Eddie Liberatore, the late Dodger scout, said before he died in 2001, "One story I don't like to tell, there were certain guys in the organization who referred to him as 'a gutless Jew' because he was wild. When he got control and began to be a big winner, he was probably the most idolized pitcher of this time. They all jumped on his bandwagon, these same critics."

Among his black teammates a degree of bias was presumed. Like Ozark, they noticed who pitched on Opening Day, whose face appeared on yearbooks and press guides and newspapers. "Don was blond and blue-eyed and more marketable as far as being the Dodger image," Wills said. "Sandy was second fiddle. All the black players felt that. Don was the poster boy: It was always Don and Sandy. We knew it was Sandy and Don."

Rumors started flying on the bus on the way back to the hotel. Coaches, rookies, other members of the pitching staff all weighed in. Opinion was unanimous. "You don't have to ask our ballclub, 'Who do you want to see pitch?'" said Gomez. "The whole world is going to say, 'Give the ball to the Jew.'"

Wills: "We might not have gone on the field if he hadn't."

Koufax and Drysdale arrived at the ballpark the next morning unshaved—a signal that neither knew the skipper's decision. In fact, it was a ruse. Koufax knew but wasn't supposed to tell anyone, not even his roommate, Trixie. Alston announced his decision at a team meeting before the game, explaining with soothing if impersonal logic why he had chosen Koufax. "He says, 'We're going to start the left-hander,'" Tracewski remembered. "'After that we have Drysdale in the bullpen and if we need it we'll finish off with Perranoski. And if that's not good enough, we are in trouble.'

"It was a very quiet meeting and it was a very quick meeting and Sandy said, 'He called me the left-hander,'" Tracewski said. "He felt he should have called him by his name."

Watching the videotape of the seventh game of the 1965 World Series is like looking at a piece of American folk art. There is an innocence about the broadcast as primitive as the production values. There were marching bands and decorous cheerleaders, skinny ties and vendors selling straw boaters to polite Minnesota fans. "Not a smokestack crowd," as infielder Frank Quilici described them. "Nice." The Twins' front office sat Dodger wives behind home plate. In Los Angeles, the Twins' wives were given seats way out in right field. Between innings, go-go dancers did a decorous frug; and Gillette hawked a new super stainless-steel blade with Miracle Edges to a clean-shaven nation. Harry Coyle, the director, had only a couple of cameras to work with, and a batboy who kept wandering into the frame. The narration is uncluttered and understated, so quiet you can hear the sound of an airplane buzzing the outfield. On the pregame show, Vin Scully and Ray Scott talked about the pitching matchup: Sandy Koufax and Jim Kaat for the third time. No one mentioned Yom Kippur. Today, ESPN would be doing man-on-the-street interviews at the Wailing Wall.

The broadcast is a staple of *Classic Sports* television. Sam Mele, the Twins' manager, has seen it nine, maybe ten times. "Lost every goddamn game," he says. He, too, remembers the quiet. "They normally weren't that quiet," Mele said. "I think everybody could sense—even my bench and me— that it's Koufax out there. You know what I mean? You can't get too excited because this guy's going to knock the jubilance out of you, you know?"

That morning a thunderstorm of biblical proportions inundated the Twin Cities. Helicopters were brought in to dry the field. By game time, the skies had cleared. Temperatures were in the fifties. Osteen, who had lost Game 6, went down to the bullpen to see if he could help out, standing in an imaginary batter's box so that Koufax would have someone to throw to. Osteen had never seen his curve from that vantage point before. He remembers thinking, So that's why they can't hit it.

As they walked in from the bullpen, Koufax stopped to say hello to Joe Nossek, the Twins' rookie outfielder, playing in his first World Series. Nossek thought, "Cloud number nine just got a little more elevated." Neither Nossek nor Osteen had any intimation of how much of himself Koufax had left in the bullpen. Though they might have gotten a scent of it, as Kaat had before Game 1, when the opposing pitchers met on the field for the ritual pregame handshake. Kaat's eyes began to water, then tear, then burn. Kaat fled as soon as baseball etiquette allowed, driven away by the smell of Capsolin. "It was like walking into a steam room with camphor," he said.

Koufax was pitching on fumes. When he walked two batters in the first inning, Drysdale got up in the bullpen. He was a two-pitch pitcher without a second pitch. Roseboro kept calling for the curve; Koufax kept shaking him off. Finally, Roseboro went to the mound for a conversation. For the first time, Koufax acknowledged how bad his elbow was. "He said, 'Rosie, my arm's not right. My arm's sore.' I said, 'What'll we do, kid?' He said, 'Fuck it, we'll blow 'em away.'"

The game was scoreless when Johnson came to bat in the fourth inning. He had called his mother before the game, vowing, "I'm going to do something today, Ma. I told Sandy I was gonna get him a run."

He kept his promise, hitting Kaat's fastball long and deep to left field. It was curving foul when the foul pole got in its way. Home run! Johnson applauded as he rounded the bases. The rest of the stadium was so quiet Tracewski could hear Johnson's footsteps as he came around third. "So quiet," Johnson said, "you could hear a cat pissing on cotton."

The crowd remained nicely catatonic until the bottom of the fifth. Quilici, the Twins' second baseman, doubled, and the next batter walked. With one out, Zoilo Versailles hit a ball hard down the third-base line. It was past Junior Gilliam when he realized it was in his glove. Somehow he beat Quilici to the bag. In the press box, the game was officially declared over.

The afternoon sun waned. Koufax pitched from the shadows. His royal blue sweatshirt appeared navy; his beard darkened inning by inning. His mouth hung open after every pitch. Drysdale got up in the bullpen again. Scully wondered aloud how far a man could go with only one pitch. "Everybody sat there with their mouths open," Ozark said. "He pitched like it was going to be his last breath."

In the ninth inning, the 360th of his season, Koufax faced the heart of the Minnesota order: Tony Oliva, Harmon Killebrew, Earl Battey, and Bob Allison, a two-time batting champion, a six-time home-run leader, a four-time All-Star, and a one-time Rookie of the Year. With one out, Killebrew singled sharply to left, the Twins' third hit of the game. Battey came to the plate. One swing, he thought, and I could be the World Series MVP! By the time the words formed a sentence in his brain, the umpire had signaled, "Strike three."

Up to the plate strode Allison, a formidable slugger whose two-run home run off Osteen had forced the seventh game. He fouled off the first pitch and looked at two others for balls and then swung at the next. "It's two and two," announcer Ray Scott informed the television audience. "Koufax is reaching back. Every time he's had to reach back, he's found what he needed."

Killebrew watched from first base as Allison swung through strike three for the final out of the series. "I told Bob, 'If you'd have swung at the ball as hard as you swung at the ground after you struck out, you might have hit it.'"

The orderly Minnesota fans exited Metropolitan Stadium, taking all the air with them. The scoreboard congratulated them for being the best fans in the world. The Dodgers were almost as low-key. Parker, the young first baseman, wasn't sure what to do with himself. "I'd been dreaming about this my whole life. I was ready to go nuts. I'm running toward the mound and there's no noise. I'm wondering if someone called time. But no, the Minnesota fans were filing out. I looked at Sandy. Sandy wasn't doing anything. He didn't pump a fist or jump in the air. He was just walking toward Roseboro."

It was his second shutout in four days, his 29th complete game of the season. The locker room was joyously subdued, partly because a phalanx of sportswriters had gotten stuck between floors in the press elevator and partly because everyone was so drained. Scully wrapped an arm protectively around

Koufax, the bright light of live television highlighting his fatigue. "Here's the fella who gave the Dodgers the championship. Sandy, in Los Angeles, when you pitched a seven-nothing shutout, you were quoted as saying, 'I feel like I'm a hundred years old.' So today, Sandy, how do you feel?'"

Koufax was too tired to do anything but smile and tell the truth. Viewers at home saw a grin so wide his dimples threatened to implode. "Well, Vinnie, I feel like I'm a hundred and one. I'm just glad it's over and I don't have to do this again for four whole months."

Time devoted a page in its next issue to baseball, a cut-and-paste story cobbled together from Series coverage, recycled quotes, and McWhirter's unused file. The tone was decidedly "cool"—grudgingly appreciative at best. It got right to the point: "Just because a man does his job better than anybody else doesn't mean that he has to take it seriously—or even like it."

And it continued:

> Alone among ballplayers, Koufax is an anti-athlete who suffers so little from pride that he does not even possess a photograph of himself. TV and radio interviewers have learned to be careful with personal questions—or risk a string of billingsgate designed to ruin their tapes. . . .

> To his teammates, even to his few close friends, Koufax's aloofness is often downright annoying. "Imagine," says Dodger catcher John Roseboro, "being good-looking, well-off, single—and still be so cool. I know guys who would be raising all kinds of hell on those stakes." Dodger vice president Fresco Thompson considers him a heretic. "I don't think he likes baseball," mutters Thompson. "What kind of a line is he drawing anyway—between himself and the world, between himself and the team?"

In the fall of 1965, you'd have to have been decidedly square to miss Roseboro's meaning. Cool as in hip. What had been intended as a compliment was construed as evidence of a "taciturn" personality. What Koufax had said to Scully in a moment of utter depletion was interpreted as further evidence of his dislike for baseball. In the great American fiction known as the World of Sports, Our Hero is a selfless, square-jawed exemplar of uncommon grace and modesty, who always plays for the Love of the Game, no matter how much he earns. Thus, to say he doesn't love it is to deny him the status of Our Hero. To label Koufax as an "anti-athlete" was to damn him forever for being different. It is what author Roger Kahn calls "a genteel form of anti-Semitism."

After the series, Ed Linn, newly hired as the ghostwriter for Koufax's proposed autobiography, went to Hawaii to meet him. Koufax was staying by himself on the beach on a remote part of the Big Island. Bill Hayes, Koufax's lawyer and business manager, gave Linn explicit directions: "You will pass two dirt roads very close together, a little variety store in between. You take the second dirt road; if you pass it and miss it, you'll never find it. Go to the end. There will be a link fence. There's a door that will be open. Sandy's there. He will be in a beach house."

"I found it without any difficulty. I get to this fence. There's no open door. There's a chain lock. There's a half-dozen workmen. I say, 'Have you seen Sandy Koufax?'

"One said, 'You talking about Sandy Koufax, the ballplayer? Boy, are you lost. He's three thousand miles away.' Just at that moment, out of this little shack comes Koufax in bathing trunks. I said to the guy, 'No, he's maybe 50 yards that way.'"

After Linn climbed the fence and they began to talk, he learned how hurtful the *Time* magazine story was, particularly the perception of aloofness for a man who was a consummate team player. So when he sat down to write, Linn composed an impassioned 14-page protest, in Koufax's voice, aimed at the editors of *Time* magazine and all other reductionist thinkers.

I have nothing against myths. But there is one myth that has been building through the years that I would just as soon bury without any particular honors: the myth of Sandy Koufax, the anti-athlete. The way this fantasy goes, I am really a sort of dreamy intellectual who was lured out of college by a bonus in the flush of my youth and have forever after regretted—and even resented—the life of fame and fortune that has been forced upon me.

Mordecai Richler reviewed the book in the November 1966 issue of *Commentary* magazine. The fact of the review by the distinguished Jewish author in the distinguished journal of Jewish thought was testament to Koufax's standing among his people, especially the literary intelligentsia. The review was scathing, damning the effort as a "very bush-league performance, thin, cliché-ridden." In short, a typical ghostwritten sports autobiography. (Had Richler read more closely, he might have heard an authentic voice in the opening cri de coeur.)

Getting to the heart of the matter, Richler wrote: "Anti-Semitism takes many subtle shapes and the deprecating story one reads again and again, most memorably recorded in *Time*, is that Sandy Koufax is actually something of an intellectual. He doesn't mix. Though he is the highest paid player in the history of the game, improving enormously on Lipman E. Pike's $20 a week, he considers himself above it."

Then he goes further: "In fact, looked at one way, Koufax's autobiography can be seen as a sad effort at self-vindication, a forced attempt to prove once and for all that he is the same as anybody else. Possibly, Koufax protests too much." In denying his putative intellectualism, Richler seemed to be saying, Koufax was denying an essential part of his Jewishness. Which no doubt accounted for the deluge of letters to *Commentary*'s editors accusing Richler of being anti-Semitic.

Having held himself to a higher standard, Koufax was then impaled upon it. To wit: The Minnesota rabbi, who still insists that Koufax was in his synagogue, said nothing at the time because he wasn't too thrilled with Koufax's lack of piety. "That's why I couldn't build him up," Raskas said. "He's not such a good Jew because he didn't marry a Jewish girl. So I don't get too excited about it."

The significance of Koufax's decision has been debated ever since in synagogues and at dinner tables, by Talmudic scholars and baseball players.

How much did he change the way Jews are perceived? How much did he change the way Jews perceive themselves? "He gave little Jewish boys some hope," said pitcher Steve Stone, who was one of them. "The Series went seven games instead of four," said general manager Buzzie Bavasi. "I always told him, 'You made Walter O'Malley a million dollars.'"

Four decades after the fact, two best-selling Jewish authors, Scott Turow and Mitch Albom, engaged in a heated polemic about the significance of a ham sandwich Koufax allegedly was seen eating in the hotel elevator in Minnesota that week. Albom's friend, a rabbi's son still a young man in 1965, was apparently still devastated at having seen pork touch Koufax's pitching hand. Turow responded indignantly: "Who's to say what is Jewish enough? Who's to say what a Jew is?" Except that Jew himself.

Peter Levine, author of *Ellis Island to Ebbets Field: Sports and the American Jewish Experience*, argues that Koufax's symbolic potency was attenuated by world events. Who needs Koufax when you have Henry Kissinger playing realpolitik? "However tough and strong a pitcher Koufax was," Levine wrote, "he clearly was no match for Moishe Dayan and his legions of commandos when it came time to search for heroes and deeds symbolic of the contemporary Jewish experience—far more relevant than anything Koufax offered."

Rabbi Lustig, who as a boy wired a transistor radio to his seven-year-old person and took the World Series into the synagogue, understands why Koufax is hardwired into the psyche of the American Jewish community and his congregation—why grown men are transformed by putting on Koufax's jersey. The decision not to pitch was a transforming event, providing the catalyst for an unknown number of lawyers and Little Leaguers to acknowledge and honor their religion in like kind. Koufax made them brave. By refusing to pitch, he both reinforced Jewish pride and enhanced the sense of belonging—a feat as prodigious as any he accomplished on the field.

"The Six-Day War was important to Zionism," Lustig said. "It changed the image of the Jew in the world. He could be a true soldier. The World Series was important to the whole community. What could be so American?

We had finally made it. We had earned the right to be as interested in baseball as in our Jewish identity."

The discussion and debate proceed without any comment from him. Some have attributed his silence to modesty; others to the realization that nothing he could say would improve upon what he did. But this too is true. It's embarrassing being a religious icon, especially an inadvertent one. Later, friends say, he would become a reader of Holocaust literature and quit driving German cars. He came to appreciate the significance his decision had for others. After the old lady at Herbie Scharfman's funeral finally let go of Koufax's right arm, Tom Villante said to him, "You know, Sandy, in my lifetime there's three guys I've known who have transcended their sports and become a symbol for their race or nationality: Jackie with the blacks, Joe D. with the Italians, and you with the Jews."

"He said, 'I know it.' And he said it as if he knew it and accepted it. This is something he carries around with him. And he is very proud of it."

Koufax refused to be a Jew's Jew or a gentile's Jew. He may have been different but he refused to be anything other than himself. In the Talmud, it is written that some attain eternal life with a single act. On Yom Kippur, 5726, a baseball immortal became a Jewish icon.

1969: Mets vs. Orioles

The Miracle Mets

from *The New York Mets: The Whole Story* by Leonard Koppett

Can a World Series be an anticlimax?

Sure. And it often has been. Who remembers that the Giants lost the World Series to the Yankees after Bobby Thomson's home run had given them the pennant? Who cares that the Dodgers, after inflaming Brooklyn's chauvinism to unprecedented heights by winning their first pennant in 21 years under Leo Durocher in 1941, went on to lose the World Series in five games? Who in New England, wallowing in memories of the 1967 Red Sox and their last-day victory, dwells on the World Series then lost to the Cardinals? And even when the end result is a victory in the Series, what Yankee fan recalling the glorious finish of 1949 (Stengel's first year), in which the Red Sox were beaten on the final two days, goes on to gloat about another routine five-game Series with the Dodgers?

But a World Series can also be the most exciting, most memorable feature of an entire season. In Pittsburgh, they talk about Mazeroski's home run in the seventh game against the Yankees in 1960, not about the long stretch drive to that pennant; in Los Angeles, they still thrill to the way Koufax and Drysdale stifled the mighty Yankees in a four-game sweep in 1963, ignoring the race that preceded that; and . . . in 1968, a dramatic seven-game Series in which the Tigers beat the Cardinals redeemed two runaway pennant races.

It took the Mets, however, to produce a World Series that was anticlimactic and the supreme thrill, both at the same time.

There were two senses in which the 1969 World Series was an anticlimax for the Mets. One was peculiar to them. So much had already happened that one's reactivity was numbed; the overwhelming significance of their rise from the bottom to the top could not be obliterated by any World Series event: It had been achieved by the winning of the pennant, and nothing could ever change that. The other sense was one that most teams share: both in terms of money and in professional pride, the big thing about the World Series is reaching it. It takes a full season to win a pennant (and now it took a playoff besides); but "anything can happen in a short series," and players know this better than anyone. When you win a pennant you prove yourself the best team, by definition, because good luck and bad luck are supposed to cancel out over 162 games; but a seven-game series is too subject to the fortunes of a particular bounce to prove anything. Financially, the big jump is between getting in and not getting in. The loser's share in the Series is still substantial money; the winner gets a few thousand more, but the loser has still had a good year. But the difference between finishing second (in the past) or losing the playoff (now) and even the loser's share in the Series is more meaningful.

So the Mets approached the Series with at least some feeling that nothing mattered that much any more, now that the pennant had been won. They were entertained privately at Governor Rockefeller's Fifth Avenue apartment, besieged by agents and offers of money, publicly adored to the highest degree. They had made it.

On the other hand, there was the artistic side: If the Mets lost the Series, the future memories in themselves and their followers would of necessity revert to the season itself—but there would be a flaw. Having come so far, the compulsion to go to the summit was very great. In the long run, their pennant achievement could not be dimmed; but at the moment, defeat and disappointment could be felt deeply. In a perverse way, winning the World Series became all-important, to cap what could now be a perfect year.

In a way, and on a much more rarefied level, this was a repetition of the rooting situation Met fans had developed for themselves in the early years, the one-way-vision sort of rooting. It was impossible to be really hurt by defeat—then, because defeat was inevitable anyhow; now, because so much had been won already; but it was distinctly possible to be whipped into ecstasy by victory—then, because it was so rare; now, because it would be the ultimate one. That old observation about the Polo Grounds' faithful—"They get their money's worth anytime the Mets score, and it's as if the other team's turn at bat simply didn't exist"—applied now on a broader scale.

In short, the Series could be shrugged off as an anticlimax if they lost, yet hailed as the greatest triumph in baseball history if they won. One couldn't ask for a more enviable position.

The events of September had educated the entire country in the mystical quality of Met victories. All the key incidents of their march to the pennant—winning a game in which 19 Mets struck out, sweeping two 1–0 games in Pittsburgh, the Marichal game with the four-man outfield, the lucky bounces, the timely hits by .213 hitters, the way the hitters overcame the pitchers' semicollapse in the playoff with Atlanta—were cited as proof that gremlins, or God, or Destiny, or something was seeing to it that the Mets won. The Orioles, who had left their own league far behind and had whipped Minnesota in three straight games in their playoff, were subjected to a full dose of such half-joking comment. Baltimore was a big favorite to win the Series, and legitimately so: Its regular lineup was being hailed as one of the "strongest ever," and its pitching had been dominant beyond the individual reputation of its starters. Yet, at every turn, someone came to Manager Earl Weaver, or a player, with another story about how some unlikely circumstance had produced a Met victory. No more imaginative than most baseball people, and no less self-centered, the Orioles took such talk to be threatening rather than amusing. To them, it had a sacrilegious tinge, an implication that fate was supposed to be against Baltimore; and it carried a vague suggestion that their skills, of which they were so proud, were being demeaned by the idea that some supernatural force would be the deciding factor, not those skills.

So when the Orioles had won the third game in Minnesota, and wrapped up their pennant, Frank Robinson's remark summed up their attitude:

"Bring on Ron Gaspar."

"Not Ron—Rod, stupid!"

"OK, bring on Rod Stupid."

Robinson, a prospective big-league manager himself, who had managed a team in Puerto Rico over the winter, knew perfectly well who Rod Gaspar was, as he knew all his opponents. The point he was making was simply that the Orioles were great, famous, and intimidating, whereas the Mets were young nobodies who might have won a National League pennant but hadn't proved anything yet to the American League.

And much of the country felt the same way. If black magic was an element in Met success, surely it lost its potency when the National League race ended.

The Oriole lineup would certainly test Met starters, who hadn't seemed so overpowering against Atlanta. Don Buford, Paul Blair, Frank Robinson, Boog Powell, and Brooks Robinson, the first five batters, were undoubtedly the most effective run-making unit in baseball. Dave Johnson, the second baseman, could hold his own. When Elrod Hendricks caught (against righties), another dangerous hitter was in the lineup; Andy Etchebarren, the catcher against lefties, was less feared. Mark Belanger, the superb shortstop, had always been considered a weak hitter, to be carried only because of his defense—until, in 1969, he had suddenly produced a .289 batting average and had batted in 50 runs.

And Baltimore pitching, the Orioles felt, could match anyone's, no matter what they said about Seaver and Koosman. Cuellar, obtained from Houston over the winter, had won 23 games (and would eventually be chosen the American League's outstanding pitcher); Dave McNally, who had pitched a shutout in the final game of the 1966 World Series and pitched an 11-inning 1–0 victory in the second playoff game against the Twins, had won his first 15 games during the season. Both were left-handed, which meant they would face the potentially less-dangerous, right-handed platoon of the Mets; all the slugging against Atlanta had been done by the lefty platoon, which included Shamsky, Kranepool, and Boswell (although Grote caught no matter who pitched). And for a third starter, the Orioles had Jim Palmer, restored to health, a fireballer who had shut out Sandy Koufax in the 1966 World Series and who had pitched a no-hitter less than two months ago. Behind them the Baltimore bullpen was well stocked. In fact, the earned-run average of the Baltimore staff, 2.87, was actually better than the 2.99 the Mets had.

Finally, the relatively long layoff fed the idea that natural forces would reassert themselves in the World Series. Because both playoffs had lasted only three games, they had ended on Monday; the Series would not start until Saturday, October 11. At this stage of a competition, four days was a long time to go without a real game.

On Wednesday, the Mets were supposed to work out at Shea Stadium, but it rained. So they worked out Thursday and went straight to the airport, where Mayor Lindsay was present for a send-off ceremony which included a piece of doggerel he read proudly. The charter flight took off an hour late, and the hotel in Baltimore turned out to be totally unequipped (in terms of telephone switchboard and room service) for a World Series crowd. Well, that was the rule rather than the exception at every "Fall Classic." In undergoing their particular inconveniences Friday night, the Mets were having their first true World Series experience.

On Friday, when both teams worked out at Memorial Stadium (and the Orioles, in uniform, were paraded in open cars through downtown Baltimore), a political story broke. It was reported that Seaver had announced he would take an ad in the *New York Times* if the Mets won the Series, saying "If the Mets can win the World Series, the United States can get out of Vietnam." This was five days before the antiwar Moratorium, originally planned for college campuses but now a national issue, and Seaver's position as the supremely successful young American was of interest to all sides. Just what the logic of such a message might be he wasn't quite clear, but its anti-Vietnam flavor was plain enough, and it stirred a storm within the fundamentally conservative, jingoistic baseball community. A day later Seaver put the matter in a different perspective: Yes, he had been approached by someone connected with the Kennedys about giving his support to such an ad, and he was considering it; and yes, he had strong feelings about the war; but he considered these his private business and did not want to be "used" as a baseball celebrity for any external purpose. The thing that concerned him today was trying to win the World Series first. If that happened and if it encouraged people to think, "If this is possible, anything is possible," well and good. But it hadn't happened yet.

And the next day, a glorious October Saturday with warm sunshine, it didn't seem that it would happen.

The first pitch Seaver threw was hit by Don Buford over the right-field fence, over an imperfectly timed leap by Swoboda whose back hit the canvas barrier.

Cuellar held the Mets to two hits for the first four innings, and with two out in the Baltimore fourth, Hendricks singled through the right side, and Seaver was suddenly in trouble. He couldn't seem to get the ball where he wanted it and walked Johnson. Belanger lined a single through the right side, and it was 2–0. Cuellar looped a single to center, and it was 3–0. Buford hit a line drive double on one bounce against the right-field wall, and it was 4–0.

And that was plenty. Cuellar did give up a run on a couple of singles, a walk, and Weis's fly in the seventh, and with two on and two out, the Mets "brought on" Rod Gaspar. He tapped weakly toward third, and Brooks Robinson, racing in and making a bare-handed scoop, threw him out on a magnificent play.

In the ninth, with two on and two out, the Mets got the tying run to bat in the person of Shamsky. If the fates, or whatever, were still at work, this was the spot for a homer. But Shamsky bounced to Johnson, and Baltimore had won the first game, 4–1.

Orthodoxy heaved a sigh of relief.

Koosman and McNally, on another beautiful day, were backed up by spectacular fielding plays (Belanger, Harrelson, Brooks Robinson) in the early innings Sunday. Then Clendenon led off the fourth with a curving drive sliced over the right-field fence, just about where Buford had hit his homer the day before. It was the first postseason run off McNally in 24 innings—and the only run in the game as Koosman went into the seventh inning with a no-hitter going.

But Blair spoiled that with a clean hit through the left side opening the inning, and with two out he stole second. Brooks Robinson promptly singled through the box, and it was 1–1.

When McNally got the first two Mets out in the ninth, he was pitching a three-hitter. But Charles succeeded in bouncing a single past Brooks Robinson and made it to third on a hit-and-run play as Grote grounded a single past Belanger. Weis promptly lined a single to left on the next pitch, and Koosman had a 2–1 lead, with the head of the Baltimore batting order up in the ninth.

He made Buford pop up and Blair ground out, and Hodges ordered his four-man outfield again, to keep Frank Robinson from getting an extra base hit. Robinson didn't but in an unexpected way: He walked on a full count—and so did Powell. So Hodges brought in Taylor, who fell behind to Brooks Robinson, three balls and one strike. However, Brooks fouled off the next pitch and then bounced to Charles, who started to tag third, saw the runner had him beaten, and threw to first, where Clendenon dug the ball out of the dirt.

The Mets had won, 2–1—on a hit by Weis. Maybe the gremlins weren't dead yet.

There was no game Monday, the "travel" day of every World Series between the second and third game, and it was a cloudy but mild Tuesday when play resumed at Shea Stadium. The Mets were still underdogs, using their rookie, Gentry, against the reinvigorated Palmer, which meant New York's lefty platoon could go to work, its first game in eight days.

Agee, the double-platoon man, greeted Palmer with a home run.

With two out in the second, Palmer walked Grote, and Harrelson singled. Whereupon Gentry lined one between the fielders in right center (really over Blair's head) for a two-run double, and the Mets had a 3–0 lead.

And Gentry didn't even give up a hit until Frank Robinson singled with one out in the fourth. Powell's single sent him to third, Brooks struck out—and Hendricks belted a curving drive, high and deep to left center, sure to produce two runs.

Agee, throwing his gloved hand across his body, reached up and caught the ball, running at a fast but controlled speed, just as he hit the fence. The white of the ball was plainly visible in the top of the webbing of his glove—but he held it.

Believe?

Grote's double made it 4–0 in the sixth, and in the seventh, after two long flies to Agee, Gentry walked three men in a row, bringing up Blair as the tying run. Hodges brought in Ryan, who had relieved Gentry so spectacularly in the third playoff game, and it worked again—but not on a strikeout. Blair hit a long, curving drive to right center; Agee ran as far as he could, lunged as he reached the running track, slid on one knee, and got his glove under the ball inches off the ground.

("The second one was easier for me," he actually said later, "because it was on my glove side.")

Even the Mets found that one hard to believe.

In the eighth, Kranepool hit a home run—a home run unsurpassed for personal satisfaction and symbolic vindication. With a 5–0 lead, Ryan let the bases get filled in the ninth on two walks and a scratch hit, but he threw a called third strike past Blair.

The Mets were leading in the World Series, 2 games to 1.

Wednesday was Moratorium Day, and Seaver's turn to pitch, and there were people giving out mimeographed handouts all around the ballpark, but nothing really impinged on the sports drama now: A six-month saga was entering its last couple of hardly credible pages.

Seaver pitched eight scoreless innings, aided by two great stops by Clendenon (one that killed a potential Baltimore rally in the third, when with two on and none out and the Mets playing in for a bunt, Buford swung and hit a one-hop liner that Clendenon speared like a hockey goalie). And he nursed a 1–0 lead from the second inning on, thanks to Clendenon's homer off Cuellar.

With one out in the ninth, Frank Robinson singled to left, Powell singled to right, and the tying run was on third.

Brooks Robinson lined a sure hit to right center.

Swoboda thundered into the gap. He dove, full length, gloved hand outstretched—and caught the ball, just as his face smacked the ground hard.

Frank Robinson tagged up and scored, but it was only tied, and when Swoboda caught Hendricks's fly after almost overrunning it, it remained a tie.

Believe? Believe?

The Mets got two on in the ninth, but Shamsky, pinch-hitting, couldn't end the game. An error by Garrett helped Baltimore put two on in the 10th, but Seaver ended the threat by striking out Blair.

By now, Coach Billy Hunter was running the Orioles, because Weaver had been chased by umpire Shag Crawford in the third inning for protesting a pitch. It was Hunter who had to make the decisions in what followed.

Grote led off the 10th with an ordinary high fly to medium short left.

Buford, blinded by the sun, or gremlins, or something, never broke in.

Belanger raced out. Blair came from center. Buford, finally, started to race in. None reached it. Grote reached second, with a double.

And the Mets had reached the threshold of ultimate victory: From this point on, it was all in their hands to achieve.

This little fly ball was Turning Point No. 9. The Mets could still lose, but only if they beat themselves, if they failed to carry out the normal things now expected of them. If Blair had caught it, Seaver was probably through pitching anyhow; even if he stayed in, he would be less and less effective as extra innings mounted. But now the Mets had a chance to win this game, right here, and that would give them a 3–1 grip on the Series with Koosman ready to pitch and Seaver available for a seventh game if it came to that.

And wherefore were these 1969 Mets different from all other Mets? In that they cashed in on their opportunities and did not beat themselves.

Gaspar ran for Grote. Harrelson was purposely passed. Martin batted for Seaver. Pete Richert, a left-hander, came in to pitch: all standard moves. And Martin would have to bunt, also a standard move.

He did. Hendricks was a little slow starting after the ball. Richert reached it first. He fired toward first—too close to the runner. The ball hit Martin's left wrist and ricocheted into short right field. Gaspar, who had stopped safely at third, ran home and jumped on the plate. The Mets spilled out of the dugout and pounded him, and Martin (whose wrist hurt), and Seaver (who had led the charge). The stands were in turmoil. The Orioles were bewildered.

The threshold of Paradise had been reached. Believe?

(Richert for one, had doubts. Without making an issue of it, he wondered if Martin had run outside the foul line, as he was supposed to, so that he wouldn't interfere with a throw to first. Photographs that evening showed that Martin had, indeed, run well in fair territory when hit by the ball; he should have been declared out, and there was an 18-hour cause célèbre requiring a public statement by Crawford, the umpire, the next morning. In his judgment, Crawford said, Martin had touched the foul line with his right foot, and that was good enough for him; it was a judgment call; and, of course, it was—but a good thing for the Mets that Crawford's judgment ran that way.)

Anyone with the slightest faith in inevitability had to doubt that the Series would ever return to Baltimore.

Game No. 5, on Thursday, October 16, was played on a cold, cloudy day. If the Orioles won it, the next game would be in Baltimore Saturday. If the Mets won it, the perfect ending would take place in the presence of the Met fans (or at least that small portion that could crack the World Series ticket barrier), poetic justice of the highest order—and the fans could repeat their field-destroying act, invented so spontaneously on September 24 and repeated so callously after the Atlanta series.

The day started badly for New York. McNally walked two Mets in the first inning, but Swoboda left them on base, striking out. Belanger singled, and McNally, instead of bunting, hit a home run off Koosman in the second. Two outs later, Frank Robinson hit one out of sight ("over a building," as Stengel liked to say), and the Orioles had a 3–0 lead.

And, if you thought about it rationally, what would be so unlikely about the Orioles winning two games at home if they won this one?

In the sixth inning, one of Koosman's pitches hit Frank Robinson on the thigh. (It did; pictures proved that, later.) But umpire Lou DiMuro ruled it hit his bat first. There was a long argument, Robinson disappeared for repairs, came back, took a third strike. Powell singled, Brooks Robinson flied out. The umpire's mistake had prevented a threatening inning from getting started.

The first Met batter in the sixth was Jones. A pitch by McNally hit him on the foot. Again, DiMuro didn't believe it—but now Hodges produced the ball, which had bounced into the dugout, with a smudge of shoe polish on it. DiMuro was convinced ("The ball never left my sight so I knew it was the same one," he said afterwards). Jones was allowed to take first base.

Opportunity, right?

Right. Clendenon hit a home run, his third of the series, and the Mets were in business, trailing only 3–2.

The first Met batter in the seventh was Al Weis.

He hit a home run.

Honest.

It didn't clear the left-field fence by much, but it did clear it. Score tied, 3–3.

Al Weis, whose only two previous homers that season had burned the Cubs so badly in July, had saved his last shot for the best time. Al Weis, who had come to spring training with extra muscles. The glove man, the utility man, the silent one, the one who had made that incredible play in the 15th inning in June, the one who had wrecked his knee while wrecking Frank

Robinson's vision, the "useful" player Hodges had liked from his American League days. The man who "could help you in a lot of little ways."

But with a World Series homer?

Now do you believe?

Koosman believed. Brought even, he would give up his life easier than another run. He would hang on somehow until the Mets scored again.

They needed only one inning. Ed Watt, a right-hander, was the pitcher now. Jones led off the eighth with a blast that just missed clearing the fence at the 395-foot mark in left center. It bounced back in for a double.

Clendenon bounced softly to Robinson at third, and Jones took third.

Swoboda ("He may be the first true Met hero," they said back in 1965) ripped a sharp line drive, right down the left-field line. Buford raced over. He didn't dive; he backhanded the ball on a short hop. Swoboda had a double.

And the Mets had a 4–3 lead.

And the rumbling crescendo was beginning in the stands, in the streets, in offices, in homes, wherever a television set or a radio could be tuned in.

The Orioles messed up a bouncer wide of first, and Swoboda scored. It was 5–3. Koosman even had an extra run to work with. Three outs to go.

Frank Robinson walks, and Koosman is mad at himself for committing a pitching sin. Now a home run can tie it, and Powell certainly is the man who can hit one. But Koosman makes him hit on the ground, to Weis, who forces Robinson at second. No chance for a double play. One out.

Brooks Robinson hits a fly to right field. Swoboda is under it. (This used to be considered a Met adventure: Swoboda under a fly ball.) He catches it. Two out.

Johnson up. A fly ball to left, fairly deep. Cleon is under it. He waits. He catches it and holds it there, motionless for a second or two, almost down on one knee.

Then he races, faster than he ever did on a football field, with his friend Agee, for the bullpen gate, to escape the onrushing crowd.

And so, at 3:14 p.m., Eastern Daylight Time, October 16, 1969 A.D., at 40 degrees 45 minutes North Latitude, 73 degrees 50 minutes West

Longitude, on the third planet of a solar system in the spiral arm of one of uncounted billions of galaxies, the New York Mets became baseball champions of the whole expanding universe.

At least, so far as we can tell.

The clubhouse celebration was properly hysterical. The fans tore up the field. A cascade of torn paper hit downtown Manhattan like a tidal wave. Someone's joy erupted in every corner of the country and in some places overseas.

Mrs. Payson cried. Casey Stengel hugged Gil Hodges. Joan Hodges and Joe Pignatano worried as they tried to keep the crowd around Gil within bounds, and as they tried to get him home before it went on too long. George Weiss, a trifle embarrassed but thrilled to his marrow, wandered around the clubhouse with Grant and the other Directors. Murphy, as always, showed on the outside only a small fraction of what he felt inside. Dick Young and Jack Lang, whatever they felt, hustled harder than ever, with so much to be written. The "young writers," who had always taken the Met Mystique and the Met players to their hearts, moved as if they belonged in the general congratulatory haze. Kiner, Nelson, and Murphy, who had seen every bit of it, were as talked out as the fan with the multiple signs, who had held up the one that read: "There Are No Words."

And, of course, there weren't. When you come right down to it, myths aren't told, they are felt. In the intricate mythology that America had created around baseball, fashioning it so lovingly for more than a century, the Mets had produced a submyth of transcendent power. A cascade of interpretation inundated their victory: They represented the power of faith, love, the common man, the underdog uplifted, democracy in action; they had unified the soul of a city rent by dissension, had justified America, glorified sport, ennobled youth, deified the team spirit, enriched the quality of life, redeemed mankind—whatever the particular editorialist decided to extol was attributed freely to the Mets. Perhaps the one great contribution a mass-amusement athletic team can make to a culture is to turn itself into such a lightning rod for the ambient idealism adrift in the system.

What the Mets had really done, of course, was merely win a flock of ballgames, within a period of exactly two months. They won because they had real, prosaic assets—two pitchers like Seaver and Koosman, a manager like Hodges who could instill and maintain a winning attitude, talented players like Jones and Agee, an essential pickup like Clendenon and a fine mix of gifted young players and less-gifted experienced men—and because, like many teams before them, they "got hot." Their organization had built its club, painstakingly, with this in mind—but it was as astonished as anyone that it all came to fruition between August 17 and October 16, 1969.

Stengel, as always, put it concisely and inimitably:

"They came slow, but fast."

The celebrations went on. A ticker-tape parade (like those for Lindbergh, the astronauts, military heroes) was held on Monday; a reception at Mayor Lindsay's residence (Gracie Mansion) that evening; a party here, a personal appearance there; a trip to Las Vegas for seven of them, to do an act with Phil Foster; a tour of Vietnam hospitals for Ed Charles and Ron Swoboda, at some sacrifice of personal earning power; a good rest for Hodges; a spate of books, articles, interviews, television shows, recording sessions, business offers, family conferences.

It would take a while to unwind. Each Met player, each Met official, each Met fan had his personal future to think of, brightened by what had happened. The general public, its mythological feast over, was already thinking of other things. The unitary, 60-day super-event of the New York Mets was over, and the historical Met Mystique was twisted into a new shape, to be seen from new perspectives.

Only one thing seemed quite certain: A baseball team wearing New York Met uniforms would have to play in 1970.

Heavenly Finale

In Heaven, the victory party went on for eons; being immortal, the ecstatic elect who were the members of the Celestial Chapter of the New York Met Fan Club had plenty of time.

They celebrated on a cosmic scale. The nectar, flowing like cheap champagne, was sloshed, spilled, squirted, and splattered more than guzzled. They were all as excited as children. They tore out huge chunks of firmament, with no purpose in view, and tacked two signs to every cloud within reach—one reading "No. 9," and the other, much larger, declaring "We're No. 1." They danced, sang, laughed, exulted, embraced, shouted, pounded one another on the back. The Heavenly Decorum was shattered cheerfully.

"I'm sure they haven't had anything so noisy here since the Revolt of Lucifer," said John Milton, a blind poet, beaming. "It's enough to wake the dead."

"Now that's one of your typically fatuous observations, John," said George Bernard Shaw, also beaming, "but this time, even I will forgive you. No one can deny that we are the dead and the Mets have awakened us."

"They have shown the mortals, and us too, that miracles are still possible," cried the usually shy Bernadette of Lourdes, grinning broadly.

"It just didn't figure, I never would have postulated it," muttered Euclid through his beard, "but you have to give them credit, they earned everything they got. There is no royal road to the World Championship."

The largest single center of attention was Dante, who had actually been there, sent down in June as the special correspondent of the immortals. He was pelted with endless questions: "What's Swoboda really like? Isn't Harrelson underrated? How about that Weis? Is Seaver really that good? Hodges is a genius, isn't he? When did they first think they could win it? Why was Shamsky platooned so much? Did you get Yogi's autograph?"

And all Dante could say, over and over, was "Amazing . . . amazing . . . amazing."

Already, bids were being made for the right to accompany the Mets to spring training. An especially sincere Russian named Leo Tolstoy would make his pitch to anyone he could corner.

"Always I believed," he would say, tears streaming down his cheeks, "that all happy families were alike. That's why I became a Met fan: They were, naturally, unhappy in their own way. But now they have taught me a new vision: They are a happy family, and yet they are like nothing else in Creation. I must go with them, humbly, like a pilgrim, to rethink again all my philosophy, to reject again all my previous work, to spread the new gospel . . . and just think, to see again St. Petersburg. . . ."

And no one would have the heart to explain to him that it was St. Petersburg, Florida.

Over by the harp sector, glorious music poured forth from a chorus of thousands, directed by George Frederick Handel:

"Donnnn—Clen-den-on . . . Hallelulia . . . Hallelulia . . . Jehhh-ry Koos-man . . . Hallelulia . . . Hallelulia!"

"A toast, a toast!" shouted Epicurus. "Let us eat, drink and make merry, for tomorrow the Mets may have to play again. A toast to the Mets!"

"To Boswell," roared Dr. Sam Johnson, lifting a glass.

"To Charles the Great—the new Charlemagne," shrilled Joan of Arc.

"Hail to thee, blithe Agee," sang Percy Bysshe Shelley, "bird thou never wert—but you sure could go and get 'em."

"To Taylor," called out Thomas Edison, always partial to electrical engineers.

"To Gaspar—*de la nuit* and *du jour,* too," said an obscure but prosperous musician named Maurice Ravel.

"To all the K's," squeaked Immanuel Kant, "who made Met victory a Kategorical Imperative: Kranepool, Koosman, Koonce, Kardwell, Kleon-Chones, Klendenon, Muh-Kandrew and Duffy Dyer."

"If you're toasting K's," broke in Hegel, always prone to argue, "why Duffy Dyer?"

"Why not?" demanded Kant.

And the assemblage obviously sided with that sentiment.

The great scientist-philosophers, as usual, were off in a corner talking to themselves.

"It was as I tried to tell you," Einstein explained, "a simple matter of relativity. Turn the standings upside down, and the last-place Mets become first."

"But the standings weren't turned upside down," demurred Aristotle, a stickler for detail. "They were merely split into two divisions. Do you mean that helped?"

"Didn't hurt," answered Einstein.

"They certainly made a bum out of my laws of gravitation," sighed Newton. "All summer I kept waiting for what went up to come down. They never did."

"Everyone insisted they couldn't reach the top," said Galileo defiantly. "Nevertheless—they moved."

"To me," said Madame Curie, her eyes shining, "they were simply radiant."

"It came as no surprise to this writer," boasted Nostradamus.

Elsewhere, some saints were feeling more benign than ever. Many of those who had been, in earthly lives, members of religious orders had naturally become baseball fans then, so they felt in fullest measure the magnitude of the Met triumph.

"For the very first time," admitted Saint Francis of Assisi, referring to the World Series, "I found myself rooting against the Birds."

"I made no attempt to understand it," said Saint Thomas Aquinas, "I just sat back and enjoyed it."

"For a while,"chuckled Saint Nicholas, "it seemed like every day was Christmas."

"I must confess one thing distressed me," said the gentle Saint Theresa. "When the fans tore up the field that way, I couldn't help thinking, pigeons on the grass, alas."

They were joined by Molière and a more recent arrival from Russia.

"Did you hear the gossip?" Molière announced. "Shakespeare and Mozart have decided to collaborate on a musical about the Mets."

"An ambitious undertaking," remarked his companion, Konstantin Stanislavski, in his methodical manner. "The only really successful musical ever done about a baseball team was *Damn Yankees*."

"They're calling theirs *Blessed Mets*," replied Molière.

The revel might have gone on for eternity had not The All-Pervasive Voice interrupted.

"Bless you, my children, and the capacity for joy that you express. The selflessness of your pleasure in a triumph, which can have only spiritual meaning to you, is a reflection of the worthy aspect of your imperfect race—which has always claimed a special place in My scheme. But even you, the most exalted of the humans, must be reminded not to lose perspective. In a few millennia—a mere blink of cosmic time—it will all be forgotten.

"Some have been so carried away by enthusiasm as to suggest that My influence was brought directly to bear on these remarkable but trivial events. That this is presumptuous does not matter; that it demeans the true accomplishment of your darlings should be clear; that it shows again such deep ignorance of My true scope is no longer surprising. But, having enjoyed yourselves, try to regain that most precious and rare attribute of sentient life, a sense of proportion.

"So celebrate a little longer, toast your Mets—and then return to your true function: contemplation. There is a time for all things, as you have been told before; a time to live, a time to love, a time for the Mets, a time for others. Even now, another baseball season is playing itself out on that little planet of yours; even now, new events, new melodramas, new heroes and new hopes are being manufactured—all equally absorbing for the moment, all equally transitory. It is, after all, only a game, that even children can play.

"But—" and now The Voice acquired an indescribable warmth, an infinitely compassionate chuckle, an indulgent smile—"even My Omniscient Omnipotence must confess, it was fun while it lasted. Let it be said, one more time: 'Let's Go Mets.'"

And all was serene in a cosmos that had produced, at least once, the Mets.

1970: Orioles vs. Reds

The Brooks Robinson Show

from *Sports Illustrated,* "That Black and Orange Magic," by William Leggett

All the Orioles seemed to have a hand in casting a spell over Cincinnati, but there was no one to compare with Brooks Robinson, the friendly ghost, who made the Reds disappear in five games.

Andy Etchebarren was sitting in the Baltimore dugout before the fifth and final game of the 1970 World Series, his eyes transfixed by the strange patterns created by raindrops falling on a heavy green tarpaulin covering the infield. Brooks Robinson sat down beside him and tapped him on the knee.

"Feeling OK, Andy?" asked Robinson.

Etchebarren smiled. "Brooksie," he said, "make it stop raining."

"Thanks," Robinson said, "but I'm not going that good."

Maybe not, but as the cold winds moved up Chesapeake Bay, a warning of Halloween just around the corner, there were those in Baltimore who swore they could feel the swooping presence of some great hobgoblin in an orange and black uniform with the number 5 on its back moving about the countryside. It had a very high forehead and a smile on its face and it was beating the bejeezus out of everything in sight with a 33-ounce bat. And what escaped, it caught with its glove.

Well, maybe not everyone in Baltimore had this vision, but that is almost surely the way the Cincinnati Reds are going to see the whole horrible thing in their nightmare this winter. A fine baseball team that had the misfortune to run into the Orioles—and Brooks Robinson—in this Series, the Reds will swear they were the victims of witches and warlocks. And maybe they were. Somebody stopped the rain. Against this kind of magic, even a group of such superlative hitters as the Reds could only hope to survive; they were a part of as fine a five-game Series as baseball could have hoped for—but they never seemed to be in any danger of winning it. When the torture was over, Johnny Bench said, "I hope we can come back and play the Orioles next year. I also hope Brooks Robinson has retired by then."

Sixteen times the Reds smashed hard line drives into the infield or deep into the outfield only to see an Oriole, usually Robinson, make an impossible play and stuff a sure hit into his glove. If somehow they had become disoriented enough to believe that this was last year and that they were the Orioles playing the New York Mets in 1969, they could have been forgiven. For the Reds, bad luck never seemed to take a holiday.

There were all sorts of cases in point, but take what happened in the second game, which Baltimore won 6–5. It ended when Oriole center fielder Paul Blair raced to the wall in deep center to catch what looked like at least a triple off the bat of pinch hitter Jimmy Stewart. In Game 3 Baltimore made the lesson stick. The Reds got their first two runners on, and then Tony Perez hit a screamer into a double play—started by Robinson. Bench followed with a brutal liner—at Robinson. The great revival died. Final score: 9–3.

If the defeats depressed the Reds, they exhilarated the Orioles, who needed some sort of vindication after the flop against the Mets. They also showed why the Orioles are considered the liveliest team in the major leagues today. Granted, the American League is not as strong as the National, nor does it have the depth of competition or the caliber and quantity of starter. Still, as can be seen by merely watching them play, the Orioles are an exception, a 1970 team undiluted by expansion. They have managed to retain their excellent pitching, especially in the persons of 20-game winners

Mike Cuellar, Dave McNally and Jim Palmer, and four Gold Glove winners at critical defensive positions, Robinson at third, Mark Belanger at shortstop, Dave Johnson at second, and Blair in center. And then of course there are Frank Robinson, Boog Powell, and Don Buford, who bring the bats.

Millions of people undoubtedly wonder why it is that the Mets could beat the Orioles so soundly last year, then finish third to Pittsburgh, a team that was in turn so easily mashed by the Reds in the playoffs. The chief difference between the 1969 and 1970 Mets is pitching. Met pitching a year ago held the Orioles to the lowest five-game Series hit total ever, 23. This time Blair and Brooks Robinson, who together batted .077 against New York, batted .450. Their hits against Cincinnati (18) were only five short of the team aggregate in 1969.

Cincinnati, unfortunately, was forced to use 18 pitchers in the five games. Not all of them were entirely healthy, and one of the best, Wayne Simpson (14–3), was too sore even to try. Aside from the injuries, the Reds are basically a very young team that usually makes up for its mistakes with muscle. But it takes experience and exceptional technique, as well, to beat a team like Baltimore. One example of a department where the Reds did come up woefully short was in throwing the ball from the outfield. Black magic had nothing to do with the occasional offending throw that just missed its mark. Next spring the Reds will have to work on marksmanship if they intend to be Series material again.

Baltimore plays with a natural flair. As Brooks Robinson said, "We just seem to do things automatically at times. I believe we do it that way because our guys are good enough that they don't need too many lessons to pick things up. Sure, we work in spring training on hitting the cutoff man and backing up the plays. If you make a mistake on things like those a whole big inning will open up against you."

Robinson was signed by the Orioles on the basis of a letter sent to Paul Richards, then the manager–general manager of the team, by a former teammate, Lindsay Deal. The letter was dated Feb. 13, 1955.

Dear Paul, it began,

I am writing you in regard to a kid named Brooks Robinson. I think he measures up to having a chance in major league baseball. I think he is a natural third baseman although he has been playing both second and third.

He will be 18 years old May 18 and graduates from Little Rock Senior High School on May 27. He is 6 feet 1 inch in height and weighs 175. His physique is outstanding for a boy this age. He bats right and throws right. . . .

Brooks has a lot of power, baseball savvy and is always cool when the chips are down. This boy is the best prospect I've seen since Billy Goodman came to Atlanta to play when I was playing there. That is the reason I am contacting you.

I thought you might be interested in him and able to make as good an offer as anyone else. Otherwise, I wouldn't have bothered you with it.

Richards passed the letter on to the team's farm department, and Robinson, seven months later, became the first prospect to make the team since its move from St. Louis, where, in kindlier moments, people called it the Browns.

How good are the Orioles? "We like to think," says Earl Weaver, the man who manages them, "that we do not have too many holes." Over the last seven seasons Baltimore has won more games (672) than any other team. The club closest to them in that period is Minnesota with 635. Next are San Francisco (633), Detroit (625), and St. Louis (617). When the Tigers, world champions in 1968, tried to repeat in 1969, not even their 103 victories of the previous year would have won for them. Since they managed to win only 90, they finished 19 games behind Baltimore.

"Certain people believe that we have had the finest team in baseball for the past two years," said Weaver last week. "It must be pretty good because it has played in two World Series and it has won one more game in the last two World Series than the New York Mets ever did."

The quote is more than a statement. It is an exposition of the Earl Weaver baseball personality. A brilliant tactical manager known in the trade to "never box himself," Weaver, now 40, took over the Orioles in midseason of 1968, and since then the team has won 265 games and lost only 141. He is a man who believes in keeping every possible statistic, then studying his lists carefully before reaching a decision, and he usually has about six reasons for everything he does.

When Cincinnati did bounce back in the fourth game of the Series, there was hope on the team that it could rally and take the Orioles back to the mod sod in Cincinnati and beat them. The Reds had stopped a 17-game Baltimore winning streak, and they felt that maybe the old idea that every winning streak is usually followed by a losing streak would hold true. Not only was the thinking fallacious; Baltimore quickly reminded the Reds that here was no ordinary team, especially where losing streaks were concerned. This season its longest bad spell lasted three games. A year ago the worst was five.

Much was made of the fact that during the year the Reds, with their preponderance of right-handed hitting power, chewed left-handed pitching up and spit it into the Ohio River. Little was made of Baltimore's record of the last two seasons against right-handed pitching. Yet the Orioles were 77 games over .500 during that period and they maintained their lifetime record against the American League's best pitchers: Denny McLain (11–13), Jim Perry (14–14), Mel Stottlemyre (7–9), Dean Chance (11–16), Joe Horlen (9–10), and Luis Tiant (2–10).

Cincinnati's record against left-handers (33–12) and the fact that the Orioles felt somewhat apprehensive about pitching McNally and Cuellar against the Big Red Machine (after the Series some of the players called it the Big Red Edsel) and its right-handed power brought a fine reaction from Frank Robinson. Presiding as judge in the kangaroo court at the Oriole victory party several hours after the last game, Robinson fined superscout Jim Russo for even suggesting that the Reds might be able to rough up McNally and Cuellar. (Frank also fined Brooks Robinson for "showboating it during the entire Series.") Before the Series began Russo suggested to Weaver that the 40-year-old right-handed reliever Dick Hall start one of the games against the Reds' righties. After thinking the matter over, Weaver decided against the plan, because if Hall started he could not be used in relief more than once and Weaver did not want to eliminate his option of using Hall more often. Hall did come into the second game, where he faced seven batters and got all of them out.

Given all of his statistics, Weaver might have known another fact. This has not been a very good year for left-handed pitching in the National League, which could explain why the Reds were death on them. The Reds' own Jim Merritt was the winningest left-hander with a 20–12 record, but his ERA was 4.08. Luke Walker of the Pirates (15–6) had only five complete games; Steve Carlton of the St. Louis Cardinals lost 19 times; and Jerry Koosman of the New York Mets had only one shutout. The San Francisco Giant staff worked 50 complete games, but only three of those were by lefties.

"There can be little doubt," said Clay Carroll, the one Cincinnati pitcher who was effective in the Series, "that we came in with a crippled staff and that the Orioles crippled what was left of it." He was not talking about the personal shelling that they took, but he might well have been. The Orioles drove five balls back at or through Cincinnati pitchers in the last game alone. Two ricocheted off bodies while the other three flew by so quickly that the pitchers, dodging, couldn't field them.

The Orioles clinched their second world championship almost exactly one year to the day after they had lost to the Mets. Then they were totally dejected, but 5,000 people showed up at the Baltimore airport to greet them, and when 5,000 people show up in Baltimore for anything it is usually free or a Colt workout. "Our players got a tremendous lift out of that," said Harry Dalton, the man who is most responsible for assembling the Oriole club. "Some of our players had tears in their eyes and their wives were crying. There are those who would have you believe that a rah-rah spirit in professional sports doesn't mean anything, but it does. Just as the fans had helped the Mets, the fact that ours still thought so much of us made our players dedicate themselves to returning and getting another chance to win the Series.

"Even though we beat the Dodgers in four straight games in 1966," Dalton continued, "beating Cincinnati is more rewarding because the Reds are such an excellent team. Pitching through the heart of their batting order was like walking through a shooting gallery."

For all their obvious strength, it is doubtful that the Orioles will stand pat during the off season. Their pitching needs some additions because, as Dalton says, "Any department that has 10 men in it can be improved upon." Weaver, too, feels that the Orioles will change, but not much. "We are not going to open up any holes just for the sake of change," he said.

All along they have had the problem of whom to play. Merv Rettenmund, for instance, did not get a chance to start in the Series until the fifth game. Playing in only 106 games during the regular season, he batted .322, hit 18 homers and batted in 58 runs. He is a superior fielder. He responded to his one Series chance by driving in two runs, one with a single and the other with a homer hit to the opposite field. Right behind Rettenmund are six other players ready to challenge the regulars. Their averages with Triple A Rochester of the International League this season ranged from .304 to .384.

The two men who probably will be challenged the least are Powell and Brooks Robinson. Powell, still only 29 years old, has hit 34 homers or more in three of the last five seasons and driven in an average of 97 runs. And Brooks? He is 33, but like some things—say, the replica of the flag that was still there that waved in center field during the Series—he will stay around Baltimore as long as people appreciate third basemen who can snub out bombs bursting in air. Or run the National League all the way back to Cincinnati with only a bat and a glove.

And a little magic, of course.

1975: Red Sox vs. Reds

Carlton Fisk's Game 6 Home Run

from *Beyond the Sixth Game* by Peter Gammons

The established dynasty, Cincinnati's Big Red Machine, meets the dynasty of the future, the Boston Red Sox, and the Red Sox win the most memorable game of the most memorable World Series of a baseball generation.

Then all of a sudden the ball was suspended out there in the black of the morning like the Mystic River Bridge. Carlton Fisk broke forward for a step, then stopped and watched. He later remembered none of the clumsy hula dance that NBC made famous, only that "It seemed like the wait for Christmas morning" as he watched to see on which side of the fine line it would land: home run/victory or foul ball/strike one.

When it finally crashed fair off the mesh attached to the left-field foul pole, Fisk raised his fists above his head in applause in the midst of his convulsive leap, and as if conducted by Charles Munch, the reaction unfurled. Fenway Park organist John Kiley boomed the opening notes of Handel's Hallelujah Chorus, Fisk gamboled his way around the bases, teammates passionately staggered to home plate, and from the bleachers to Presque Isle people looked at one another as the first shock warmed into reality. In Raymond, New Hampshire, an Episcopal minister named James Smith burst out of his house, ran across to St. Bartholomew's Church, grabbed the rope, and began ringing the church bell about the same time that, in Yardley, Pennsylvania, the wife of another Episcopal minister, Gretchen Gammons, ran across the street to St. Andrew's and did the same.

It had been back in the 10th inning that Pete Rose had turned from his place in the batter's box and said to Fisk, "This is some kind of game, isn't it?" At 12:34 a.m., in the bottom of the 12th inning, Fisk's histrionic, 304-foot home run brought Red Sox shortstop Rick Burleson running to home plate saying to teammate Rick Miller, "We just might have won the greatest game ever played."

So it seemed at the moment, frozen in time. Judged soberly, rationally, there are undoubtedly dozens and hundreds and thousands of baseball games staged from Old Orchard Beach to Los Angeles that one would have to say had more technical brilliance. But this one had captured all that baseball could be. Fisk's home run had virtually altered the autumnal equinox. By the time the ball had caromed off the screen and 35,000 people had stood to sing "Give Me Some Men Who Are Stout-Hearted Men" as Fisk gallivanted across the field to an interview room, the entire emotional scale had been played.

After three days of rain, the Red Sox had begun this fight for survival with a three-run, first-inning homer by wonderchild Fred Lynn. Then they watched in resigned silence as, slowly but surely, the heavily favored Reds chipped away at the mortality of a hero named Luis Tiant. When Cincinnati center fielder Cesar Geronimo homered in the top of the eighth inning, El Tiante left, trailing 6–3, to heartfelt but polite applause that accepted the finality of the situation.

If some clock had been allowed to run out at that point, the sixth game of the 1975 World Series would have been no more, no less than a game from the, say, 1961 World Series or 1969 National League Championship Series. But, turn after hairpin turn, it became the Sixth Game. First, in the bottom of the eighth, Bernardo Carbo hit a stunning two-out, three-run homer that tied it. In the ninth, when Boston had the bases loaded and none out, Cincinnati left fielder George Foster caught Lynn's fly ball and threw Denny Doyle out at the plate to kill what was apparently a certain game-winning rally. In the 11th, Dwight Evans made a catch that Reds manager

Sparky Anderson insisted was "given its significance, one of the two greatest catches ever made" to rob Joe Morgan of a game-winning double, triple, or homer and turn it into a double play. Then, in the 12th inning, against Pat Darcy, the record 12th pitcher in the 241-minute game, came Fisk's shot, the cherry on the top of this all-time banana split of a game.

The Sixth Game was an abridgment of the entire splendid series in which Boston led in all seven games and lost the lead in five of them, in which five games were decided by one run, two were decided in extra innings, and two others in the ninth inning. But there was much more to this game, and this Series, than statistics, however dazzling they might be. Baseball was coming out of an era of five consecutive vanilla-bland World Series won by teams from Baltimore, Pittsburgh, and Oakland, hardly centers of media excitement. Immediately preceding those five World Series were the years when no one could score runs, which came just a few years after an era in which a team from New York or Los Angeles had been in the World Series for 20 consecutive Octobers. Nineteen seventy-five was the year television coverage of baseball came of age, with the split image of Fisk's rumba and the ball suspended against the morn, a fitting symbol of TV's ascendancy.

There, too, like a Christmas carol service, at the end of a decade that decried all customs and history, were all the traditions of a sport whose lineage is steeped in history. Cincinnati and Boston, in fact, were the first two professional baseball cities. Fenway Park, with its nooks and crannies and its promise that no two games will ever be alike, is the romanticists' ideal. The matchup of the two teams presented emotional extremes: the IBM image of the Big Red Machine, the best team in baseball, with its short hair and the kind of puissance that earns the Pete Rozelle Trophy, against the Olde Towne Teame, the last great white team, which had come out of nowhere that year with the only rookie ever to be Most Valuable Player (Lynn), an institution (Carl Yastrzemski), a Brahmin New Englander (Fisk), and some characters named Tiant and Carbo and Bill "Space Man" Lee. Riverfront Stadium, which could have been ordered from a Sears catalogue, as contrasted with the idiosyncratic Fenway Park.

The Reds' characters were submerged in and by a team perfection, and in the end, they won the Series because they simply played the game more perfectly than Boston, for whom Doyle was the sixth runner in six games tagged out at the plate. It was the Red Sox who did the spectacular in the Series, the Red Sox who did so much to bring individualism and personality back into the sport. "When tonight is over," Lee was credited with saying before he pitched the seventh game, "Don Gullett is going to the Hall of Fame, and I'm going to the Eliot Lounge."

What few remember about the Sixth Game was that despite its days of dramatic rainout buildup, it was seven outs from having all the drama of the Astros playing the Giants in August, from a routine conclusion of the Reds defeating the Red Sox in six games. It had begun with Lynn's three-run homer off Cincinnati starter Gary Nolan—who, like all the Reds starters that year, would be gone within three years—in the first inning. That was the final, dramatic blow of what was one of the greatest rookie seasons in baseball history. There was a Joe Hardy air about Lynn, a private, loping kid a year and a half out of the University of Southern California. One week into the season, which the Red Sox had started after a horrible September 1974 collapse, the inability to deal (in the wake of the Yankees getting Bobby Bonds, the Orioles Lee May, and the Tigers Nate Colbert), and a 10–21 spring training, Yankee manager Bill Virdon said, "Don't bother talking about Bonds. Fred Lynn may be the next DiMaggio." Virdon completed his statement with an "I told you so" when Lynn's spectacular diving, bouncing, ninth-inning catch in Shea Stadium in August saved a 1–0 Boston victory that marked the Yankees absent the remainder of the season. Lynn batted .331. He drove in 105 runs, scored 103, rapped 47 doubles and 21 homers, and made one tumblers' catch after another en route to being named both Rookie of the Year and his league's Most Valuable Player. In the fifth inning of the Sixth Game he banged into the center-field fence leaping for Ken Griffey's triple, slid to the ground in a heap, and lay there. The stands fell silent as if witness to a presidential assassination, and Red Sox owner Tom Yawkey turned to scouting director Haywood Sullivan and said, "Those walls must be padded before next season."

For more than a month, it had been Tiant—likened by the *Boston Globe's* Leigh Montville to the old man in *The Old Man and the Sea*—who had pulled the Red Sox together. El Tiante was listed at 34 and rumored to be closer to 40, but he was the central nervous system of the team. He had been sidelined for weeks with a bad back, and when September came (Baltimore manager Earl Weaver kept promising his team's annual comeback and one Baltimore columnist labeled the Red Sox the Boston Chokers), it was Tiant who stepped forth. On September 11, he returned from a three-week absence, took a no-hitter into the eighth, and beat Detroit 3–1. Four days later, with what Red Sox officials later admitted was a crowd in excess of 45,000 (prior to standing-room fire laws), he rode the home runs of Fisk and Rico Petrocelli to a 2–0 win over the Orioles' Cy Young Award winner, Jim Palmer, on the night that the chant "LOO-EEE, LOO-EEE" came into being. He shut out Cleveland on the final Friday night of the season to all but clinch the pennant. When the A's began the playoffs as the experienced favorites, he shut them out in the first game and began a three-game sweep. When the Reds began the World Series as heavy favorites, he shut them out, and comically out of place at bat but somehow effective, he started the winning six-run, seventh-inning rally. When, in Cincinnati, the Red Sox were down 2–1 in games, he pitched the game by which he always said he'd like to be remembered: 163 pitches, a 5–4 lead in the fourth, two runners on in each of the last five innings, and a 5–4 victory that was as gutsy as John Garfield in *Body and Soul*.

But this night, El Tiante's marionette abracadabra could carry them no more. A walk to designated bunter Ed Armbrister began a three-run fifth inning that not only broke Tiant's skein of 40 consecutive scoreless innings in Fenway but tied the game. Foster made it 5–3 with a line drive off the center-field fence in the seventh, and when Cesar Geronimo angled his homer inside the right-field foul pole leading off the eighth, Tiant left as *Sport* magazine editor Dick Schaap began collecting the MVP ballots in the press box. No one much noticed when the Red Sox got two on leading off the eighth; Cincinnati's prized rookie reliever Rawlins Eastwick III came in and struck out Evans, got Burleson to fly out, and had only to get the pinch hitter, Carbo, to bring the Reds to within an inning of their first championship in 35 years.

Bernardo Carbo. He was a cartoon character of sorts, a frizzy-haired kid who traveled with a stuffed gorilla dressed in a Cardinals uniform and named Mighty Joe Young. After running into the bullpen wall to save a home run in the crucial June series with the Yankees, Carbo delayed the game for 10 minutes while he scoured the warning track for the chaw of tobacco that had popped out of his mouth; when he found it, he put it back in his mouth and the game continued. Carbo was a streak hitter who, in both of the two years since being obtained from the Cardinals, had hit spectacularly for the Red Sox until mid-May, then ended up relegated to the bench. He never accepted that, once charging up to general manager Dick O'Connell's office immediately before a game to protest Evans's presence in the lineup. Bernardo always had trouble accepting authority, which is why Sparky Anderson and the Reds had traded him to St. Louis in the first place. He had hardly played at all in the second half of the season, but in Game 3 had pinch-hit a homer, and with two outs in the bottom of the eighth of Game 6, he got his second chance.

With two strikes, Eastwick threw him a fastball that befuddled Bernardo as if it were the Pythagorean theorem. He pulled his bat up in self-defense, deflecting the third strike off to the left. "That might have been the worst swing in the history of baseball," Fisk would tease Carbo later, but it wasted the pitch. Eastwick came in with another fastball and Carbo drove it into the center-field bleachers. "The crowd willed it up into the seats," claims Rose.

6–6. "Bernie," said Lee, "is the only man I know who turned fall into summer with one wave of his magic wand."

The Red Sox had a chance to win it in the ninth, with the bases loaded and none out. When Lynn lofted a fly ball down the left-field line halfway between third base and The Wall and George Foster settled under it 170 feet from home plate, third-base coach Don Zimmer yelled to base runner Denny Doyle, "No, no."

Doyle, however, thought Zimmer was saying "Go, go." He took off, Foster's throw to Johnny Bench cut him down easily, and the threat passed. Then with Griffey on first, one out in the 11th, Red Sox reliever Dick Drago pitched to Joe Morgan.

When the Series was over, Anderson was to say that the Boston player who had impressed him most was Evans. Dwight was only 23 at the time, but his three-year major-league career had been a struggle to approach others' expectations. He arrived in September 1972 with the promise of superstardom, but youth, two serious beanings, and personal problems and insecurities had complicated his baseball life. Once the Gold Dust Twins, Fred Lynn and Jim Rice, arrived in 1975, it was Evans who the media constantly suggested should be traded for a pitcher or a power-hitting third baseman. That only added to his problems. But, whether he hit .223 as he did as a rookie or .274 as he did in '75, Evans never wavered in the field. He was at that point in his career a defensive offensive player and an offensive defensive player, the premier defensive right fielder in the American League, playing the most difficult right field in baseball. In this series it was his dramatic ninth-inning, two-run homer off Eastwick that took the third game into extra innings and to the Armbrister interference controversy.

As Red Sox reliever Dick Drago went into his stretch, Evans tried preparing himself for all possibilities. "In all important situations, Doyle would give me a signal if Drago were throwing a breaking ball to a left-handed hitter so I could be leaning for him to pull," Evans said. "One of the great things about playing the outfield with Fisk catching was that he moved so much you could tell the location of the pitch. Knowing the pitching and seeing Fisk set up, I was thinking that the worst thing that could happen would be that Morgan could pull a line drive directly over my head, so I was mentally leaning in that direction." Morgan indeed smashed the worst, a line drive directly over Evans's head. But, breaking as the ball was hit, Evans scrambled backward, stabbed the ball at full stride as he crossed the warning track, ricocheted off the wall, whirled, and fired back to the infield; Yastrzemski, the first baseman, grabbed the throw halfway between the coach's box and the dugout and tossed to Burleson—who'd raced across from shortstop —to complete the double play. "It probably wouldn't have been in the seats," said Evans, "but it would have been the game." As it turned out, it was a catch that shares a place in World Series history with such other historic defensive plays as Willie Mays's in 1954, Al Gionfriddo's in 1947, and Harry Hooper's in 1912.

Pat Darcy, the seventh pitcher, began the bottom of the 12th by running a sinker down and in to Fisk's wheelhouse. "He's a lowball pitcher, I'm a lowball, dead-pull hitter, so I was looking for that one pitch in that one area," said Fisk. "I got it, then drove it." He chopped his woodcutter's swing and sent his line drive searing toward the foul pole. The problem was keeping the ball in fair territory, as with that short, chopping swing Fisk had spent much of his career setting unofficial records for foul homers. But this was Fisk's season of retribution—after a knee injury that nearly ended his career in 1974, he had broken his arm in the first exhibition game of 1975 and came back in June to bat .331 the remainder of the season. So he found retribution for Game 3. That night he impaled his mask onto the screen as Morgan's game-winning line drive soared over Lynn's head and Geronimo danced across the plate in front of him; it had been Geronimo whom Armbrister was trying to advance with his bunt attempt, but after the controversial collision as Fisk tried to pounce on the ball, his off-balance throw to start what could have been a double play sailed into center field to launch what would be a long winter's argument with and torment for home-plate umpire Larry Barnett.

But this 12th-inning drive crashed against the mesh attached to the foul pole, and as Fisk was madly running and skipping and clapping around the bases, George Frederick Handel echoed across the Back Bay and church bells pealed out for both the New England town team and baseball itself.

No seventh game was really necessary, at least from the romanticist's viewpoint, and that encompassed much of the audience, since so much of baseball and its tradition from Abner Doubleday to Babe Ruth to Fernando Valenzuela is romance. "Instead of playing a seventh game, they should spread tables and checkered tablecloths across the outfields and just have a picnic, a feast to a glorious World Series, and toast one another until dawn," suggested television journalist Clark Booth. There was a seventh game, of course, which served to put it on the record that the Cincinnati Reds won—albeit by one run in the ninth inning—and that the Boston Red Sox still had not been world champions since 1918, when Ruth was their best pitcher and Yawkey was a 15-year-old student at the Irving School in Tarrytown, New York.

The deciding game was dotted with essences of both teams. Once again, the Red Sox had a 3–0 lead, forged from Gullett's sudden wildness in the fourth inning. Once again, the Red Sox could not put Cincinnati away, either with their bats (Burleson had struck out with the bases loaded to end the fourth) or with their pitching or with their defense. Once again, it was the Hun, Rose, who led their charge, as he'd led it from the first at bat of the first game when he snarled, "Tiant is nothing," a declaration he continued to make for two weeks.

With his beloved moon staring down over his left shoulder, Bill Lee had cruised along into the sixth inning with the 3–0 lead. No one entertained America during the series more than The Space Man, as he happily discussed Vonnegut ("In nonsense is strength"), organic gardening, violence ("I'd have bitten Barnett's ear off—I'd have Van Goghed him"), and Boston politics with any journalist who would listen—and most of them did. That he was even on the October stage was surprising: After August 24, when he shut out the White Sox in the rain throwing Leephus bloopers and had a 17–6 record, he did not win another game, finishing the season lost in the bullpen until the Boston scouting reports suggested that his screwball and off-speed stuff would be more effective against Cincinnati's potent lineup than the conventional hard sinker-slider repertoire of late-season Reggie Cleveland. He'd pitched brilliantly in the rain-delayed second game, coming within an inning of a 2–1 victory that would have done in the Reds. But Johnny Bench, showing his experience, looked for the screwball, got one inches off the outside corner on the first pitch of the ninth, and drove it into the right-field corner. Then a David Concepcion infield hit and a Griffey double off Drago took the Reds home to Cincinnati 3–2 winners.

By the sixth inning of the final game, Rose was stomping around the dugout like a whiffling Che Guevara. He screamed, hollered, and slapped his teammates, then stomped up to the plate and led off the inning with a single, one of the extraordinary 11 times he reached base in his final 15 plate appearances. An out later, Bench pulled a Lee sinker into the ground for what appeared to be an inning-ending double play to Burleson. "There are some things you just can't allow to happen," said Rose. "At that moment, a double play was one of them." He sent himself into a kamikaze orbit toward Doyle. "He saw me coming for 10 feet in the air," Rose later chortled. "I made sure of it." He wanted his take-out slides to go to Cooperstown with his base-hit records.

Doyle had another problem besides Rose. The baseballs used then were made in Haiti, and once in a while the force of the bat would literally tear the cover off a ball. "The cover had almost entirely torn off when Bench hit it," Doyle revealed the next spring. "When I went to get rid of it to first, it just flew out of my hand." Utility infielder Bobby Heise retrieved the ball in the dugout, an unenviable trophy that Doyle would keep. The only postseason opportunity of Doyle's career was not one bathed in heroics, for he had lost another Bench double-play ball in the whiteness of Bench's uniform in Game 5.

So, instead of being out of the inning, Lee then had to face Tony Perez. For the first four games, Perez had been mired in a hitless slump. But in Game 5 he walloped two tremendous home runs off Cleveland to provide Gullett the margin for the 6–2 victory. The scouting reports told Lee not to throw Perez, a deadly off-speed hitter, any junk. But The Space Man did what he wanted to do whenever he wanted to do it—which is how he became one of baseball's first and foremost counterculture idols—and he insisted on throwing Perez one of his Moon Curves or Leephus pitches. A blooper ball. He had thrown three earlier, two for strikes, one for a pop-up, and had even thrown one to Perez that was taken for a strike. "Lee was throwing that hard screwball so well, I never thought he'd throw another one of those bloopers," said Perez. "Sure, I was surprised, but I was geared up for the fastball, and that's so slow it's easy to adjust to." Rumor has it that the ball ended up in Kokomo, Indiana, having landed on a truck in the westbound lane of the Massachusetts Turnpike. Fact had the Red Sox lead cut to 3–2, and an inning later Lee developed a blister. "All of a sudden I found myself pitching to Griffey and I couldn't get the ball to go anywhere near where I wanted it," explained Lee, and when he walked Griffey, manager Darrell Johnson had to bring in left-hander Rogelio Moret. Griffey stole second, and after an out and a walk, Rose slapped another single that tied it. Right-hander Jim Willoughby, a tall, floppy sinker-baller who looked as if he were falling out of a tree when he pitched, came on to retire Bench with the bases loaded, pitched a 1-2-3 eighth, and looked forward to the ninth. He had pitched 6¹/₃ Series innings without allowing an earned run.

After Evans led off the bottom of the eighth with a walk, Burleson failed to put down a bunt, grounding into a double play that would have brought Willoughby, the most effective reliever of the Series, to the plate. Johnson sent up Cecil Cooper. Thus was another link in the chain of Boston's problematic baseball legacy forged.

Three months later, a man sat in the Abbeyfeale Café in Inman Square in Cambridge, drinking 50-cent shots with 25-cent drafts, blankly staring at the television mounted up in the corner of the bar. He had been there for nearly four hours, watching, when he turned for the first time to a group of three men down the bar. "Why," he stammered, "did Johnson bat for Willoughby?"

"Where were you," replied one of the men, "when you heard Denny Galehouse was pitching against the Indians?"

"How," asked another, "could Slaughter have scored from first?"

At the time, Cooper was going through what Gil Hodges had experienced in 1952, and what Eddie Murray and Willie Wilson and Dave Winfield would later have to face. He had gone into a dreadful slump that at that point had reached 1-for-18, a dour ending to what had been an emerging (.311) season before he had been hit in the face by a pitch thrown by Milwaukee's Billy Travers September 7.

Manager Johnson, too, was experiencing a public flogging of sorts. Lee, ired at being passed over for the sixth-game start when rain allowed Tiant to come back, said, "Darrell's been falling out of trees and landing on his feet all season." Johnson was a quiet man, whose inability to articulate had made him the butt of press conference jokes by the national media. He'd been the minor-league manager who helped direct most of the extraordinary young talent to Boston, and he'd organized and expertly handled a pitching staff to get as much out of it as one ever could have asked. But Johnson also was nearly fired in June, when, as the team went on a 9–4, job-saving road trip, the front office talked to Detroit officials about luring away Tigers manager Ralph Houk. Second baseman Doug Griffin, replaced by Doyle in mid-June, stated, "We're going to win this thing in *spite* of the manager." Such fragments of disrespect clouded the season. Fisk and Lee walked out of a meeting in the manager's office in Baltimore, claiming Johnson was incoherent. When the Red Sox clinched the division championship the last Saturday, Johnson refused to grant Yastrzemski permission to fly home to Florida and miss the final day of the season and the next couple of workouts prior to the playoffs; Yastrzemski went anyway. When they won the playoffs in Oakland, Johnson never went in and joined in the clubhouse celebration, instead sitting in his tiny office a few feet away, sipping champagne with Oakland outfielder Joe Rudi, his off-season hunting companion.

Replacing Willoughby, Cooper went out, and rookie lefthander Jim Burton came in to pitch the top of the ninth, since Drago had pitched three innings the night before. Burton promptly walked the man he was brought in to face, the left-hand-hitting Griffey leading off. Two outs later, Griffey was on second. Burton wisely walked Rose and pitched to the National League's Most Valuable Player, Morgan. It doesn't matter how the ball got out there, that Burton threw a pitch Morgan described as "a breaking ball on the outside corner that two years earlier I couldn't have handled," or that Morgan's bloop barely carried the infield into shallow left-center. The Reds had scored what would be the winning run in the ninth inning of the seventh game, and when Will McEnaney finished off the bottom of the ninth and watched Yaz—who

The Sixth Game, October 21, 1975

Cincinnati	AB	R	H	RBI	Boston	AB	R	H	RBI
Rose, 3b	5	1	2	0	Cooper, 1b	5	0	0	0
Griffey, rf	5	2	2	2	Drago, p	0	0	0	0
Morgan, 2b	6	1	1	1	Miller, ph	1	0	0	0
Bench, c	6	0	1	2	Wise, p	0	0	0	0
Perez, 1b	6	0	2	0	Doyle, 2b	5	0	1	0
Foster, lf	6	0	2	0	Yastrzemski, lf–1b	6	1	3	0
Concepcion, ss	6	0	1	0	Fisk, c	4	2	2	1
Geronimo, cf	6	1	2	1	Lynn, cf	4	2	2	3
Nolan, p	0	0	0	0	Petrocelli, 3b	4	1	0	0
Chaney, ph	1	0	0	0	Evans, rf	5	0	1	0
Norman, p	0	0	0	0	Burleson, ss	3	0	0	0
Billingham, p	0	0	0	0	Tiant, p	2	0	0	0
Armbrister, ph	0	1	0	0	Moret, p	0	0	0	0
Carroll, p	0	0	0	0	Carbo, ph	2	1	1	3
Crowley, ph	1	0	1	0					
Borbon, p	1	0	0	0					
Eastwick, p	0	0	0	0					
McEaney, p	0	0	0	0					
Drissen, ph	1	0	0	0					
Darcy, p	0	0	0	0					
Totals:	50	6	14	6		41	7	10	7

Cincinnati	000	030	210	000–6
Boston	300	000	030	001–7

LOB–Cincinnati 11, Boston 9. 2B–Doyle, Evans, Foster. 3B–Griffey.

HR–Lynn, Geronimo, Carbo, Fisk. SB–Concepcion. S–Tiant.

Cincinnati

	IP	H	R	ER	BB	SO
Nolan	2	3	3	3	0	2
Norman	$^2/_3$	1	0	0	2	0
Billingham	$1^1/_3$	1	0	0	1	1
Carroll	1	1	0	0	0	0
Borbon	2	1	2	2	1	1
Eastwick	1	2	1	1	1	2
McEnaney	1	0	0	0	1	0
Darcy (L)	2	1	1	1	0	1
Tiant	7	11	6	6	2	5
Moret	1	0	0	0	0	0
Drago	3	1	0	0	0	1
Wise (W)	1	2	0	0	0	1

Tiant pitched to one batter in the eighth. Borbon pitched to two batters in the eighth. Eastwick pitched to two batters in the ninth. Darcy pitched to one batter in the twelfth.

HP–By Drago (Rose). T–4:01. A–35, 205

in 1967 had made the last out of his only other World Series—hit a gentle fly to Geronimo, they had completed a task that almost everyone in America had figured they'd accomplish with considerably greater ease.

Rose, Morgan, and company had won the 1975 World Series. But when the Sixth Game had ended with that ball suspended out in the black of the morning like the Mystic River Bridge, Carlton Fisk, Bernardo Carbo, Luis Tiant, and the Red Sox *were* the 1975 Series.

Baseball had seized the imagination of the entire country; the excitement and color of that World Series marked it immediately as one of the greatest ever. It seemed inevitable that the Red Sox would dominate their league for years, and that baseball was entering a golden era in which this most traditional of sports would enjoy unprecedented tranquility, prosperity, and popularity.

Instead, the new era was quietly ushered in a few short weeks later in the office of arbitrator Peter Seitz, who ruled that Andy Messersmith and Dave McNally were, as they had claimed, free agents not bound to their respective teams forever through the option clause in their contracts. Though no one suspected it on that glorious October night, the Sixth Game and the 1975 World Series marked the end of an old era, not the beginning of a new one.

Final American League Standings and Red Sox Statistics, 1975

	W	L	PCT	GB	R	HR	BA
EAST							
BOS	95	65	.594		796	134	.275
BAL	90	69	.566	4.5	682	124	.252
NY	83	77	.519	12	681	110	.264
CLE	79	80	.497	15.5	688	153	.261
MIL	68	94	.420	28	675	146	.250
DET	57	102	.358	37.5	570	125	.249
WEST							
OAK	98	64	.605		758	151	.254
KC	91	71	.562	7	710	118	.261
TEX	79	83	.488	19	714	134	.256
MIN	76	83	.478	20.5	724	121	.271
CHI	75	86	.466	22.5	655	94	.255
CAL	72	89	.447	25.5	628	55	.246
League Total					8281	1465	.258

Manager	W	L	PCT
Darrell Johnson	95	65	.594

Final American League Standings and Red Sox Statistics, 1975, continued

Pitcher	T	W	L	PCT	ERA	SV
Luis Tiant	R	18	14	.563	4.02	0
Bill Lee	L	17	9	.654	3.95	0
Rick Wise	R	19	12	.613	3.95	0
Reggie Cleveland	R	13	9	.591	4.43	0
Roger Moret	L	14	3	.824	3.60	1
Dick Pole	R	4	6	.400	4.42	0
Dick Drago	R	2	2	.500	3.84	15
Diego Segui	R	2	5	.286	4.82	6
Jim Burton	L	1	2	.333	2.89	1
Jim Willoughby	R	5	2	.714	3.54	8
Steve Barr	L	0	1	.000	2.57	0
Rick Kreuger	L	0	0	–	4.50	0
Team Total		95	65	.594	3.99	31

POS PLAYER	B	G	AB	H	2B	3B	HR	R	RBI	BA
Regulars										
1B Carl Yastrzemski	L	149	543	146	30	1	14	91	60	.269
2B Doug Griffin	R	100	257	69	6	0	1	21	29	.240
SS Rick Burleson	R	158	580	146	25	1	6	66	62	.252
3B Rico Petrocelli	R	115	402	96	15	1	7	31	59	.239
RF Dwight Evans	R	128	412	113	24	6	13	61	56	.274
CF Fred Lynn	L	145	528	175	47	7	21	103	105	.331
LF Jim Rice	R	144	564	174	29	4	22	92	102	.309
C Carlton Fisk	R	79	263	87	14	4	10	47	52	.331
DH Cecil Cooper	L	106	305	95	17	6	14	49	44	.311
Substitutes										
2B Denny Doyle	L	89	310	96	21	2	4	50	36	.310
3B Bob Heise	R	63	126	27	3	0	0	12	21	.214
DH Tony Conigliaro	R	21	57	7	1	0	2	8	9	.123
3B Dick McAuliffe	L	7	15	2	0	0	0	0	1	.133
1B Deron Johnson	R	3	10	6	0	0	1	2	3	.600
2B Steve Dilliard	R	1	5	2	0	0	0	2	0	.400
3B Butch Hobson	R	2	4	1	0	0	0	0	0	.250
2B Kim Andrew	R	2	2	1	0	0	0	0	0	.500
2B Buddy Hunter	R	1	1	0	0	0	0	0	0	.000
OF Bernie Carbo	L	107	319	82	21	3	15	64	50	.257
UT Juan Beniquez	R	78	254	74	14	4	2	43	17	.291
OF Rick Miller	L	77	108	21	2	1	0	21	15	.194
C Bob Montgomery	R	62	195	44	10	1	2	16	26	.226
C Tim Blackwell	B	59	132	26	3	2	0	15	6	197
C Tim McCarver	L	12	21	8	2	1	0	1	3	.381
C Andy Merchant	L	1	4	2	0	0	0	1	0	.500

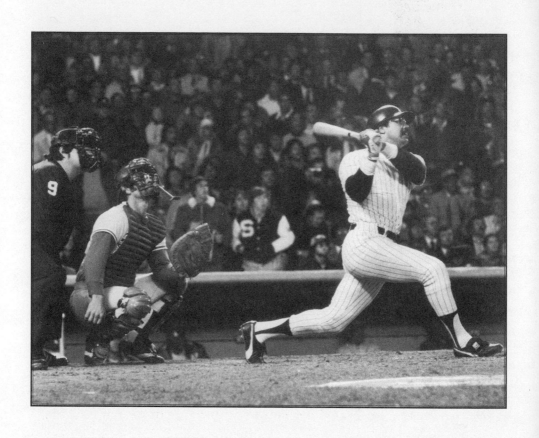

1977: Yankees vs. Dodgers

Reggie Jackson's Three Dingers

from *Ladies and Gentlemen, The Bronx is Burning* by Jonathan Mahler

If the 1977 postseason was going to be a microcosm of the regular season—and that was how things were shaping up—there was just one piece missing: the controversial magazine story.

The new issue of *Time*, which contained a story headlined NICE GUYS ALWAYS FINISH . . . ?, greeted the Yankees on their return to New York on the cold, rainy morning of Monday, October 17. In a single page of text the magazine had Steinbrenner saying that several Yankees had pleaded with him to fire Martin; Martin saying that if Steinbrenner fired him, he'd never live it down with the fans ("a little Dago like me fixed his ass"); and Reggie saying he would refuse to play another year for Martin.

To most of America and all New York none of this came as any surprise. By now everyone just wanted to see how this bizarre drama would end.

The following morning, October 18, the skies had cleared but the cool air lingered in New York through the early part of the day.

Reggie had breakfast with his agent, Matt Merola, and then lounged around his apartment with Ray Negron. He called Ralph Destino to make plans for later. Destino was going to drive his son and Reggie's father and sister home from the ballpark. Then, as was their custom, they'd meet up at McMullen's.

By dusk the temperature in New York had climbed into the mid-50s. The home team went out for batting practice. A couple of Dodgers were sitting on ball bags in front of the third-base dugout. Several more stood on the dugout steps.

Yankees' third-base coach Dick Howser pitched to the last few of his men, a group that included Reggie Jackson. As he stepped in to take his cuts at around 6:40 p.m., a crowd gathered behind the cage. Reggie smashed three balls into the third tier and a fourth off the back wall of the right-field bleachers, some 500 feet from the plate. No one recalls exactly how many Reggie hit out during batting practice that evening—or rather the estimates vary widely—but everyone remembers it as an unprecedented performance. "Every ball flew like it was shot out of a cannon," says Roger Director, an editor at *Sport* magazine who was on the field at the time. "It was an electrifying thing. People were completely buzzed and amazed."

Fran Healy was shagging flies in left-center during the show. Healy, who swears that Reggie hit every pregame pitch out of the park, couldn't help remembering the old baseball saw that a good BP was a bad omen: "I thought to myself, 'Boy, is he gonna have a horseshit game.'"

In the days that followed, some said it had to end like this, but watching Reggie Jackson's Game 6 performance now, it seems like an odd conclusion to this long season of tension and torment, not anticlimactic, but somehow unbaseball-like. There is none of the subtle jockeying, the foul tips and worked counts that usually accompany memorable at bats. Reggie simply strides to the plate three consecutive times against three different pitchers and, before the commentators can even properly set the scene, strokes the first pitch he sees into the seats. One gets the sense that if this had been the first half of a twin bill—and Martin hadn't sat him in the second—he would have hit three more, not because he was so much better than everyone else but because something had been lit inside him. For this one night the all-too-human Reggie Jackson glowed with superhuman greatness.

He first appeared on center stage in the second inning, a black turtleneck under his double knits, the top button of his uniform unfastened as usual, with the Yankees trailing 2–0. Reggie had gone 0 for 4 with a pair of strikeouts against Burt Hooton in Game 2, but the balance of power had already shifted. Hooton didn't throw him anything near the strike zone.

At the start of the fourth, the Yanks now down 3–2, Reggie knelt on one knee in the on-deck circle and watched Thurman Munson rap a single to left. Expecting something hard and inside, Reggie took his usual spot in the box and then moved off the plate about six inches, glancing back to make sure the Dodgers' catcher hadn't noticed. Reggie tapped his bat lightly on the plate and turned his gaze to the mound. Sure enough, Hooton came inside with a fastball, and Reggie smoked it—a low liner, no more than 15 feet off the ground. Unsure of the ball's fate, Reggie broke hard out of the box before it landed in the first row of the right-field bleachers. He circled the bases briskly, his upper body bent forward, slowing to a trot about 10 feet from home. As he bounded down the dugout steps, Martin—"the beleaguered little pepperpot," as Cosell referred to him on ABC—gave him an adoring pat on the cheek.

The next inning three men were scheduled to hit before Reggie, but he pulled his 35-inch bat from the rack anyway as Elias Sosa, the right-handed fastballer who had relieved Hooton, finished his warm-up pitches. Three batters later, with two out and one on, Reggie came to the plate. He mashed down his helmet and turned on Sosa's first pitch, a fastball down and in, sending it screaming over the wall in right.

It was another line drive, so Reggie again sprinted out of the box and started motoring around the bases. Between first and second, he picked at his form-fitting uniform, pulling it away from his swelling chest, as the baying—

"*Reg-gie, Reg-gie, Reg-gie*"—washed over the park. The ABC cameras found him moments later at the first base end of the dugout, the second button of his uniform now undone. In case anyone at home had lost count, he held up a pair of fingers, mouthing the word *two*.

In the home half of the eighth, a standing ovation greeted Reggie as he walked toward the plate. The din continued as he smoothed the dirt in the batter's box with his spikes. Then, for a split second, after Reggie reached down for Charlie Hough's diving knuckleball, a good pitch, the crowd fell silent—"choking on its own disbelief," as the *Washington Post*'s Thomas Boswell would write. This time Reggie knew. He stood and watched as the ball sailed toward dead center, touching down about halfway up the stadium's blacked-out bleachers, some 475 feet from where it had collided with his bat. As Reggie glided around first, Dodgers' first baseman Steve Garvey applauded softly into his glove.

Reggie's last home run put the Yankees on top 8–3. The Yankees' first World Series in 15 years was almost won, and the Bronx ballyard was ready to explode. The stadium had quadrupled its security for that night's game. More than 100 cops in riot helmets now took their positions in foul territory, crouching on the field side of the wall along the first- and third-base lines. On the other side of the wall, officers were swinging their nightsticks above their heads to keep fans back. The public-address announcements began: "Ladies and gentlemen, no one is to go on the field at the end of the game."

On his way out to his position for the final three outs, Reggie—his pinstriped shirt now buttoned only halfway up—doffed his cap and blew kisses to the crowd. It was a long half inning. Torrez was weary, but he wanted to finish it, and Martin didn't see any harm in letting him. The outs came slowly, but they came. The bleacher creatures were now sitting along the top of the outfield fence, their legs dangling over the wall in fair territory. Firecrackers and cherry bombs were exploding on the field.

With two down in the top of the ninth, Reggie called a time-out and started running toward the dugout. ABC's Keith Jackson narrated: "Reggie

Jackson is leaving the field, and I don't blame him. The home fans are chasing their most valuable player off the field."

But Reggie was pointing at his head: He just wanted a batting helmet! It took a couple of minutes to find one—the equipment had already been moved into the clubhouse to keep it away from marauding fans—but Reggie eventually trotted back out for the final out, a little pop-up that Torrez handled himself.

In an instant, thousands of fevered fans were pouring onto the field. They came from every section of the stands, charging across the tables in the press box on their way down. The extra police and their five mounted horses were no match for this mass of swarming, shaggy-haired humanity. Reggie took off his helmet and glasses and started weaving in and out of the crowd, the fullback looking for daylight. Without his specs, he had poor depth perception; he was genuinely frightened. Gaining speed now, he sent a parka-plump, blue-jeaned fan sprawling with a shoulder block and disappeared into the dugout.

Only Babe Ruth had hit three home runs in a single World Series game (twice, in fact), but never in consecutive at bats, let alone on three pitches.

A feat like this, after a summer like this, lent itself to many different interpretations. To defenders of baseball's emerging era, it was proof that free agency had reenergized the game by raising the stakes for its performers and the expectations for its fans. To baseball nostalgists, it was a vindication of content over form, a victory of on-the-field drama over off-the-field melodrama. "We live in an unprivate time, and the roar of personality and celebrity has almost drowned out the cheering in the stands," wrote Roger Angell in the *New Yorker*. "The ironic and most remarkable aspect of Reggie Jackson's feat is that for a moment there, on that littered, brilliant field, he—he, of all people—almost made us forget this."

The tabloids wove Reggie's three mighty blows into their narrative of the city's struggle for survival. "Who dares to call New York a lost cause?" a pumped-up *Post* editorialized.

After antagonizing Reggie earlier in the season, the *Amsterdam News* now canonized him, comparing his Game 6 feat to Joe Louis's knockout of Max Schmeling and Jackie Robinson's first major-league home run. "Black residents of New York City reacted with a special jubilation and sense of triumph to the sensational performance by Reggie Jackson," the paper reported on its October 22 front page. "Much of the feeling appeared to be based on the widespread feeling among Blacks interviewed by *The Amsterdam News* that the white-dominated media and whites in the crowds, as well as the Yankees' white manager Billy Martin, had been especially hard on Jackson because he was Black, arrogant, and spoke his mind."

As for Reggie, he didn't see why he should be limited to one interpretation. In the dozens of interviews he gave in the ensuing weeks, his Game 6 performance became a triumph of the Lord ("God allowed me to do that"), a humanitarian gesture ("I'll tell you what I was thinking . . . *I did this for all of us. Take it. Enjoy it. And let's do it again*"), and, naturally, an emphatic telegram from the once-embattled superstar to his enemies, real and imagined: "Those home runs delivered a simple message: Let me up now—I'm no longer gonna be held down."

After the game most of the Yankees headed to a team party at the Sheraton in Hasbrouck Heights, New Jersey.

A few hours before the first pitch, Martin had been given a $35,000 bonus, a Lincoln Continental, and the assurance that he'd have his job in 1978. Now he'd won his first World Series as a manager. But he still couldn't enjoy himself. He was exhausted, and the party was too crowded. Martin flung his scotch to the floor and repaired to a quiet bar nearby.

Reggie was late getting to McMullen's. The game ended at 10:43 p.m. and he and Destino usually met an hour after the last out. But at 12:30 a.m. Destino, who had brought along two dates for them, was still waiting.

Reggie eventually showed, pulling his blue Volkswagen up onto the sidewalk on Third Avenue. At around 2 a.m., Governor Carey arrived with a small entourage. The two parties merged and proceeded to drink champagne and eat cheeseburgers into the morning. Sometime after 3 a.m. Carey summoned two state troopers to guard Reggie's car and assured Jim McMullen that the rules that govern after-hours drinking had been suspended for the night.

At a little before dawn, Reggie dashed home for a quick shower and change of clothes and headed down to Rockefeller Center for an interview with the *Today* show. It was cool and drizzly in New York, the start of the Son of Sam's competency hearings and the day the first Concorde was scheduled to touch down at Kennedy Airport.

After the ticker-tape parade for the World Champion New York Yankees had made its way down Broadway to City Hall, Reggie went back uptown to Cartier. Soon he would start trying to persuade Destino to drive with him to spring training in his new Rolls-Royce, which was outfitted with a CB radio. (Destino's handle was the King of Diamonds; Reggie's, in honor of the forthcoming REGGIE! candy bar, was the Candyman.) For now, though, Reggie just wanted to stretch out on the couch in Destino's office and close his eyes.

1985: Royals vs. Cardinals

The Call

from *The Sedalia Democrat,* "'85 I-70 Series: Blame It on Balboni," by Phil Ellenbecker

It's Royals-Cardinals time again. Or Cardinals-Royals. Time to talk about Don Denkinger.

You know, the guy who cost the St. Louis Cardinals in the I–70 World Series of 1985, the guy who blew the call in the ninth inning of the sixth game, allowing the Kansas City Royals to steal the game on their way to their first and only Series title. His name always seems to pop up this time of year.

Well, as a nearly lifelong Kansan who grew up with the Royals, I'm here to tell you that Don Denkinger didn't cost the Cardinals the 1985 World Series. Steve Balboni did.

Let me explain. The call Denkinger clearly blew was on Jorge Orta's nubber between the pitcher's mound and first base on an 0–2 count to start the inning. Orta was called safe at first on a bang-bang play that wasn't so bang-bang when you looked at the replays.

But there's no clock in baseball so the Cardinals, with a 1–0 lead, had all the time in the world, or at least three outs—which can be an eternity in baseball—to make Denkinger's transgression forgettable.

They failed miserably. Starting with the next batter, Balboni. He should have been out when Jack Clark muffed his foul fly. And he probably should have been out when the count went to 0–2.

I can clearly remember sitting at a dive in Leavenworth, Kansas, at that time, just getting off work, and turning to the geezer next to me and saying, "He's gonna strike out."

Balboni led the American League in strikeouts that year, so that wasn't exactly a bold prediction.

So what does "Bonesy" do? He reaches down and golfs a single to left field, a nifty bit of hitting I'd never expected out of a hit-or-miss guy like Balboni.

Looking back on what transpired after that, lo these many years, I feel fairly confident that if Todd Worrell could have put Balboni away in that at bat, or better yet, coaxed a double-play ball (St. Louis was third in the major leagues in doubles turned that season), the Cardinals would have kept the Royals off the scoreboard and walked off with the Series title.

But it didn't happen, and three batters later Jim Sundberg was crossing the plate with the winning run on a single by Dane Iorg (ironically, somewhat of a Series hero for the Cardinals in 1982), giving the Royals a 2–1 victory. The Cardinals had an 89–0 record with a lead going into the ninth inning entering this game.

And let the whining begin. Cardinals manager White Herzog (known as "The White Rat," but I prefer "The White Waaah," as in the big crybaby) as much as said after the game that his team didn't have a chance in the seventh game after the horrible way they'd been wronged by that dastardly Denkinger.

And then the Cardinals went out and proved their skipper right with a horrible, embarrassing performance in Game 7, losing 11–0. Both Herzog and Joaquin Andujar got booted from the game and ace pitcher John Tudor, on his way into the locker room after being punched out by the Royals, cut his pitching hand while trying to punch out an electrical fan.

The last two games were pretty typical of the Cards' performance throughout the Series. This team had a 2–0 lead coming into three games at home and blew it. Mainly because they couldn't ever, ever hit against the Royals' pitching.

The Cardinals had a .185 batting average in the Series. As Jed Clampett would say, "Pitiful, just pitiful."

And don't tell me that Vince Coleman, the freshman phenom on the base paths for the Cardinals who got ate up by a tarp before the Series started, would have made a difference. As the saying goes, you can't steal first base.

I could go on and on. But suffice it to say, the Royals deserved to win that season. A great franchise (before Ewing Kauffman had to give up the ghost) that had always come up short in the late 1970s and early '80s, this was a team of destiny.

So enough about Don Denkinger already, Cardinals fans. Get over it.

Oh, and one more thing. Give Jorge Orta some credit. With an 0–2 count on him he did what every ballplayer from little league on is told to do in that situation: Get your bat on the ball and stay alive. He reached out and flicked Worrell's pitch between the pitcher and first, hustled his butt on down to first and made the play just close enough for Don Denkinger to live in infamy.

While visiting St. Louis last month, Don Denkinger received two things he never saw coming. The first was a new watch. The second was a standing ovation.

He was speaking at a 20th anniversary dinner for the Cardinals' 1985 World Series team, a benefit for the Whitey Herzog Youth Foundation. Bob Costas was the emcee, Denkinger the guest of honor. The longtime Major League Baseball umpire and Waterloo resident says nobody told him he had to address the crowd—some 600 guests—until he showed up. So he winged it.

He thanked Herzog and Costas and the foundation for inviting him. He dusted off some old jokes, his favorite anecdotes from 31 years of service to baseball. He recounted a time he was behind home plate while Jack Clark, then with the New York Yankees, was batting.

At one point, Clark turned and asked, "Where was that pitch at?"

"Jack," Denkinger teased, "don't you know you're not supposed to end a sentence with a preposition?"

Clark asked for a time-out and stepped out of the box.

"OK," the first baseman replied, "where was that pitch at, [expletive]?"

"That knocked them out," Denkinger, 69, says with a soft chuckle. "I left 'em falling out of their chairs. It was wonderful. It was . . ."

Cathartic?

A pause.

"No," he finally sighs. "Not really. It was really only my second trip to St. Louis. It's not that I don't want to go to St. Louis; I just don't have a reason to go to St. Louis. It's a great place, a great town. Great people. The Cardinals just have this big following."

A following with whom, 20 years down the road, Denkinger is slowly, finally, making peace.

On Oct. 26, 1985, at Royals Stadium, the St. Louis Cardinals led Game 6 of the World Series, 1–0, in the bottom of the ninth. Denkinger was working along the first-base line. Kansas City's Jorge Orta slapped a grounder between first and second. Clark, then playing first base for the Cardinals, fielded it but was slow getting it out of the glove. Pitcher Todd Worrell ran to cover the bag.

The throw was a little wide and a tad high. Denkinger had set himself in a bad position—he overran the play—and wasn't sure that Worrell's foot was touching first base.

He called Orta safe. Replays showed that not only was Worrell's foot on the bag, but the throw beat Orta by a full step.

The Cardinals pretty much imploded from there. Kansas City won in improbable fashion, 2–1. The next night, the Royals crushed St. Louis, 11–0, to take the championship, and furious Cardinals fans made Denkinger the scapegoat.

A St. Louis disc jockey gave his home number and address over the air. Callers threatened to come to Waterloo and burn down the house. Letters threatened far worse.

When Denkinger arrived home after the Series, he found police cars stationed on both ends of his street.

"I think some of the [threats] were from people involved in the gambling side," Denkinger says now. "Somebody thinks they've got a sure thing and the money's in and then it backfires, they've got to have somebody to blame it on.

"I didn't tell him to spend his money foolishly. I didn't tell him to spend his money on the Cardinals."

Time heals. The passion and pain give way to perspective. It wasn't Denkinger's fault that Vince Coleman was hurt. Or that Clark couldn't handle Steve Balboni's pop-up. Or that Cardinals catcher Darrell Porter got his signs crossed.

Still, Denkinger screwed up, no question. He admits it. He's never run from it. Ever.

When he agreed to sign autographs at a card show in St. Louis last October—his first appearance in the city since the '85 Series—he told himself: No matter what they ask for, no matter what they request, I will do it with a smile.

And he did. Even when a man dressed in Cardinal red walked up to Denkinger's table and asked if he would write:

To Dave,

I blew it.

—Don Denkinger

"I didn't back off one step," Denkinger says. "I was getting paid to do this. Whatever made them feel good. I know I missed that play. Life goes on."

Denkinger, who retired in 1998, still splits his time between Waterloo and his winter home in Arizona. He still golfs like crazy, even though drives come a little shorter off the tee. He hasn't changed. We have. ESPN Classic recently featured Denkinger as the subject of its "The Top 5 Reasons You Can't Blame . . ." series, in which long-standing fan assertions or myths are refuted. A feature on his place in baseball lore is scheduled to run tonight on HBO Sports' "Costas Now."

"My wife asks me, 'When is it going to stop?'" Denkinger says. "I said, 'I guess when I stop picking up the phone and talking to people about it.' They just keep throwing it up to you. It's something you just can't forget."

You ask Denkinger why he hung on to all those angry letters over the years. He says he thought, at one time, about writing a book. Now he's not so sure.

Some wounds are better left closed.

"There's really no animosity here toward him anymore," assures Al Hrabosky, the Cardinals' former pitcher, television analyst, and St. Louis sports icon. "Don's probably harder on himself than most of the fans."

But not all. An instant after the Herzog Foundation presented him with that gift watch, Denkinger flipped open the box. That's when he noticed something different about the face. The numbers were inscribed in Braille.

1986: Mets vs. Red Sox

Bill Buckner and the Infamous Ground Ball

from *The New Yorker,* The Sporting Scene, "Not So, Boston," by Roger Agnell

Yes, it was. Yes, we did. Yes, that was the way it was, really and truly. . . . The baseball events of this October—the Mets' vivid comeback victory over the Boston Red Sox in seven games, and the previous elimination of the Houston Astros and the California Angels in the hazardous six-game and seven-game (respectively) league-championship playoffs—will not be quickly forgotten, but disbelief is a present danger. Sporting memory is selective and unreliable, with a house tilt toward hyperbole. In inner replay, the running catch, the timely home run become incomparable, and our view of them grows larger and clearer as they recede in time, putting us all into a front-row box seat in the end, while the rest of that game and that day—the fly-ball outs, the four-hop grounders, the fouls into the stands, the botched double play, the sleepy innings, the failed rally, the crush at the concession stand, the jam in the parking lot—are miraculously leached away. This happens so often and so easily that we may not be prepared for its opposite: a set of games and innings and plays and turnabouts that, for once, not only matched but exceeded our baseball expectations, to the point where we may be asking ourselves now if all this really did come to pass at the end of the 1986 season and if it was all right for us to get so excited about it, so hopeful and then so heartbroken or struck with pleasure. To which let it be said again: Yes, it did. Yes, it was. Yes, absolutely. What matters now, perhaps, is for each of us to make an effort to hold on to these games, for almost certainly we won't see their like again soon—or care quite as much if we do.

Purists are saying that the postseason baseball this year was not of a particularly high quality. In the World Series, the first five games were played out without a vestige of a rally, or even of a retied score; that is, the first team to bring home a run won the game. Each of the first four games, moreover, was lost by the home team: not much fun for the fans. One of the games turned on an egregious muff of a routine ground ball, and another produced the decisive event (it turned out) on the third pitch of the evening—a home run by the Mets' Lenny Dykstra.

Game Five, World Series

This was less than a classic, perhaps, but there was spirit and pleasure in it. The home-team Red Sox ravaged their Fenway supporters with a 4–2 win, behind their mettlesome left-hander Bruce Hurst, and defeated Dwight Gooden for the second time in the process. This was the Sox' high-water mark (it turned out later), putting them ahead by 3 games to 2, but it also felt like the first game in which the Series competition was fully joined. The Bostons, it will be recalled, had won the Series opener down at Shea, with a splendid 1–0 effort by Hurst against Ron Darling, in which the only run had come in on an error by Mets second baseman Tim Teufel. A promised Gooden-Clemens thriller the next day came to nothing when the Sox won by 9–3, doing away with Dwight almost without effort; Clemens, for his part, was wild, and was gone in the fifth inning. This was Dwight Evans's great game: a mighty two-run homer that caromed off a tent marquee out beyond left-center field, and then a lovely sliding, twisting catch against Dykstra in right. Up in Boston, the Mets, now in a jam, rebounded strongly, with four first-inning runs against

Oil Can Boyd in Game 3; Dykstra's leadoff home run set the tone, all right, but the central figure of the evening may have been the Mets' lithe left-hander Bobby Ojeda, a member of the Red Sox pitching corps last year, who nibbled the corners authoritatively ("You don't live in one place in this ballpark," he said later) in the course of his 7–1 outing, and became the first left-hander to win a postseason game at Fenway Park since Hippo Vaughn turned the trick for the Cubs in 1918. Those two quick losses to the Red Sox in the early games meant that Davey Johnson would be overdrawn at the pitching bank in the ensuing games, but he got even at last in Game 4, when Ron Darling shut down the Sox for seven innings (he gave up no earned runs at all in his first two outings), and the Mets roughed up Al Nipper et al. with twelve hits, including two homers by Gary Carter. A rainout the next evening provided a breather for the careworn pitchers and probably improved the quality of the games over the remaining distance. (A missing figure in the Red Sox pitching rotation was Tom Seaver, who suffered a knee-cartilage tear in September and was forced to sit out all the postseason games: hard news for Sox fans—and for Mets fans, too, I believe.)

Hurst's work here in Game 6 was the kind of pitcher's outing that I have most come to admire over the years—a masterful 10-hitter, if that is possible. This was his fourth start in postseason play, and although he was not nearly as strong as he had looked during his gemlike shutout at Shea, he used what he had and kept matters in check, scattering small hits through the innings and down the lineup, and racking up ground-ball outs in discouraging (to the Mets) clusters with his forkball. ("It Hursts So Good," one Fenway fan banner said.) The pitch, which disconcertingly breaks down and away from right-handed batters, sets up the rest of his repertoire—a curve and a sneaky-quick fastball—and although Hurst resolutely refers to it as a forkball, it is in fact the ever-popular new split-fingered fastball (*sort* of a forkball), which Hurst learned in 1984, during a brief on-the-field consultation with its inventor, Roger Craig, the present Giants manager, who at that time was coaching the Tigers' pitching staff; it is probably this circumstance that has made Hurst so diplomatic in his nomenclature, for coaches are not encouraged to distribute magic potions to players on strong opposition teams within their own division. Hurst didn't actually have enough confidence to use the pitch in a game until late June last year, at a time when he had been exiled to the Red Sox bullpen, but it revived his career wonderfully, transforming him from a journeyman 33–40 lifetime pitcher (in 5¹/₂ seasons) to a 22–14 winner in the subsequent going. Hurst missed seven weeks this summer with a groin injury, but he convalesced rapidly, wrapping up his season's work by going 5–0 and 1.07 in his last five starts, which won him a league accolade as Pitcher of the Month in September. Despite all this, I think we should be wary about making too much of one particular delivery, for pitching is a lot harder than that.

Hurst, it should be noted, belongs to the exclusive Fenway Lefties Finishing School, which numbers two other polished and extremely successful southpaw practitioners among its graduates: Bob Ojeda and John Tudor, who pitched the Cardinals to a pennant last year with a tremendous 21–8, 1.93 summer and then won three games in postseason play. Ojeda, for his part, had an 18–5 record with the Mets this year, which was the best won-lost percentage compiled by any of the Mets' celebrated starters; it was the best in the league, in fact. Previously, Ojeda had toiled for six summers in Fenway Park, and Tudor for five.

The uniting characteristics of the three Wallmasters are control, extreme confidence, and a willingness to come inside. At Fenway Park, the inside pitch to a right-handed hitter is what it's all about, for it discourages him from leaning out over the plate in the hope of something he can rap onto or over the Green Monster, and requires him, in fact, to compete with the man on the mound for his—the pitcher's—part of the plate and for his sector of the ballpark, which is to say outside, and to right or right-center: a mismatch. The inside pitch, it should be added, is mostly thrown in the early innings, to plant the *idea* of it in the batter's head, but is then eschewed in the late going, when weariness is more likely to result in a tiny, fatal mistake. Actually, it doesn't have to be thrown for a strike in order to have its effect, and unless you are a Clemens or someone of that order, it's probably a much better pitch, all in all, if it's a ball. "What Ojeda does, over and over, is one of the beauties of the game," Keith Hernandez said at one point in the Series. "When you miss, you've got to miss where it doesn't hurt you. That's what pitching is all about." For his part, Hurst, who throws over the top and finishes his delivery with a stylish little uptailed kick of his back leg, works with great cheerfulness and energy, and here in Game 5 he finished his evening's work with a flourish, fanning Dykstra for the last out of the game, with Mets runners on first and third. "BRUCE!" the fans yowled. "BRUUUUCE!"

It was a great night at the Fens. A gusty wind blew across the old premises (left to right, for the most part), and a couple of advertising balloons out beyond the wall bucked and dived in the breeze, tearing at their tethers. The long cries from the outermost fan sectors (the oddly slanting aisles out there looked like ski trails dividing the bleacher escarpments) came in windblown gusts, suddenly louder or fainter. The wind got into the game, too, knocking down one long drive by Henderson in the second (it was poorly played by Strawberry) and another by Jim Rice in the fifth, which sailed away from Dykstra and caromed off the top railing of the Sox' bullpen—triples, both of them, and runs thereafter. It was the kind of game in which each player on the home team (in that beautiful whiter-than-white home uniform, with navy sweatshirt sleeves, red stirrups, the curved, classical block-letter "RED SOX" across the chest, and a narrow piping of red around the neck and down the shirtfront) seems to impress his own special mode or mannerism on your memory: Rich Gedman's lariatlike swirl of the bat over his head as he swings through a pitch; Rice's double cut with the bat when he misses—swish-*swish*—with the backward retrieving swing suggesting a man trying to kill a snake; Boggs's way of dropping his head almost onto the bat as he stays down in midswing; Buckner (with that faro-dealer's mustache and piratical daubings of antiglare black on his cheeks) holding the bat in his extended right hand and, it seems, aiming it at the pitcher's eyes as he stands into the box for an at bat. And so on. Almost everyone out there, it seemed—every one of the good guys, that is—had his moment in the game to celebrate and be put aside in recollection by the fans: Hendu's triple and double, Marty Barrett's walk and single and double (he batted .433 for the Series), a beautiful play by Boggs on Kevin Mitchell's tough grounder in the second, and, best of all, Billy Buck's painful and comical hobbling gallop around third and in to the plate in the third inning to bring home the second run of the game on a single by Evans. Buckner can barely run (can barely play) at all, because of his sore back and his injury-raddled ankles; it takes him two hours to ice and wrap his legs before he can take the field. He had torn an Achilles tendon in the September 29th game and was playing in this one only on courage and painkillers and with the help of protective high-top boots. No one wanted to laugh at his journey home after Evans bounced the ball up the middle, but you couldn't help yourself. He looked like Walter Brennan coming home—all elbows and splayed-out, achy feet, with his mouth gaping open with the effort, and his head thrown back in pain and hope and ridiculous deceleration. When he got there, beating the throw after all, he flumped belly-first onto the plate and lay there for a second, panting in triumph, and, piece by piece, got up a hero.

This was the last home game of the year for the Red Sox, and when it was over the fans stayed in the stands for a time (John Kiley gave them "McNamara's Band" on the organ again and again), clustering thickly around the home dugout and calling out for Hurst and Billy Buckner and the others, and shouting "We're Number One!" and waving their white Red Sox painters' caps in exuberance. There had been great anxiety about this game, because of the Mets' sudden revival in Games 3 and 4, but now the Sox were moving down to New York for one more win, with a rested Clemens going on Saturday and with Hurst ready again, if needed, on Sunday, and I don't think anyone there at the end that night really thought it might not happen. There is great sadness in this, in retrospect, since the team's eventual loss (and the horrendous way of it, on each of the last two days) has brought back the old miasmal Boston baseball doubt and despair—the Bermuda low that has hung over this park and this team perhaps since the day in 1920 when owner Harry Frazee traded a good young left-handed pitcher named Babe

Ruth to the Yankees, two seasons after Ruth had helped bring the Sox their last (to this day [1986]) World Championship. Once again, New England's fans have been sent into the winter with the dour nourishment of second-best to sustain them: Indian pudding. If they wish, they may once again ponder the wisdom of Oscar Wilde's opinion that there are two tragedies in this world: One is never getting what you want, and the other is getting it—a dictum they would love to put to the test someday.

But enough of this. Glooming in print about the dire fate of the Sox and their oppressed devotees has become such a popular art form that it verges on a new Hellenistic age of mannered excess. Everyone east of the Hudson with a Selectric or a word processor has had his or her say, it seems (the *Globe* actually published a special 24-page section titled "Literati on the Red Sox" before the Series, with essays by George Will, John Updike, Bart Giammatti—the new National League president, but for all that a Boston fan through and through—Stephen King, Doris Kearns Goodwin, and other worthies), and one begins to see at last that the true function of the Red Sox may be not to win but to provide New England authors with a theme, now that guilt and whaling have gone out of style. I would put forward a different theory about this year's loss and how it may be taken by the fans. As one may surmise from the *Globe*'s special section, the Red Sox have become chic: Pulitzer Prize winners and readers of the *New York Review of Books* hold season tickets behind first base, and the dropped "Geddy" and "Dewey" and "Roger" and "the Can" clang along with the sounds of cutlery and grants chat at the Harvard Faculty Club. The other, and perhaps older, fan constituency at Fenway Park has not always been as happy and philosophical about the Sox. The failures of the seventies and early eighties were taken hard by the Boston sports crowd (the men and women who care as much about the Celtics and the Patriots and the Bruins as they do about the Sox), and the departure of Carlton Fisk, Rick Burleson, Freddy Lynn, and Luis Tiant, and the retirement (at long last) of Yastrzemski, left a very bitter taste, and so did the team's persistent, almost stubborn unsuccess in the 1980s. (It finished fifth, fourth, and sixth in the American League East in the three years before this one, an average 19 games behind the leader.) The ugly "Choke Sox" label was much heard, and the team's ancient, stubbornly held style of play, characterized by insufficient pitching, insufficient or nonexistent speed, a million ground-ball double plays (by the Sox, I mean), and an almost religious belief in the long ball, had become a byword in the game, a "pahk your cah" joke around the league. Nothing could change this, it seemed.

But this year it changed: a baseball miracle. This year, the Red Sox not only won their division and the American League playoffs and, very nearly, the World Series but became a different sort of team, to themselves above all. Nineteen eighty-six turned around for the Red Sox because of Roger Clemens (and perhaps because of Schiraldi's sudden midseason arrival as a bullpen stopper), but a more significant alteration was one of attitude—a turnabout that began when Don Baylor came over from the Yankees and almost immediately became the team leader, something the Sox had been lacking for as long as anyone could remember. He told the young pitchers that they had to pitch inside if the team was to win; he persuaded the batters to take the extra base, to look for ways to get on base in the late innings (like getting hit with pitches, for instance: a Baylor specialty), to find that little edge—the one play or moment or lucky hop—that turns games around. Tom Seaver came aboard in June, and deepened this same aura with his maturity, his ease, and his sense of humor and proportion. The Sox grew up this summer: you could see it on the field—in Jim Rice choking up on the bat by an inch or so when he got to two strikes (this for the first time ever) and stroking the ball to right-center now and then, so that though his homers went down by seven (to 20), his batting average improved by 33 points and his hits by 41—and in the results. The players spoke of it themselves. "We have more character," they said, and "We're going to win"—words unheard by this writer from any Boston club of the past.

What fans think about their team is subtle and hard to pin down, but I am convinced that everything was changed this year by one game—by that stubborn and lucky and altogether astounding Red Sox return from near-defeat in the fifth game out at Anaheim, when they came back from extinction and a three-run deficit in the ninth inning and won by 7–6. It almost carried the month, and it is startling to notice, in retrospect, that the Red Sox actually won five games in a row right in the middle of the postseason—the last three of their championship playoffs and the first two of the World Series. There is no prize for this, of course, but no other team in October played quite so well for quite so long. In its killing last-minute details, their loss to the Mets in Game 6 (they fell after holding a two-run lead in the 10th inning, with no one on base for the Mets) was so close to what the Angels had experienced that their fans—even the most deep-dark and uncompromising among the bleacherites, I think—must have seen the connection, and at last sensed the difficulties of this game and how much luck and character and resolve it takes to be a winner in the end. History and the ghost of Sox teams past had nothing to do with it. The Choke Sox died in Anaheim, and this losing Red Sox team will be regarded in quite a different way in New England this winter. It will be loved.

Game Six, World Series

The Mets are not loved—not away from New York, that is. When the teams moved up to the Hub, with the Mets behind by 2 games to none, there was a happy little rush of historical revisionism as sportswriters and baseball thinkers hurried forward to kick the New York nine. Tim Horgan, a columnist with the Boston *Herald*, wrote, "Personally, I don't think anything west of Dedham can be as marvelous as the Mets are supposed to be. I wouldn't even be surprised if the Mets are what's known as a media myth, if only because New York City is the world capital of media myths." Bryant Gumbel, on NBC's Today show, called the Mets arrogant, and ran a tape of Keith Hernandez's bad throw on a bunt play in Game 2, calling it "a hot-dog play." Sparky Anderson, the Tigers manager, declared over the radio that the Indians, the traditional doormats of his American League division, put a better nine on the field than the Mets, and a newspaper clip from the heartland (if San Diego is in the heart of America) that subsequently came my way contained references to "this swaggering band of mercenaries" and "a swaying forest of high fives and taunting braggadocio."

Much of this subsided when the Mets quickly drew even in the games, and much of it has nothing to do with baseball, of course; what one tends to forget is that there is nothing that unites America more swiftly or happily than bad news in Gotham or a losing New York team. Some of these reflections warmed me, inwardly and arrogantly, as Game 6 began, for I was perched in a splendid upper-deck-grandstand seat directly above home plate, where, in company with my small family and the Mets' mighty fan family, I gazed about at the dazzlement of the ballpark floodlights, the electric-green field below, and the encircling golden twinkle of beautiful (by night) Queens, and heard and felt, deep in my belly, the pistol-shot sounds of clapping, the cresting waves of "LETSGOMETS! LETSGOMETS! LETSGOMETS!" and long, taunting calls—"Dew-eee! DEW-EEEE!" and "Rog-errr! ROG-ERRRR!"—directed at some of the Bosox below: payback for what the Fenway fans had given Darryl Strawberry in the last game in Boston. And then a parachutist came sailing down out of the outer darkness and into the bowl of light and noise—a descending roar, of all things—of Shea. "Go METS," his banner said as he lightly came to rest a few steps away from Bob Ojeda in mid-infield and, encumbered with minions, went cheerfully off to jail and notoriety. We laughed and forgot him. I was home.

Game 6 must be given here in extreme précis—not a bad idea, since its nonstop events and reversals and mistakes and stunners blur into unlikelihood even when examined on a scorecard. I sometimes make postgame additions to my own scorecard in red ink, circling key plays and instants to refresh my recollection, and adding comments on matters I may have overlooked or misjudged at the time. My card of Game 6 looks like a third grader's valentine, with scarlet exclamation points, arrows, stars, question marks, and "Wow!"s scrawled thickly across the double page. A double arrow connects Boggs, up on top, to Spike Owen, down below, in the Boston second—a dazzling little hit (by Wade)-and-run (by Spike) that set up Boston's second score of the game. Two red circles are squeezed into Jim Rice's box in the Boston seventh—one around the "E5" denoting Ray Knight's wild peg that put Rice on first and sent Marty Barrett around to third, and the other around the "7–2" that ended the inning, two outs and one run later, when Mookie Wilson threw out Jim at the plate. A descendant arrow and low-flying exclamation points mark Clemens's departure from the game after the seventh (the Red Sox were ahead by 3–2, but Roger, after 131 pitches, had worked up a blister on his pitching hand), and an up-bound red dart and "MaZZ PH" pointing at the same part of the column denote Lee Mazzilli's instant single against Schiraldi, while the black dot in the middle of the box is the Mazzilli run that tied the score. But nothing can make this sprawling, clamorous game become orderly, I see now, and, of course, no shorthand can convey the vast, encircling, supplicating sounds of that night, or the sense of encroaching danger on the field, or the anxiety that gnawed at the Mets hordes in the stands as their season ran down, it seemed certain, to the wrong ending.

The Red Sox scored twice in the top of the 10th inning, on a home run by Dave Henderson ("Hendu!" is my crimson comment) and a double and a single by the top of the order—Boggs and then Barrett—all struck against Rick Aguilera, the fourth Mets pitcher of the night. Call it the morning, for it was past midnight when the Sox took the field in the bottom half, leading by 5–3. Three outs were needed for Boston's championship, and two of them were tucked away at once. Keith Hernandez, having flied out to center for the second out, left the dugout and walked into Davey Johnson's office in the clubhouse to watch the end; he said later that this was the first instant when he felt that the Mets might not win. I had moved down to the main press box, ready for a dash to the clubhouses, and now I noticed that a few Mets fans had given up and were sadly coming along the main aisles down below me, headed for home. My companion just to my right in the press box, the *News'* Red Foley, is a man of few words, but now he removed his cigar from his mouth and pointed at the departing fans below. "O ye of little faith," he said.

It happened slowly but all at once, it seemed later. Gary Carter singled. Kevin Mitchell, who was batting for Aguilera, singled to center. Ray Knight fouled off two sinkers, putting the Red Sox one strike away. (Much later, somebody counted up and discovered that there were *13* pitches in this inning that could have been turned into the last Mets out of all.) "Ah, New

England," I jotted in my notebook, just before Knight bopped a little single to right-center, scoring Carter and sending Mitchell to third—and my notebook note suddenly took on quite a different meaning. It was along about here, I suspect, that my friend Allan, who is a genius palindromist, may have taken his eyes away from his set (he was watching at home) for an instant to write down a message that had been forming within him: "Not so, Boston"—the awful truth, no matter how you look at it.

Schiraldi departed, and Bob Stanley came on to pitch. (This was the Steamer's moment to save what had been an unhappy 6–6 and 4.37 season for him, in which his work as the Sox' prime right-handed stopper had received increasingly unfavorable reviews from the Fenway bleacher critics; part of me was pulling for him here, but the game was out of my hands—and evidently out of his as well.) Mookie Wilson, batting left-handed, ran the count to 2 and 2, fouled off two more pitches, and then jumped away, jackknifing in midair, to avoid a thigh-high wild pitch that brought Mitchell flying in from third, to tie it. Wilson fouled off two more pitches in this at bat of a lifetime and then tapped a little bouncer down toward first, close to the baseline, that hopped once, hopped twice, and then slipped under Buckner's glove and on into short right field (he turned and stared after it in disbelief), and Knight thundered in from around third base. He jumped on home plate with both feet—jumped so hard that he twisted his back, he said later—and then disappeared under an avalanche of Mets.

The postmortems were nearly unbearable. "This is the worst," Bob Stanley said.

"I'm exhausted," Ray Knight said. "My legs are trembling."

"As close as we came . . ." whispered John McNamara. "As close as we came, I can only associate it with California."

"It's baseball," said Dave Henderson. "It's baseball, and we've got to live with it."

Questions were asked—they always are after major accidents—and some of them must be asked again, for this game will be replayed, in retrospect, for years to come.

Q: Why didn't Davey Johnson double-switch when he brought in Jesse Orosco to get the last out of the eighth inning? Without an accompanying substitute at some other slot in the order, Jesse was forced to depart for a pinch-hitter an instant later, in the Mets' half, thus requiring Johnson to wheel in Aguilera, who was a much less certain quantity on the mound, and who quickly gave up the two runs that so nearly finished off the Mets. A: I still don't know, for Davey is a master at the double switch—a textbook maneuver in National League tactics manuals, since there is no designated hitter—and a bit later on he made a much more questionable switch, which removed Darryl Strawberry from the game. It came out all right in the end, but I think Davey just forgot.

Q: Why didn't McNamara pinch-hit for the creaking Buckner in the 10th, when another run could have nailed down the Mets for sure? And, having decided against this, why didn't he at least put the much more mobile Stapleton in to play first base in the bottom half—perhaps to gobble up Wilson's grounder and make the flip to the pitcher? More specifically, why didn't he pinch-hit Baylor, his designated hitter, who batted in the No. 5 slot throughout the regular season and in the playoffs but rode the bench (no DH) almost to the end during the games played at Shea? A: Johnny Mack has defended himself strongly against both of these second guesses, citing Buckner's excellent bat (a .267 year, with 18 home runs and a 102 runs batted in) and Buckner's glove ("He has good hands," he said), in that order. His answer to the Baylor puzzle is to say that Baylor never pinch-hits when the Red Sox are ahead—sound strategy, one can see, until a game arrives when they might suddenly fall behind at the end. McNamara also claims that Stapleton normally substitutes for Buckner at first base only if there has been an earlier occasion to insert him as a pinch-*runner* for Buckner; this is mostly true (it wasn't the case in Game 5), but the fact remains that Stapleton was playing first base in the final inning of all three games that the Sox did win. My strong guess is that McNamara is not beyond sentiment. He knew the torments that Buckner had gone through to stay in the lineup throughout the season, and the contributions he had made to bring the club to this shining doorstep, and he wanted him out there with the rest of the varsity when the Sox seemed certain to step over it at last.

We need not linger long on Game 7, in which the Mets came back from a 3–0 second-inning deficit and won going away (as turf writers say), 8–5. It was another great game, I suppose, but even noble vintages can become a surfeit after enough bottles have been sampled. A one-day rainout allowed us to come down a little from the sixth game and its astounding ending, but then we came to the last day of all, and the sense of that—a whole season rushing to a decision now—seized us and wrung us with almost every pitch once play resumed. Ron Darling, who had given up no earned runs in the Series so far, surrendered three in the second inning (Evans and Gedman whacked home runs on successive pitches) and was gone in the fourth. Hurst, for his part, permitted only a lone single in five full innings, but ran dry in the sixth, when the Mets evened the game. They had specialized in this sleeping-dragon style of play all through the championship season, and this last time around they showed us once again how dangerous they really were: nine hits and eight runs in their last three innings of the year.

Somehow, the anguish of the Red Sox mattered more than the Mets' caperings at the very end, because it was plain by now that it could have just as easily gone the other way. In the Boston clubhouse, Al Nipper, who was badly battered during his very brief appearance in the New York eighth, sat at his locker with his back turned and his head buried in his hands. Dennis Boyd, who had not been called on in the Sox' extremity, rocked forward and back on his chair, shaking his head in disbelief. Friends of mine said later that they had been riveted by a postgame television closeup of Wade Boggs sitting alone in the dugout with tears streaming down his face, and a couple of them who are not fans asked me how it was possible for grown men to weep about something as trivial as a game. I tried to tell them about the extraordinary heights of concentration and intensity that are required to play baseball at this level, even for a single trifling game in midseason, but I don't think they believed me. Then I remembered a different moment on television—something I saw a couple of years ago on a trip abroad, when the captain of the All-England cricket team was interviewed over the BBC just after his 11 (I *think*) had lost a protracted test match to Australia. I listened to the young man's sad recapitulations with predictable American amusement—until I suddenly noticed that there were tears in his eyes. He was crying over *cricket!* I suppose we should all try to find something better or worse to shed tears for than a game, no matter how hard it has been played, but perhaps it is not such a bad thing to see that men can cry at all.

The acute moment in Game 7 was produced in the Mets' sixth, when Keith Hernandez came up to bat against Hurst with the bases loaded and one out and the Red Sox still ahead by 3–0. Anyone who does know baseball understood that this was the arrangement—this particular batter and this precise set of circumstances—that the Mets wanted most and the Red Sox least at the end of their long adventures. It was the moment that only baseball—with its slow, serial, one-thing-and-then-another siftings and sortings—can produce from time to time, and its outcome is often critical, even when reexamined weeks later. I think the Red Sox would have won this game if they had got Hernandez out. As it was, he took a strike from Hurst (a beautiful, dipping off-speed breaking ball) and then rocketed the next pitch (a fastball, a bit up) to deep left-center for a single and the Mets' first two runs and the beginning of their championship comeback. I'm not sure that anyone remembered at the time, but we should remember now that Hernandez, then a member of the Cardinals, hit a crucial two-run single up the middle in the sixth inning of the seventh game of the 1982 World Series, to start that team on its way to a comeback 6–3 victory over the Milwaukee Brewers.

Many fans think of Gary Carter as the quintessential Mets player, while some may see Lenny Dykstra or Wally Backman or Dwight Gooden, or even Ray Knight (who won the Series MVP award), or perhaps Mookie Wilson in that role (Mets-haters despise them all, for their exuberance, their high fives, their cap-waving encores, their vast publicity, their money, and their winning so often: Winning is the worst mannerism of all), but for me the Mets are Keith Hernandez. His game-long, season-long intensity; his classic at-bats, during which the contest between batter and pitcher seems to be written out on some invisible blackboard, with the theorems and formulas being erased and rewritten as the count progresses; his style at the plate, with the bat held high (he is bare-armed, always), and his pure, mannerism-free cuts at the ball; and, above all, his demeanor afield—I would rather watch these, I think, than the actions of any other player in the game today. Watching him at work around first base—he is sure to earn his ninth consecutive Gold Glove for his performance at the position—you begin to pick up the little moves and glances and touches that show what he is concerned about at that instant, what dangers and possibilities are on his mind. Holding a base runner close, with a right-handed pull hitter up at bat, he crouches with his left foot planted on the baseline and toeing to right—a sprinter's start, no less—and he moves off so quickly with the pitch that he and the runner appear to be tied together, one mass zipping along the base path. When there's a left-handed batter in the box under the same circumstances, Keith leaves his post just as quickly once the pitcher lets fly, but this time with a crablike backward scuttle, quicker than a skater. He makes the tough 3–6 peg down to second look easy and elegant, and he attacks bunts with such assurance that he sometimes scoops up the ball on the third-base side of the invisible pitcher-to-home line (I have seen only two or three other first basemen pull this off even once; Ferris Fain, of the late-1940s Athletics, was one of them) and then gets off his throw with the same motion. If you make yourself notice where Hernandez has stationed himself on the field, you will sometimes get a sudden sense of what is really going on down there. Wade Boggs, the best hitter in baseball, usually raps the ball up the middle or to left, even though he is a left-handed swinger, but his failure to pull even one pitch up the line to right in the course of the World Series allowed Hernandez to play him more and more into the hole as the Series went on, and contributed to Boggs's problems at the plate in these games. Even one pulled foul would have altered his positioning, Keith said after the Series ended; he was amazed that Boggs hadn't attacked him in this way.

Hernandez is probably not an exceptionally gifted athlete, but his baseball intelligence is remarkable. Other Mets players say that he always seems to be two or three pitches ahead of the enemy pitcher and catcher, and that he almost seems to know the other team's coaches' signals without looking, because he understands where they are in their heads and what they hope to do next. He shares all this with his teammates (keep count in a game of the number of different players he says something to in the course of a few innings), and the younger players on the club, including Darryl Strawberry, will tell you that Keith's counsel and patience and knowledge of the game and its ways have made them better ballplayers, and winners. All this comes at a price, which one may guess at when watching Hernandez chain-smoke and put away beers (there is a postgame ice bucket at his feet by his locker) in the clubhouse as he talks and comes down after the game. The talk is a season-long seminar that Mets writers attend, day after day, taking notes and exchanging glances as they write. The man is in the game.

Davey Johnson also has some baseball smarts, and in this last game he showed us, if we needed showing, how far ahead he had been all along. Sid Fernandez, the Mets' dumpling left-handed strikeout pitcher—their fourth starter this year, and during some stretches their best—came into the game in the fourth inning, with the Mets down by 3–0, and stopped the Sox dead in their tracks: a base on balls and then seven outs in succession, with four strikeouts. "That did it," Keith said afterward. "When Sid was in there, we began to feel that we might win this game after all. He was the necessary hero." Johnson had passed over Fernandez as a starter in the Series (he is streaky and emotional), but he had brought him along, all right. Fernandez had pitched a shaky one-third of an inning in Game 2, surrendering three hits and a run late in a losing cause; in Game 5, which the Mets also lost, he had pitched four shutout innings, with five strikeouts. He was Series-tested by the end, and he became Johnson's last and best move.

The Sox, for their part, mounted a courageous rally in their eighth inning, when three successive solid blows accounted for two runs and closed the score to 6–5 before Orosco came in and shot them down for good. By this time, the Mets hitters had done away with Schiraldi and were loose in the Boston bullpen—John McNamara's worst dream come true. Strawberry's homer and the cascade of Mets runs at the end released the fans at last, and their celebrations during the final outs of the year—the packed thousands together chanting, roaring out the Freddie Mercury rock chorus "We will, we will . . . Rock you!" while pointing together at the Boston bench—were terrific fun. There was a great city party there at Shea, and then all over town, which went on into the parade and the ticker tape (it's computer paper now) the following afternoon, but when it was all over I think that most of us, perhaps all of us, realized that the victory celebration didn't come up to the wonderful, endless 16 innings of Game 6, back during the playoffs. As one friend of mine said later, "For me, that night was the whole thing. Whatever there was to win had been won."

There was a surprise for me, there at the end. I am a Mets fan. I had no idea how this private Series would come out, but when the Mets almost lost the next-to-last game of the Series I suddenly realized that my pain and foreboding were even deeper than what I had felt when the Red Sox came to the very brink out in Anaheim. I suppose most of my old Red Sox friends will attack me for perfidy, and perhaps accuse me of front-running and other failures of character, but there is no help for it. I don't think much has been lost, to tell the truth. I will root and suffer for the Sox and the Mets next summer and the summers after that, and if they ever come up against each other again in the World Series—well, who knows? Ask me again in 167 years.

1988: Dodgers vs. Athletics

Kirk Gibson's Walk-Off Home Run

from *The Los Angeles Times,* "It Could Happen Only in Hollywood," by Jim Murray

Well, **you can** believe that if you want to.

As for me, I know a Warner Bros. movie when I see one. I've been around this town long enough to spot a hokey movie script.

Kirk Gibson's two-run homer gave Los Angeles a 5–4 win over Oakland.

I mean, this is *Rambo IV,* right? That was Sylvester Stallone who came out of the dugout in the ninth inning of Game 1 of the 1988 World Series. That wasn't a real player? Believe this one and you'll think *Superman* is a documentary.

The country is never going to buy it. This is the thing Hollywood does best. But it never happens in real life. In real life, the hero pops up in this situation. In an Italian movie, he dies. He doesn't hit a last-minute home run with two outs and two strikes and the best relief pitcher in baseball throwing. This is John Wayne saving the fort stuff. Errol Flynn taking the Burma Road.

A guy who can hardly walk hits a ball where he doesn't have to. A few minutes before, he's sitting in a tub of ice like a broken-down racehorse.

Kirk Gibson is the biggest bargain since Alaska. He should be on crutches—or at least a cane. He wasn't even introduced to the World Series crowd in the pregame ceremonies. He wasn't even in the dugout till the game got dramatic. Some people were surprised he was in uniform. Some were surprised he was upright.

The odds against his hitting a home run in this situation were about the odds of winning a lottery. The manager was just milking the situation, trying to keep the crowd from walking out early. No one seriously expected a guy with two unhinged knees to get a hit, never mind *the* hit.

Here was the situation: The Oakland Athletics, who are less a team than a packet of mastodons, baseball's answer to a massed artillery attack, had the game all but won, ahead by one with two out, one on.

Somehow, a quartet of Dodger pitchers had held this mass of muscle to four measly runs. The Dodgers had somehow pasted together three. They got two of them when Mickey (Himself) Hatcher, who may be himself a figment of the sound stages, hit his second home run of the year.

Oakland got back four when Jose Canseco hit his 46th homer of the year.

So, the score was 4–3, in favor of Oakland. Two were out, the crowds were streaming out, the traffic jam was starting, when pinch-hitter Mike Davis drew a walk.

Out of the dugout came Our Hero. Tom Mix, Frank Merriwell, the Gipper never had a better part.

The wonder was, they didn't have to carry him up there. There should have been a star in the East or lightning playing around his forehead the way this postseason has been going for Kirk Gibson. He had posted the most devastating .154 average in the history of playoffs (his slugging average is .800) this fall. Every hit he gets wins a game. Three out of three of them have been home runs.

A World Series crowd doesn't know much about baseball. But a Hollywood crowd does know all about happy endings. They know an MGM finish when they scent one, too. They began to holler and scream.

You wanted to say, "OK, nice touch," to the manager, Tommy Lasorda, but you wanted to tell the crowd, "Grow up! This isn't Disneyland."

On the mound, Oakland pitcher Dennis Eckersley didn't believe in fairy tales or Horatio Alger Jr. dime novel plots, either. Nor did Oakland Manager Tony La Russa.

If they did, they would have walked Kirk Gibson. Even when the count went to 3 and 2, they were putting their money on logic, reason, percentages.

Hah!

Eckersley threw a here-hit-this! pitch.

If you saw *Sands of Iwo Jima, Rio Hondo,* or even *Singing In the Rain,* you know what happened. When last seen the ball was headed to the moon.

Fadeout. Up the music. Roll the credits. The guys in the white hats win again. The big bad rustlers from Oakland, the hit men, the seat-breakers, had to stand there helplessly while the good guys won again.

It had everything but a schoolmarm and a dog. Or Gibson riding slowly off into the sunset.

You knew it would happen. A movie is nine reels of disaster and calamity befalling the star. But the last act finds him getting fanned into consciousness by his horse and led by Rin Tin Tin to where the outlaw has his fiancée and he rescues her in the nick of time, the ninth inning, so to speak. It's the way we do things here in Hollywood. You have to figure that's what happened. Somewhere out there, the screenwriter in the sky brought in this ending where the hero takes a called strike three while everybody cries. Or he pops up to the pitcher. But somewhere out there, C.B. or L.B. takes a disgusted look and says, "You call this a picture! What's this dreck! Take it back and write me something for Doug Fairbanks and Mary Pickford, something that'll sell in Dubuque. When I want a three-handkerchief picture I'll remake *Camille.*"

Well, look at it this way: You got a better explanation for what happened at Dodger Stadium Saturday night? You believe it, do you?!

Nah!!

1988: Dodgers vs. Athletics

Orel Hershiser's Pitching Mastery

from *Sports Illustrated,* "A Case of Orel Surgery," by
Peter Gammons

The night after he finished off the Oakland Athletics, Orel Hershiser
was sitting on Johnny Carson's set and singing "Praise God, from Whom all
blessings flow. . . ." Even with all of Hershiser's new honor and fame, his Los
Angeles Dodger costar, Kirk Gibson, asked an apt question: "Does everyone
really appreciate what Orel has done? I don't know if we will ever again see
the likes of what he's done through all of this. It may be that no pitcher in
history stayed in that kind of groove so long or so well."

The recent accomplishments of Orel Leonard Hershiser IV are every
bit as impressive as Gibson suggests. After finishing the season with his
unprecedented streak of 59 scoreless innings, he allowed all of three earned
runs in three starts and one relief appearance, culminating in a seventh-game
shutout, against the New York Mets in the league playoffs. Next came his
three-hit shutout of the Athletics in Game 2 of the World Series and, finally,
his 5–2 four-hitter in Game 5. Perhaps someone will eclipse the 59 scoreless
innings some day, and perhaps someone will top his postseason totals of

three wins and a save. (That save, Gibson says, "is unforgettable because it shows how he always places the team above himself.")

But, taken together, what Hershiser did in the final 46 days of baseball in 1988 most likely will never be duplicated: seven wins, no losses, one save, seven shutouts (plus 10 scoreless innings in a no-decision) and a 0.46 ERA. As if that weren't enough, he tied a World Series record by batting 1.000 in three at bats.

Sandwiched between Hershiser's 19–3 record of 1985 and his 23–8 record in '88 were 14–14 and 16–16 seasons, and fans naturally assume that he was an average pitcher in those two years. But Los Angeles pitching coach Ron Perranoski says, "He was as good in '87 as he was this year, but we didn't have the people like Alfredo Griffin to catch the ball."

Don't compare him with former Dodger greats like Sandy Koufax, you say? Koufax's lifetime earned run average was 2.76, Hershiser's is 2.77. Hershiser has been a starter for five seasons, and in four of them he has ranked in the top three in the National League in ERA. The only two active starting pitchers with 1,000 innings whose ERA is less than 3.00 are Hershiser and Dwight Gooden of the Mets (2.62). Over the past four years Hershiser has won 72 games, a total exceeded only by Frank Viola (75) of the Minnesota Twins and Gooden (74). Hershiser's lifetime winning percentage is .629, and yet in three of his five seasons the Dodgers were a sub-.500 team.

"I couldn't figure out why I was missing his pitches in Game 2," said Oakland's José Canseco, who was 0 for 8 against Hershiser. "Then I looked at the videos and I saw how much the ball was moving. In Game 5, I got a dose of his curveball, which is in Bert Blyleven's class. Great stuff, great pitcher."

Because Hershiser doesn't put up big strikeout numbers like those of Nolan Ryan or Roger Clemens, there is a tendency to not think of his stuff as being dominant. "The only pitcher I've seen in 30 years with a similar combination of the hard-running sinker and deadly overhand curveball was Clem Labine," says Perranoski, referring to one of his predecessors as the Dodgers' bullpen ace. Hershiser's sinker moves so much that the Athletics were convinced he was throwing a spitter. "He gets to two strikes and his ball defies any law of physics," said an Oakland coach. "It's got to be a spitter."

The Dodgers have heard that before. When Hershiser was a rookie, he struck out Claudell Washington, then an Atlanta Brave; as Washington strolled to his position, he told LA coach Mark Cresse, "That boy's got a nasty spitter."

"He didn't then, and doesn't now," says Cresse. "But I understand why they think he throws one. I've never seen a sinker dart and run like his."

Few pitchers can claim two pitches that are among the very best in the game, but Hershiser can, with his sinker and curveball. "After the sinker, he changes speed on the curveball," says his catcher, Mike Scioscia. "He has a straight change and a cross-seam running fastball that he gets up and in on right-handed batters. And he can drop down and throw his curveball from a crossfire angle. That's a lot of artillery for a hitter to contend with."

Perranoski points out that Hershiser's rhythm seldom falls out of sync. "It takes a pure athlete as coordinated as he is to maintain that kind of groove for so long," says Perranoski. "It would be like a bowler rolling 300 games every day for six weeks."

Still, it's how Hershiser puts his ability to work that has raised him to his present plateau. He habitually studies videotapes of opposing hitters, and also uses videos to check on his own delivery; he did just that between innings when he struggled a bit early in his seventh-game playoff shutout of the Mets.

"He has the ability to figure out what he's doing wrong while he's on the mound," says Scioscia. "He'll slow down the game, make a few throws to first, talk to the catcher, until he finds what he needs." In World Series Game 5, Hershiser, by his own admission, was "very erratic." The A's were trying to slap his sinker through the middle like a team of Charley Lau disciples. So Hershiser went away from his sinker and threw a lot of curveballs at different speeds and some cross-seamed fastballs up in the strike zone.

Teammates and opponents marvel at Hershiser's pitching instincts. "With National League hitters, he knows their tendencies and knows how to pitch them," says Scioscia. "But with the A's, he made immediate adjustments. I think some of that comes from the fact that he understands hitting." When Canseco came up for a final chance at redemption with two on and one out in the eighth inning of the finale, Dodger manager Tommy Lasorda had his bullpen working. "Normally, I would never throw inside to him late in the game because he's so quick and so strong," Hershiser said later, "but sometimes a surprise is all you need. So I threw Canseco the only inside fastball I'd thrown him in eight at bats." Canseco popped it up. Hershiser then struck out the wallowing Dave Parker on what he called two "55-foot curveballs." The final threat was over. "And I thought he was done," said Lasorda. "He never stops amazing me."

"Don't ever underestimate how tough he is," says the Dodgers' Mike Marshall. "He's the most competitive person I've ever known." And Marshall knows Gibson and John Tudor.

What's most refreshing about Hershiser is that he has perspective on what he has done. Unlike most players, who think baseball was invented the day they signed their first pro contract, Hershiser clearly understands his place alongside the Koufaxes and Drysdales. Still, he's no prima donna; after both World Series wins, he told reporters, "I'll sit in front of my locker all night answering questions if you want me to."

But the bulldog in him came out when, after the Athletics were disposed of, he walked down the hallway to the interview room in the Oakland Coliseum and an A's fan yelled, "You were lucky, Hershiser." A couple of dozen steps later, Hershiser blurted out, "Oh yeah—grab a bat." He wasn't smiling.

1989: Giants vs. Athletics

The Earthquake Series

from *The Mercury News,* "Remembering the World
Series Earthquake," by Horace Hinshaw

Last weekend the San Francisco Giants honored the 1989 team. That
year the Giants won the National League pennant and played the Oakland
Athletics in the World Series, what has become known as the "Earthquake Series."

The quake is best remembered as the Loma Prieta earthquake, which
occurred on October 17 at the beginning of Game 3 at Candlestick Park.
The earthquake caused a 10-day disruption in play.

Over the past 20 years many people talk about that Series, and in
particular that day, and can recall just exactly where they were the moment
the quake hit—at 5:04 p.m.

My wife, Marian, and I were among the 60,000 fans attending the
game. We had obtained tickets and were seated high atop the bleachers in
center field.

Last Saturday night at AT&T Park, 20 members of that 1989 team
returned to be reunited for an on-field ceremony before the game. The player
getting the biggest applause was Will "The Thrill" Clark, who finished as

runner-up to Kevin Mitchell for the Most Valuable Player award that year. The fans also remembered José Uribe, the 1989 shortstop, who died as a result of a [motor] vehicle accident last year. His wife was introduced and presented with her husband's jersey (No. 23). It was really a neat tribute to the Giants players. All 20 former players were introduced to the fans.

The day following the earthquake, and through the next week, was chaotic for a lot of people.

The quake was caused by a slip along the San Andreas Fault. The quake lasted 15 seconds and measured 6.9 on the moment magnitude scale. Unfortunately, the quake killed 63 people throughout northern California, injured more than 3,500 people and left some 8,000 to 12,000 people homeless. Many people were affected by the quake and many public service agencies were actively involved for weeks.

I was working for the Postal Service at the time. Working with the Giants I had coordinated a promotion to make available for fans at Candlestick Park a souvenir envelope depicting the dates of the World Series games. Needless to say, following the moment of the quake, that souvenir envelope for Game 3 became a very popular philatelic item. People were requesting to purchase the envelope for months after the Series.

Coincidentally, I had just left the postal booth at the stadium and returned to join Marian in our seats prior to the start of the game. For that game, I had a portable television with me.

Approximately at 5 p.m. the pregame formalities got underway as both teams took the field for introductions. Unbeknownst to the people in the stands, just minutes later a 6.9 earthquake rocked the entire bay area.

People appeared relatively calm. Then suddenly, there was a loss of power, people were screaming, police were coming onto the field and players were walking off the field. I'm sure that for many of the players not living in the Bay Area, this was their first experience of an earthquake. Players were looking for their families.

Nobody knew the extent of the damage outside the park. I turned my TV to another channel and we were getting images of the Bay Bridge collapsing, fires erupting, and crumbling buildings being damaged. I drew a crowd of people around me, looking over my shoulder to view the pictures.

Being October, it was getting dark. The lights at the stadium were out. The announcement was made by loudspeakers from the police to evacuate the stadium. Amazingly, even leaving the stadium people were very orderly.

Remember, this was years before cell phones became popular! Marian and I had to go to the postal booth to make arrangements with the staff. Much to my surprise, the booth was doing a land-office business. The day of the game was posted on the envelope; that's a big deal for stamp collecting enthusiasts. We soon made fans mad because we were ordered to close the booth and leave the premises.

Players were leaving the park still wearing their uniform. The parking lot—normally very difficult to egress—was really a mess with vehicles trying to exit. Buses were overcrowded. Marian and I made our way to the bus; we had left our vehicle at the Daly City BART and took the game bus to the stadium. Normally, it takes no more than 15 minutes to reach BART; however, that night it took the bus an hour and a half to maneuver through traffic before finally arriving at BART. The city was a total blackout. It was a very long night. We didn't know what to expect when we arrived home. To our surprise, there was no sign of an earthquake at our home—not even a picture frame off the wall.

That's certainly was not the case in San Francisco. Fires were erupting. People were dying. San Francisco was becoming the most televised city in the world. Images of the Bay Bridge kept being shown.

It was a very hectic time for the Post Office. Our infrastructure was impacted. Mail delivery was affected. Collapsed streets, damaged buildings, and people being evacuated from their homes prevented mail from being delivered. Portable mail delivery stations were set up around San Francisco. People had to have identification to receive their mail.

The Marina district was the most affected. I recall talking with Joe DiMaggio, standing in line at a portable postal station set up in the neighborhood, and explaining to him and others how the post office was helping people get their mail.

Being from Arkansas, all my relatives lived in the South. They were attempting to call us, but to no avail. It was a couple of days before we talked with my brother. They thought we had dropped off into the ocean.

As it turned out, being at Candlestick Park was probably one of the safest places in the Bay Area. Because of the World Series being held in early evening, many people left work early or gathered at taverns to watch the game. This made the rush-hour traffic lighter than normal; otherwise, the death toll could have been much higher.

At Candlestick Park, only half of the fans had arrived when the earthquake hit. This helped reduce the load and strain on the stadium structure. The stadium was not seriously damaged. The World Series was postponed for 10 days, moving the third game to October 27.

The Giants were never able to recover. When the Series resumed, Oakland won Games 3 and 4. A rested Dave Stewart allowed just six hits in the 13–7 Oakland win in Game 3. The A's wrapped up the Series with a 9–6 Game 4 victory.

It was the first World Series in which the losing team never had the lead and never had the tying run at the plate in its final turn at bat.

1991: Twins vs. Braves

Kirby Puckett's Game 6 Performance

from *ESPN: The Magazine,* "11 Innings," by Tim Kurkjian

To appreciate the greatness of Kirby Puckett's 12-year career, all you had to see was 11 innings.

They came in Game 6 of the 1991 World Series, perhaps the greatest World Series ever played. The Twins were behind in the series, 3–2, when Puckett almost single-handedly beat the Braves with one of the best one-game performances in postseason history. He hit the game-winning home run that sent the Twins to a 4–3 victory—it was his fourth hit and third RBI—and he made a fabulous leaping catch against the center-field fence in the third inning.

"This isn't the first time he's had that kind of game," Twins manager Tom Kelly said after the game.

He had many games like it, but very few players have ever had a game like that in the World Series or the postseason, especially in an elimination game. It was right there with the best of Joe DiMaggio, Mickey Mantle, Yogi Berra, George Brett, Roberto Clemente, Brooks Robinson, Babe Ruth, and

Reggie Jackson. It was the kind of unforgettable performance that elevates a player to legendary status. Puckett's career numbers were Hall of Fame material, but Game 6 of the '91 World Series went a long way in getting him into Cooperstown on the first ballot in 2001.

And the best part is, Puckett basically predicted it.

"I went to the clubhouse, and I gathered [everyone] up. I said, 'Everybody together, we're going to have a short meeting,'" Puckett said, retelling the story years later. "Everybody comes in, and I said, 'Guys, I just have one announcement to make: You guys should jump on my back tonight. I'm going to carry us.'"

Then he did.

"We were in a bad way; we needed someone to step forward in a major way," Twins teammate Gene Larkin said. "He told us to jump on his back. Not many guys can talk the talk and walk the walk, but Kirby always could. After he spoke to us, we just knew that Kirby was going to do something special. We've seen him do that many times. That time it was on the biggest stage."

Teammate Kent Hrbek said: "Great catch, great home run, great player. I know if there were a line of players standing on a block and I had the first pick, I would pick Kirby Puckett. But I don't remember him for that game, I remember him for playing hard every night."

In the first inning of Game 6, Puckett tripled home a run, then scored. In the third inning, with one out and a runner at first, Atlanta's Ron Gant hit a fly ball to deep left-center field.

"I thought it was gone," Puckett said. But Puckett, who was 5-foot-8, scaled the Plexiglas fence in left-center and caught it—making one of the greatest catches in World Series history.

"If he hadn't made that catch," Larkin said, "we might have lost the World Series in six games."

Puckett hit a sacrifice fly in the fifth to give the Twins a 3–2 lead, but the Braves tied it, setting up the dramatic 11th inning. The Braves brought in left-hander Charlie Leibrandt, a starting pitcher, to work in relief. Puckett hit a 2–1, hanging changeup over the wall in left-center to end the game.

As he rounded the bases, pumping his fist and screaming at the top of his lungs, the Metrodome was almost indescribably loud. The fans chanted "KIRBY! KIRBY!" He was mobbed at home plate.

"It was so loud in the Metrodome, it was like a plane taking off on the runway," Larkin said.

The Twins won Game 7, 1–0, in 10 innings behind a masterful performance by Jack Morris.

"After Game 6, Jack said something like, 'Now it's my turn to do my job; Kirby did his job,'" Larkin said.

It was one of the greatest Game 7s ever played, but it only happened because of what Puckett did in Game 6. It will forever be known simply as the Puckett Game, and no further explanation is needed. It was the night that a team's best player and leader played his best, and his best was as great as the World Series has ever seen.

1991: Twins vs. Braves

The Game 7 Duel

from *The Star Tribune*, "Morris vs. Smoltz," by Joe
Christensen

*The Twins' Jack Morris faced Atlanta's John Smoltz in the deciding game of the
1991 World Series. Morris, now retired, and Smoltz, still pitching for Atlanta,
reminisced about that Fall Classic.*

Jack Morris went looking for John Smoltz on Wednesday and
found his nemesis from Game 7 of the 1991 World Series walking outside
the Atlanta Braves clubhouse.

Until that moment—shortly after 5 p.m.—they never had spoken about
the events at the Metrodome that night in 1991, when Smoltz pitched 7$\frac{1}{3}$
innings and Morris pitched all 10 in the Twins' 1–0 triumph.

Morris said he told Smoltz, "If he wouldn't have gotten taken out, we'd
have both been out there in the 14th [inning]."

Two of the best pitchers in postseason history stood there for about 15
minutes—Smoltz in full uniform, Morris in a blue Tommy Bahama shirt—
reminiscing.

At one point, Braves outfielder Jeff Francoeur walked up and introduced
himself to Morris.

Francoeur, an Atlanta native, was a seven-year-old watching Morris shatter his favorite team's dreams that night. He pointed at Morris and told Smoltz, "I always hated that guy."

Sixteen years later, Smoltz said the memory that sticks with him the most is the eighth inning. After pitching a 1-2-3 seventh, Smoltz retreated to the clubhouse, hoping he could change the team's luck by watching [the game] on TV.

Smoltz, then 24, saw Lonnie Smith single, leading off the eighth. Then, the Twins caught a huge break. Terry Pendleton doubled to deep left-center field, but Smith fell for a phantom play by middle infielders Greg Gagne and Chuck Knoblauch. Smith looked confused at second base and barely made it to third.

Still, the Braves had runners at second and third. Nobody out. Smoltz decided he'd better get back to the dugout.

"I wanted to see us score the run," he said. "I knew the game was going to be over. And I guess the worst possible scenario happened. You watched the air go out of the balloon. That might have been the toughest inning I've seen in my professional career."

Early Lesson

Smoltz knew all about Morris. Growing up in Michigan, he was 17 when Morris pitched a no-hitter and led the Detroit Tigers to the 1984 World Series title.

Smoltz signed with the Tigers the next year and was rising through their farm system when they traded him to Atlanta for Doyle Alexander in 1987.

Now, Smoltz sat in disbelief as Morris pitched out of that eighth-inning jam. A harmless groundout from Ron Gant. An intentional walk to David Justice. And then Sid Bream hit a grounder right at Kent Hrbek, who started a 3-2-3, inning-ending double play.

"It's everything I admired about [Morris] growing up," Smoltz said. "And it was everything that became our undoing as it unfolded."

The Twins finally chased Smoltz in the eighth, when Randy Bush and Knoblauch singled, putting runners at first and third with one out. That prompted Braves manager Bobby Cox to summon reliever Mike Stanton, and he escaped the jam when Hrbek lined into an inning-ending double play.

But as Morris kept going, all Smoltz could do was watch.

"Both guys were dominant," former Twins manager Tom Kelly said. "If you had to pick a guy who pitched better, I don't know if you could separate those two guys."

'Let's Get It On'

Morris carved his legend that night. After Kirby Puckett's home run off Charlie Leibrandt had ended Game 6, officials gathered Morris and Smoltz for a news conference.

It was about 1 a.m. when Morris said, "In the words of the late, great Marvin Gaye, 'Let's get it on.'"

Morris set down the Braves 1-2-3 in the ninth. At that point, Kelly told Morris this was all the Twins could ask: nine scoreless innings. Thanks. Rick Aguilera was ready in the bullpen.

But when Kelly walked away, Morris told pitching coach Dick Such he wasn't leaving the game.

"I know [Kelly] wanted to hear me say I was fine—which I was," Morris said. "I was getting stronger. I had no reason to leave the game at that point. I think I had several innings left in the tank. What the heck? We were all going home the next day. You've got all winter to rest."

Morris retired the side again in the 10th. It was one of his easiest innings of the game.

"The first five innings, you're kind of running on emotion, and all of a sudden, you just dial it in," Morris said. "And then my adrenaline took over. I felt every inning after the fifth I was getting stronger. I didn't lose any velocity. My location was getting better."

Finally, in the Twins' 10th, a breakthrough.

Dan Gladden hit a leadoff double against Braves reliever Alejandro Pena. Knoblauch bunted Gladden to third. Cox ordered Kirby Puckett and Hrbek intentionally walked.

"The thing I remember most," Kelly said, "is sitting there in the dugout going, 'How on earth are we going to find a way to score one run?'"

With the bases loaded, Kelly sent up Gene Larkin as a pinch hitter, and Larkin lifted a fly ball over left fielder Brian Hunter's head.

Gladden scored, the Twins dogpiled as champions, and Smoltz retreated with his teammates to a silent clubhouse.

Morris, now 52, went on to win another World Series over the Braves the next year for Toronto. He retired in 1994 with a 6–1 career postseason record.

The 1991 postseason was the first for Smoltz, and now he is the all-time leader in postseason victories (15) and strikeouts (194). [Andy Pettite surpassed Smoltz and is now the current leader.]

That Game 7 often replays on ESPN Classic. Smoltz, now 40, said he's never been able to watch the whole thing.

"I will," he said. "I know when I'm sitting in my chair bored someday, 50 years old, I'll definitely pop that game in—and have the same feelings as if I was right there."

1993: Blue Jays vs. Phillies

Joe Carter's Walk-Off Home Run

from *Sports Illustrated,* "Home Sweet Homer," by Steve
Rushin

*After his dramatic home run gave the Blue Jays a second straight World Series title,
Joe Carter touched home plate and touched off a SkyDome mob scene.*

Every day and never, that's how often this happens. Every day a boy
hits a come-from-behind home run in the bottom of the ninth inning to win
the World Series. And never, in 89 Fall Classics, has this actually come to
pass. Of course it hasn't. Even in the big leagues, hitting a home run is called
leaving the yard, and that is the only place where such a thing can happen:
the backyard.

"An unbelievable dream fantasy," then, is how Blue Jay reliever Al Leiter
described what happened at 11:39 on Saturday night in Toronto. "This
happens in the backyard. Bottom of the ninth, down by one, and Joe pops
one out of the park? You dream it all those years as a kid, and then here you
are, in the World Series, and it happens?"

This is what happened in Game 6 of the 90th World Series: Joe Carter
hit a three-run home run in the bottom of the ninth inning to give the Jays an
8–6 victory over the Philadelphia Phillies and their second consecutive world
championship. As Phillie reliever Mitch Williams left the field in torment,

Carter joyously triple-jumped around the base paths at the SkyDome, bounding up and down like Neil Armstrong on the moon. Which is, in effect, who Joe Carter had just become.

He said he understood that his life had changed with that swing, that he was now a piece of history, the kind of athletic artifact that Kirk Gibson is wherever he goes. So be it. "This is like, Do you believe in miracles?" said Carter, when he had found the home team's clubhouse through tear-stung eyes. "Yes, I do believe in miracles."

Every day and never. Understand, no other man has done this. When Bill Mazeroski hit his historic home run for the Pittsburgh Pirates in Game 7 in 1960, the only other year in which a home run ended the Series, the game had been tied when he came to the plate. That isn't the way it was in Oklahoma City, where Joe Carter first left a yard. On the asphalt at his father's filling station, the boy was always clowning around when he shot rubber bands off his fingers and into the wind. He pretended they were flying baseballs. "If the rubber band landed on the roof, it was a home run," said Carter. "If it didn't land on the roof, it was a foul ball or something. Tonight, it didn't land on the roof, but over the fence was good enough."

The ball—a 2–2 fastball, down and in—landed 379 feet from home plate, in the Blue Jay bullpen behind the left-field wall. It detonated fireworks inside the Dome and outside in the cold Canadian night, and it occasioned a string of heartbreakingly corny scenes . . . everywhere.

John Sullivan, the Blue Jays' 52-year-old bullpen coach, who is retiring after this season, retrieved the very baseball that ended his 34-year career in the major and minor leagues. Sully, in shower slippers and a T-shirt, would soon see Carter in the clubhouse and say, as if handing him a leftover orange, "I thought you might want this." Of course, a man from the Hall of Fame was already waiting at Carter's locker, like a grim banker come to repossess. Carter let that guy have only his bat. He had no idea where his cap was. The ball, Carter was keeping.

The hero had stepped from the thundering field into the clubhouse, where a bottle of champagne was thrust into his left hand. He had stepped from the raucous clubhouse into the corridor outside, on his way to a press conference, when a World Series program was thrust toward his right hand. Carter kept walking through the bowels of the SkyDome as he signed for a boy, maybe 10 years old, whose chin was quivering, whose eyes were watering, who looked about to burst out sobbing when he said to the departing Carter, "You're the best, Joe."

Really. The kid said that.

There was a lipstick smudge on the sleeve of Carter's T-shirt, left there by his wife, Diana. Invisible were the buss marks of his teammates, a collection of men who, on an ordinary night, make Stonehenge look expressive. These men had swallowed Carter whole at home plate. "I just went nuts," insisted Blue Jay first baseman John Olerud, who seldom goes nuts or anywhere near it. "Oh, yeah. Look at the replay. You'll see me bouncing up and down out there."

In fact, Carter looked at the replay when the moment was but an hour old, ducking into the Blue Jays' video room to see the insanity one more time and emerging with newly moist eyes. "The fans in Philadelphia saw a great 15–14 ballgame," Carter said, by way of explaining his feat. "I guess we had to give something to the fans in Toronto."

Ah. The home run, to hear Carter tell it, was only a fair exchange for the Great 15–14 Ballgame, the epic—James A. Michener's Philadelphia—which had concluded three nights earlier in the City of Brotherly Love. The Great 15–14 Ballgame was Game 4 at Veterans Stadium, the highest-scoring game in the 532-game history of the World Series. It set or tied 13 records in all. It was the longest nine-inning night game ever played in the major leagues, four hours and 14 minutes of imponderably poor pitching that somehow made for powerful entertainment. "It was," veteran Toronto scout Gordon Lakey said afterward, "the most exciting game I've ever seen."

The Blue Jays led the series 2–1 when Game 4 began in a relentless drizzle. Major League Baseball officials sat morosely in a roofless Plexiglas box behind home plate, each one of them looking like a man in a dunk tank, as untold indignities were visited upon their pastime. In the top of the first, Phillie starter Tommy Greene walked in the first Blue Jay run. In the bottom of the first, Toronto starter Todd Stottlemyre walked in the first Phillie run. All told, there were six walks in the first inning, at the end of which the score was Philadelphia 4, Toronto 3.

If Carter's home run was the enduring heroic image of this Fall Classic, then a Classic Pratfall in the second inning of Game 4 was a slapstick memory that also will remain: Stottlemyre inexplicably attempting to go from first to third on a single by Roberto Alomar; Stottlemyre sliding facefirst as if he were sniffing for truffles around third base; Stottlemyre being thrown out, improbably, 8 to 6 to 5; and Stottlemyre, his chin bloodied, being asked by trainer Tommy Craig to read the unfathomable scoreboard (of all things) to prove his coherence.

After three innings of this nonsense, the Blue Jays led 7–6. In the fifth, Jay reliever Leiter, one bead in a very long necklace of relievers who would pitch on this night, was contemplating his first major league at bat. "See how this feels," teammate Ed Sprague suggested, offering one of his bats.

"I don't give a _____ how it feels," said a laughing Leiter, whose last hit came for Central Regional High in Bayville, New Jersey, where he batted .220 in 1984. He wasn't going up there to hit, for Pete's sake. And yet Leiter immediately doubled to left-field and felt a little silly afterward for worrying about one little AB.

After all . . . "What's the worst thing that can happen?" Phillie center fielder Lenny Dykstra had asked last week, apropos of playing in the World Series, before answering his own question. "You can become a hero." That's the worst thing that can happen to you in the World Series.

So Dykstra became a hero in Game 4, hitting two home runs, missing a third by two feet and driving in four runs altogether. The Phils drove Leiter out of the game in the fifth inning, when they scored five times to take a 12–7 lead. Then, and only then, did all hell break loose.

Blue Jay manager Cito Gaston had called for reliever Tony Castillo to come in from the bullpen to replace Leiter. But the bullpen phone didn't work. It kept ringing and ringing but—Great Cito's Ghost!—there was never a voice at the other end. And no one was eager to answer the bell, anyway. As Leiter would note of the bullpen phone on this October evening of carnage,

"You just say, I hope it's not for me." So Mark Eichhorn, a right-hander, had mistakenly come in from the pen to relieve Leiter, and Cito wanted to know why Castillo, a southpaw, wasn't there instead.

Well, 23 people eventually congregated in the infield during this pitching change: There were guys in business suits, umpires, players, the Vet grounds crew spreading water-absorbent kitty litter around the bases and the batter's box . . . there were clowns juggling, men on unicycles spinning plates (or so it seemed, anyway). From overhead the game looked like an Esther Williams routine. Cito was given walkie-talkies to communicate with his relievers, but they didn't work either, and he eventually made do with human carrier pigeons running back and forth between the dugout and the bullpen.

In the sixth inning, in a game in which 19 runs had already been scored, Phillie manager Jim Fregosi, whose phone, alas, was working just fine, brought in reliever David West. Entering the game, West had a World Series earned run average of infinity: He had faced eight batters, and eight batters had reached base against him. As did the first two batters on this night. When, finally, Carter flied out to right, West had reduced his lifetime Series ERA to 162.00.

It was unimaginable, then, and downright unheroic, when the Jays gave up in the seventh inning. Down 13–9, Gaston sent his pitcher, Castillo, to the plate to lead off the inning. "_____," said Dykstra little more than an hour later, recalling the moment in disbelief. "They gave up."

They gave up in a World Series game; and what's more, in the bottom of the seventh inning, Castillo hit Phillie catcher Darren Daulton with the bases loaded. For the love of god, Castillo HBP'd in a run, making the score 14–9. You don't see that often in the World Series, but then, you don't see this often either: The Blue Jays scored six runs in the top of the eighth off Phillie relievers Larry Andersen and Williams, run after run lapping up at home plate. The Blue Jays gave up, but Phillie pitchers gave in, and Toronto won the Great 15–14 Ballgame, 15–14.

And so, after Toronto center fielder Devon White tripled in the last two of the half-dozen runs and then in the ninth caught a fly ball for the final out of the game, Blue Jay pitcher Dave Stewart, who played his first professional game in 1975, was asked for perspective. "Never seen one like it," said Stew. Not in spring training. Not in high school. Not in high school football, he said. "Two touchdowns," said Stewart, "is usually safe."

So how can it be that the next night, in Game 5, all the Phillies needed was a safety in Curt Schilling's hellacious 2–0 complete-game win over the Blue Jays? "Why do you have steak one night," asked Alomar, "and chicken the next?" A good question. And speaking of food, a fan in Philadelphia held a sign during Thursday night's game that read, WILL PITCH MIDDLE RELIEF FOR FOOD. As the team flew to Toronto for Game 6 on Saturday, trailing in the Series 3–2, things were that bad for the Phils' bullpen.

Of course, few people knew that the Phillies had received two calls from some yahoos threatening the life of Williams on Thursday night, and it would have been forgivable if Game 6 were not the foremost thing on his mind on Saturday. That night, behind the 37-year-old Series MVP Paul Molitor and the four-hit pitching of Stewart, the Blue Jays led 5–1 after six innings. But the Phillies threw up a ridiculous five-spot in the seventh inning—three of the runs coming on Dykstra's sixth home run of the postseason—and took a 6–5 lead into the eighth, when the Jays failed to score with the bases loaded. Thus, the one-run lead remained in the ninth, when Williams entered.

On this night Toronto leadoff hitter Rickey Henderson walked on four pitches. White flied out to left field, but Molitor singled. And then Carter came to the plate and was served that fastball down and in. "Ninety-nine times out of 100," Carter said later, "I hook that pitch way foul. I don't know why, but thank God this one stayed fair."

The ball stayed fair, but Carter lost it in the lights. He didn't pick it up again until he neared first base, heard the tinnitus-inducing din and began his jubilant romp. He still isn't sure if he touched second base—"I hope they don't appeal," he said—on his way to third, where he turned the corner and fought his way through a gauntlet of delirious teammates. When he stepped on home plate, the Blue Jays officially became the first team to repeat as champions since the 1978 New York Yankees.

Every day and never. Carter always dreamed of hitting the home run to win the big game, of course. Who hasn't? But in 11 seasons in the big leagues, Carter had hit only one ninth-inning, game-winning home run, period: Against Dan Quisenberry of Kansas City in a meaningless game, seven years ago. But now . . .

Now, he said, children will emulate his trip around the bases after he hit the come-from-behind home run to win the World Series. Carter has three children of his own, and when he returns to his home in Kansas City, he likes to play ball with kids in the neighborhood. Kids for whom the neighbor's fence is the left-field fence at the SkyDome. What would he say to those children who may still have been awake at 11:39 on Saturday night?

"Don't be afraid to live out your dreams," said Carter. "Don't be afraid of failure, either. If you fail, so what? If I was out in the ninth inning, there was another guy coming up behind me."

In other words, what's the worst thing that can happen when you dream?

You can become a hero.

1994

World Series Canceled

from *The New York Times*, "Lost Games, Lost Dreams," by Jack Curry

Initially, Buck Showalter didn't pack a box. Neither did Felipe Alou. In their clubhouses, the players stuffed everything in dozens of boxes, making August 1994 feel like early October. But the two managers did not even stick a sheet of paper in an envelope. There was no reason for packing because they expected to be back at work soon.

With the players poised to strike, Showalter called his behavior at the time a combination of optimism, naïveté, and denial. Alou recalled his state of mind as a blend of hope, idealism, and denial. They would be out a week or so, they figured. The season would resume and their opportunities to continue a magical season, Alou with the Montreal Expos and Showalter with the Yankees, would be given a reprieve.

But the days without a labor agreement stretched from one week to more than a month. Showalter drove his daughter to her first day of second grade and scouted the minor leagues. Alou waited in Montreal, went to Florida, and then went to his home in the Dominican Republic.

Finally, 34 days after Showalter and Alou watched their first-place teams pack, Bud Selig, then the interim commissioner, told the world that the rest of the regular season and postseason had been canceled. It was the first time since 1904 that there would be no World Series, and the managers of the teams with the best records in the American and National Leagues were shattered.

"We were right where we wanted to be at the time of the strike," Showalter, who is now an ESPN analyst, said. "I felt as good about where that club was headed as any club I ever had. We had great karma. We were the little engine that could."

Alou called the season devastating, recalling how he journeyed to the Dominican Republic for his 89-year-old father's funeral on August 3, came back a few days later and then got blindsided by the strike. The 67-year-old Alou spoke wistfully about one of the worst months of his life.

"It's not the sweetest thing to talk about," he said. "It took away an opportunity. I only managed that one club. That took away my only opportunity to be in the playoffs. It's frustrating. It's emptiness. That was it."

Those feelings could overtake managers again, like the Yankees' Joe Torre and Arizona's Bob Brenly, whose teams have the best records in their leagues. But they have each managed in the World Series before. A better comparison to Alou and Showalter would be Los Angeles' Jim Tracy and Anaheim's Mike Scioscia, who are trying to manage in the postseason for the first time.

"Our plan is to be perennial contenders," Scioscia said, deflecting talk about the possibility of losing the season.

But, obviously, plans get disrupted. The last strike all but destroyed baseball in Montreal. Ransacked it. Trampled it. The Expos were 74–40, had a six-game lead, and were loaded with players in their prime when their splendid ride was derailed. Moises Alou, Felipe's son, was hitting .339. Ken Hill had 16 victories. Larry Walker was at .322. John Wetteland had 25 saves. Marquis Grissom had 36 steals.

By the time baseball resumed in 1995, the Expos were gutted. They let Walker depart as a free agent and unloaded Hill, Wetteland, and Grissom because they could not afford the salaries the players would receive in arbitration. The finest team in Montreal history was silenced and ruined.

"I don't think you'll ever have a small-market team with as much talent as we had," Alou said. "After they came back, the Expos didn't have enough to pay those guys."

Alou might have lost as much as anyone in the strike. That season was Alou's chance to finally manage a team in the World Series. The Expos averaged 72 victories over the next six seasons and Alou was fired in 2001.

Alou is now a bench coach for the Detroit Tigers and knows it is doubtful he will ever manage in the postseason.

"It's not anyone's fault," he said. "It's fate. It's what life gives you."

Showalter was in his third season managing the Yankees, and they were soaring with a 70–43 record and a 6½-game lead. Paul O'Neill led the league in hitting with a .359 average, but some players wondered if the five-time batting champion Wade Boggs (.342) might catch him. Jimmy Key was 17–4. Finally, Showalter thought, the months of molding a dysfunctional team into a cohesive club were paying off. The team had lost 86 games in 1992.

Then the strike happened.

"When you grow up in an organization and you get an opportunity to build it, you get near the top of the mountain and, all of a sudden, the mountain crumbles," he said. "If you lie in bed and start thinking about it, you're up all night."

Of course, Showalter thinks about it. He left the Yankees after the 1995 season, and they won a title under Torre in 1996. He managed the expansion Arizona Diamondbacks until 2000, and they won a championship in 2001.

While Showalter often thinks about what might have been in 1994, 1996, and 2001, he said that 1994 "hurts more than any" because he felt helpless. Something was taken away, something special.

Showalter remembers watching his kitchen television as Selig canceled the season as vividly as he remembers hearing that Thurman Munson had died in a plane crash in 1979. He said the Yankees thought they were the best team in 1994 and "got nothing to show for it."

Alou said the Expos "had everything to win it all."

Neither manager had a chance to prove he was the best, a feeling they hope no one else has to experience.

"I didn't think there was any way they would do it, because there was no precedent for losing a season," Showalter said. "I'm not that naïve anymore."

1995: Indians vs. Braves

Glavine and Maddux Pitch Atlanta to Victory

from *Sports Illustrated,* "Brave Hearts," by Tom Verducci

On its third try in five years, Atlanta finally won the World Series.

As rain and darkness fell like a soggy blanket over Atlanta last Friday afternoon, two men sat in a car slogging north through downtown traffic, two men who over the past five years have accounted for every National League Cy Young Award, 181 victories and a .691 winning percentage. This is how the Atlanta Braves would win the 1995 World Series: with Tom Glavine in the driver's seat and Greg Maddux riding shotgun.

It was on their ride home from a workout that Maddux talked an uncertain Glavine into a game plan for Game 6 the following night. Glavine, having watched the Cleveland Indians get to Maddux in Game 5, wondered what adjustments the Indians had made against him with their second look. "I don't think they adjusted well," Maddux said. "I was off a bit. It was more me than it was them. Just go out and pitch your game. Don't change."

Glavine decided that he would live on the outside corner, mostly with his changeup again, even though he beat Cleveland 4–3 in Game 2 with just about no other pitch working for him. "What Greg had to say reassured me,"

Glavine said. "To hear it from a pitcher like him meant a lot." Glavine also remembered how Steve Avery had pitched Game 4 and won, 5–2. "Avery couldn't believe they never adjusted to his changeup," said Atlanta pitching coach Leo Mazzone. "So he just kept throwing it."

For the fourth time in five years the Braves would play a game that could bring Atlanta its first world championship. They were 0–3 in the other tries, with each game started by a different Brave pitcher and ending with the same maddening margin of defeat: a single run. This would be Glavine's first crack at the clincher.

He was ready to be rid of the blabbering Indians—who during the Series sometimes acted like louts crashing a black-tie affair—especially after reading in the morning newspaper that Cleveland's punchless shortstop, Omar Vizquel, had said of the Braves, "They know they can't win a World Series."

Said Glavine, "That statement made me madder than anything else."

So he took the mound intending to throw his best pitch, the changeup, until the Indians proved they could hit it. They never did. Glavine did not paint the lower outside corner so much as he coated it with lacquer, pitch after pitch after pitch. Asked how many times Glavine ventured inside with a delivery, Atlanta catcher Javy Lopez replied, "I can count them on one hand."

Glavine, with last-inning relief from Mark Wohlers, came within one bloop single of a no-hitter; Tony Peña's leadoff hit in the sixth—off one of those nasty changeups—checked up in center field like a wedge shot. Supported only by a solo home run by David Justice in the bottom of that inning, Glavine pitched the Braves to a 1–0 victory.

Can't win a World Series? Well, shut your mouth. At last, Atlanta.

It may have been the best-pitched game among the 91 that have ended a World Series. It definitely was the only one-hitter among them. The mystery to Glavine's mastery was how the Indians could lunge and flail time and time again at pitches that almost never varied in location. "His changeup is that good," Maddux said. "He throws it with the exact same arm speed as his fastball, so it's impossible to pick up. Yeah, you may be looking for something away, but is it hard or soft? And every time he did come inside, he got them out. And that plants a seed."

"Number one, you've got to trust yourself," said Glavine, who was voted Most Valuable Player of the World Series. "I've got so much confidence in my changeup that I can stand on the mound and tell you it's coming and, if it's a good one, you're not going to hit it."

The Indians never did adjust to the way Atlanta pitchers worked away from them, particularly with changeups. "They knew not to challenge our hitters," said Vizquel, whose .174 Series average contrasted with his brilliant play in the field. "They didn't come inside against them."

Cleveland scored more than five runs 69 times in the regular season, winning all but three of those games. They scored that many just once in the World Series, in Game 3—the only time an Atlanta starter, John Smoltz, came at them with fastballs and sliders instead of good off-speed pitches. The best-hitting team in 45 years was held to six hits or fewer in all four losses, and batted .179 overall.

Maddux and Glavine put ornate bookends on an otherwise ordinary Series (only once did the winning run score after the seventh inning, and only one player, Cleveland second baseman Carlos Baerga, drove in more than two runs in a game). Maddux opened it with a two-hitter, and Glavine closed it with the combined one-hitter. Not until they ran into the Braves did Cleveland have fewer than three hits in any game this year. "That says more about their pitching than our hitting," said Indian coach Buddy Bell. "They pitched that well. They should get the credit for this."

Baerga, who made the last out of all three losses in Atlanta, was not as gracious as Bell. "I think we have a better team than them," he said. "It's hard for me to take." That was typical of the tough talk of the Indians, the kind of team you would not want to bring home to Mom. Hanging in their clubhouse is a framed and matted essay called "The Art of Getting Along," by Wilfred Peterson. Now if only they would read it.

Cleveland's comportment took some of the shine off Game 3, a tense 7–6 Indian win, in which the two closers, Wohlers and José Mesa, combined for 5²/₃ shutout innings and 92 pitches—most of them unleashed at or near 100 mph. The night began with one Indian, Albert Belle, unloading a profanity-laced tirade at reporter Hannah Storm of NBC, one of baseball's national television rights holders, and ended with another Indian, Eddie Murray, refusing to talk to reporters about his game-winning hit in the 11th inning. From his training-room bunker Murray issued an innocuous statement through the team's PR director. Two little Indians.

On the same day as his altercation with Storm, Belle snapped at a photographer near the first-base line during batting practice. "Move your ass out of the way," Belle said. When the photographer did not move quickly enough for him, Belle added, "I said move your ass out of the way."

Then, after banging six straight pitches over the left-field wall, Belle ordered a TV cameraman to move away from the batting cage. "And turn the _____ camera off," he said. The cameraman did not move. Belle poked him in the shoulder with the butt of his bat and said, "Put the damn camera down."

This was the first World Series in which a team's general manager (Cleveland's John Hart) fielded a question in the interview room before the deciding game about whether his cleanup hitter required psychological testing. The commemorative World Series patches on the sleeves of the Cleveland uniforms, which included baseball's hollow slogan WELCOME TO THE SHOW, needed an addendum stitched underneath: NOW GET THE _____ OUT OF MY FACE.

On those occasions when the Indians did choose to talk, they didn't know when to shut up. Pitcher Orel Hershiser annoyed the Braves with his proselytizing, his chirping that Atlanta felt pressure from not winning the 1991 and '92 World Series, and his public scolding of Maddux in Game 5 for buzzing a fastball that nearly trimmed the whiskers of Murray's mustache. Murray glared at Maddux as if he were a sportswriter, causing benches and bullpens to empty. Hershiser approached Maddux on the grass near the mound and asked, "Did you try to hit him on purpose?"

"No," Maddux said. "I'm just trying to come in."

"You can do better than that," scoffed Hershiser, and shot him a look of warning. Or as Hershiser explained later, "It's kind of like, 'I can have as good control as you have.'"

Said one Brave, "[Hershiser] thinks he's pitching coach, hitting coach and PR director." Atlanta chafed, too, at how Tribe third baseman Jim Thome stopped to marvel at his home run in Game 5, as if it were the space shuttle *Discovery*—well, it did travel almost as far—and flung his bat away with an arrogant flourish. "They're a cocky team," said Glavine, "and they don't need to be. You hoped that some guys over there would be more professional than they were. Those guys don't need to be talking [trash] and tossing bats on home runs practically into our dugout. We don't play that way."

So annoyed were the Braves at what Hershiser and Vizquel later dismissed as meaningless psychological warfare that they called a team meeting before Game 6 to get over it. "We were a little too concerned about it," Glavine said, "and a couple of guys got up and said it didn't matter what they said. We controlled the Series, and if we just played our game, we'd win it."

The Indians were bullies in the regular season, coasting to the American League Central title by a record 30 games while pounding the back end of opposing rotations. But, as Mazzone said, "They found out we don't have a back end to our rotation."

When Cleveland needed to beat Avery, the Braves' No. 4 starter, at home to even the Series at two—Atlanta manager Bobby Cox took some heat for not using Maddux on short rest—the Indians failed miserably, losing the only game not decided by one run, 5–2.

Atlanta pitched Belle magnificently throughout the Series. The only player ever to slug 50 homers and 50 doubles in the same season did not pull a hit to left field in the six games. He batted only seven times with a runner on base and was walked on four of those occasions. At a paltry .235 he led all Cleveland hitters with more than two at bats. Likewise, Murray's play was nothing to talk about. He batted .105 (2 for 19), dragging his average in 18 World Series games down to .169.

The Braves and the gritty Glavine were almost beyond remonstration, especially from a team that, according to its own general manager, "took a couple of ball games to get a sense and feel for what the World Series is about." Atlanta's skin has been thickened by 47 postseason games since 1991, during which Glavine has logged a 1.83 ERA in 86²/₃ innings.

While everyone talked about Atlanta's unfulfilled world championship quest starting with the torturous 1991 World Series, the time line actually began in the summer of 1987: Starting in July the Braves called up shortstop Jeff Blauser from the minor leagues, traded pitcher Doyle Alexander for Smoltz, and promoted Glavine to the majors. Smoltz was assigned to the minors and Blauser returned there for half the next season, leaving Glavine as the current Brave with the longest continuous service with the club. All three of them spent time with the 1988 Braves, who lost 106 games and finished 39¹/₂ games out. "See that light tower up there?" Blauser said, pointing to the rim of Atlanta–Fulton County Stadium on the first-base side. "One night a lightbulb fell out and came crashing down into the stands. It didn't come close to hitting anybody. That's how empty this place was. There must have been about 2,500 people."

Last Saturday night the place swelled with 51,875 people and the anxiety of a city that had never before celebrated a championship in a major professional sport. TONIGHT'S THE NIGHT proclaimed one banner. [Up until that time] only two other World Series ended so late in the year—Daylight Savings Time ended just after the game—and those were delayed by a strike (1981) and an earthquake (1989).

This was a year that began late, too, because of another strike, one in which Glavine played a prominent role as the team's player representative. For that he was booed when Opening Day finally arrived on April 26. "It hurt, sure," he said late Saturday night. "I hope now I've given them something else to associate me with."

Glavine allowed only one runner as far as second base. He dominated the Indians even when he was tired in the eighth inning. "I really got out of the inning without making a good pitch," he said. He could thank Cleveland manager Mike Hargrove, who allowed Thome (0 for 8, including four punch-outs against left-handers) and weak-hitting Peña and Ruben Amaro to bat that inning while leaving two of his better hitters against lefties during the season, Sandy Alomar (.364) and Herbert Perry (.344), on the bench.

It was after the eighth inning that Glavine told Cox and Mazzone he was done. "Look up at that scoreboard," Mazzone said to Glavine. "You've got a one-hitter in the World Series. What if it was a no-hitter?" Said Glavine, "Whew. Tough call."

The last three outs belonged to Wohlers, whose ability to slam the door on a game plugged the last hole on the team. The very last out, the one he had dreamed about "since I was five years old," was too much for him to even watch. When Baerga lifted the baseball in the air toward left center field, Wohlers looked away, into the stands. When the crowd let loose a great cathartic roar, he knew the end had been secured in Marquis Grissom's glove. "I kind of blacked out," he said. "Then I saw Javy running at me, and I figured I'd better do something before he ran my butt over."

Almost two hours later Glavine kicked off his spikes and handed them over to a representative of the Hall of Fame for transport to Cooperstown. He thought out loud about the victors' spoils. "A putting green," he said. "[Atlanta president Stan Kasten] promised us a putting green in the new stadium if we won the World Series."

Next door, a new stadium is going up. It will serve as an Olympic venue for the Summer Games in Atlanta next year and, after some downsizing, as the Braves' new home in 1997. It rises like a monument to baseball's team of the 1990s, promising all the proper amenities. It will have luxury boxes, the finest grass field, and, now, besides the putting green, a world championship banner. They say the lightbulbs will stay in place, too.

1996: Yankees vs. Braves

Jimmy Leyritz's Game 4 Home Run

from *The New York Times,* "For Yanks, Game Isn't Over
Till They Win It in the 10th," by Jack Curry

It will be remembered as the most rewarding victory of the season. It will be remembered for the way the Yankees miraculously rallied from a 6–0 deficit to beat the Atlanta Braves, 8–6, with Game 4 of the World Series ending this morning in 10 memorable innings. Now it is a three-game series to determine the best team in the sport.

No baseball team has a richer history in the postseason than the Yankees. But among all their accomplishments, the Yankees had not overcome a six-run deficit in a playoff or World Series game. Until now.

On the brink of moving to within one loss of elimination, the Yankees, champions of the comeback in this postseason, rallied for three runs in the sixth inning, three more in the eighth—on Jim Leyritz's three-run homer—and two in the 10th to win this four-hour-17-minute marathon, the longest game in World Series history.

For all the hitting, the deciding runs crossed on a two-out, bases-loaded walk to Wade Boggs, then on an error by Braves first baseman Ryan Klesko.

The stunning comeback against the defending-champion Braves evened the 4-of-7 World Series at two victories apiece and guaranteed that it would return to Yankee Stadium for at least Game 6 on Saturday night.

Game 5 will be played here tonight, with the Braves' John Smoltz, the Game 1 winning pitcher, opposing the Yankees' Andy Pettitte, the losing pitcher in the opener.

Game 4 turned on a curious decision, in the 10th inning, which the Yankees capitalized on. With Yankee runners on first and second and two outs, manager Bobby Cox of the Braves made a daring strategical move when he opted to walk Bernie Williams, one of the Yankees' stars and hottest hitters in the postseason, to fill the bases and face the rookie Andy Fox.

Cox later called it the smart decision, but it backfired as Yankees manager Joe Torre inserted Boggs as a pinch-hitter and Steve Avery walked him on a high 3–2 pitch that scored Tim Raines with the go-ahead run.

"That's probably the biggest walk I've ever had in my 15-year career," Boggs said. "We've been doing this all season. It's not like we just started inventing comebacks in the playoffs. We've done this before."

The Yankees added an extra run in a bizarre manner. Charlie Hayes blooped Brad Clontz's pitch to first base, where Klesko lost the pop-up in the lights. Hayes was the fifth straight Yankee to reach in the 10th after Avery retired the first two batters.

"I just never saw it," Klesko said. "It went into the lights and it never came out."

Cox said, "A lot of things went wrong for us."

Graeme Lloyd, the eventual winning pitcher, had saved the Yankees in the Braves' ninth when he relieved Mariano Rivera and induced Fred McGriff to hit into an inning-ending double play.

The Yankee comeback was completed in the eighth when Leyritz— who was using Strawberry's bat—hit his three-run homer off Mark Wohlers to tie the score. It shocked an angry Wohlers and caused most of the 51,881 fans at Atlanta–Fulton County Stadium to do a double-take.

"I thought if we won tonight, we're going to win it," said Yankee reliever

Jeff Nelson, who pitched two scoreless innings, the sixth and the seventh. "I don't think they ever thought we'd be going back to New York. They were up 2–0.

"Everybody was writing us off and wondering whether they were going to win in four or five games. We're shocking the world."

They did this morning.

The Yankees were seemingly out of luck and out of hope. Their season was five outs away from turning into a must-win situation for three straight games. They trailed the Braves by three runs and they were opposing Wohlers, the most intimidating closer in the National League.

But something stunning happened as the Braves were preparing the champagne for a possible celebration in Game 5 and everyone else was writing the Yankees' World Series obituary.

Leyritz slashed a 2–2 slider from Wohlers and deposited it above a leaping Braves left fielder Andruw Jones and over the fence.

It was one of the biggest postseason homers for the Yankees since the same Leyritz hit one against Seattle's Tim Belcher to win Game 2 of the 1995 division series in 15 innings by a score of 7–5.

"My wife is happy because I played that one so many times during the off season, so now I got another one to play," Leyritz said. "That was definitely the biggest hit of my career."

1997: Indians vs. Marlins

Edgar Renteria's Game 7 Walk-Off Hit

from *Sports Illustrated,* "Happy Ending," by Tom
Verducci

The Marlins' stirring, 11th-inning come-from-behind defeat of the Indians in
Game 7 redeemed an otherwise lackluster Series.

You think you have busted loose from its orbit, gladly leaving behind
the endless three-ball counts, the batters taking aimless strolls after every
pitch and games that end long after most television sets have clicked off. The
1997 World Series surely lost you as a result of some of the worst pitching in
Series history; some of the worst weather; the longest games, on average; and
in general, such laggardly play that even baseball's No. 1 spinmeister, acting
commissioner Bud Selig, threw up his arms before Game 6 and said, "We
need to address the pace of games and quit talking about it. In the next 30 to
45 days changes will be in place."

Then, just as you begin to feel untethered, the gravitational pull of the
game tugs you back. What the Florida Marlins and Cleveland Indians did
on a steamy night in Miami on Sunday did not just save their Series from
ridicule, but also proved one of the fundamental laws of sport: Nothing on
the American sports landscape is more powerful than Game 7 of a World
Series.

We had waited six years for baseball to stage a Game 7, the longest span that has elapsed between such games since 1924. And after what had transpired in the first six games this year, we have never needed one more. What separated the Marlins and the Indians after nine innings of the last game of the 93rd World Series, the 2,300th game of the year, was . . . nothing. They were tied at 2—only the fourth time a Game 7 had extended into extra innings. Not until two men were out in the 11th inning, and six minutes had passed since midnight, did the 1997 season end. It did so when shortstop Edgar Renteria gave Florida its first World Series championship with a line drive that flicked off the glove of right-hander Charles Nagy and into center field, a single that sent second baseman Craig Counsell bounding happily home with the winning run. No one complained that, at four hours, 11 minutes, the 3–2 victory took too long. This was seventh heaven.

"We put on a show for the whole nation that baseball can be proud of," said Cleveland righty Orel Hershiser. "It's just fortunate that two organizations were able to rise above everything baseball people are doing to [the sport]."

Super Bowl Sunday is a national holiday in which the game itself is dwarfed by the hysteria of its buildup. The Stanley Cup and the NBA Finals, which have staged only one seventh game apiece since 1988, lack the historical weight of the World Series and don't usually match its level of drama. Baseball's showcase, even when it appears to be at its worst, is seldom disappointing. Every World Series this decade has ended on a game-winning hit (three times) or with the tying run on base or at bat (four times).

"Around the seventh inning I started to think it was going to be a classic, maybe go to extra innings," Florida pitching coach Larry Rothschild said. "The tension was there with every pitch. When you get to the seventh game of a World Series, whatever people have said about it before doesn't mean anything."

Only a Game 7 could make the 76 walks in this year's Series (a record), and the 81 runs (one short of the record), forgettable. Posterity, too, might overlook the fact that the television ratings hit all-time lows; none of the five pitchers to earn a victory had more than 38 career wins; a 14–11 Florida win in Game 3 included 17 walks, six errors, and an unprecedented 11-run ninth inning that prompted Indians manager Mike Hargrove to groan, "That was as ugly a game as you'll ever see"; and Cleveland's 10–3 victory in Game 4 was played in 18-degree windchill with flurries that made Jacobs Field resemble a gargantuan version of those snow globes you can buy at a knickknack shop.

Instead, Game 7 gave us more lasting souvenirs. It reminded us of what is best about baseball. The game is still about fathers and sons—four second-generation major leaguers played in the Series finale: catcher Sandy Alomar Jr. and right-hander Jaret Wright for the Indians, and outfielder Moises Alou and closer Robb Nen for the Marlins. Sometimes it is about mothers and sons, too. About an hour before the game, 22-year-old Florida right-hander Livan Hernandez walked into suite 251 of Pro Player Stadium in full uniform and threw his arms around his mother, Miriam Carreras. It was the first time he had seen her in two years, since he had defected from Cuba. She had just arrived from the island on a special visa, which was made possible in part by a petition signed by the Marlins players and sent to the Cuban government after the league championship series. The mother and son embraced, teary-eyed, for 10 minutes without speaking. Then they were introduced to a special guest in the suite: Joe DiMaggio.

Carreras left the stadium in the sixth inning for Hernandez's apartment. He came home with some hardware: the MVP trophy, which he earned by becoming the first rookie in 50 years to win two World Series games.

Baseball is also about confirming that players are human with a single letter: E. When Cleveland second baseman Tony Fernandez muffed a grounder to make the winning run possible, he took his place in October infamy alongside Fred Snodgrass, the New York Giants' center fielder whose dropped fly ball in 1912 allowed the Boston Red Sox to win in their last at bat. "I believe," Fernandez said in explaining the play, "the Lord doesn't send you more than He thinks you can bear."

The Indians made Game 7 possible by beating Florida's ace right-hander Kevin Brown 4–1 in Game 6, the second time in the Series that

Brown had lost. That night left-hander Al Leiter, who would start Game 7 against Wright, went home and said to his wife and mother, "I don't want to see, read, or talk about baseball. I know what tomorrow means." On the day of Game 7 his telephone rang about 40 times. He took only two calls: from former New York Yankees teammate Dave Righetti and former minor league coach Gil Patterson, both of whom encouraged him to throw more curveballs to keep the Indians from sitting on his fastball and cutter.

Not long before the first pitch, Florida manager Jim Leyland assembled the Marlins in front of their teal lockers in the clubhouse. He had spoken to them before every game of the Series, often invoking the name of Muhammad Ali. So often did Leyland mention the former heavyweight champion that the Marlins were thinking about asking Ali to visit them before one of the games in Cleveland. Leyland decided against it, not wanting to subject Ali to the inevitable swarm of media that would descend upon him.

Instead, Leyland, in a throaty voice made scratchy by too many cigarettes and too much coffee over the 3,721 pro games it took him to get to the World Series, made this promise to his team before Game 7: "When you come back here, you will be world champions." The room fell silent. Then the 52-year-old manager, always seeming to push the right buttons at the right time, cracked up his players by saying, "Since I couldn't get Ali, I tried to get Elvis, but he couldn't be here."

Leiter pitched gallantly, allowing only two runs over six innings on a third-inning single by Fernandez. Wright was even better. He took a one-hit shutout into the seventh, and even after allowing a home run to third baseman Bobby Bonilla and leaving the last eight outs to the bullpen, he was in line to become the first rookie in 88 years, since Babe Adams of the Pittsburgh Pirates, to win Game 7.

The Indians wasted a chance to add to their 2–1 lead in the ninth when they put runners at first and third with one out. Center fielder Marquis Grissom, batting against Nen, bounced to Renteria, who shocked Alomar by throwing him out at home rather than trying for a double play. "I was a dead dog," Alomar said. Nen then retired pinch-hitter Brian Giles on a fly ball.

"The last few innings seemed to take forever," Cleveland shortstop Omar Vizquel said. "The minutes trying to get to the end went so slowly."

In the ninth inning Hargrove gave the ball to his closer, right-hander José Mesa. An NBC crew began setting up a wooden platform draped with red-white-and-blue bunting in the Cleveland clubhouse, to interview the apparent world champions. A sheath of clear plastic was draped over the lockers to protect clothing from the spray of champagne. But then Alou, who put the Marlins ahead to stay in Games 1 and 5 with three-run homers off Hershiser, grounded a single into left field.

The 67,204 fans at Pro Player Stadium quaked in anticipation. In Cleveland, the insecurity capital of the country, Indians fans quaked with dread. Their Tribe had not won a World Series since 1948. The town has not won a championship in a major sport since its departed Browns won the 1964 NFL title, the longest drought among cities that have fielded teams in three major sports. John Elway, Earnest Byner, Michael Jordan, and even current Indians DH-outfielder David Justice, who won the 1995 World Series with a Game 6 home run for the Atlanta Braves, have ruined would-be championship seasons in Cleveland. Die-hard Indians fans buy up more home-team merchandise than any baseball fans but the Yankees'—in Game 3 the entire stadium was sold out of merchandise, sending club vice presidents to a warehouse for emergency restocking before Game 4. A city with a terrific orchestra, a beautiful ballpark, and the Rock and Roll Hall of Fame desperately yearns to be validated by a trophy. Or as one of Cleveland's cabbies put it, "All we want is a winner."

Mesa struck out Bonilla, bringing the Tribe within a double-play grounder of finally becoming champions. But catcher Charles Johnson cracked a single to right field, sending Alou to third. Counsell then tied the game with a sacrifice fly. "What's so hard is that we were one pitch, one batter, however you want to put it, from winning," Vizquel said later in the clubhouse, where the plastic wrap had been hastily shoved into a corner behind a refrigerator. "We were so close. It's just so hard to describe." Mesa departed in the 10th inning, leaving a two-out, two-on mess for Nagy,

Cleveland's best starter during the regular season, whom Hargrove had skipped in favor of Wright because "right now Charlie gives you the body language that tells you, 'I don't want to be on this earth.'" As Nagy warmed up with the World Series in the balance, Vizquel said to Renteria, the runner at second base, "Do you drive a convertible? You've got a nice tan." Then he asked, "Where did you go last night? Did you go out after the game?"

Fernandez joined the oddly timed bit of frivolity, asking Renteria, "Aren't your legs tired? Do you think you could score on a base hit?"

The question was left unanswered. Alou flied out.

The 11th began with a base hit by Bonilla, whose nightly facial theatrics and gimpy play caused by a strained left hamstring recalled lengthy death scenes in spaghetti Westerns. Nagy got one out when Greg Zaun, who had pinch-run for Johnson in the ninth and then replaced him behind the plate, popped up a bunt. Then, just as the scoreboard clock showed 12:00, came the stroke of midnight for the Indians: Counsell sent a bouncer to the left of Fernandez. In his haste to get Bonilla at second base, Fernandez missed the ball, and Bonilla flopped into third.

After an intentional walk to Jim Eisenreich filled the bases, center fielder Devon White forced Bonilla at home with a grounder to Fernandez. It was Renteria's turn to cement the legacy of this Series and his team.

The win was Florida's 28th in its last at bat this season, and Renteria had provided eight of those game-winning hits. The Marlins' victory legitimized the wild card, which was their ticket to the postseason. Having knocked off Atlanta, the winningest team in baseball, and by overcoming a deep Cleveland offense that had held the lead in every game of the Series, the Marlins proved to be worthy world champions. A sign at Game 6 said it all: WE BELONG.

As the Marlins rushed to mob Counsell and Renteria, for the second time in three years the last ball of the World Series wound up in the glove of Grissom in center field. As a Brave in 1995, he caught the final out, a fly ball by Cleveland's Carlos Baerga, then absently flung it into the air in jubilation. This time he picked up the baseball hit by Renteria and squeezed it in the pocket of his glove as he trudged off the field. Just before he reached the dugout steps, he looked back over his shoulder and saw the celebration raging.

What, he thought, do I want this for? With a quick underhand flip and the disdain of a fisherman throwing back a catch not worth keeping, he tossed the baseball toward the middle of the diamond and the mass of people. It rolled among the spiked feet of world champions too busy to notice—too busy jumping, hugging, and sending up a roar that will echo forever with the clear resonance of a Game 7.

2001: Diamondbacks vs. Yankees

Luis Gonzalez's Series-Winning Single

from ESPN.com, "Luis Gonzalez's Single Wins 2001 Series," by Rick Weinberg

He had not been in this situation before. No one ever had, in fact. Not in 96 previous World Series.

Game 7 of the World Series, bottom of the ninth, bases loaded, tie game, one out, the game's premier closer on the mound.

This is exactly where Luis Gonzalez of the Arizona Diamondbacks found himself on November 4, 2001, with the baseball world's spotlight shining right down on him.

As Gonzalez walked to the plate to face Mariano Rivera, trying to beat a team which had won three straight World Series championships, his mind was a blur. But he quickly gained the clarity to think to himself, "Choke up."

This concept was totally unfamiliar to Gonzalez, who had hammered the staggering total of 57 home runs during the season. "It was the first time I choked up all year," he would later admit to the media.

Considering Rivera's stuff—a vicious, nasty cut fastball—and the nature of the situation, Gonzalez's call to choke up illustrated his baseball intelligence and experience.

The Moment

The crowd at Bank One Ballpark is in a nervous frenzy for the bottom of the ninth inning. A team from Arizona has never been this close to a professional championship, but on the mound is the impenetrable Rivera, who has registered 23 successive postseason saves and never blown a save in the World Series. Rivera blew out all three Diamondbacks that he faced in the bottom of the eighth, protecting New York's 2–1 lead, setting the stage for the ninth—and final—inning of this epic World Series and classic Game 7 that began with Roger Clemens dueling Curt Schilling.

"When we all reached the dugout [for the bottom of the ninth], we all said, 'Believe. You gotta believe!'" Arizona first baseman Mark Grace would say later. "And we did believe. We knew we could win. We had come too far. We weren't going to walk away without the fight of our lives, without scrapping and clawing for as long as we could. All we had to do was put together a few quality ABs."

That they did, starting with Grace. The last of the ninth begins with Grace looking at ball one. On the next pitch, Rivera throws one of his trademark cutters. Grace, who had waited 14 years to get into a World Series after spending his career with the Chicago Cubs, fights off the pitch and loops it into center field for a single. David Dellucci is sent in to run for Grace. Damian Miller then lays down a bunt—right in front of the mound. Rivera fields the ball and spins around. He sees he has Dellucci dead at second base. This could actually be a double play because Miller is slow. But Rivera's throw sails wildly past shortstop Derek Jeter and into center field.

Instead of being an out away from elimination with no one on base, the Diamondbacks have runners on first and second and no outs. Bank One is rocking—and the Yankees are reeling. Never did they ever consider that they'd be in this position. Not with Rivera on the hill. "Losing never entered our minds," Jeter would say later. "Not for a second." Not until

Rivera commits that throwing error. But the Yankees' ace closer comes back by fielding a second straight bunt, this one by Jay Bell, into an out at third base, leaving the Yankees two outs away from a fourth straight World Series championship.

Next up is Tony Womack, who had kept the Diamondbacks' postseason alive with a game-winning hit in Game 5 of the National League Division Series against St. Louis. He does it again, lacing a 2–2 pitch for a double down the right-field line to tie the game. Bank One is simply delirious as Craig Counsell steps to the plate. Shockingly, Rivera hits Counsell with a pitch, sending the crowd into a wilder frenzy. The bases are now juiced for the team's best hitter.

The electricity in the stadium is off the charts as Gonzalez fouls off the first pitch. The next pitch is a classic Rivera cutter, veering in on Gonzalez's hands. He swings, cracking the bat, just below the trademark. "I got jammed, but I knew I didn't have to hit it hard," Gonzalez says. "I knew I just had to hit the ball in play."

The ball floats toward shortstop, spinning in the air, like a cue shot, and away from a backpeddling Jeter, who was playing in to cut off the run at the plate. As Gonzalez runs toward first base, Jeter races back and lunges in vain as the ball floats over him and lands on the lip of the outfield grass. Bell—the first free agent signed in Diamondbacks history —races across the plate with the Series-winning run as absolute bedlam breaks loose on the field and in the stands.

"Not a day has passed that I haven't thought about it," Gonzalez says today. "Not one. And not a day has passed that I haven't thought about how fortunate I was to be in that position, how fortunate we all were. It was so wonderful to be a part of that. It's one of those moments where the memory never fades away."

2002: Angels vs. Giants

Angels' Game 6 Comeback

from *The Los Angeles Daily News,* "Touched by an Angel," by Steve Dilbeck

Logic made an exit. Disbelief swept through the crowd. Insanity ruled.

The Angels lived to play one more day.

And not just any day, but baseball's best day, its most dramatic, most storied, and most treasured day.

Game 7 of the World Series.

All it took for the Angels to make it to baseball's greatest game was the greatest comeback in their history, a 6–5 victory that was also one of the biggest comebacks in World Series history.

The Angels were headed for the sports obits, for talk of a nice season falling just short, of having at least made it to their first World Series.

They trailed the Giants 5–0 Saturday in Game 6 going into the bottom of the seventh. Their offense had consisted of an infield hit and a broken-bat single. Mummies have shown more life.

But an Angels team that has specialized in coming back all season had saved its best, most unbelievable comeback for last.

The Angels had one more rally in them. One more gut-check, one more night of looking straight into the abyss and somehow walking away.

"Until that last out is made again (tonight), we'll never give up," said first baseman Scott Spiezio. "We're going to go out, be aggressive, play, our game and have the same attitude we've had all year."

The Giants had every reason to believe they'd won their first World Series since moving to San Francisco. They were in complete control. Barry "Puffy" Bonds was making shelf space for his World Series MVP trophy, having hit his fourth Series homer.

The Giants had to figure they'd be announcing plans for a parade today, fighting a hangover, instead of playing in a dramatic Game 7.

"There was definitely confidence, but we knew the game wasn't over," said Giants manager Dusty Baker. "They proved it wasn't over."

Giants right-hander Russ Ortiz had been all but dominating. He was a man on a mission, a pitcher determined to avenge his Game 2 loss.

It didn't seem like much when Troy Glaus singled with one out in the seventh. But when Brad Fullmer followed with another hit and Ortiz's pitching count hit 98, Baker called on reliever Felix Rodriguez to face Spiezio. It was his sixth appearance in as many games.

The crowd, again decked out in all red, was pleading for something to happen, banging thousands of noise sticks, standing, almost demanding one more night of magic.

And then Spiezio delivered, sending a 3–2 Rodriguez pitch high to right field.

"I didn't know it was gone when I hit it," Spiezio said. "I was saying, 'God, please, just get it over the fence.'"

It landed about two rows deep, maybe 335 feet deep. About the same distance as Shawon Dunston's home run for the Giants in the fifth to the opposite corner.

Suddenly the Angels were down only 5–3. The bench was alive, the crowd electric.

"I know this team," Spiezio said. "All it needs is a little spark."

Then, in the eighth, Darin Erstad led off with a home run against

Tim Worrell. The Angels were down by a lone run. Belief was rising. The impossible seemed within reach.

Tim Salmon singled. Garret Anderson blooped a hit to right that Bonds overran and then slipped trying to pick up for an error. The tying run was at third, the winning run at second.

Baker called on his stopper, Robb Nen, to face Glaus. Nen, one of the greatest closers in baseball history. One more stomach-turning postseason moment.

Glaus was hoping for a single or a sacrifice fly to just tie the score, but Nen got a slider up and Glaus lined it for a two-run double.

And then, Edison Field simply exploded.

"I go back to the Kirk Gibson game in '88," said Angels manager Mike Scioscia. "I think there was about as much electricity in that stadium as there ever was. I think tonight surpassed that."

The Angels had an improbable 6–5 lead. It was the kind of turnaround, the cause of such utter disbelief, that can make sports so special.

No team facing elimination had ever come back from a 5–0 deficit in World Series history.

And so, tonight, the Angels and Giants, two teams that refuse to back down, to give any quarter, are going to go at it one more memorable time.

"We're both going after it hard," Scioscia said. "When you have two teams like that, there's always special things that can happen."

The rest of the country is missing one special World Series. It's missing some great sports drama.

The Giants, if they're not demoralized, will try a second time to win the World Series tonight by sending out Livan Hernandez, who had been 6–0 in the postseason until losing Game 3.

The Angels, if they can come down from Saturday's high, are going to send a rookie, John Lackey, out tonight to try and pull down their first World Series.

"[Tonight] we'll go with everybody," Baker said.

So will the Angels. It's all or nothing now. Baseball's dream game is here. And all it took was the Angels' greatest comeback.

[The Angels won the 2002 Series 4 games to 3.]

2003: Marlins vs. Yankees

Young Marlins Surprise the Yankees

from *The New Yorker*, The Sporting Scene, "Gone South," by Roger Angell

In a last surprise, the young Marlins are champs.

Baseball Commissioner Bud Selig, in a surprise news conference two days after the conclusion of the recent World Series, announced that Major League Baseball will undertake a radical change in scheduling next fall, when the Divisional and League Championship eliminations will come after the World Series, not before. "Tradition matters," Selig said, "but the fans have made it clear that they much prefer the interest and drama of the earlier rounds of postseason play, and we're going to oblige them. From now on, it's the Fall Classic first and then heartbreak." The commissioner confirmed reports that he had called in some top metaphysicians to tackle the contradictions implicit in such a plan. "They're gung-ho for the plan, conceptwise," Mr. Selig said. "Once we have this in hand, we're looking to clear up the designated-hitter dilemma, as well. Ambiguity is tough, but so is Roger Clemens."

Well, maybe not, but after the vibrant and confounding baseball scenes in the weeks just past, no possibility can be wholly excluded. Look what did happen:

- In the ceremonials before the third game of the American League Divisional playoffs between the Red Sox and the Oakland Athletics, a Red Sox relief pitcher named Byung-Hyun Kim heard prolonged boos from his home-team Fenway Park fans when his name was announced, and responded digitally.
- Another bird, the Yankee Stadium celebrity eagle Challenger, lost his way while performing his ceremonial flight from the center-field bleachers to a handler on the pitcher's mound before the first game of the Red Sox–Yankees American League Championship Series, wobbled past Derek Jeter (who flinched away, snatching off his cap), and flumped to the ground near home plate. Fired on the spot, the famous fowl unexpectedly emerged from retirement prior to the third game of the World Series, but now with a Sunbelt employer, and made a safe journey home for the Florida Marlins during the anthem at Pro Player Stadium, in Miami. Redemption.
- At Wrigley Field, in Chicago, Cubs left fielder Moises Alou leaped and stretched for a fly ball descending in foul ground beside a steep bank of seats, and had the ball deflected from his glove by a lifelong Cubs fan, Steve Bartman, whose name, on the instant, became inextricably woven into the 128-year-old history of the franchise. (As is perhaps not known to schoolchildren in Mukden or Petrozavodsk, the Cubs have not won a world championship since 1908 and the Boston Red Sox since 1918.) The incident still left the good guys three runs ahead in the game and an easy inning and two-thirds away from a victory over the Florida Marlins in the National League Championship Series and their first trip to the World Series in 58 years, but the Cubs now swiftly yielded a base on balls, a single, a clanking error by their shortstop, and an eventual eight-run rally. They lost, lost again the next night, and were eliminated. The sight of Bartman being pelted with insults and threats and cups of beer, and taken away, hiding his face, by the cops for his own safety, has stuck in mind,

however. Cubs players and coaches quickly came forward to say that his instinctive grab had nothing to do with the outcome, but Bartman was subjected to later vilifications on the Internet and in the papers, and felt forced to issue a lengthy apology. Baseball is the only sport that fingers individual spectators this way and remembers their names: Sal Durante, who caught Maris's Ruth-breaking 61st home run in 1961; Jeffrey Maier, who reached for that short home run to right field in Yankee Stadium in a 1996 playoff against the Orioles; and Alex Popov and Patrick Hayashi, the bleacher fans at Pac Bell Stadium who ended up in a scuffle for the ball and the court costs, after Barry Bonds's 73rd. Ask not for whom that ball falls.

At the Boston games, fans saw separate interference plays by Red Sox infielders in the same inning nullified when two different Oakland Athletics base runners forgot to touch home plate; witnessed the 72-year-old Yankee bench Kewpie Don Zimmer throw a punch at Red Sox ace Pedro Martinez (who deflected the attack in the manner of Belmonte dealing with a heifer) during a team brawl; and (by television from the Bronx) watched Sox manager Grady Little perform a gruesome public seppuku by failing to remove the selfsame Pedro from action in the eighth inning of the ALCS seventh-game finale, after successive hits by the Yankees. The Yanks tied the game on a bloop double by Jorge Posada, and won it—against a different pitcher—in the 11th, on a lead-off, walk-off home run by Aaron Boone. Getting either or both of the Cubs and Red Sox into the World Series on their hallowed home fields had been a happy possibility nationally discussed and op-edded since July, and when the two teams were again dispatched winless into winter their fans were left with a last gnawing weirdness: Both clubs had led by an identical three-run margin at a moment when they stood the same bare five outs away from a pennant, and both blew the chance.

Even as the World Series began, friends of mine were saying how much they mourned the absence of these famous losers in the finale. They'd yearned to see the sweet and accursed old teams have at each other in their grand old parks—a lore-off, so to speak. Part of me felt the same way, but when Juan Pierre, the speedy Marlins center fielder, touched off the first inning of the first Series game with an unplayable bunt, scooted to third on a single, and scored on a sacrifice fly, my mind began to clear. I didn't know this team, but their anonymity and lack of history suddenly felt like a gift. Most of the Yankees and Red Sox we'd been watching carried an almost visible weight of expectation and precedent and prior exploit or failure with them whenever they stepped up to the plate or delivered a pitch, and looked wearied by it; as the *Globe* columnist Dan Shaughnessy put it, the uniform had become too heavy. When Pierre came up to bat again in the fifth, with base runners on second and third, and rapped a little single to left, third baseman Aaron Boone cut off the peg to the plate, allowing the second run to score. Watching, you knew that Boone had glimpsed Pierre, or the idea of Pierre, whirling past first base, and wanted him stopped there. He'd given up the run—the winning run, as it turned out—because he was afraid of the next one, or a bunch more. Call it a forced mistake, and as I put the play into my scorecard I circled it, for elegance.

These wild-card Florida Marlins, who finished the regular season ten games behind the Atlanta Braves in the National League East, entered the postseason as an assemblage of attractive outsiders who'd posted the best record in their league since the beginning of June under a fresh manager, 72-year-old Jack McKeon, called out of retirement to take the post early in May. With a lineup featuring the perpetual All-Star catcher Ivan Rodriguez; the leggy and engaging 21-year-old flinger Dontrelle Willis, who could start and finish games with equal ardor; and a 20-year-old Venezuelan, Miguel Cabrera, up from Double-A ball, at cleanup, the Marlins appeared elated by the odds against them, even when they fell behind. They didn't go away, in the parlance, but burned steadily and imperturbably through October, winning the last three games in a row in successive elimination series against the power of the Giants, the celebrated pitching of the Cubs, and now the Yankees—and with the last one, of course, the World Championship. Their closest call, you could say, came when the Giants' J. T. Snow, representing the tying run, charged frantically down the line toward home with two out in the ninth of the final divisional game, and slammed into Rodriguez at home. The throw in from left field beat him by yards, and Pudge held onto the ball.

This was the second crown for the Marlins in seven years, but the new champs fielded only one player, third baseman Jeff Conine, who played for them in 1997—a returnee signed aboard this summer after interim stints with the Royals and the Orioles. The current owner, Jeffrey Loria, was allowed to buy the franchise two years ago, after epochal sufferings with his prior fief, the Montreal Expos. By consensus, most of the credit for the Marlins' sudden rise goes to some brilliant draft signings by the carryover general manager, Dave Dombrowski, who has since accepted the same post with the Tigers, and prior owner John Henry, who now owns the Red Sox, of all things. A uniting thread between these Marlins and the 1997 group—aside from chronic low attendance at steamy Pro Player Stadium, which was built for the NFL's Miami Dolphins—is that neither champion visited first place after April.

The upbeat Marlins will soon drop out of this account (we are following the Selig fantasy formula), but they leave behind a trail of bright images, including that of the expressionist lefty Dontrelle Willis—who appeared in five postseason relief turns and two starts—tilting and flailing like a reborn Goose Gossage, with his tongue stuck out and his excited eyes alight under that down-to-his-nose, flat-brim, street-chic cap. In Game 3, another outsized pitcher, the goat-bearded, sulky-faced Josh Beckett, struck out 10 Yankees in $7^1/_3$ innings, amid tropical Miami showers, but was beaten by Derek Jeter's three hits for the night, the last a double up the right-field line, after a terrific mound duel against Mike Mussina. The win put the Yanks one up in the Series, and when they rallied late the next night . . . to carry the game into extra innings, and loaded the bases with one out in the 11th, a customary Yankee outcome appeared at hand. They didn't deliver, and the winning Florida poke—a lead-off homer down the left-field line in the 12th by shortstop Alex Gonzalez—bore such an uncanny resemblance to the Aaron Boone walk-off that had killed the Red Sox, days before, that it looked like a mistake in the screening room. Hey, hold it—wrong guys!

The Yankee offense, unreliable all season, was so creaky by now that Torre benched Jason Giambi and the wholly discombobulated Alfonso Soriano the next night—and shortly had to do without his starter, David Wells, who suffered back spasms after one inning's work and could not return. (Jolly in the interview room the day before, Boomer had boasted that he had a rubber arm and could leave the rigors of conditioning to other pitchers forever.) The Marlins' seven hits over the next four innings helped build the 6–4 win and the parvenus' second lead in the series. The teams came back to the Stadium, where the Yankees win big games by force of habit, but they'd finished scoring for the year. The silencing 2–0 win delivered by Josh Beckett was the first Series-ending shutout suffered at home by the Yankees since Lew Burdette did it for the Milwaukee Braves, in 1957. The Marlins were outscored in the Series, and outhit, as well, but it had begun to be noticed by the irritated Yankee pitchers that most of those scores—nine of the latest 12 Florida runs, in fact—had come with two outs. Just when you thought you had them, you didn't. And here it happened again, with two down in the sixth: a bloop against Andy Pettitte by Gonzalez, a drive up the middle from Pierre, and Castillo's sliced mini-hit to right, to bring in the first run of the game—the only one required, it turned out. The peg from right had a chance, but the front runner, Gonzalez, came skidding past home on a slide that fell away from Posada's swipe, and he caressed the plate with his outstretched left hand as he flew by. Marlin-style ball, and a recognizable marque by now.

Beckett's opponent, Pettitte, was making his 30th postseason start here and his 10th in the World Series, but it was the younger man who looked suave and untroubled on this evening, jumping ahead in the counts and delivering ceaseless heat and late-moving curveballs in a thrilling, manner-free flow. He was in the mid-to-upper-90-mph range all night, and here and there edged higher. Beckett, who is 23 and 6-foot-5, has the contemptuous air of the overgifted athlete, but, having earned the sneer now—he'd added nine more strikeouts, and by the time he was done had surrendered but three runs in his last 29 innings, along with two shutouts—he appeared to forgive us a little at the end. He holds an apprentice's 17–17 record for his three years in the majors to date, with a 9–8 won-lost record and a 3.04 earned-run average this season, when he had to sit out seven weeks with an inflamed elbow. "He's just starting to pitch," said the Florida utility infielder Mike Mordecai, shaking his head in awe. He compared Beckett to a teammate of his from a decade ago, the left-handed Atlanta phenom Steve Avery, but I had a better model in mind: 21-year-old Bret Saberhagen, who gave up a lone run to the Cardinals over 18 innings during the 1985 Series, and effortlessly won the MVP, just as Beckett did here. Watching them both, you could see Cooperstown in the mists ahead—or else the waiting rooms of Dr. James Andrews, the celebrated Birmingham shoulder surgeon, et al., which was Saberhagen's path, as it turned out. This is a tough trade.

Young players who win a championship are clueless about its rarity, but Jack McKeon, lighting a cigar in the corridor outside the champagne-damp Marlins clubhouse, knew what they'd accomplished. His 55 years in baseball include managerial tenures with four other major league teams, and a decade as baseball-operations vice-president of the Padres, who made the World Series in 1984 but swiftly lost to the Tigers. Now he had that ring. McKeon grew up in South Amboy, New Jersey, but has acquired the skipperish, plainsman's mien, behind rimless glasses, that comes to so many elder baseball guys. In conversation before the finale, he and I had discussed the way that "72-year-old" prefix had become welded to his name these past weeks. "You notice that, too, I bet," he said, throwing an unexpected arm around my shoulder, "but, hell, this beats retirement. Never retire—right?" He'd been idle at home in Elon, North Carolina, when Marlins owner Loria came calling in May. McKeon said that he'd not minded the daylight hours at home, or the garden work, but hated what came afterward. "Sitting in the same damned chair till midnight, watching games," he said scornfully. "That used to be my working day."

I hope Jack McKeon saw the *Post* headline the day after he'd won, and is having it framed: YANKEES SLEEP WITH THE FISH.

This October, the closeness of the postseason games and the sight of so many celebrity teams—A's, Yankees, Red Sox, Braves, Cubs, and Giants—suddenly fighting for their lives in the early rounds of play made these eliminations feel like a different sport altogether: baseball with a 30-second clock. Counting the World Series, 38 games were required to produce a champion, with 11 of them settled by one run, and six going into extra innings. The easy, almost endless run of summer ball was not just over but obsolete, and it requires effort to bring any part of it back, even the Mets. Place should be reserved, however, for the achievement of the switch-hitting Red Sox infielder Bill Mueller, who twice hit home runs from different sides of the plate in the same game. The second time he did this, against the home-team Texas Rangers, the dingers—first right-handed, then left—came in consecutive innings and were both grand slams. Never before—never nearly before.

For a single game, I will keep the drizzly, foggy evening of June 13th, at Yankee Stadium, when Roger Clemens, after failing in his three previous tries, at last nailed down his 300th win. He was the 21st pitcher to enter this particular club, but on the same night also notched his 4,000th lifetime strikeout, a level previously attained only by Nolan Ryan and Steve Carlton. Clemens, who is 41, was retiring after this season, his 20th, and he had wanted these certifications before the end. The landmark K was odd, because Roger had just given up a home run and a double to the previous Cardinal batters here in the second inning (it was an interleague game) and because the cheers greeting the whiff, by shortstop Edgar Renteria, now began to blend with a welcome for the next batter, designated hitter Tino Martinez, an old Yankee hero making his first appearance at the Stadium since his departure two years ago. Tino, sensing the moment, stepped back to allow the Roger ovation to reach its full, 55,214-fan volume while the ball was being handed off to a ball boy like a Brinks package, and then at last got into the batter's box for his own "TI-NO! TI-NO! TI-NO!"

Nothing came easily on this night, in fact, in a game that repeatedly threatened to be delayed or wiped out by rain, or even won by the wrong team, until a two-run homer by Raul Mondesi in the seventh brought the score to 5–2 Yankees, and safety. Clemens had departed in the top of the same inning (he struck out ten batters) but came back onto the field after the final out, while the scoreboard played Elton John's "Rocket Man" and the fans flashed their digital cameras and wept. Clemens hugged his catcher, Jorge Posada; hugged his other teammates and coaches; hugged the Yankee PR honcho, Rick Cerrone; hugged his wife, Debbie; hugged his sons, Koby, Kory, Kacy, and Kody; hugged the ballpark.

I am not big on lifetime records, but this 300th win changed Clemens and changed the fans' view of him as well. Almost from the beginning of his career, he has been an enigmatic presence in the clubhouse and in midaction—a tree in the living room, a dangerous object left on the highway. There have been six Cy Young Awards and those two epochal 20-strikeout games, 10 years apart, and also the fugues: his early ejection from a league championship start in 1990 for muttered curses on the mound; his nailing Mike Piazza with a fastball on the side of the helmet in 2000; and its sequel, the flung-bat-stump mystery in the World Series that same fall. But now and for the rest of this season Clemens became calmer on the mound and less mumbly or Esperantoid with the media. Planet Roger had produced a sunset. "Since the 300 he's not so hard on himself all the time," Joe Torre said. "It's like he's come through something and out the other side." Clemens was not less of a pitcher, however, keeping a live fastball (and that Kilroy stare-in at the batter over the fence of his glove) and going 17–9 for the season, with 190 (or 4,099) strikeouts, fifth best in the league. He also won two huge starts in the postseason—the third game against the Twins in the divisionals, which put his team in command at last, and that roily Game 3 in Boston, where he stood cool amid the schoolyard punchings and pushings. He wanted to stay useful, and did so, besting his duellist Pedro in every category in his six innings and coming off with the win.

The Sox fans taunted Clemens all that afternoon, but I believe they still remembered his last local appearance, at the end of August, his 100th victory in this old park, when he'd come out of the game after seven, a winner once again, and received a substantial, echoing "O" from the width and breadth of the Fenway multitudes, who had loved him here in his celebrated 13-year tenure and foully vilified him ever since.

Some writers and television sports guys have been saying that Roger won't stay retired—he'll miss it all too much—and I just hope they'll bring their money around, come spring. I think they're the ones who don't want to say good-bye. "I'm dead serious on what I'm doing," Clemens said in Florida. "I'm pretty set on it." This was about his departure, but it fits a career as well.

At 2:37 in the morning, Steve Wulf, a Red Sox fan who is also the executive editor of *ESPN: The Magazine,* was alone in the living room of his house in Larchmont watching on television the first game of the Sox-Athletics American League divisional playoff from Oakland. The A's had loaded the bases in the bottom of the 12th inning when catcher Ramon Hernandez dropped down a killer bunt, to bring home the winning run. "Fuck," Wulf said to himself, turning off the set—and heard the same summarizing blurt softly repeated from above by his wife, Bambi, who had long since gone to bed, and, still more faintly, by their 17-year-old son, Bo, on the top floor. Here was a harbinger, the first leaf of another hard Bosox autumn ahead—11 more games of breathless and mindless, heroic and incomprehensible ball, ending in a fresh seismic shock to the Red Sox Nation, by consensus the worst one of all. I was at Fenway Park for most of the action, but cannot offer a reliable summary— certainly not of the divisional third game, which featured a collective six errors and several base-running grotesqueries by the visitors.

Scrolling ahead, we alight in Game 3, Scene 4 of the next series, the ALCS, at Fenway Park, just as Pedro Martinez lets fly that fastball aimed behind Yankee batter Karim Garcia, grazing him high on the left shoulder as he flinches away. Vintage Pedro or something, but there's no doubt about his intention. Handed a two-run first-inning lead against Roger Clemens, Martinez has given back a run in the second, then a solo homer to Jeter, and, just now, a walk and a single and an RBI double to Hideki Matsui. The Yankees lead, and will hold on to win, despite chaotic distractions. When play resumes, Garcia bangs irritably into second baseman Todd Walker at the front of a double play, and in the ensuing pushing and grabbing,

Martinez glares at Jorge Posada in the Yankee dugout and aims a finger at his own forehead: You're next! After the teams change sides Manny Ramirez comes out at Clemens, bat upraised, in response to an eye-level pitch that was actually over the plate. ("If I'd wanted it near him he'd have known it," Clemens said later.) Benches and bullpens empty, old Zimmer swings at Martinez and goes down—what was that?—and will be taken away tenderly as the players at last disperse and the umps confer. Later, there's a mini-fracas in the Yankee bullpen, where reliever Jeff Nelson and right fielder Garcia (vaulting the fence to get there) get into a street scuffle with a Red Sox employee. This game had been billed as a classic between the best pitcher of his day and the best of his era, but turned into low farce.

The next day, a rainy Sunday, Zimmer wept and apologized, fines were assessed ($50,000 to Martinez on down to $5,000 for Zimmer), and the Red Sox management, defying a team-silence edict from the commissioner's office, staged an embarrassing press conference while attempting to put a Sox spin on the debacle. "This is a band of brothers," explained chief executive officer Larry Lucchino. Fra Pedro, whose team's record had just gone to 9–15 in games he'd started against the Yankees, dismissed Zimmer's apology but offered none of his own. "It's not a good feeling to have to apologize," he said. "I don't know if you realize this." With a 14–4 record and a 2.22 ERA this year, Martinez is not exactly in decline, but after this weekend you had the sense that even in the stoniest New England precincts he will no longer be defined by his numbers. In his *Globe* column, Dan Shaughnessy wrote, "Pedro was an embarrassment and a disgrace to baseball Saturday. . . . And the Sox front office enables him, just as they do Manny Ramirez. Just as they did with Roger when he was here and Yaz when he was here and Ted when he was here."

Don Zimmer, who has retired, deserves at least a footnote, here at the end of one of those "Glory of Their Times" baseball careers. His 55 years in the game included a marriage (it's still going) at home plate at Elmira when he was a young infielder in the Eastern League; a dozen years in the majors, with five different teams; and a manager's post with four more, including the Red Sox. Just this past season, he turned up in a dazzling new baseball trivia question, in good company. Q. Name four guys who were ejected from major-league games in six different decades. A. Casey Stengel. Leo Durocher. Frank Robinson. Zimm.

It comes to a seventh game—could anyone have doubted it? This will be the 26th time the Red Sox and Yankees have faced off this year—a record for any two teams in the annals—and while there have been stretches when the latest renewal held all the drama of a couple of cellmates laying out a hand of rummy, this is another killer dénouement. For all we know, it's up there with the 1978 Bucky Dent playoff and the DiMaggio late return of 1949. There's a wired, nonstop holiday din at the Stadium, which dies away only with the first intensely watched pitches. Everything matters now. Clemens is back and so is Pedro—but this Roger appears frail and thought-burdened. The No. 2 Boston batter, Todd Walker, raps a safe knock after a 10-pitch at bat, and Nomar Garciaparra lines out hard to right. An inning later, Kevin Millar singles, and Trot Nixon, from his flat-footed left-handed stance, delivers a businesslike homer into the stands in right: his third two-run job in the postseason. With two out, the bearded, dadlike Jason Varitek doubles into the right-field corner. Johnny Damon's grounder looks like the last out but—geez!—third baseman Enrique Wilson mishandles the ball and his throw pulls first baseman Nick Johnson off the bag, as Varitek turns the corner and scores. It's 3–0, and when the teams change sides the Stadium has gone anxious and pissed-off conversational: fans up and down the stuffed tiers complaining to their seatmates or sending the bad news home on their cells, with gestures: . . . plus Wilson is in for defense, right? . . . our only chance was stay close to goddamn Pedro.

Martinez, for his part, survives some first-inning wobbles and is soon in rhythm: the stare-in from behind his red glove, the velvety rock and turn, and the strikes arriving in clusters. After each out, he gloves the returning ball backhand, and gazes about with lidded hauteur. No one else in the world has eyes so far apart. The Yanks go down quickly again, and we're at the top of the fourth—and the startling sound, it's like a tree coming apart, of Kevin

Millar's solo shot up into the upper-deck left-field stands. Clemens, down 4–0 and almost helpless, gives up a walk and a hit-and-run single to Mueller and departs, maybe for the last time ever. A 10-year-old Yankee fan I know named Noah has by this time gone down on his knees on the concrete in front of his seat near first base, hiding his head.

There were Sox fans here, too, of course—you could see them in red-splashed knots and small parties around the Stadium, and pick up their cries. The Boston offense had been a constant for them all year, including the 16-hit outburst in the series-tying 9–6 win the night before. This year, the Sox set major-league records for extra bases, total bases, and slugging percentage. The Boston front office, headed by the 29-year-old GM, Theo Epstein, had traded vigorously to build a batting order with no soft sectors or easy outs in it. Mueller, the double-grand-slam switch-hitter, was batting eighth today. For me, Kevin Millar, a free agent acquired for cash from the Marlins last winter, was the genius pick. On April 1st, the second day of the season, he contributed a 16-inning game-winning home run in Tampa, and in June pinch-hit a grand slam that helped pull off a seven-run turnabout against the Brewers. With his blackened cheekbones and raunchy grin, he became the model for the Sox' newfound grunginess—dirt-stained uniforms and pine-smudged helmets, and an early-October outburst of shaved heads that transformed sluggers and pitchers and old coaches into plebes or pledges. His "Let's cowboy up!" rallying cry from the dugout and the on-deck circle caught on with DJs and schoolkids and Green Line subway riders, inundating Greater Boston in "Cowboy Up!" caps and T-shirts and fan towels and diapers and souvenir glassware. Somebody found a clip of 18-year-old Kevin mouthing the lyrics to Bruce Springsteen's "Born in the U.S.A." in a Beaumont, Texas, karaoke solo, which became a staple on the Fenway message board. The unimaginable had happened: The Sox were loose.

Mike Mussina, called into the crisis with Boston runners at first and third, and no outs—Clemens had just gone—went into his ceremonial low-bowing stretch and struck out Varitek, the first batter, on three pitches. Three more brought a handy 6-6-3 double play at Damon's expense. "MOOOOSE!"

the bleacherites cried. It was Mussina's first relief appearance after 400 lifetime starts, but he understood the work. Jason Giambi, struggling at .190 in the series, hit a homer barely into the center-field seats, for a first dent in Pedro, and, liking the range, did it again to the same sector in the seventh, bringing us to 4–2, with the old house roaring and rocking. The press-box floor thrummed under my feet, as I had felt it do on an autumn late night or two before. Young Noah had lifted himself off the deck by this time and stood by his seat, yelling.

I had been looking about the familiar Stadium surround in valedictory fashion—the motel-landscape bullpens, the UTZ Potato Chip sign over in right—but from here to the end sat transfixed by the cascade of events, scarcely able to draw a full breath. No other sport does this, and even as we stare and cry, "Can you believe this?" we forget how often it comes along, how it's built into baseball.

Joe Torre, patching in relievers after Mussina's three-inning stint, produced David Wells, whose first pitch was sailed deep into the bleachers by Sox DH David Ortiz. 5–2 now. Checking the video monitor, I saw Wells's top teeth hit his bottom lip with the expletive. But Pedro had been long at his tasks, and when Jeter doubled to the right-field corner in the eighth and was singled home by Bernie Williams, the margin narrowed again to two, and here came manager Grady Little, out to hook his ace and pat him on the rump as he left. Little likes to stand below a pitcher, on the downslope of the mound, and here again, looking up at Pedro like a tourist at the Parthenon steps, he said a few words and walked away. This could not be. Martinez had thrown 115 pitches, and given up ringing hits to five of the last seven batters. A Sox-fan friend of mine, Ben, watching in his apartment on West 45th Street, had gone on his hands and knees, screaming. But Pedro stayed on: a ground-rule double by Matsui, then the dying bloopy double by Posada that landed untouched out beyond second base, for two runs and the tie. "There's a lot of grass out there," Posada explained later. Grady Little, in his own brief postgame, said, "Pedro Martinez has been our man all year long, and in situations like that he's the one we want on the mound," which was understandable but untrue. This had been only the fifth game in 31 starts in which Martinez was allowed to pitch into the eighth.

It was Mariano Rivera time—the waiting Boston bad dream—and Mo, defending the tie, poised and threw, poised and threw, whisking through the ninth. There was a scary double to left by Ortiz with two gone in the 10th, but Rivera, sighing, delivered the cutter to Millar, who lined gently to Jeter. Midnight had come and gone, but the Yankees could do no better against Embree and then Timlin, the tough Sox relievers Grady Little had slighted in extremis (the two surrendered no runs at all in this series, in 16-plus combined innings). The top of the 11th went away, to noisy, exhausted accompaniments; the latest Boston pitcher was Tim Wakefield, the tall knuckleballer who had embarrassed the Yankees with his spinless stuff, twice beating Mussina in close, low-scoring games. Mo was done: The balance had swung the other way. I looked at my scorecard to confirm the next Yankee batter—Aaron Boone, who had come into the game as a pinch-runner in the eighth—looked back, and saw the ball and the ballgame fly away on his low, long first-pitch home run into the released and exulting and rebelieving Yankee crowds. I yelled, too, but thought, Poor Boston. My god.

News and reviews of this game poured in even while the World Series was cranking up. A woman I know, riding a late taxi downtown that night with a friend, was stopped at a light at 23rd Street and Seventh Avenue when she heard the earphoned, Urdu-speaking driver suddenly shouting "Aaron Boone! Aaron Boone!" A man in the Abbey Tavern, around the corner from the Piazza Navona in Rome, turned to say something consoling to a new Sox-fan acquaintance after the Boone homer—it was 6:15 in the morning—and found the seat empty. In Gramercy Square, light from his home TV screen illuminated the patrician visage of 86-year-old Gardner Botsford, a retired editor and writer who was wearing the first messaged garment of his life, a classic white cotton T-shirt, with "Yankees Suck" in 75-point blue capitals. Botsford is no Red Sox fan, but his shirt, the gift of a friend just back from Fenway Park, summed up his convictions: Voltaire could not have put it better. When Boone had done his deed, Botsford took off the shirt and went upstairs. "Didn't work," he said to the silent form across the bed. Eighteen-year-old Pat Sviokla had asked a bunch of friends and classmates over to watch the game at his house in Newton, outside Boston, but when Boone's shot went out the party disappeared. "Nobody said a word," Pat's mother, Eileen, said later. "Six or seven of them going out the door, single file. They looked like POWs." Bill Buckner letting the ground ball go through his legs at Shea Stadium had happened in 1986, when these young men were one-year-olds. Bucky Fucking Dent, Joe Morgan, Jim Willoughby taken out, and Throw the ball in, Johnny, was stuff their fathers and grandfathers talked about. Now they belonged.

Much of the buzz collected around Grady Little. "Grady Sutton is a better manager than Grady Little" was the gist and entire content of a note I had from an unknown correspondent—who'd somehow realized that I would recognize Grady Sutton as the moonfaced ninny in the old W. C. Fields flicks. "Grady Little is the George Bush of managers," a friend across the hall from me in my office came by to announce. "Letting Pedro stay in is like George Bush staring into Putin's soul."

Now, a month later, a little of New England's pain and anguish may have dispersed, helped along by the Yankees' loss in the World Series and that late footage of Derek Jeter, still with his cap and spikes and wristbands on, sitting disconsolate in front of his Stadium locker a full hour after the Yanks' elimination.

Grady Little has been let go, and the Red Sox have offered waivers on Manny Ramirez, hoping to trade him and his $20-million-a-year contract for new pitching. If you want to tap into the Sox fans' psyche now, you have to consult a new Web site, www.redsoxhaiku.com, where it comes in eloquent triplets:

> *Bright leaves falling. Clear*
> *Blue sky. Frost at dawn. Autumn.*
> *Red Sox lose again.*

Or:

Buckner or Little
It doesn't really matter
Someone will fuck up

And:

Hey, wait till next year:
Every eighty-six years
Like clockwork. Go Sox.

Joe Torre, who called the Red Sox the best team his Yankees had faced during his eight-year tenure as manager, was short of a haiku by a beat or two in the interview room just before that seventh game, but also on target: "This really is fun, but you don't know it's fun until it's over."

2004: Red Sox vs. Cardinals

Red Sox Win!

from *Faithful* by Stewart O'Nan and Stephen King

"You want to know how I feel? I'm at a loss for words."

—Curt Schilling, October 28, 2004

October 23rd/World Series Game 1

SK: I think Wake is a GREAT choice for Game 1. Sure he's a risk, but he'd be MY choice; he might tie those big thumpas in knots. Even if he doesn't, I give Francona kudos for giving Timmy the ball. And for God's sake, he's gonna put Mirabelli behind the plate, right? Right. Seeya 5:30,
Steve "I Still Believe" King

Reflections of Stewart O'Nan

I'd violently disagree with Steve—Wake is his boy as much as Dave McCarty is mine, and Wake's been plain awful this year, besides the few usual wins in Tampa; the best thing he did was volunteer to mop up in Game 3 against the Yanks and give Lowe his spot in the rotation*—but I'm out the door and

---

*All right, I'm no ingrate: he saved our bacon in extras in Game 5, holding the Yanks scoreless for three nervous, passed-ball-filled innings and picking up the win.

sailing across 1-84 before Steve's e-mail reaches me. It's been a long time since I've been to a World Series, and I aim to get my fill.

The souvenir shops around the park don't open until noon. At eleven-thirty, lines of eager buyers stretch far down the block. The amount of free junk people are handing out is astounding—papers, posters, buttons, stickers, pictures, temporary tattoos, Krispy Kreme doughnuts. Fans are staggering around with bags of the crap, in total material overload. When the stores open, barkers with bullhorns herd customers into switchbacked ropes—"This line only for World Series and AL Champion merchandise—this line only!"

Hanging out by the parking lot eight hours before game time, the autograph hunters are treated to an impromptu concert by Steven Tyler as he runs his sound check for tonight's anthem. Steven doesn't actually sing the song, he just blows an A on his harmonica and runs through an ascending series of bluesy scales, and sounds great—a cool reminder that Aerosmith started out as an electric blues band influenced by the early Stones, the Yardbirds, and Muddy Waters.

After that, PA announcer Carl Beane warms his pipes, rumbling: "Ladies and gentlemen, please welcome . . . the National League Champion, St. Louis Cardinals," over and over, as if he might have trouble with it later. He goes through a fantastical lineup: "Batting first, number one . . . Carl . . . Beane." A minute later, "Batting fourth, number nine . . . Ted . . . Williams," and the crowd outside applauds. "Batting fifth, number six . . . Stan . . . Musial."

And speaking of old-timers, rumor is that Yaz is throwing out the first pitch, a sentimental touch, and overdue, since it's said that Yaz and the club haven't had the best of relationships since he retired. The new owners may be trying to patch things over. We also witness—well in advance—the return of Lenny DiNardo and Adam Hyzdu, two guys who spent time with the club early in the year. It's nice to see the Sox are giving them a taste of the big show (though, of course, the guy we really want to see is Dauber).

Two other early arrivals of note: team physician Dr. Bill Morgan and, 15 minutes later, wearing a brace on his right leg and no shoe in the cold,

Curt Schilling. Before Game 6, Dr. Morgan sutured Schili's tendon to his skin, a procedure he practiced first on a cadaver. Rumor (again, rumor, the outsider's substitute for information) is that he's going to stitch him up again for tomorrow's start in Game 2. On those few threads, our whole season may depend.

Inside, there are more banners than I've seen all year—a lifting of the normal ban, for TV's sake, I expect. It's cold, with a wind whipping in from straight center, which should give Wake's knuckler more flutter. Even the stiff wind isn't enough to keep David Ortiz in the park tonight. In the first, in his very first World Series at bat, El Jefe busts out with a three-run golf shot OVER the Pesky Pole. We chase Woody Williams early, giving Wake a 7–2 lead going into the fourth.

Beside me, Steve is smiling. Kevin, the usher who comes down between innings with a camp chair to keep people off the wall, is overjoyed with how things are going. "No," I say, glum, "just watch: Wake'll start walking people. He always does when we give him a big lead." And I don't say this to jinx anything, I say it because I've seen Wake all year long, and that's just what he does.

And that's just what he does—walking four in the fourth to break a World Series record, and soon after he's gone it's 7–7. It's like they used to say about Fenway when it was a launching pad: No lead is safe here.

Reflections of Stephen King
"Man, that was ogly," Orlando Cabrera said in a postgame interview. He paused, then added, "But we won." *Ogly* pretty well sums up the first game of this year's World Series, which ended with a thing of beauty. Keith Foulke striking out Roger Cedeño a few minutes after midnight.

Speaking of ogly, Orlando wasn't looking so good himself in that interview, and he seemed uncharacteristically solemn. A Woody Williams pitch hit him on the shoulder in the first inning, then bounced up into his face, leaving him with a bruised chin, a fat lip, and a temporary inability to smile—which, under ordinary circumstances, Mr. Garciaparra's replacement does often. Pain or no pain, Cabrera must have been at least tempted to test that smile when the Red Sox finally escaped with an ogly but serviceable 11–9 win in spite of four errors (one by Bronson Arroyo—starter Tim Wakefield's fourth-inning relief—one by Kevin Millar, and two by Manny Ramirez). Every one of those errors led to runs, leading me to wonder if any of the Red Sox players felt tempted to visit the Cardinals' clubhouse after the game and assure them on behalf of the home team that Boston doesn't play that way *every* night.

Cabrera might have been even more tempted to test his swollen lip if informed of this statistic: In World Series history, the team drawing first blood has gone on to win the Fall Classic 60 percent of the time. Still, there's that other 40 percent . . . and the fact that the Cards have yet to lose during this postseason on their home field. But—fingers crossed, now—you've got to like the Red Sox going into Game 2. They're nice and loose (what could be looser than four errors and four walks issued by Red Sox pitching?), their demonic archrivals are behind them, and they're riding a nifty five-game winning streak.

Last night's game began with a moment of silence for Victoria Snelgrove, the young woman killed by a pepper-gas ball during riot-control operations outside Fenway following Boston's final victory over New York, and while it was both decent and brave of the current ownership to remember her (one is tempted to believe that the previous bunch of caretakers would have swept Ms. Snelgrove under the rug as fast and as far as possible), it was also a reminder of what is *truly* ogly in our brave new world, where all game bags are searched and the clocks tick on Osama Mean Time.

There were lines of Boston police, looking like puffy Michelin Men in their riot gear, watching impassively as the happy and largely well-behaved crowd left the old green First New England Church of Baseball with the strains of "Dirty Water" still ringing in their ears and the memory of Mark Bellhorn's game-winning, foul-pole-banging home run still vivid in their minds. To me those dark lines of armed men outside such a place of ancient and innocent pleasure are a lot harder to look at than the mark on Orlando Cabrera's face, or his swelled lower lip.

11–9 is a crazy score for a World Series game; so is a total of 24 hits and 5 errors. But the bottom line is that we won, Father Curt takes the mound tomorrow night on home turf with his freshly restitched ankle, and that's a beautiful thing. (A remarkable one, anyway.)

I only wish Torie Snelgrove was around to see it.

Reflections of Stewart O'Nan

The most surprising thing to me about Game 1 was how the Faithful booed Dale Sveum during the pregame introductions. I suppose it's a delayed (or should I say sustained?) reaction to Johnny being thrown out at home in the first inning of Game 7 of the ALCS. Whatever it is, I don't like it.

And despite the win, I don't like the way Kevin Millar played, leaving 10 men on, making essentially two errors on the same play (double-clutching that cutoff, then throwing the ball into the dugout), and later not getting anywhere near a ball hit down the line that both Mientkiewicz and McCarty handle easily.

By contrast, the Cards' Larry Walker took to the big stage in a big way, making two great catches in right (a Manny liner down into the corner with men on, and a windblown pop he had to run a long way and then lunge for at the last second), and hitting a double, a homer, a single and another double. This is Walker's first World Series, after a long and brilliant career in the hinterlands of Montreal and Colorado, and it was heartening to see him show the world his A game. If Pujols, Rolen, and Edmonds had done anything to help him out, we'd be down 0–1.

Mark Bellhorn, meanwhile, seems determined to enforce the curse of the ex-Cubs (that is, the team with more ex-Cubs is bound to lose the Series—the Cards have five while we only have two, Marky Mark and Billy Mueller). Before his home run off Julian Tavarez, he was 2 for 3 against him lifetime, so his success didn't surprise me, only the magnitude of it. It was no fluke. Tavarez didn't fool him at all. Marky Mark ripped the pitch before his Pesky Pole shot high and deep down the line in right, but foul. All he had to do was reload and straighten it out, making him one of a very rarefied club—players who've homered in three straight postseason games.

October 24th/World Series Game 2

On the street outside the players' lot I run into Andrew on his way out to buy some salads for the guys. We're surrounded by a crowd of tourists hoping to catch a glimpse of the stars. Camera crews, cops. Andrew still can't believe this is all happening—a common reaction among the Nation, even those deep inside it. I ask him about Schill's ankle, and tell him about seeing Dr. Morgan yesterday. Yeah, he says, they had him on the table, but he tried to stay away from there.

"How's he look?" I ask.

Andrew just shrugs. "We'll have to see."

Inside, I catch Tony Womack along the left-field wall, joking with an old friend in the stands about beating him at golf next week. When he gets a break, I ask him how his collarbone feels after taking that David Ortiz smash off it last night.

"I'm fine," he says, and I tell him how much I'd been rooting for him in spring training.

"You ran great, bunted great, stole bases. I wish you could have played the field."

"Man," he says, shaking his head, "they didn't want me."

We shake hands, and a minute later he calls Larry Walker over.

Walker looks puzzled until he sees Tony's friend.

"You know this guy?" Tony asks.

"Know this guy?" Walker says. "This guy owes me eight grand!"

It's Sunday, and in the concourse crowds are gathered around the wall-mounted TVs watching the Patriots beat the Jets for their 21st consecutive win. If the Pats can win 21 straight, the logic goes, why can't we win eight?

Our seats are down in the corner where I normally post up for BP—better seats than I'm used to. How good? Above us in the Monster seats is Jimmy Fallon, and two rows in front of us, so close I could lean forward and tap his shoulder, is Eagles QB Donovan McNabb. He played an outstanding game today in Cleveland, his long scramble setting up an overtime win. He must have showered and gotten right on the plane. He's so tired that the only time he stands up during the game is to go to the restroom, but, like us, he stays for every drizzly, windswept pitch.

October 25th

Reflections of Stephen King

One summer night in the mid-1960s, right around the time the Beatles were ruling the American music charts, a young music producer named Ed Cobb happened to be walking with his girlfriend beside the Charles River in the quaint old city of Boston, Massachusetts . . . or so the story goes. Out of the shadows came a thief who tried to mug him out of his wallet (or maybe it was out of her purse; on that the story is not entirely clear). In any case, the musically inclined Mr. Cobb foiled the thief and got an idea for a song as a bonus. The song, "Dirty Water," was eventually recorded by a group of Boston proto-punks called the Standells and released by Capitol, who wanted a record Cobb had produced for Ketty ("Anyone Who Had a Heart") Lester. No one expected much from the raw and raunchy* "Dirty Water," but it went to No. 11 on the *Billboard* pop charts and has remained a standard on the Boston club scene ever since.

It was revived by the new Red Sox management and has become the good-time signature of Boston wins. For the Fenway Faithful, there's nothing better than seeing the final out go up on the scoreboard and hearing that six-note intro with the familiar first-note slide leading into the verse: *Down by the riiiiver. . .* And so it seemed a particularly good omen to see the resurrected Standells in deep center field before the game last night, a lot grayer and a little thinner on top but still loud and proud, singing about that dirty water down by the banks of the River Charles.

---

*In my high school, the phrase "lovers, muggers, and thieves" was routinely construed to be either "lovers, junkies, and thieves" or "lovers, fuckers, and thieves."

A great many things about baseball in general and the Red Sox in particular are about the bridges between past and present—this was just one more provided by a current Yawkey Way administration that seems pleasantly aware of tradition without becoming enslaved to it. And when the Red Sox had put this one away in the cold mists of a late Sunday evening, the sounds of "Dirty Water" rang out again, this time with the tempo a little faster and the tones a little truer. And why not? This was the one recorded when the Standells were young. This is the version that hit the charts four months before Curt Schilling was born.

He was awesome last night. The word is tired, clapped-out from overuse, but I've had a 170-mile drive to try and think of a better one, and I cannot. The crowd of just over 35,000 in the old green Church of Baseball knew what it was seeing; many of them may have been in Fenway Park for the first time last night (these Series-only fans are what *Globe* writer Dan Shaughnessy so rightly calls the "Nouveau Nation"), but even they knew. The galaxy of flashbulbs that went off in the stadium, from the plum dugout seats to the skyviews to the distant bleachers to those now perched atop the Green Monster, was chilling in its cold and commemorative brilliance, declaring by silent light that the men and women who came to the ballpark last night had never seen anything quite like it for sheer guts and never expected to see anything quite like it again. Not, certainly, with their own eyes.

Edgar Renteria, the Cardinals' leadoff hitter, battled Schilling fiercely—first six pitches, then 10, then a dozen, running the count full and then spilling off foul after foul.* He might have been the game's key batter, and not the ones Schilling had to face following more Boston miscues (another four) that allowed the Cardinals extra chances upon which they could not capitalize.

Before finally hitting sharply to shortstop (and the often-maligned Kevin Millar made a fine pick at first to complete the play), Renteria tried every trick in the book. Every trick, that is, save one. He never attempted to

---

*To prolong or deepen this drama, the pitch-speed display above the wall in left-center was tantalizingly blank for this half-inning. Who knew what Schill had? Only Tek and the hitters. SO

lay down a bunt. In three starts on his bad peg—two against the Yankees and now one against the Cardinals—no one has tried to make Curt Schilling field his position. I'm sure the Red Sox infielders have discussed this possibility and know exactly how they would handle it . . . but it has simply never come up. And when this thing is over, when the hurly-burly's done, all the battles lost and won, someone needs to ask the Yankee and Cardinal hitters *why* they did not bunt. Of course I can imagine the boos that would rain down on a successful bunter against Father Curt at Fenway, but is it beyond the scope of belief to think that even Yankee or Cardinal fans might find it hard to cheer such a ploy for reaching first (well . . . maybe not Yankee fans)?

Could it have been—don't laugh—actual *sportsmanship?*

Whatever the reason, the Cards played him straight up last night—I salute them for it—and for the most part, Father Curt mowed them right down. Tony Womack and Mike Matheny had singles; Albert Pujols had a pair of doubles. And, as far as hits against Schilling went, that was it. He finished his night's work by striking out the side in the sixth.

For the Red Sox, it was a continuing case of two-run, two-out thunder. Two runs scored after two were out in the first; two more after two were out in the fourth; two more in the sixth, the same way.* By the end of the game (Mike Matheny, groundout), the deep green grass of the field and the bright white of the Red Sox home uniforms had grown slightly diffuse in the thickening mizzle. The departing fans, damp but hardly dampened, were all but delirious with joy. One held up a poster depicting a Christlike Johnny Damon walking on water with the words JOHNNY SAVES beneath his sandaled feet.

I heard one fan—surely part of Mr. Shaughnessy's Nouveau Nation—actually saying he hoped the Red Sox would *lose* a couple in St. Louis, so the team could clinch back on its home soil (yes, Beavis, he actually said "home soil"). I had to restrain myself from laying hands on this fellow and asking

---

*Respectively: Tek with a triple to the triangle that's out if the wind isn't blowing straight in; Marky Mark with a similar bomb off the wall in dead center; and O-Cab, who was uncharacteristically ahead in the count all night, bonking one off the Monster. SO

him if he remembered 1986, when we *also* won the first two, only to lose four of the next five. And when a team is going this well (RED HOT RED SOX, trumpets this morning's *USA Today*), one loss can lead to others. Winning two at home, within a sniff of the River Charles, may have been vital, considering the fact that the Cardinals have yet to lose a single postseason game in their own house.

Tomorrow night, Pedro Martinez will face the Cards near the dirty water of a much larger river, in a much larger stadium. It will be his first World Series start, and given that no team has ever climbed out of an 0–3 World Series hole (and surely that sort of thing can't happen twice in the same postseason . . . can it?), I think it's going to be the most important start by a Red Sox pitcher in a long, long time. Certainly since 1986.

October 26th/World Series Game 3

SK: Dear Stewart-Under-the-Arch: Here's my idea of the doomsday scenario, also known as the Novelist's Ending. The BoSox win *one* game in SaintLoo. Come back to Boston up *3 games to 2*. Lose *Game 6*. And . . . have to start Father Curt for all the marbles in Game 7. Stewart, this could *actually* happen.

SO: I'm hoping we can steal one out there, and hey, if we get two, I won't be crying about eating my Game 6 tickets. It's just like the Yankee series: We just have to win one game—the game we're playing.

SK: All lookin' good. Now, if Pedro can only do his part.

You know, I think he will.

SO: Pedro remains inscrutable. We can't hit like it's a regular Pedro game; we have to pretend it's John Burkett out there. Think seven or eight runs. Go Sox!

Reflections of Stewart O'Nan

The Sox are up 4–0 as the game rolls into the ninth, and I find I can't sit down. As Foulke comes in, I'm muttering the lyrics to his Fenway entrance music, Danzig's "Mother" ("And if you want to find Hell with me, I can show you what it's like"). He gets Edgar Renteria, then has Larry Walker 0–2 when he just lays a fastball in there, and Walker golfs it out. I watch Johnny turn and watch it, then I'm out of the room, swearing and pacing through the house. It's okay, we've got a three-run lead and there's no one on. Foulkie just has to go after hitters and not walk anybody. Pujols gets behind and jaws at the ump after a borderline call, then skies one deep to left (oh crap) that Manny settles under (whew)—that's two. Scott Rolen, 0 for the series, is taking, gets behind, then inexplicably takes the 1–2 pitch, which, while slightly in, is clearly a strike, and the ump punches him out to end the game. We're up 3–0 and I'm jumping around the room.

Petey came through so big, and Manny, and Billy Mueller hitting with two down. We're a game away. I've been a strike away before, so I'm already trying to play it down, but, damn, I didn't expect us to ever be up 3–0 on the Cards. The idea of winning it all sends me romping through the house, bellowing the Dropkick Murphys' "Tessie," even though I don't know all the words: "Up from third base to Hun-ting-ton, they'd sing another vic-t'ry sooooooong—two, three, four!"

Reflections of Stephen King

Boston has now won seven in a row (tying a postseason record), pushing the Cards to the brink where the Red Sox themselves stood only a week ago. The most amazing thing about the World Series part of the Red Sox run is that the Cardinals have yet to lead in a single game. Their manager, Tony La Russa, certainly knows this, and while his part of the postgame news conference seemed long to me, it must have seemed interminable to him. He looked more like a middle-level racketeer being questioned in front of a grand jury than a successful baseball manager. Part of the reason for La Russa's long face may have had to do with the game's key play, which came in the third inning, when Cardinals base runner (and starting pitcher) Jeff Suppan was thrown out at third.

Suppan led off the inning with a slow roller to third. Mueller handled it cleanly, but not in time to get Suppan at first. Edgar Renteria followed with a double to right that had Trot Nixon falling on his ass because of the wet conditions in the outfield.* Suppan probably could have scored right there, tying the game, but perhaps he was held up by the third-base coach. (We'll give him the benefit of the doubt, anyway.) So with runners at second and third and nobody out, up came Larry Walker, a gent who is absolutely no slouch with the stick. He hit a ground ball to Mark Bellhorn.

At that point the Boston infield was playing back, conceding Suppan's run, which would have tied the score, 1–1. But Suppan didn't score when Walker made contact, nor did he when Bellhorn threw Walker out. Instead he broke toward home, broke back toward third base, then broke toward home a *second* time. Meanwhile, Boston's new kid on the block at first base, David Ortiz, in the lineup because the designated hitter doesn't exist in National League parks, was observing all this. From Ortiz's side of the diamond, Suppan must have looked as frantic and disoriented as a bird trapped in a garage. He fired across the diamond to Bill Mueller just as Suppan darted back toward third base a second time. Suppan dove for the bag, but Mueller was able to put the tag on him easily.

The result of this beer-league baserunning was that instead of tying the score against one of the American League's craftiest power pitchers with only one out, the Cardinals found themselves with two outs and no runs scored. Albert Pujols followed Walker, grounding out harmlessly to end the inning. The Cards would not score until the bottom of the ninth, and by then it was too late. The irony (La Russa's long postgame face suggested he did not need this pointed out to him) was that the National League team had been screwed by the very rules that were supposed to tip the scales in their favor. It was *their* pitcher who made the baserunning blunder, and *our* erstwhile designated hitter who saw it happening and gunned him down.

---

*It rained heavily in St. Louis right up until game time, and the warning track was a swimming pool. I hate it when teams are forced to play ball under these conditions, but it's the same old sordid story: When Fox talks, Major League Baseball walks. If this is going to continue, the Players Association ought to consider insisting on pads and helmets (at least for the outfielders) after October 15th.

Although Boston got a pair of insurance runs in the fifth, more two-out thunder from Manny Ramirez in the first* and Bill Mueller (batted home by Trot Nixon) in the fourth were all the run support Pedro Martinez needed; he, Mike Timlin, and Keith Foulke spun a gem. Following Edgar Renteria's double in the third inning, Red Sox pitching retired 18 Cards in a row. Larry Walker broke up the string with one out in the ninth, turning around a Keith Foulke fastball to deep left center for a home run.

So now the St. Louis deficit is 0–3. One would like to say that lightning cannot strike twice on the same patch of ground, and certainly not so soon, but in truth, one *cannot* say that. Especially not if one happens to have been a Red Sox fan for the last 50 years and has had the cup snatched away from his lips so many times just before that first deep and satisfying drink.

I don't think I've ever been so aware of the limitations of this narrative's necessary diary form until today. You sitting there with the finished book in your hand are like an astronaut who can see the entire shape of the earth: where every sea ends and every coastline begins again. I just go sailing along from day to day, hoping to avoid the storms and writing in this log when seas are calm. And now I think I can smell land up ahead. I hope I'm not jinxing things by saying that, but I really think I can. Not just any land, either, but the sweet Promised Land I've been dreaming of ever since my Uncle Oren bought me my first Red Sox cap and stuck it on my head in the summer of 1954. "There, Stevie," he said, blowing the scent of Narragansett beer into the face of the big-eyed seven-year-old looking up at him. "They ain't much, but they're the best we got."

Now, 50 long years later, they're on the verge of being the best of all. One more game and we can put all this curse stuff, all this Babe stuff, all this 1918 stuff, behind us.

Please, baseball gods, just one more game.

---

*Followed, in the bottom of the inning, by Manny's perfect one-hop peg on a short fly to nail Larry Walker at the plate and keep us up 1–0. This moment of redemption after Manny had made errors on consecutive and very *ogly* plays in Game 1. Cardinals third base coach José Oquendo, like so many other baseball people, mistook Manny's spaciness for lack of ability. Anyone who's watched Manny throw knows he's amazingly accurate and that Walker had no chance. SO

SK: Ah, but I begin to smell exotic spices and strange nerds . . . er, nards . . . could these be the scents of the Promised Land? I can only hope they are not scents sent by false sirens on hidden stones beyond a mirage of yon beckoning shore . . .

But I digress.

We rocked tonight, dude.

SO: It's good to be up 3–0 instead of down 0–3, but the job's the same: Win the game we're playing. The guys have to stay on top of it.

SK: You must have been eating the postgame spread with Tito.

October 27th/World Series Game 4

Reflections of Stewart O'Nan

It's Trudy's and my 20th anniversary today. We were supposed to be in Chicago last weekend, eating at Charlie Trotter's and the Billy Goat Tavern (the honest-to-God home of the Cubs' curse as well as the chee-burger, chee-burger skit from *SNL*), but those plans dissolved in the face of Games 1 and 2. Tonight, at Trudy's insistence, I call and cancel our long-standing dinner reservations at the best restaurant in town. I don't tell the maitre d' why. "Enjoy the game," he says.

Signs and portents everywhere. Tonight's the 18th anniversary of our last World Series loss—Game 7 to the '86 Mets. Not only is there a full moon, but right around game time there's a total lunar eclipse. By the time I go outside to see the lip of the earth's shadow cross the Sea of Tranquility, Johnny has us up 1–0 with a leadoff home run. Later, when Trot doubles on a bases-juiced 3–0 green light to give us a 3–0 lead, the eclipse is well under way, casting a decidedly red stain—blood on the moon, or is it a cosmic nod to the Sox?

For the third game in a row, Lowe pitches brilliantly, giving up just three hits in seven innings. Arroyo looks shaky in the eighth, but Embree relieves him and is perfect for the second straight outing. As Foulke closes, I'm standing behind the couch, shifting with every pitch as if I'm guarding the line. At this point, for no other reason it seems than to torture us, Fox decides to show a montage combining all the horrible moments in Red Sox postseason history, beginning with Enos Slaughter, moving through Bucky Dent and Buckner, and finishing with Aaron Boone. I hold a hand up to block it out (to eclipse it!). At this moment in Red Sox history, I do *not* want to see that shit. It's not bad luck, it's bad *taste*, and whoever thought it was appropriate is a jerk.

With one down, Pujols singles through Foulke's legs, right through the five-hole, a ball Foulke, a diehard hockey fan, should have at least gotten a pad on. We're nervous—another runner and they'll bring the tying run to the plate—but Foulke's cool. He's got that bitter disdain—that nastiness, really—of a great closer. He easily strikes out Edmonds (now 1 for 15), then snags Edgar Renteria's comebacker and flips to Mientkiewicz, and that's it, it's that simple: The Red Sox have won the World Series!

While we're still hugging and pounding each other (Trudy's crying, she can't help it; Steph's laughing; I'm just going: "Wow. Wow. Wow.") Caitlin calls from Boston. In the background, girls are shrieking. She's at Nickerson Field, formerly Braves Field, where BU is showing the game on a big screen. I can barely hear her for the noise. "They did it!" she yells. "They did!" I yell back. There's no analysis, just a visceral appreciation of the win. I tell her to stay out of the riots, meaning keep away from Fenway, and she assures me she will. It's not until I get off the phone with her that I realize the weird parallel: When I was a freshman there, my team won the World Series, too.

It's more than just a win; it's a statement. By winning tonight, we broke the record for consecutive playoff wins, with eight straight. Another stat that every commentator unpacks is that we're one of only four championship teams to have never trailed in the Series.* Thanks to Johnny, O.C., Manny, and Papi, we scored in the first inning of every game, and our starters, with the exception of Wake, shut down St. Louis' big sticks. Schill, Petey, and D-Lowe combined for 20 shutout innings. Much respect to pitching coach

---

*Along with Tony La Russa's 1989 A's, the '66 O's, and the '63 Dodgers. All three, like the Sox, had a pair of aces—Dave Stewart and Bob Welch with the A's, Jim Palmer and Dave McNally with the O's, and Sandy Koufax and Don Drysdale with the Dodgers.

Dave Wallace and his scouts for coming up with a game plan to stop the Cards. As a team, they batted .190, well below the Mendoza Line. Scott Rolen and Jim Edmonds went 1 for 30, that one hit being a gimme bunt single by Edmonds against a shifted infield. Albert Pujols had zero RBIs. Reggie Sanders went 0 for 9. It's not that we crushed the ball. We scored only four runs in Game 3 and three in Game 4. Essentially, after the Game 1 slugfest, we played NL ball, beating them with pitching, and in the last two games our defense was flawless. In finally putting the supposed Curse to rest, we dotted every *i* and crossed every *t*. And to make it all even sweeter, the last out was made by Edgar Renteria, who wears—as a couple of folks noted—the Babe's famous #3.

October 28th
Reflections of Stephen King
It came down to this: With two outs in the St. Louis half of the ninth and Keith Foulke on the mound—Foulke, the nearly sublime Red Sox closer this postseason—only Edgar Renteria stood between Boston and the end of its World Series drought. Renteria hit a comebacker to the mound. "Stabbed by Foulke!" crowed longtime Red Sox radio announcer Joe Castiglione. "He underhands to first! The Red Sox are World Champions! *Can you believe it?*"

I hardly could, and I wasn't the only one. A hundred miles away, my son woke up *his* five-year-old son to see the end. When it was over and the Red Sox were mobbing each other on the infield, Ethan asked his father, "Is this a dream or are we living real life?"

The answer, it seems to me this morning, is both. The only newspaper available at the general store was the local one (the others were held up because of the lateness of the game), and the *Sun-Journal's* huge front-page headline, of a size usually reserved only for the outbreak of war or the sudden death of a president, was only two words and an exclamation mark:

AT LAST!

When the other New England papers finally do arrive in my sleepy little pocket of New England, I'm confident they will bear similar happy headlines of a similar size on their front pages.

A game summary would be thin stuff indeed compared to this outpouring of joy on a beautiful blue and gold New England morning in late October.* Usually when I go to get the papers and my 8 a.m. doughnut, the little store up the road is almost empty. This morning it was jammed, mostly with people waiting for those newspapers to come in. The majority were wearing Red Sox hats, and the latest political news was the last thing on their minds. They wanted to talk about last night's game. They wanted to talk about the Series as a whole. They wanted to talk about the guts of Curt Schilling, pitching on his hurt ankle, and the grit of Mr. Lowe, who was supposed to spend the postseason in the bullpen and ended up securing a magickal and historickal place for himself in the record books instead, as the winner in all three postseason clinchers: Game 3 of the Division Series, Game 7 of the League Championship Series, and now Game 4 of the World Series. And while none of those waiting for the big-time morning papers—the Boston *Globe*, *USA Today*, and the *New York Times*—came right out and asked my grandson's question, I could see it in their eyes, and I know they could see it in mine: *Is this a dream, or are we living real life?*

It's real life. If there was a curse (other than a sportswriter's brilliant MacGuffin for selling books, amplified in the media echo chamber until even otherwise rational people started to half-believe it), it was the undeniable fact that the Red Sox hadn't won a World Series since 1918, and all the baggage that fact brought with it for the team's long-suffering fans.

The Yankees and *their* fans have always been the heaviest of that baggage, of course. Yankee rooters were never shy about reminding Red Sox partisans that they were supporting lifetime losers. There was also the undeniable fact

---

*And the summary is simple enough: Once again last night we hit and pitched. The Cardinals did neither. Only one Cardinal starter—Jason Marquis—managed to stay in a Series game for six innings, and the heart of the St. Louis batting order (Pujols, Rolen, Edmonds) got only a single run batted in during the entire four-game contest. It came on a sac fly.

that in recent years the Yankee ownership—comfy and complacent in their much bigger ballpark and camped just downstream from a waterfall of fan cash—had been able to outspend the Red Sox ownership, sometimes at a rate of $2 dollars to $1. There was the constant patronization of the New York press (the *Times*, for instance, chuckling in its indulgently intelligent way over the A-Rod deal, and concluding that the Yankees were still showing the Red Sox how to win, even in the off-season), the jokes, and the gibes.

The ball through Bill Buckner's legs in 1986 was horrible, of course, but now Buckner can be forgiven.

What's better is that now the Bucky Dent home run, the Aaron Boone home run, and the monotonous chants of *Who's your Daddy?* can be forgotten. Laughed off, even. On the whole, I would have to say that while to forgive is human, to forget is freakin' *divine*.

And winning is better than losing. That's easy to lose sight of, if you've never done it. I can remember my younger son saying—and there was some truth in this—that when the Philadelphia Phillies finally won their World Championship after years of trying, they became "just another baseball team." When I asked Owen if he could live with that as a Red Sox fan, he didn't even hesitate. "Sure," he said.

I feel the same way. No one likes to root for a loser, year after year; being faithful does not save one from feeling, after a while, like a fool, the butt of everyone's joke. At last I don't feel that way. This morning's sense of splendid unreality will surely rub away, but the feeling of lightness that comes with finally shedding a burden that has been carried far too long will linger for months or maybe even years. Cubs fans now must bear the loser legacy all by themselves. They have their Curse of the Billy Goat, and although I am sure it is equally bogus,* they are welcome to it.

Bottom of the ninth, two out, Albert Pujols on second, Red Sox Nation holding its breath. Foulke pitches. Renteria hits an easy comebacker to the mound. Foulke fields it and tosses it to Mientkiewicz, playing first. Mientkiewicz jumps

---

*Not so! That one's real, and solidly documented. SO

in the air, holding up the index finger of his right hand, signaling *We're number one*. Red Sox players mob the field while stunned and disappointed Cardinal fans look on. Some of the little kids are crying, and I feel bad about that, but back in New England little kids of all ages are jumping for joy.

"*Can you believe it?*" Joe Castiglione exults, and 86 years of disappointment fall away in the length of time it takes the first-base ump to hoist his thumb in the *out* sign.

This is not a dream. We are living real life.

Reflections of Stewart O'Nan

While the Babe may be resting easier, I barely sleep, and wake exhausted, only to watch the same highlights again and again, seeing things I missed while we were celebrating. As the Sox mob each other, in the background Jimmy Fallon and Drew Barrymore are kissing, shooting their fairy-tale ending to *Fever Pitch* (nice timing, Farrellys!).* In short center, right behind second base, Curtis Leskanic lies down and makes the natural grass equivalent of a Patriots snow angel. The crawl says RED SOX WIN WORLD SERIES, and I think, yes, yes they did.

It did happen. It was no dream. We're the World Champions, finally, and there's that freeing sense of redemption and fulfillment I expected—the same cleansing feeling I had after the Pats' first Super Bowl win. The day is bright and blue, the leaves are brilliant and blowing. It's a beautiful day in the Nation, maybe the best ever.

And yet, the season's over, too. There will be no more baseball this year, and while I've said I wouldn't mind eating my tickets to Games 6 and 7, it feels wrong that I won't be back in Fenway again until April.

Just for fun, I go to the website (choked with new World Champions merchandise) and poke around, looking for spring training information.

---

*So many story lines wrapped last night: Manny, who went unclaimed on waivers, is the World Series MVP (and very possibly the regular-season MVP as well); Lowe totally vindicates himself, making him an incredibly attractive free agent; the same with Pedro; Terry Francona goes from The Coma to a legendary Red Sox manager; Orlando Cabrera, who stepped up big in the number two slot and fielded brilliantly in the postseason, makes us forget Nomar. The year is signed, sealed, and delivered. All that's left now is the Boston Duck Tours parade and the team deciding who gets a World Series share. As always, I hope Dauber's not forgotten.

There's a number for City of Palms Park, but when I call it, it's busy. It's going to be crazy there next year. If I want to get in, I'd better start working on it now. I flip the pages of our 2005 calendar to February and March and wonder when Trudy's school has its break. I wonder if there's a nicer hotel closer to City of Palms Park, and whether they'd have any rooms left at this point.

I have to stop myself. Okay, calm down. There's no need to hustle now, the very morning after. I can take a day off and appreciate what we've done—what they've done, the players, because as much as we support them, they're the ones out there who have to field shots we'd never get to, and hit pitches that would make us look silly, and beat throws that would have us by miles. And the coaches and the manager, the owners and the general manager, who have to make decisions we'll never take any heat for. They did it, all of them together, our Red Sox.

Congratulations, guys. And thank you. You believed in yourselves even more than we did. That's why you're World Champions, and why we'll never forget you or this season. Wherever you go, any of you, you'll always have a home here, in the heart of the Nation. Go Sox!

SO: You know how the papers are always saying you bring the team bad luck? Well, the one year you write a book about the club, we win it all. Another fake curse reversed.

Not in your lifetime, huh? Well, brutha, welcome to Heaven!

SK: How do you suppose Angry Bill is doing?

SO: He's in that box of a room in Vegas, grumbling about something— probably the Bruins.

SK: Are you going to the V-R Day Parade?

SO: No, but tonight I ate that Break the Curse cookie I got on Opening Day. A vow's a vow. Washed that stiff six-month-old biscuit down with champagne and enjoyed every morsel. Life is sweet.

Off to drink more champagne. You (and Johnny D) are still The Man.

SK: No, Stewart, you (and Papi) are The Man. I'm giving you the two Pointy-Finger Salute.

SO: Right back atcha, baby. Keep the Faith.

2008: Phillies vs. Rays

Phillies' Suspended Game Victory

from *Worth the Wait: Tales of the 2008 Phillies*

by Jayson Stark

Game 5–Act I: October 26, 2008

Philadelphia—The Phillies came to the ballpark for Game 5 thinking they were about to hand the World Series over to Mr. October, Cole Hamels.

Little did they know they were about to hand it over to Bud Selig's favorite Doppler 10,000.

And because they did, this World Series was never going to be the same. You understand that, right?

It was no longer going to be known for Carlos Ruiz's 2:00 a.m. walk-off squibber or Joe Blanton's Babe Ruth impression or Cliff Floyd's mad dash home on the most improbable squeeze bunt of modern times.

Nope.

This one was now going down in a whole different chapter of World Series lore: Weather lore.

We can figure out exactly where it fits into the grand history of baseball meteorology one of these years. But in the meantime, all anyone knew when they exited the ballpark was this: One of these days, one of these weeks, one of these months, whenever the commissioner decided to lift the first suspended game in the history of postseason baseball, the Phillies, the Rays, and the rest of humanity were going to find Game 5 of this World Series, in theory, exactly where they left it.

Halfway through the sixth. Tie game, 2–2. The Phillies still leading the Series, 3 games to 1. So they remained, again in theory, precisely where they were after Game 4—one win away from the second World Series championship in franchise history.

Yeah, it was all exactly the same, all right. Except nothing was the same.

A mere one day earlier, the Phillies had this Series set up in their ultimate dream scenario—one win away, with their most dominating starting pitcher lined up to pitch it.

Now, one soggy half-baked suspended-animation debacle later, they'd essentially wasted a Cole Hamels start.

And they were certain, at the time, that they were looking at having to deal with the terrifying prospect of facing David Price when play resumed.

And the two Rays hitters who were 0-for-the-Series—Carlos Peña and Evan Longoria—had finally remembered how to hit.

So you knew exactly what every Phillies fan in America was thinking as that rainwater was dripping all over their dreams: *Uh-oh.*

That would be the polite terminology for it, anyway.

In Philadelphia, nothing is ever easy. Nothing. So this mess just fit in.

"Of course. We've gotta make the World Series memorable," laughed Hamels, after what was supposed to be the greatest night of his life had turned into Bud Selig's remake of *Singin' in the Rain.* "And this definitely will do so."

Hey, ya think?

Hamels tried his best to put a happy face on this insanity. But all you need to know about how his teammates felt about it was the sound of deafening silence all around him.

The manager, Charlie Manuel, wouldn't talk to the media afterward. And neither would many of the most prominent members of his team—Jimmy Rollins, Pat Burrell, Shane Victorino, and Jayson Werth, just to name a few.

You can draw your own conclusions as to why that was. But here are the conclusions we would draw if we were you:

- They were furious that this game wasn't stopped until Hamels had surrendered the tying run in the top of the sixth, even though the field had begun looking like a veritable Sea World attraction at least a half-hour earlier.

- They weren't happy that it was started in the first place, since glop had already begun falling out of the sky during batting practice and the worsening weather forecast was the No. 1 topic of pregame conversation—just ahead of how many layers of clothing they were all going to have to wear to avoid frostbite.

- And, most of all, they were incensed by the whole situation— having their best-laid World Series plans steamrolled by the needless rush to play a game in conditions more suitable for an Iditarod than the most important game of their careers.

"Hey, it sucks. Let's be honest," said closer Brad Lidge, one of the few Phillies who did address the media afterward. "But what choice do you have? We just have to come back here tomorrow and try to finish the job."

So how *were* these decisions made? Why did they start? Why did they keep on playing? Why did they stop play when they did?

Selig brought two umpires, Rays president Matt Silverman, and Phillies GM Pat Gillick to the postsuspension press conference afterward to try to explain it all—not to mention to try to make it as clear as possible that you couldn't hang this whole nightmare on him.

He talked about all the upbeat weather forecasts he'd been handed as late as 45 minutes before game time. He talked about the pregame meeting he'd convened with the umpires, the grounds crew, the managers, the GMs—in short, everybody but Al Roker—in which they all decided, "Let's play."

And it was only in the fourth inning, Selig said, that he found himself "getting very nervous." Which caused him to make two different visits with the groundskeeper, in the fourth and fifth innings, to inquire about the state of the field.

Selig claimed he was told that it wasn't until the sixth inning that the field turned into a total river delta. And that's why the game was halted when it was.

But when players started describing the conditions afterward, suffice it to say they weren't quite as, uh, sunny about those elements as the commish.

Asked when *he* would have stopped this game, Rays reliever Trever Miller replied, "I would have said no later than the fourth inning. As soon as Jimmy Rollins had trouble with that fly ball [Rocco Baldelli's uncaught pop-up leading off the top of the fifth], right then and there that would have told everyone that conditions were not conducive to playing good baseball.

"That's what you want in the World Series," Miller said. "You want good baseball being played by the best players of the season. When Mother Nature is robbing you of that, it's time to put the tarp on and come back another day."

"Let me tell you," said his teammate, Carlos Peña. "That was bad. That was probably the worst conditions I've ever played under in my life. It was really, really cold. Windy. And it was raining nonstop. I mean, when do you ever see a puddle at home plate?"

Hamels said it was so hard to grip the ball, he never tried to throw a single curveball. And he could never get the right grip on his best pitch, his David Copperfield disappearing changeup. So he pumped about twice as many fastballs as he would on any other night. And this, remember, was supposed to be the most important night he'd ever spent on a pitcher's mound.

And then, when the fateful top of the sixth inning rolled around, the rain clearly changed the way the most pivotal inning of this game unfolded.

With two outs, nobody on, and an ocean pouring out of the heavens, B. J. Upton thunked a ground ball up the middle. It looked like a hit off the bat. But Rollins got there, got a glove on it, and then watched it wiggle out of his hands like a fish that had just slipped off his hook.

Within moments, Upton had stolen second—sliding right through a puddle the size of Delaware—and scored on Peña's two-out, two-strike single to left. And we had ourselves a tie game.

Before we get to the ramifications of that tie, though, let's go back to that fateful rally. Asked if he thought Rollins would have thrown Upton out had this been regular old weather—as opposed to monsoon season—Hamels had no doubt.

"On a normal day? Oh, yeah," he said. "Definitely. I think he might have caught Longoria's ball, too [i.e., the ground-ball single that drove in the Rays' first run, in the fourth]. But you know, that's the way luck [works] in baseball."

Yeah, and that luck worked for the commissioner, too. Because this game was now tied, he was able to walk into that press conference with his handy-dandy rulebook and read off Rule 4.12.6—which allows for tie games that were already official to be suspended.

"I'll tell you what," said the Phillies' Matt Stairs. "To have a tie game, sixth inning, that makes Bud Selig and the boys pretty happy, because they didn't have to make a big decision, to let that game go through a 10-, 12-, 13-hour delay. . . . So the Big Man's happy. He didn't have to make that decision."

Ah, but what Matt Stairs didn't know—what, apparently, none of these players on either team knew—was that Selig had already made his big decision.

If the rules weren't going to permit him to suspend this game, he was going to have to go to Plan B. He was just going to have to impose martial law—or at least Selig's Law—and, essentially, suspend it anyway. By simply declaring the world's longest rain delay. Whether that took 24 hours, 48 hours, or all the way to Thanksgiving.

But whatever, Selig vowed, these teams were not going to finish this game "until we have decent weather conditions."

Gee, it's a shame he didn't have that same feeling before he allowed this game to start in the first place. But whatever, on this point, he made the right call. Players on both teams made it clear they would have been embarrassed to decide the World Series on a game that got rained out in the sixth inning.

"I truly think that would have been the worst World Series win in the face of baseball," Hamels said. "And I would not pride myself on being a world champion on a called game."

"The clinching game," said Miller, "should always be decided by nine innings and down to the last out. Not by Mother Nature or whatever else could be thrown at us. That's what the fans pay to see, and that's what we've worked our entire season to get to.

"For us not to get that hit right there . . . that would be awful. That would be the most miserable off-season I would have ever had, trying to swallow that one down. That stuff doesn't digest. Hopefully they recognize this, and in the winter meetings they establish some sort of protocol and this doesn't happen again."

Hey, good plan. Nothing like a little protocol, so that both teams at least would have gone into this situation knowing the rules they were playing under.

But now here's a better idea, an even better rule of thumb: We're pretty sure this won't be the last attack Mother Nature springs on a postseason baseball game. In fact, with the World Series scheduled to stretch into November in the future, the chances of a meteorological disaster way worse than this are almost a lock.

So how about if baseball makes a pact—right here, right now. The heck with the Fox primetime schedule. The heck with the old both-sides-have-to-play-in-it mind-set. How about this mind-set: If the weather forecast is scary enough before *any* postseason game to give the commissioner, in his own words, "significant trepidation" about playing, let's not start it. Okay?

It's that simple. What happened to the Phillies in Game 5 should never happen to any team in this situation. And Bud Selig knows it.

And here's what he also knows: It's a good thing the Phillies went on to win this World Series. Because if they hadn't, the always-magnanimous residents of Philadelphia weren't going to blame Charlie Manuel, the next three losing pitchers, or good old Mother Nature. They were going to blame him, Bud Selig.

And in the annals of Sports Figures Most Likely to Get Off the Hook in This Town, Bud should know this: There's a better chance that Philadelphians would forgive Joe Carter, T. O., and possibly even J. D. Drew than a commissioner whose inability to recognize a rain cloud cost these people a World Series parade.

The Wait for Game 5 Goes On: October 27, 2008

In Philadelphia, folks are used to seeing the sky fall on their greatest sports parades.

Just usually, it's not quite this literally.

In Philadelphia, a place I confess I've lived most of my life, they know stuff happens in sports. They just wonder why it's mostly bad stuff. Especially when things seem way too good—by which we mean way too non-Philadelphian—to be true.

So Game 5 of the 2008 World Series fits right in. It's so utterly Philadelphian, they should place a DVD of it in William Penn's hand, way up there on top of City Hall.

One day, these folks were pouring through the gates of a ballpark they love, certain they were about to watch a team they love do something they'd witnessed once in their lives, their parents' lives, their grandparents' lives, the founding fathers' lives, and, when you get right down to it, even the dinosaurs' lives: Win a World Series.

Next thing they knew, there was more water falling on their heads than flowing between the banks of the Schuylkill. Their sure-handed shortstop couldn't catch a pop-up. Their best pitcher couldn't grip the pitch that has made him what he is. And their happy little march to the parade floats had turned into an all-time weather debacle.

Only in Philadelphia.

Sooner or later—they hoped—Bud Selig was going to invite them all back to the ballpark to finish Game 5. And maybe, they hoped, it would all turn out fine for the Phillies and the millions of human beings whose mental health depended on them.

But that isn't what most of those humans were thinking 24 hours later, as those raindrops kept descending. Ohhhhh no. They were thinking even Mother Nature didn't want them to win. They were thinking it was their meteorological Bartman Moment. But above all, they were thinking this could only happen in Philadelphia, a place where heartbreak in sports is the specialty of the house.

Little did they suspect that the one thing they should have been remembering was that the team they'd surgically attached their psyches to wasn't thinking the way they were all thinking.

Asked, on the day after that deluge, if he was worried about his players' ability to put this weird turn of events behind them, Phillies manager Charlie Manuel replied, "I don't think there's going to be any problem at all. I think we've been resilient now for the last couple of years. I think we know exactly where we're going and what we want to do. We're going to be ready."

Asked the night before what he would tell the fans who had shown up for Game 5 at Citizens Bank Park believing they were about to see their team win the World Series, Phillies ace Cole Hamels retorted, "That's what we're believing. And that's what we still believe. Now it won't obviously be tonight. But tomorrow. That's what we really want to do. We want to do it in Philly, in front of the fans who have really been there for us all year."

Of course, every team says stuff like that about its fans this time of year. But this time, it was different. This time, it was those fans—those weary, desperate, beaten-down, angst-ridden, broken dreamers—who had become one of the most intriguing parts of this plotline.

These people had spent the last parade-free quarter-century walking around with such a profound, universal sense of dread that every one of them should have had their own personal psychological counselor assigned to them.

They weren't merely aware of all the natural sporting disasters that had befallen their teams through the years—from Chico Ruiz to the Fog

Bowl, from Black Friday to Smarty Jones. They'd spent much of their lives contemplating just how and when their next nightmare was about to demolish their spirit, with one swing of the big old sporting wrecking ball.

But then something amazing happened. There was something about this team that gave them faith and the courage to conquer that dread.

They'd just seen their team win one game on a 2:00 a.m. dribbler down the line and another on a mighty home run by a pitcher they'd never before confused with Mike Schmidt. They found their team leading this World Series 3 games to 1. And all of a sudden, for once in their lives, they were convinced this was their time, that it was finally safe to trust this team.

That's a phenomenon, you understand, that's more rare in this universe than the Aurora Borealis. So when it erupted, it was so striking that even these players themselves noticed it.

"Even when we'd lose a game late in the season," said third baseman Greg Dobbs, "the stuff we'd hear was, 'That's okay, boys. Get 'em tomorrow.' Not, 'Boo, you suck.' We got none of that. So you know how people say you learn more about yourselves and others when you face adversity? I think that's something I learned from the fans. I realized that these fans have actually turned the corner."

But in Philadelphia, it's never a shock that, just when they least expect it, the corner is always waiting to turn on them. So of course it turned. One more time.

And, naturally, it wasn't even the first time the weather gods did the turning. It was 31 years since another October monsoon washed away another Phillies team's dreams—31 years since the Phillies and Dodgers played an entire LCS-ending game in conditions right out of the set of *The Perfect Storm*. And, *of course*, people in Philadelphia spent every waking waterlogged hour reminiscing about that day—because no good Philadelphia sports horror story deserves to be put out of its misery. Ever.

But at least, unlike that day, the commissioner of baseball didn't pretend that this time around it wasn't even raining. At least this time, the commish noticed those raindrops and placed this game in a state of suspended animation.

So at least this time—with 3¹/₂ innings left to be played in Game 5—there was still a chance for this Phillies team to rewrite this story.

Or not.

So that was the plotline hovering over this World Series as the planet waited for Game 5 to resume.

If, somehow, the Phillies hadn't gone on to win, this World Series would have left a scar on their fan base the size of the King of Prussia Mall.

But because they did, it turned this goofy weather mess into something to laugh about during every October deluge for the next thousand years.

So Part 2 of this game would be more than a mere sporting event, friends. It would be a life-altering event for an entire community. Would these people get their parade and release their demons? Or would one horrendously ill-timed act of nature drive them deeper into the Cuckoo's Nest?

It was all about to be played out on a soggy October baseball field. Only in Philadelphia.

Game 5—Act II: October 28, 2008

For a quarter of a century, they'd waited for this night, waited for this moment.

For a quarter of a century, they'd watched these scenes happen in somebody else's town, on somebody else's field of dreams.

Seasons came. Seasons went. Baseball seasons. Football seasons. Basketball seasons. Hockey seasons. They never ended this way—not one stinking one of them. Not in Philadelphia—the city where these sorts of dreams never came true.

And then, on a wintry night in October, in the cliffhanger episode of *A Funny Thing Happened on the Way to the Parade Floats*, it happened.

It was 9:58 p.m. in the Eastern Time Zone. The perfect closer, Brad Lidge, finished off the perfect season with the perfect pitch.

The hitter standing 60 feet away, Tampa Bay's Eric Hinske, swung through one last invisible slider. And as Brad Lidge collapsed to his knees and euphoria erupted all around him, you could almost feel the sky clearing and the universe shifting.

The Phillies had won the World Series, won it in five astounding games, won it by finishing off a 4–3 win over Tampa Bay they'd had to wait 46 waterlogged hours just to complete.

But that's not all. For the city they play in, the wait was over. A wait that had consumed every man, woman, and child; every Mummer; every pretzel baker; every cheesesteak chomper; every boobird.

A wait that had dragged them all through 25 years and 98 combined seasons of misery and heartbreak, seasons whose only common trait was that they'd all managed to last just a little too long.

It was the longest wait, by far, of the 13 metropolitan areas in America with teams in all four major sports. No other metropolis out there—anywhere—was within eight years.

And then, with one pitch, with one euphoric shriek in the night—in 45,000-part harmony—it was over. And life in Philadelphia may never be the same.

"For all these years," said Jimmy Rollins as fireworks crackled through the night, "the part of playing here that upset me the most was that I was always home in October, watching somebody else celebrate.

"But not this year," said the man who first opened his mouth and dared them all to reach for this chunk of the sky. "This year, *we* get to celebrate."

If you live in Kansas or New Mexico or Maine, you may not fully understand the meaning of all this. So we'll try to spell it out for you.

How long did Philadelphians have to wait? In between championships, their four pro teams played a combined 9,029 games without ever producing a night quite like this.

There were titles in Green Bay and Edmonton and East Rutherford, New Jersey. There were parades in Charlotte and Calgary and San Antonio. But never in Philly. Not once.

Philadelphia's four teams reached the postseason 47 times in all those years—and got bounced out of the postseason in all 47 of them. Seven of those teams made it all the way to the final round of that postseason. All seven watched somebody else spraying the champagne.

But of all those franchises, none dragged its fans through the funny farm more than the Phillies.

From 1984 through 2006, they reached the postseason just once in 23 seasons. They lost more games in that time than any team in their league except the Pirates.

They watched the Royals win a World Series. They watched the Diamondbacks win a World Series. They watched the Marlins win two of them. The Red Sox finally won. The White Sox finally won. But the Phillies just kept wallowing in that muck, looking for the formula that would lead them to a night like this.

So what were the odds that, in the 4,416th game they'd played since the last title in their town, it was the local baseball team that finally parted the polluted waters?

"When I was a kid, back in 1980, baseball was still exciting here," said Jamie Moyer, the only Phillie who could say he actually attended the parade of the 1980 World Series champs. "Back then, people lived for the game around here. So it's funny. Last year, one of our beat writers said to me, 'Do you realize you guys, as a team, brought baseball back to Philadelphia?'

"I never really looked at it that way. I never really thought about it that way, that we had brought baseball back to Philadelphia. He said, 'It's something that had been lost here for a lot of years.' And I said, 'You know what? If that's the case, that's really cool. That in our own small way, we've been able to bring baseball back to Philadelphia, to bring the Phillies back on the map.'"

And now, of course, they're the team that actually owns that map.

What a concept.

Before this night, they'd won one World Series in the first 125 years in their history. They'd lost more games than any team in any professional sport in North America. They were a team that hadn't just dropped off their own city's map. There was a time they'd practically toppled off their own sport's map. But not anymore.

As late as mid-September, these Phillies were a team dangling from the National League cliff—3½ games behind the Mets in the NL East, four games back of the Brewers in the wild-card free-for-all. No one could have seen then that a parade was in their future.

But all they did after that was go 24–6. Yeah, 24–6. Only four World Series winners in history—just two of them in the last 94 years—ever had a better finish than that.

"You always see that every year, don't you?" said outfielder Geoff Jenkins. "There's always that one team that gets hot at the right time."

Yeah, you always see it, all right. You just never saw it in this town, from this team. Until now.

These Phillies were so hot, they won games in this World Series they had no business winning. A game in which they went 0 for 13 with men in scoring position. A game that lasted till 1:47 a.m. A game in which Joltin' Joe Blanton was their home-run hero.

But they saved their grand finale for the goofiest game of all. A game with a 46-hour rain delay. A game divided into a two-part soap opera. A game so strange that even though it ended on a Wednesday night, history will always tell us it was played on a Monday night, thanks to that tricky suspension passage in Bud Selig's rulebook.

It was all so bizarre, all so unprecedented, it was hard to know what these teams would encounter when the glop finally stopped falling out of the sky and it was safe to come back to the ballpark.

One of the big questions in the minds of Phillies players, Moyer said, was whether the seats would even be full. Who knows how many of the 45,000 people sitting in those seats after the Game 5 rain delay had left town, had other stuff on their plate, or had even lost their ticket stubs, he wondered.

Text Credits

The First World Series
Excerpt from *When Boston Won the World Series* copyright © 2004 Bob Ryan. Reprinted by permission of Basic Books, a member of the Perseus Books Group.

The World Series That Wasn't
"The World Championship," from *The Year They Called Off the World Series*, by Benton Stark, copyright © 1991 by Benton Stark. Used by permission of Avery Publishing, an imprint of Penguin Group (USA) Inc.

Red Sox Game 7 Extra-Inning Win
Excerpt from *Red Sox Nation: An Unexpurgated History of the Boston Red Sox*, copyright © 2005 by Peter Golenbock. Reprinted with permission.

Black Sox Scandal
Chapters 8–9 from *EIGHT MEN OUT: The Black Sox and the 1919 World Series* by Eliot Asinof. Copyright © 1987 by Eliot Asinof.
Reprinted by arrangement with Henry Holt and Company, LLC.

Casey Stengel's Inside-the-Park Home Run
Excerpt from Stengel: *His Life and Times* by Robert W. Creamer reprinted by permission of SLL/Sterling Lord Literistic, Inc. Copyright by Robert W. Creamer.

Athletics' 10-Run Inning
Excerpt from *Connie Mack's '29 Triumph: The Rise and Fall of the Philadelphia Athletics Dynasty* copyright © 2005 [1999] William C. Kashatus by permission of McFarland & Company, Inc., Box 611, Jefferson, NC 28640. www.mcfarlandpub. com

Babe Ruth's Called Shot
Excerpt from *The Big Bam: The Life and Times of Babe Ruth* by Leigh Montville, copyright © 2006 by Leigh Montville. Used by permission of Doubleday, a division of Random House, Inc.

The Gashouse Gang
Excerpts from St. *Louis Globe-Democrat, Chicago Daily News, St. Louis Post-Dispatch*, pp. 303–307,

from *The Dizziest Season: The Gashouse Gang Chases the Pennant* by G.H. Fleming, copyright © 1984 by G.H. Fleming. Reprinted by permission of HarperCollins Publishers.

Mickey Owen's Dropped Third Strike
"Owen, Henrich, Say Casey Threw a Curve" by Dave Anderson appeared in the *New York Times* on June 12, 1988. Reprinted with permission of the author.

The Hapless Browns Meet the Legendary Cardinals
Excerpt on pages 109–32 reprinted from *The Boys Who Were Left Behind: The 1944 World Series Between the Hapless St. Louis Browns and the Legendary St. Louis Cardinals* by John Heidenry and Brett Topel by permission of the University of Nebraska Press. Copyright © 2006 by John Heidenry and Brett Topel.

Enos Slaughter's Mad Dash
pp. 372–79 from *The Spirit of St. Louis* by Peter Golenbock copyright © by Peter Golenbock. Reprinted by permission of HarperCollins Publishers.

Billy Martin's Game 7 Catch
Excerpt from *The Era, 1947–1957* by Roger Kahn © 1993 by Roger Kahn. Reprinted with permission of the author.

Willie Mays's Catch
Excerpt from *A Day In the Bleachers* by Arnold Hano Copyright © 1995 by Arnold Hano. All rights reserved.

Dusty Rhodes Comes Through
Excerpt from *Triumph and Tragedy In Mudville: My Lifelong Passion For Baseball* by Stephen Jay Gould. Copyright © 2003 by Turbo, Inc. Used by permission of W.W. Norton & Company, Inc.

Jackie Robinson Steals Home
Excerpt from *What I Learned From Jackie Robinson*, by Carl Erskine, © 2005, reproduced with permission of the McGraw-Hill Companies.

Sandy Amaros's Game 7 Catch
Excerpt from *Praying for Gil Hodges*, by Thomas Oliphant, copyright © 2005 by the author and reprinted by permission of Thomas Dunne Books, an imprint of St. Martin's Press, LLC.

Excerpt from *The Perfect Yankee: The Incredible Story of the Greatest Miracle In Baseball History*, by Don Larsen with Mark Shaw, reprinted with permission of Sports Publishing LLC.

Bill Mazeroski's Series-Winning Home Run
Excerpt from *The Pirates Reader*, ed. by Richard Peterson, copyright © 2003 by University of Pittsburgh Press. Reprinted with permission.

Bob Gibson's Gutty Game 7 Performance
Excerpt from *October 1964* by David Halberstam, copyright 1994 by The Amateurs Limited. Used by permission of Villard Books, a division of Random House, Inc.

Sandy Koufax, Yom Kippur, and Game 7
Excerpt from pp. 181–95 from *Sandy Koufax: A Lefty's Legacy* by Jane Leavy, Copyright © 2002 by Jane Leavy. Reprinted by permission of HarperCollins Publishers.

The Miracle Mets
Excerpt from *The New York Mets*, by Leonard Koppett, reprinted with the permission of Scribner, a Division of Simon & Schuster, Inc., from *The New York Mets* by Leonard Koppett. Copyright © 1970 by The Macmillan Company. Copyright 1970 by Information Concepts Incorporated. All rights reserved.

The Brooks Robinson Show
Reprinted courtesy of *Sports Illustrated*: "That Black and Orange Magic," William Leggett, October 26, 1970, copyright © 1970 Time Inc. All rights reserved.

Carlton Fisk's Game 6 Home Run
"1975: The Sixth Game" from *Beyond the Sixth Game* by Peter Gammons. Copyright © 1985 by Peter Gammons. Reprinted by permission of Houghton Mifflin Harcourt Publishing Company. All rights reserved.

Reggie Jackson's Three Dingers
Excerpt from *Ladies and Gentlemen, The Bronx Is Burning: 1977 Baseball, Politics, and the Battle For the Soul of a City* by Jonathan Mahler. Copyright © 2005 by Jonathan Mahler. Reprinted by permission of Farrar, Straus and Giroux, LLC.

The Call
"'85 I-70 Series: Blame It on Balboni," by Phil Ellenbecker appeared in *The Sedalia Democrat*, May 21, 2009. Reprinted with permission.

Bill Buckner and the Infamous Ground Ball
"Not So, Boston," by Roger Angell, reprinted by permission; © Roger Angell. Originally published in *The New Yorker*. All rights reserved.

Kirk Gibson's Walk-Off Home Run
"It Could Only Happen In Hollywood," by Jim Murray, appeared in the *Los Angeles Times*, October 16, 1988. Reprinted with permission.

Orel Hershiser's Pitching Mastery
Reprinted courtesy of *Sports Illustrated*: "A Case of Orel Surgery," Peter Gammons, October 31, 1988, copyright © 1988 Time Inc. All rights reserved.

The Earthquake Series
"Remembering the World Series Earthquake" by Horace Hinshaw, June 18, 2009, reprinted with permission of the *San Jose Mercury News*/YGS Group.

Kirby Puckett's Game 6 Performance
"For 11 Innings, Puckett's Greatness Took Center Stage," by Tim Kurkjian, appeared in *ESPN the Magazine*, March 6, 2006. Reprinted with permission.

The Game 7 Duel
"Morris vs. Smoltz: A pitchers' duel that set the standard," by Joe Christensen, appeared in the *Star Tribune* on June 14, 2007. Reprinted with permission.

Joe Carter's Walk-Off Home Run
Reprinted courtesy of *Sports Illustrated*: "Home Sweet Homer," Steve Rushin, November 1, 1993, copyright © 1993 Time Inc. All rights reserved.

World Series Canceled
"Baseball: Lost Games, Lost Dreams," by Jack Curry, from the *New York Times*, © the *New York Times*, August 26, 2002. All rights reserved. Used by permission and protected by the Copyright Laws of the United States. The printing, copying, redistribution, or retransmission of the Material without express written permission is prohibited.

Glavine and Maddux Pitch Atlanta to Victory
Reprinted courtesy of *Sports Illustrated*: "Brave Hearts," Tom Verducci, November 6, 1995, copyright © 1995 Time Inc. All rights reserved.

Jimmy Leyritz's Game 4 Home Run
"For Yanks, Game Isn't Over Till They Win It In the 10th," by Jack Curry, from the *New York Times*, © the *New York Times*, October 24, 1996. All rights reserved. Used by permission and protected by the Copyright Laws of the United States. The printing, copying, redistribution, or retransmission of the Material without express written permission is prohibited.

Edgar Renteria's Game 7 Walk-Off Hit
Reprinted courtesy of *Sports Illustrated*: "Happy Ending," Tom Verducci, November 3, 1997, copyright © 1997 Time Inc. All rights reserved.

Luis Gonzalez's Series-Winning Single
"Luis Gonzalez's Single Wins 2001 World Series" by Rick Weinberg appeared on ESPN.com. Reprinted with permission of the author.

Angels' Game 6 Comeback
"Touched By An Angel," by Steve Dilbeck, appeared in the *Los Angeles Daily News*, October 27, 2002. Reprinted with permission.

Young Marlins Surprise the Yankees
"Gone South," by Roger Angell, reprinted by permission; © Roger Angell. Originally published in *The New Yorker*. All rights reserved.

Red Sox Win!
Excerpt from *Faithful: Two Diehard Boston Red Sox Fans Chronicle the Historic 2004 Season*, by Stewart O'Nan and Stephen King, reprinted with the permission of Scribner, a Division of Simon & Schuster, Inc. Copyright © by Stewart O'Nan and Stephen King. All rights reserved.

Phillies' Suspended Game Victory
Excerpt from *Worth the Wait: Tales of the 2008 Phillies*, copyright © 2009 by Jayson Stark. Reprinted with permission.

Photo Credits

Bill Buckner: © The Boston Globe/Stan Grossfield/Landov

Willie Mays: © AP

Yogi Berra and Don Larsen: © AP

Carlton Fisk: © AP photo/Harry Cabluck

Kirk Gibson: © AP photo/Rusty Kennedy

Joe Carter: © Rick Stewart/Allsport/Getty Images

Reggie Jackson: © Louis Requena/MLB photos via Getty Images

Jackie Robinson: © Mark Kauffman/*Sports Illustrated*/Getty Images

Babe Ruth: © B. Bennett/Getty Images

Index